The Auberge of the Flowering Hearth

BOOKS BY ROY ANDRIES DE GROOT

Feasts for All Seasons

Cooking with the Cuisinart

Revolutionizing French Cooking

The Auberge of the Flowering Hearth

The Wines of California, the Pacific Northwest and New York
Including the First Classification of the Best Wineries and Vineyards

The Auberge of the Flowering Hearth

of the

Flowering Hearth

Roy Andries de Groot

Library of Congress Cataloging-in-Publication Data
De Groot, Roy Andries, 1912–
The Auberge of the flowering hearth / Roy Andries de Groot.
p.   cm.
"First published by the Ecco Press in 1983"—T.p. verso.
Includes index.
1. Cookery, French. 2. Gastronomy. 3. Alps, French (France)—
Social life and customs. I. Title.
TX719.D37   1992   641.5944—dc20   91-33229
ISBN 0-88001-504-7

9 8 7 6 5 4

For Ñusta and Jupy, who were happier
in the Valley, together,
than anywhere else on earth.

CONTENTS

PART II   THE RECIPES

Acknowledgments

Many friends have helped in trying to solve the almost insuperable central problem of this book: how to interpret in words the overwhelming ambiance of an enclosed mountain valley in the High Alps, how to bring its food, its wines, its kitchen preparations, its way of life across the Atlantic to the United States. Some friends came with us to La Vallée and joined in its exploration by "lending their eyes," so to speak, toward the absorption of the immense scene.

To Berenice MacFarquhar, who climbed the mountains, drove up the impossibly steep and rocky roads, explored the forest footpaths and spent innumerable hours in the kitchen of the Auberge of the Flowering Hearth, watching and taking notes.

To other friends who came with us to the Valley and contributed their ideas and impressions, including Petra Chu, Christa and Riquet Hess and Bonnie Messenger.

To the residents of the Valley and the Carthusian monks of the monastery of La Grande Chartreuse, who, having lived there for 900 years, were best able to outline the background of history, including the Prior-General, Dom André, and Brother Marie-Bernard.

To the residents of the village of Saint-Pierre-de-Chartreuse, and especially to the young men and women of the high mountain region of the Dauphiné who spoke to me with so much love and so much despair of this "undeveloped" region of France, including Cécile Drevet and Marie-Odile Franconie.

To Michel Legris, who first brought me to the Valley and was always its most imaginative, knowledgeable and lucid interpreter.

To my many friends at home in the United States who helped in transforming a huge mass of notes into a practical and serviceable manuscript, including Jan and Joe Flaherty, both highly imaginative amateur cooks, who joined in testing the recipes and translating them into workable terms for American kitchens and food markets; also to Jean and John Tingley, who reviewed and retested a number of the recipes.

To other friends who read the manuscript and contributed valuable suggestions, including Don Erickson and Virginia Léon de Vivero.

To Odile Sersiron and Mary Lyons of Foods from France, Inc., who advised on native French cheeses and ingredients which were imported into the United States and incorporated into the menus and recipes.

To my editors, researchers, proofreaders, tasters, testers and typists, for devoted determination to get every detail right, led by Lynne Spearman and including Jill Davenport, Beatrice Frankard, Edna Gengerke, Alice Thomas and Johanna Wright. Also, to Leonor Dalmas Wolf of the research staff of the New York Public Library for her valuable help in documenting the historical background of the Valley.

Finally and above all, of course, to Vivette Artaud and Ray Girard, whose collaboration will always remain with me as a memorable experience.

PREFACE

*to the Revised
Ecco Edition*

*I*t is now fifteen years since I first approached the forbidding granite
wall of rock, found the jagged cleft cut by the rushing torrent of
the river, negotiated the narrow road on the ledge above the ravine,
swung around the hairpin bends and plunged through one rock tunnel
after another, until I found myself in the sun-splashed forest, surrounded, it seemed, by an orchestra of a thousand birds singing in
harmony a hundred songs. The trees parted, as if they were a stage
curtain, to bring me, for the first time, into the extraordinary valley
of La Grande Chartreuse. Within a few minutes, I was sitting at a
perfectly laid table, with a snow-white cloth, the warm October sun
reflected from the wine glasses, the porcelain plates and the silver, in
the garden of The Auberge of the Flowering Hearth. We were high
on the slope of the valley. From far below, on the banks of the river
in the tiny village of Saint-Pierre-de-Chartreuse, floated up the sounds
of a lazy noontime: the cries and shouts of children, the barking of an
excited dog, a buzz-saw cutting logs in sharp bursts of power, the bells
of a small herd of cows, the bleating of sheep, the pealing of a church

bell, a young woman singing, a shot from high on one of the surrounding mountains. . . . A bright Alpine Crépy was poured, flashing in the sunlight. A plate was placed before me with a feather-light soufflé of the local Alpine velvety rich Beaufort cheese, accented by farm butter churned this morning. My story had started. . . .

It is now almost ten years since the first edition of this book was published. It was five years in the writing. I went back, again and again. I did not—as some publicists and readers have suggested—stay on indefinitely, that first time, postponing my departure day-by-day, gradually eating myself into a stupor through twenty-two magnificent breakfast, lunch and dinner menus. In fact, at the first visit, I explored the entire region, dining many times outside the valley, including meals at some of the best restaurants in the city of Grenoble. But I always returned to the ladies of The Auberge of the Flowering Hearth with immense satisfaction. They did not try to compete with the showy extravaganzas of the famous "starred" restaurants. They had their own style of a completely honest, entirely simple, perfectionist ideal of country cooking—using the iron hooks and rotating spits built into the great hearth—sliding their black iron pots into the "braising wells" bricked in under the glowing embers of the huge wood fires. The final results, on the table, were irresistibly superb. I recorded it all on my tapes and, then, using the techniques of a good sauce cook, I concentrated it, refined it, reduced it, adjusted the accents, tested and tasted, until I was quite sure that every written recipe would reasonably reproduce the balanced beauty that was the cuisine of The Auberge of the Flowering Hearth.

This is the one point I must hammer home hard. The recipes in this book are a permanent and unchanging record of a lovely way of life in an extraordinary place at a particular time. These recipes work precisely as well today as they did ten years ago. I wrote this as a cook book. If you will reread my original foreword, you will find me making it perfectly clear that: "This book is not a tourist guide."

After ten years of opening thousands of letters from readers, I have been astonished and disturbed by the acrimonious tone of quite a substantial number of them. The theme is always the same. "We went to 'your valley' and we failed to find 'your ladies' and the food wasn't nearly as good as you said it was." As each letter progresses, it becomes perfectly clear that the writer expected to drive straight to The Auberge of the Flowering Hearth, sit down at a table in the dining room, whip out a copy of this book and order any one of the menus (which I took five years to assemble)—regardless of whether it was Spring, Summer,

Fall, or Winter! The problem became so severe for the young husband-and-wife owners of The Auberge that they had a form letter printed, which they automatically send to all Americans who write for reservations. The letter points out that "Mr. de Groot's book was written over a period of several years and represents a concentration of an enormous amount of kitchen work, so that, while some of the dishes he describes are still available, it is entirely impossible, within a stay of a few days, to reproduce the full ambiance of all the menus." The letter also points out certain hard factual changes that have taken place in a decade, such as, for example, "that French federal forestry conservation laws have become so tight that we can no longer easily obtain hardwood logs for burning and cannot, any more, cook over wood fires in our great hearth" —also that "game conservation is now so strict that it is virtually impossible to get the Chartreuse chamois and venison, while many of the birds are no longer permitted to be hunted."

If, in spite of my warnings, you decide to go to the valley of La Grande Chartreuse, I do at least beg you to differentiate between the eternal verities and the temporal things. The glorious solitude of Le Grand Som and the other surrounding mountain peaks is forever. The life of the Carthusian monks and their huge monastery at the top of the pass is unchanging and, in a way, protects the primeval beauty of the valley. But this is hard on the people who live there, who must earn a livelihood and would like to encourage tourism. So the floor of the valley is changing. More auberges and restaurants are being opened. Small ski slopes are being developed. Death has come to a number of the characters in my book. During the very dry season, there is always a problem with water and it is difficult to fight fires in the village. Several of my favorite old buildings, including some described in this book, have burned down. Above all, food and restaurants come and go and change. The Auberge of the Flowering Hearth is still there, but you certainly must not expect the food to be the same, a decade later. I am not even sure that they still keep flowers in the hearth! If you do go, may I ask a favor. If you fail to find some of the people I mention, or a few of the buildings I describe, don't come back and tell me—as some readers have done—that the people in this book are fictional. The village of Saint-Pierre-de-Chartreuse is a very small place and everyone in it, from the Mayor to the owner of le drugstore, knows me and my book. Just mention the name of any person in this book and ask questions about them. You will be told precisely what has happened to them, whether they are dead, or, if not, exactly where they are now.

Finally, a decade has brought some changes to my own gastronomic philosophy. It seems to me, now, that modern biochemical research has raised persuasive questions about health dangers in the regular use of MSG (monosodium glutamate). Originally, when this derivative of vegetable protein was produced by hand in small quantities in China (as MEI JING) *and Japan (as* AJI-NOMOTO), *it may have been a natural product and an essential part of the cooking techniques when many of their ingredients were dried and not always, to put it mildly, entirely fresh. But today, in our Western world, where MSG is chemically manufactured by the millions of tons, under various commercial trade names, I firmly believe that its use in substantial quantities in everyday cooking may be a potential danger to health. For this reason, I have eliminated it from my kitchen. I would have liked to have taken out every reference to it in this book, but that would have involved large technical problems in reprinting. So I suggest that, if you agree with me, you will simply disregard the MSG as an ingredient wherever it appears in any recipe.*

For my wife, Katherine, as for me, these recipes remain among our favorites of all time. Feasting by the Seasons of La Vallée de la Grande Chartreuse and the rules of L'Auberge de l'Atre Fleuri remains an unchanging and unending joy.

Roy Andries de Groot

The 15th of November, 1982.

FOREWORD

*The Mysterious Label
Led to the Strange Journey*

*This book was an accident. The idea came out of a journalistic
journey. For many years I have enjoyed, as an after-dinner drink,
the ancient and famous liqueur Green Chartreuse. It was so much
a part of the routine of my ordinary living that I guess I never
thought about it much. There were various bottles in my cellar, with
different shapes and different labels. When these bottles were placed
on the dining table, it was my guests who read the words and began
asking the questions. Questions I found I could not answer.*

*Some of the labels were so old and stained that they were hard
to decipher. What did the rather mysterious words and phrases mean?
Who were these "Pères Chartreux" who distilled the liqueur at "La
Grande Chartreuse" by "a secret process" known only to them? One
old label was dated 1944 in honor of the "Liberation of France from
the German armies." Another, dated 1940, had been laid down "in
honor of the return of the Pères Chartreux to France after an exile
of thirty-seven years." Who kicked them out? Where did they go
for thirty-seven years? And where was "La Grande Chartreuse"? The*

labels had all been printed in Grenoble and the liqueur had been bottled in Voiron, a small town in the region of the Dauphiné in the High Alps of southeastern France. I was now thoroughly intrigued.

The next day, I happened to be lunching with my editor, Curt Anderson. I wondered if he knew the answers to the questions about Green Chartreuse. He did not. He said: "Why don't we make it an assignment for the magazine? Why don't you go to La Grande Chartreuse and, if there is really some secret, find out what it is and write a story?"

I consulted my reference books and maps. I pinpointed the places. I learned that the liqueur was made by a group of hermits who lived in a lonely and wild valley high in the mountains. They had rejected the world and had vowed to pass the rest of their lives in isolation and silence. But the French government, using military force, had twice thrown them out of France. Why? I put in a telephone call to La Grande Chartreuse. A few seconds later I was talking to unconcerned operators in Paris, then Lyon, then to a troubled young lady at the exchange in Grenoble. "But, Monsieur," she said, her voice sounding almost terrified, "do you not know that Les Pères Chartreux are vowed to a life of silence? They do not even speak to each other. They live on top of a mountain. It is inconceivable that they would have a telephone."

I was not going to give up so easily. I told her that I was a journalist and that it was absolutely essential that I speak to someone representing these Pères Chartreux. I mentioned the town of Voiron. Instantly her voice was eager and relieved. "Wait a minute, Monsieur. They do have a civilian office, in Voiron at the foot of their mountain. A telephone is listed there. Attendez un moment, I will ring it."

That was how I found Monsieur Michel. I was at once charmed by the cultivated French voice with the slightly professorial tone. He had been a teacher of French history. He had all the facts. Yes, indeed, there was a secret process known only to Les Pères Chartreux. Yes, it was perfectly true that they lived at the top of their high valley in complete isolation and silence. Yes, it was possible to visit the valley, and if I came he would be glad to be my guide. There was now a direct jet flight from New York, via Paris, to Lyon. He would meet me at the Bron airfield in Lyon and drive me the few hours it took to reach the Valley of La Grande Chartreuse. I said I would make my arrangements and cable him.

Then, in somewhat hesitant and questioning tones, as if trying to test out my attitude over that three-thousand-five-hundred-mile telephone line, he asked: "Monsieur, where would you like me to make a reservation for you to stay? Would you prefer one of the large establishments in Grenoble? Perhaps the Grand Hôtel, with almost a hundred luxurious rooms including a restaurant with all the classic 'haute cuisine' dishes and great wines of France? Or . . . would you prefer something simpler and closer to the mountains? A small auberge in the Valley itself. . . . Only six rooms . . . the country dishes of our mountain region . . . the local cheeses and game meats . . . the local wines . . . ?" I said I would prefer the small auberge in the Valley.

A few days later I booked my direct flight from New York to Paris and on, in the same plane, to Lyon. This is where we begin. . . .

What I found in Monsieur Michel's valley (and at the small inn to which he took me, the Auberge of the Flowering Hearth) has made it, for me, not just another place, but a point of view, a way of life. I have been drawn back there again and again. Each time I have felt the deepest sense of relief from the pressures which seem to smother me in the modern man-made world. Whenever I have driven along the highway from the congested and ugly suburbs of Lyon toward the purity of the mountains, I have felt myself gradually disengaged from the chaos and fear in the cities where I normally live and work. Each time I have reentered the Valley and again sensed its natural peace, I have felt as if I were reawakening into the real world after a nightmare. Sharing the life of this small world, I have felt neither deceived nor menaced. Sharing the food— always the basic element of life—I have felt a graceful rhythm of unity with the land and the people.

When I began setting down my feelings in this book, I faced a difficult decision. Should I try to protect the isolation of the Valley by keeping its location a secret? Should I change the names of the people and the places? I decided not to change or hide anything. This involves an obvious danger. It is easy to find the Valley on a map. It is perfectly simple to follow my route and go there. But if the Auberge of the Flowering Hearth were to be invaded by thousands of tourists, almost everything that I write about it would cease to be true. It would at once lose its character, the simple perfection of its style, the balance of its way of life.

There is also another danger. If you went to the Valley, you might be disappointed. Hard as it has fought for its isolation, it has not avoided some invasion by the modernistic, mass world. Although most of the land is protected by State ownership of the forests, some small plots of pasture have been sold to tourists and some blaringly ugly summer cottages have been built. A few small ski lodges, in imitation Swiss chalet-style, contrast too sharply with the simple stone cottages of the ancient village of Saint-Pierre-de-Chartreuse. There is, in one corner, an advertising sign for a small trailer park.

The Auberge itself is an old stone farmhouse. It is not a fairy-tale ivy-clad dream house hidden away in mysterious woods. It stands squarely at the side of the road. It has never been "dolled up," or "made over," in changing its role from farmhouse to inn. It remains rigidly simple. It cannot afford show-off luxury. It is too small and too far from the normal tracks of tourist traffic.

If you look for them, you can see small blemishes on the vast panorama of forests and mountains, of colors and forms. Nothing is ever quite perfect. But to me the imperfections are unimportant. I firmly believe that nothing of deep and abiding value is ever seen with the eyes alone. It must also be seen with the heart. I am concerned, in this book, with experiences deeply felt. I am concerned with food as an expression of the vitality of the natural and simple life of the Valley. I am not much involved with geography or the points of the compass. I hardly care whether the pine forests in which I first heard the haunting hoot of the coq de bruyère was on the east or west side of the peak of the Grand Som. I cannot remember whether the pool where the red-spotted speckled trout slapped the water as they leaped was above or below the village. This book is not a tourist guide. It is in praise of a way of life.

When the ladies who own and run the Auberge of the Flowering Hearth, Mademoiselle Vivette Artaud and Mademoiselle Ray Girard, set their table with the animals and birds of their valley and its surrounding mountains, with the fish caught by their friends in the nearby lakes, with the cheeses carefully made and the fruits and vegetables laboriously grown by their farmer neighbors, with the wild mushrooms they pick themselves in the woods, with the wines from the nearby mountain vineyards, they are fulfilling the unity of that way of life—a unity which seems to me to be of the deepest value but which the world seems to be rejecting. It is even being rejected by the young people of Saint-Pierre-de-Chartreuse. In 1870 the population of the village was about one thousand, seven hundred. In 1970 it was about seven hundred.

Most people like to bring back some memento of a faraway and lovely place. I asked to be allowed to bring back some of Mademoiselle Ray's extraordinary recipes. I recorded them in her kitchen as she prepared each in the form of a lesson. I have prepared them again in my kitchen in New York. I have found many of the authentic French ingredients among the imported foods on the store shelves. More and more of the small, freshly creamy Alpine cheeses are now being brought here. An increasing number of the refreshing, simple Alpine wines are now being shipped here. Even when they are transplanted far from their natural home, these menus and recipes have brought to my dining table a special glow. May they bring it also to yours.

Roy Andries de Groot

New York, 27 April, 1973

PART ONE

The High and Lovely Place

ONE

*Journey to a
High and Lovely Place*

It was raining over Paris. Our jet from New York glided above the layer of mist and polluting smoke, shaded in the dawning light from grey to yellowish brown. The colors of the city were muted, as if by an immense fallout of dust. On the long runways of Orly airport, the wetness outlined, as if on a map, the shapes of the oil slicks on the concrete. When the doors of our plane opened, there was nothing particularly Parisian about the smell of the smog. I used to boast that if I were to be deposited blindfolded in any one of the great gastronomic cities, I could identify it within a few seconds by sniffing the air and recognizing its particular smells from its kitchens and food shops. Now every city smells the same.

The loudspeakers told us there would be a slight delay before continuing our flight to Lyon. We were asked to leave the plane. The café au lait in the terminal waiting room tasted vaguely chemical. The au lait was a white powder flowing from the corner of a small plastic envelope. Forty minutes later we were descending over the blast furnaces and steel mills of Lyon. Below the mushroom

3

cloud of black smoke, there was an immense display of fireworks. Tongues of flame rose out of the mouths of furnaces, licked the foul air and withdrew. Showers of sparks fountained up from the cone-shaped converters. It seemed as if our plane could never find its way down to the Bron airport through the thick smoke.

We were met by Monsieur Michel, who packed us into his Citroën DS-21 and turned at once off the main highway to avoid the terrifying midtown traffic of the steel city. He took the small suburban roads. He wanted to put Lyon behind us as soon as possible and head out toward the southeast.

There was a bright and hopeful road sign with a large red arrow: N. 6—Grenoble, Chambéry, Genève. We passed through the blackened industrial slum of Saint-Priest. Abandoned, collapsing warehouses, the smell of garbage and rats. Posters announced that the area was being redeveloped into a "Nouvelle Zone Industrielle."

At the bedroom town of La Verpillière we were on the main N. 6 highway toward Switzerland. The traffic was solid. We crawled. La Verpillière was dominated by high-rising slabs of garishly colored concrete apartment towers which had been implanted in what were once flower and vegetable gardens or green pastures. These had to be sacrificed to the needs of the industrial city, which had to have bedrooms for its workers. The arms of its bus lines and commuter roads stretched out, hungrily seizing the green land for concrete living space.

Not only for living space. Every few miles, billboards proclaimed, "Nouvelle Zone Industrielle." The industry of Lyon had to be decentralized. The industry of Paris had also to be decentralized, and part of it was being relocated here. More space needed for fire and smoke.

Gradually, almost imperceptibly, the green land began to resist the invasion. Gently undulating cornfields surrounded an old stone farmhouse. A few cows grazed on the far slope. At the top, the sunlight sparkled on the bright roof of a small church—bright with gaily colored lozenge-shaped glazed tiles—its grey spire rising above its protecting circle of dark poplar trees.

Then there were more high-tension electric towers and transformers. There was a smell of gas in the air. The village was called Saint-André-le-Gaz. How sad for Saint-André!

As we drove beyond these suburban towns we seemed suddenly to have turned a decisive corner, and the atmosphere of our journey was completely changed. The multilane highway to Grenoble forked to the right, taking all the traffic with it. We curved to the left on a two-lane road marked for Chambéry. We began slowly climbing; we rounded the bend. There, in the far distance, was our first view of the mountains. One can come upon this view a hundred times, from a dozen different directions. The first flush of excitement is always overwhelming. One recognizes the tier upon tier of the lower hills. One is lifted above them to the shoulder upon shoulder of the masses of granite. One senses the promise of the still-invisible peaks.

The farm fields were now blending into moorland pastures. There were bare rocks on the upper slopes. Woods of beeches below. Forests of pines on the skyline. The road curved and descended to the small town of Les Abrets. An avenue of chestnuts rose to the manor house on the hill. Circling around it, the country houses stood in their landscaped gardens, behind stone walls and wrought iron gates. At every point there was individuality and variety. They stood apart from the industrial world.

We climbed again to the small hill town of Pont-de-Beauvoisin, famous for its fishing grounds of carp and rainbow trout in the surrounding lakes and rivers. The narrow street descended sharply between stone houses with steeply sloping four-sided roofs designed to prevent the winter snows from settling too thickly and heavily. At the bottom of the hill we crossed the bridge for which the town was named, over a clear, smooth river, its waters reflecting the cloud patterns of the sky.

Monsieur Michel told us about the double life of this river which would be our traveling companion from here to the end of our journey and was inseparably bound up with the high and lovely place to which we were traveling. In fact, without this river we might never have been able to reach our objective. The river is called Le Guiers (pronounced *gay*). It rises from two separate springs, about six miles apart, in the High Alps. One is on the slopes of the Dent-de-Crolles, the other at the foot of the Cirque de Saint-Même. So at first there are two rivers, both tumbling down the mountains to the high plateau. There, like an adolescent boy and a spirited girl, they achieve different reputations. The boy river is said to be dreamy, lazy, slow—with jade green waters and deep, smooth pools. His official name, on the maps, is Le Guiers Mort. But is he really dead? In spring, when the melting snows flood down into the valleys, he is as wildly alive as any torrent. His floods have destroyed several villages and again and again have drowned the cattle and ruined the crops.

The other, the girl river, has the reputation of being always spirited and wild—of running a course of speed and violence, plunging, frothy white. Her official name is Le Guiers Vif. Yet she is hardly so alive during the summer droughts. She can be as dead as the lily pond in a cemetery. Boy and girl finally meet and merge at a village called Entre-les-Deux-Guiers. By then they have already completed the work for which we must be grateful. They have cut a path for us through a wall of rock almost five thousand feet high.

Across the bridge at Beauvoisin, we climbed steeply and steadily. Our road became a ledge cut into the side of a granite cliff. Below us, to the right, was the deep and narrow Gorge des Chailles. We swung and twisted with the curving cliff. Across the gorge, the granite wall rose perpendicular for perhaps a thousand feet. The gorge opened out into a wide, wild valley, rising to a high plateau. Now there was a much closer view of the first of the great Alpine "massifs," looking like an immense and impregnable fortress wreathed in a pure white mist. Its granite walls rose up, sheer and straight for almost five thousand feet, from the floor of the plateau. Behind this seemingly unscalable wall the white peaks mounted higher still.

We reached the mountain village of Les Echelles, once a fortified stopping place on the Roman road across the Alps to the provincial capital at Vienne on the Rhône. In the center of the village, we left the main highway and continued on the narrow mountain road.

The air was scented by wood smoke. Carried on the mountain air, it seemed fresh, natural, pure. The road ran as level and straight as any Roman highway, among the trees, on the plateau. When there was a break in the trees, the gigantic wall of the massif seemed to be leaning over us. The forest opened out to make room for the historic mountain town of Saint-Laurent-du-Pont, named for its bridge over the River Guiers which guards the secret gateway through the impregnable wall to our high and lovely place. We stopped for a midmorning *petit déjeuner* at the small Auberge des Deux Mondes. I wondered about the name. The inn must have been at least two hundred years old. Was the original owner a prophet? In the uncomplicated time in which he lived, could he have foreseen this place as a dividing line between two worlds? Here, now, it seemed at last as if we were leaving the polluted world behind. Here, one felt the anticipation of the pure world through the gateway.

Our *petit déjeuner* was supposed to be a mere snack, but the chef-owner of the auberge was a Savoyard who followed the mountain tradition of solid eating. His idea of breakfast was a terrine of locally hunted wild boar, a grill of rainbow trout from the nearby Guiers, a roast of tiny whole larks served on a Gratin Dauphinois of creamed potatoes, and a bottle of cold, crackling white Seyssel from the Savoy mountains. And while we savored these pleasures, Monsieur Michel told us why the high valley remains so aloof and isolated—why it is called "La Vallée du Désert."

TWO

Seven Men Came and Made It Forever Different

S aint-Laurent-du-Pont is the town "of the bridge." Here the narrow road crosses the River Guiers, turns and begins to rise sharply towards the almost secret narrow Porte de la Fourvoirie, "the gateway of the fortified road." The name takes us back two thousand years. When Roman soldiers entered the Valley they were so sure that this pass could be impregnably defended that they called it Forta Via, "the fortified entrance." Forta Via, on the modern maps, has become Fourvoirie. The gateway of La Fourvoirie is a narrow cleft in the five-thousand-foot granite wall. Through the mountainous barrier, the turning and twisting pass cuts inward and upward to the high secluded interior valley. There would be no gateway at all had it not been for the erosion of the rock, over millions of years, by the River Guiers. The fast-flowing water has cut a slot three thousand feet deep in the wall of granite. The rock has given way. The other defenses of the Valley have not.

The road up from Saint-Laurent-du-Pont is assaulted and often made impassable on the average of one hundred and twenty days a year by raging storms, torrential gushes of rain or piling drifts of snow. On the average of one hundred days, the wind, reflected back by the granite wall, is as solidly cold over Saint-Laurent-du-Pont as a block of ice. These are the fierce outer defenses. Behind them, at the center of the inner valley, the air is milder and softer. There is seldom the cutting bite of the wind. The storms cannot penetrate the surrounding mountain walls. The snow falls gently, with feathery lightness, straight down. The seeds of the trees fall directly to the earth. The forests of beeches and pines creep forward, year by year. They plant themselves as they expand.

Throughout its history the Valley has been involved with romantic adventure. It has been more impenetrable, more legendary, more mysterious than any fictional Shangri-La. Since men first struggled up into the Valley and made their homes there, they have loved it and fiercely defended it.

It may have been Roman soldiers who first explored the Valley. They were building their roads across southern France. When the Romans took control of the Valley, they defined it by two Latin words which have become inextricably bound up with its history. They called the place *desertum*, meaning that it was "deserted" because it was too inhospitable, too wild for men to live in. The word remained. The name is still La Vallée du Désert. The word does not mean a desert of sand, without life. This "desert" is teeming with animals and birds. Its earth is rich with wild fruits and mushrooms. Its fields are lush pastures.

The Romans built two tiny settlements where men could stay for a while. One, to guard the gateway through the granite cliffs, became Saint-Laurent-du-Pont. The other, on the floor of the high valley itself, consisted of a few huts which the Romans defined as *catursiani*. The word meant "a little house where one is alone in an isolated and wild place." The word has remained. It became *chartreuse*. The Roman settlement is today the village of Saint-Pierre-de-Chartreuse.

The Romans departed, leaving almost no record of their stay. They were followed, decade after decade, by other strong men fascinated by the dangers and difficulties of climbing into this "impossible" valley. In the fifth century the Burgundian knights are thought to have made it their base and stronghold for their running battles against the Saracens across southern France and into Spain. Later, when the Burgundians settled down, they founded the great landowning families of Seigneurs and left their serfs in La Vallée du

Désert to work the land and pay the tithes. In the historical records of the region, one begins to find some details of the early life of Saint-Pierre-de-Chartreuse. The families of the serfs were exceedingly poor. They baked their own rough bread. They grew haricot beans and lentils. They had a few chickens, goats and pigs. They made sausages, called Les Biaux, of goats' meat and pork, flavored with the aromatic herbs they picked on the mountainsides. They are still made by some families in the nearby villages of Les Entremonts.

In the eighth and ninth centuries parties of itinerant Benedictine monks stayed in the Valley for a time. The ancient records report that one of them said, "We could not bear the horror of so vast a solitude." Eventually they abandoned their buildings and departed. For another two hundred years, the wilderness of *le désert* remained unchallenged. Then, on a single day, the balance of power was changed. Seven men came to the Valley with a determination greater than the force of the wilderness. They took the Valley into their hands and shaped it into something forever different.

It was on the twenty-fourth of June in 1084 that a group of men, dusty and tired after struggling over the mountain road from Grenoble, appeared at the gateway to the Valley. One was in the robe of a bishop. Beside him walked a friar, his hood drawn over his head against the heat of the sun. Their followers carried heavy shoulder packs. The man with the inner power to conquer *le désert* was the friar Bruno. The extraordinary thing was that he was almost fifty-five years old. His decision to come to the Valley had arisen from his revulsion against the disintegration of the world.

Bruno had been born in the German city of Cologne. He had decided to be a priest and had come to France to study at the great cathedral center of Reims. He showed brilliant gifts and was rapidly promoted to positions of high leadership and power, but he was increasingly disillusioned by the dishonesty and immorality of his time. He saw himself surrounded by graft and greed. He watched the irresponsibility of political and religious leaders inside and outside the Church. When the struggle for political power and wealth in Reims cracked wide open and the Archbishop was expelled on charges of worldly ambition, Bruno's patience also cracked. He packed some clothes and food into his shoulder bag, turned his back on Reims and walked southward toward the forests of Burgundy. He wanted no more part of any society of men. He would be a hermit in the loneliest and wildest place he could find.

At the Burgundian monastery of Molesmes, he was advised by its head, the Benedictine Abbé Robert, to continue southeastward toward the Alps and to discuss his desire to be a hermit with Bishop Hugues of Grenoble. It was said that this man (at twenty-seven, one of the youngest bishops of France) was also a believer in solitude. He had found it again and again at times of stress by exploring the loneliest and wildest places of the Alpine mountains.

On his way Bruno found, one by one, six other men so much fired by his idea of getting out of the world that they packed their bags and came with him. When these seven men talked to Bishop Hugues in Grenoble, the bishop at once thought he knew the place where there was a spring in the middle of a forest, on a high plateau almost level with the peaks of the mountains above an isolated valley. He agreed to lead them to the place.

So—late on the sunny morning of the twenty-fourth of June in 1084—the seven men (with Hugues leading them), dusty and tired, climbed the steep mountain path and entered La Vallée du Désert.

THREE

Almost Nine Hundred Years Later— The Same Path to the Same Grandeur

We took the last sips of our coffee at the Auberge des Deux Mondes. Monsieur Michel drove the car across the old bridge over the River Guiers. We turned sharp left and climbed steadily in first gear toward the cleft in the granite wall towering above us. We were heading toward the same valley of peace as were Hugues and Bruno with their six companions almost nine hundred years before.

The cleft has been widened by blasting out a rock ledge for the road above the white-foamed river. The sign at the entrance pointed upward: Route de la Forêt Domaniale—Saint-Pierre-de-Chartreuse. The road turned and twisted blindly. It rose sharply. Our engine whined in low gear. The cliffs seemed to be leaning over us. On our right, there was a sheer drop into the gorge of the tumbling river. On our left the cliff stepped forward and blocked our way. The road tunneled through it. A right-angle bend. Another small tunnel. Fifty yards of sunlight. A third tunnel. A hairpin bend. One more tunnel. As soon as we were through the narrow Porte de la Fourvoirie, the rock walls opened out and we were in a forest of old beeches (many must have been almost a hundred and fifty feet high), brown, green, red and yellow. My ears were suddenly alert to every sound. My nose was aware of the essences of the earth. The scene was dominated by the orchestra of life and movement among the trees. From the gorge below there came the bass roll of rushing water. Above, the treble voices of the birds. They seemed unconcerned with our intrusion.

Monsieur Michel is intimate with these forests. He named the birds and their cries. From high on the cliff came the harsh klaxon hoot of the *coq de bruyère*, the Alpine grouse. Its mate was joyously gabbling as she fattened herself on ripe blueberries and raspberries. Nearer, there were the excited cackles and screams of the wild pheasant; also the high whistles of the mountain thrush, when she stopped gobbling juniper berries. There was the angry chattering of the rock partridge; lonely calls from the quail; and the raucous complaints of woodcocks. Farther away and higher up, there came piercing cries of wild moorhens and hazel grouse. Skunks and squirrels darted across the road as we traveled slowly.

Monsieur Michel said that sometimes at night his headlights had caught leaping foxes and hares. In the fall, on the highest slopes, he had hunted the "Prince of the Valley," the long-horned chamois; on the gentler slopes, he had found mountain deer. In the deeper forests he had tracked the *marcassin*, the young wild boar. When he fished in the clear river pools, Monsieur Michel caught rainbow and speckled trout. And at night he stalked and netted angry croaking frogs.

The trees closed in above us—an airy vault of gold and green lace. Then, quite suddenly, they opened out. Our road leveled. We were inside the security of the Valley. The gorge widened between the mountains. The Valley appeared as a vast oval amphitheater. Around the highest circle, soaring against the sky, there were the sharply chiseled, dazzlingly white peaks. Just below, wreathing around each peak like a dark green collar, then merging into the second circle around the amphitheater, were the forests of evergreen pines. Below, marching down the slopes to the floor of the Valley as if they were the spectators in the amphitheater, were the brightly colored, curving sweeps of the beeches. On the floor of the Valley, in the ring of the arena, rich green pastures surrounded the now-quiet river, with miniature herds of cattle and sheep. And, in the very center of the ring, with wisps of bluish wood smoke rising from its cottage chimneys, was the tiny village of Saint-Pierre-de-Chartreuse. It was an immense and self-assured scene.

Our paved road skirted the northern slope of the Valley. It remained high, with the downward sweep to our right. Below, a narrow winding gravel road followed the river and crossed it over an ancient stone bridge. Huge rocks seemed to block the course of the river, which disappeared beneath them, under a boiling, frothing whirlpool, with a thunderous roar. Early travelers along this road reported it as a terrifying experience. But our new road remained high above the white foam, continuing toward the center of the Valley, where it would turn and descend the steep hill to Saint-Pierre-de-Chartreuse. We did not go as far as the hill. We stopped on a high spur above the village. We had come to a group of grey stone buildings. One was low, solid and square, its stone washed in light beige and partly covered by rambler roses. There was a small hand-lettered sign above the door: AUBERGE DE L'ATRE FLEURI.

From the wooden gate, the flagstone path led through the roadside front garden, with lilac and rose bushes, geraniums and hydrangea. We were met at the front door by the two ladies who own and run the Auberge. Its business manager and maître d'hôtel was a slightly plump, vivaciously voluble lady from Provence, Mademoiselle Vivette Artaud. Her partner, the lady-chef, was a slim, ascetic-looking and quietly shy lady from Marseille, Mademoiselle Ray Girard.

We stepped at once into *Le Hall*, the central lobby and meeting place of the house. There was a warm, indoor smell of bread and fruit. The first piece of furniture, near the door, was an old *levain*, a low, heavily lidded oak chest in which yeasted bread dough was left to rise. Next to it, against the wall, was a *pétrin*, a timber box with a sloping bottom in which the risen bread dough was kneaded before being transferred to a *maie*, in which it was pressed into the shapes of loaves. I wondered whether these old chests were still being used in this house.

Le Hall was a large room and its first, most striking feature was its mirror-shiny, perfectly smooth paved floor of natural *ardoise*, slate flagstones in a dark and rich green. The floor established the informality of the room.

Then one's attention was drawn to the fire in the open hearth, which dominated the room with a feeling of comfort, gastronomic satisfaction, hospitality, warmth and welcome. The pile of huge beech and pine logs crackled and roared on a firebrick platform raised above the floor. More logs were stacked below the hearth. The opening must have been almost six feet high and five feet wide, framed by golden brown tiles and covered, above, by a canopy of polished copper with a valance of heavy leather to hold in the smoke. This open hearth pierced the central wall of the house. One looked through it, past the flames, into *Le Salon.* The hearth served both rooms with its flickering glow and shining warmth. But much more than that. This hearth also played its classic medieval role in the preparation of food. From its roof there hung a black wrought iron chain with a hook for a heavy cauldron. There were grill bars and black iron basting cups at various heights. In front there was a turning spit. There were covered holes in its floor, where iron pots could be set for slow heating under the glowing embers. There were warming shelves and iron tripods. There were chimney hooks for smoking hams. In spring and summer, when there is no fire in the great hearth, it is hung with antique copper cauldrons and pots filled with flowering and green plants. This is why the house is called "The Inn of the Flowering Hearth" (L'Auberge de l'Atre Fleuri).

We climbed the curving stairs to a room with casement windows overlooking the peaks and the Valley. We settled in and rested. Then Mademoiselle Vivette announced that she thought the midday sun was warm enough for us to lunch in the sheltered garden. On the wall at the left, as we stepped out through the French windows at the back, there were two freshwater tanks filled with live crayfish and rainbow trout. The air was soft and sweet, the view overwhelming. In the noontime hush, noises floated up from the village below: children shouting, crashes from the barns, water splashing into buckets. The sun had broken up the clouds and everything glistened. In our garden we were enclosed by the sounds of bubbling and rushing water from a stream at one side racing down over the rocks. Some of the water was piped off to a fountain, sparkling and splashing. We sat down to the first of the extraordinary meals of the Auberge. . . .

MENU OF
The Arrival Lunch

APÉRITIF: KIR DE PROVENCE

Soufflé aux Fromages des Alpes
(Soufflé of Alpine Cheeses)

WHITE, CRÉPY DE SAVOIE, FICHARD

Civet de Lièvre à la Chartreuse
(Ragout of Wild Hare in Red Wine)

Homemade Buttered Noodles

RED, BEAUJOLAIS VILLAGES DE BROUILLY, EN CARAFE

Salade de Cornette au Lard
(Salad of Belgian Endive with Crisped Bacon Dressing)

Fromages:

Picodon de la Drôme   Père Ernest du Dauphiné
Pétafine des Hautes-Alpes

Glace à la Noix de Grenoble
(Homemade Walnut Ice Cream)

Café

ENZIAN BRANDY OF MOUNTAIN GENTIAN

This magnificent lunch was based almost entirely on the local specialties of the Alpine region. It immediately established the extraordinary skills of Mademoiselle Ray in preparing the foods and of Mademoiselle Vivette in perfectly serving and precisely balancing them with the right wines. From this first occasion onward, the cuisine of the Auberge was made memorable by their approach to the food as a picture set off by the frame of the wine. For each dish, the frame was never so bold as to dominate the picture, nor so shy as to be overwhelmed.

This was especially true with the cheeses. Instead of offering us a huge cheeseboard with fifteen or twenty choices, Mademoiselle Vivette limited us to three types of exactly the right strength to complement and conclude the remaining red wine.

Even her opening Kir was quite different from the usual. She proved how much variety can be achieved in even the simplest of apéritifs by varying the white wine from the traditional Chablis. Instead, she used a dry, fruity, nonvintage white Rognac from a small vineyard near the Provençal village of Marignane about twenty miles from Marseille. One can get dozens of other effects with other white wines, mixed with the usual tablespoon per glass (more or less, to taste) of a first quality Crème de Cassis distilled from the black currants of Dijon.

The soufflé was unusually aromatic and richly textured from being made with two Alpine cheeses of powerful character: the French Gruyère des Alpes and the creamy yellow Tome de Savoie. These local cheeses have a strong affinity for the charmingly light Savoy white wines. Today, Mademoiselle Vivette chose a young vintage Crépy from the French slopes above the Lake of Geneva. Its aroma filled our noses as it was poured from its slim tall bottle. It was aromatic, full-bodied, slightly crackling on the tongue. For later lunches Mademoiselle Ray prepared several more soufflés, each distinctly different, each showing the variety that is possible from the same soufflé recipe (see page 199), with different combinations of cheeses and wines.

Mademoiselle Ray's friend Georges Cloitre had brought her a wild hare which he had shot on the mountain slopes of Les Entremonts above his village of Saint-Philibert. She had hung it in the cool outside larder for a few days. Then she had cut it up and marinated the pieces with herbs and a strong red wine of the Côtes du Rhône. Finally, it had been gently, gently simmered in more red wine, and to give a slight touch of aromatic sweetness to the gamy meat, she had flamed it with a glass of the local Green Chartreuse (see recipe page 286).

The accompanying Beaujolais *de l'année* (meaning, "of the last harvest") was the one which Mademoiselle Vivette had brought back in her car from her last tasting and buying trip. The Beaujolais country, after all, is only about seventy-five miles from the Auberge.

What the French call *La Cornette,* or *La Chicorée,* is chicory to the British and Belgian endive to us. The stalks were chunked and tossed with green scallion tops, crisped, crumbled bacon and garlic-rubbed croûtons, then dressed with hot bacon fat and tarragon wine vinegar (recipe, page 369).

To finish the wine, Mademoiselle Vivette presented three very local, little-known-outside-the-region, simple cheeses. The crumbly, salty Picodon is made by shepherds from goats' milk and ripened in sandstone pots. During this process the cheeses are pricked, or *pico*ed. Hence the name.

The Père Ernest is a fresh milk, young and creamy rich cheese which comes wrapped in straw, with a quite wonderful aromatic character.

The Pétafine is made from mixed cows' and goats' milk, slightly enriched with olive oil, then faintly flavored with Champagne.

Since walnuts are one of the principal crops on the agricultural plains around Grenoble and the Alps, it was to be expected that Mademoiselle Ray would make the richest and best walnut ice cream I have ever tasted. The freshly shelled nutmeats were skinned and pounded by hand into a pulp before being mixed with the cream base (recipe, page 406).

With the coffee, there were tiny glasses of the famous Enzian, a clear dry brandy distilled from the yard-long roots of the yellow mountain gentian flower which grows on the high Alpine slopes. A remarkable half-flowery, half-nutty flavor.

FOUR

The Price of Peace and Solitude Has Been Unending Struggle

Our strength renewed by food and rest, we began to explore the Valley. Instead of driving down into the village, we continued along the high road, climbing to the forested plateau dominated by the two highest peaks, Le Grand Som ("The Great Summit") and Chamechaude. Within a few minutes, we reached the group of ancient buildings abandoned by the Benedictines a thousand years before, now known as La Correrie ("The Courier's House"). At one time in the history of the Valley it was the gatehouse, closing off the road. No traveler was allowed to pass. Nothing was permitted to disturb the silence at the top. The rule of silence is still observed. A few yards beyond La Correrie there is a steel gate. The whine of engines in low gear is not welcomed on the narrow, rough, steep road up through the forest. Visitors walk up—generally in silence. We were at once under a vault of trembling leaves in a deep forest of beeches and pines. The late afternoon sunlight shimmered through in continuous movement. Monsieur Michel said he always felt that this was the most beautiful forest he had ever seen.

Suddenly, without the first warning of a distant view, we were in front of the high walls of the monastery that has taken its name from the valley, La Grande Chartreuse. The granite walls, perhaps twelve feet high, gave the impression of a fortress. Above the enormous doors, there was a notice: *On ne visite pas.* As the path took us above the monastery, we looked down on the grey slate roofs, steeply peaked against winter snows, of the buildings within the walls.

We reached a plateau between the mountain peaks. It was a wilderness of huge tumbled rocks and the great trunks of ancient pines. At the center, water bubbled out from a spring into a small rock pool, carved with the name Bruno. This is the place to which Bruno and his companions came when they entered the Valley on 24 June 1084. Apart from the gentle splash of the water, the silence was infinite. Only the whispered sighing of the air among the pines. Monsieur Michel sat on the edge of the pool as he talked of the history of the Valley.

When Bruno and his companions first saw this spring, the huge rocks had not yet fallen upon it. The ground was reasonably level. It would not be too difficult to cut a clearing in the forest. They went down to the village in the Valley and asked for shelter for a few days. Each morning at dawn they returned to the building of their "Chartreuse," their house of solitude in the wilderness. Since they felt that they were part of this Valley, they decided to call themselves by the original Roman name for its inhabitants. They became *Cartusiensi,* Carthusians.

Immediately they faced serious difficulties. In the wilderness they could grow only a small part of their food. They could not sow wheat. They would have to buy bread. They must have money to live. Their freedom to be alone, to have the peace and solitude for contemplation, would have to be earned. During the first winter the struggle was desperate. The Chartreuse was buried under fifteen feet of snow. The cold was unbearably intense. The following spring, they began assembling small herds of cattle, goats and sheep. They bartered some of the meat, the skins and wool for bread and other necessities. They made their own cheeses. They cut wood for their fires. Other men joined them. The Chartreuse became a community of about twenty men. As they expanded, they bought land in the Valley. In time they controlled its agriculture. They also controlled its development. They kept it unified. They preserved the natural simplicity of its life.

They continued this uncomplicated economy for almost fifty years. Then came the first disaster. On 30 January 1132, a great avalanche slid down from the peak of Le Grand Som, breaking off huge rocks the size of houses and rolling them down on top of the Chartreuse. It was completely crushed, then covered by ten feet of rubble. Half the Carthusians were buried alive. The rest started at once to rebuild, but now at a more sheltered place about a mile down the Valley. They called their new home La Grande Chartreuse. It stands there today.

The new building project demanded more money. It could not be done by barter with the villagers of Saint-Pierre-de-Chartreuse. Since the Carthusians would have to buy materials from outside the Valley, they would have to find something to sell to the world outside. They learned from the villagers about small-scale mining of the iron ore on the mountain slopes. The Carthusians became miners. They built a forge and harnessed water power—to blow air onto the furnaces and to work the hammers. They became known throughout Europe as the forgers of the hardest steel outside Sweden. They had a business. They had an income.

Yet their primary objective remained the life of solitude. Apart from their necessary work, they wanted to be left alone to live as hermits. They did everything possible to keep the Valley isolated—to discourage visitors. They closed the entrance with huge doors. They set up La Correrie as the gatehouse barring the way. But they were not left alone.

The Seigneurs of the region—the great landowners—began asking questions about mining rights. These powerful men had their private armies. They invaded the Valley, attacked the Carthusians and sealed up many of the mines by rolling rocks into them. At the end of an extremely hot summer in 1300, with the Valley as dry as dust, La Grande Chartreuse caught fire and was totally destroyed. It was rebuilt. Within twenty years it was burned again. Rebuilt, it lasted only eight years. One of the Seigneurs attacked La Grande Chartreuse. The Carthusians were warned in advance and hid in the forest. The soldiers destroyed every piece of furniture, every book and document in the library, all the stores of food. There was no peace for the Men of Solitude.

The Carthusians and the people of the Valley were decimated by bubonic plague and famine. In 1371, the third fire. Rebuilt. In 1473, the fourth fire. Rebuilt. In 1509, the fifth fire. Determined not to be driven out by these disasters upon disasters, they expanded their herds and their mines. The Valley rang with the beat of the hammers, with the crash of falling trees as more wood was needed for the fires, with the jingle of the teams of horses drawing the wagons loaded with ingots of steel. The Seigneurs were equally determined to stop the mining. They again invaded the Valley and sacked La Grande Chartreuse. In 1592, the sixth fire. In 1676, the seventh fire. Then the Carthusian steel operation began to decline. All over Europe, there were the beginnings of a mass-production steel industry which would, in time, eliminate the small forges. It seemed as if the Carthusian dream would fail. Perhaps, after all, one cannot fight the world. Perhaps there is no way out of it.

At this desperate moment there came into the hands of the Carthusians an extraordinary document. It was a recipe, handwritten on three tattered pages, for a kind of old wives' herbal potion. This sort of recipe, at that time, was nothing unusual. Almost every family had its private medicine, claimed to cure virtually everything. What was unusual about this recipe was its fantastic complication. Its ingredients included 130 different fresh herbs which would have to be picked on the slopes of the mountains and were required to be macerated and dissolved in brandy. One of the Carthusians was an apothecary. He decided to try to make the potion—even though the handwriting was almost illegible and the instructions extremely vague. The job took twenty-seven years. Finally, there was a brilliant green distilled liqueur—sweet and extremely strong. The people of Saint-Pierre-de-Chartreuse tasted it and loved it. Some of it was bottled in glass demijohns and carried in the saddlebags of mules over the mountain road to Grenoble. The people of Grenoble loved it too. They were more than willing to buy it at a very fair price. The Carthusians had a new product to sell. They named the drink for the Valley where it was made: "Green Chartreuse." Its success, however, was not assured.

The French Revolution intervened. The State ordered the Carthusians expelled from France and their buildings and lands seized. The army sent 400 men to occupy La Grande Chartreuse. The men of silence and solitude escaped across the mountain passes into Switzerland with their most valuable possessions, including the secret recipe for the liqueur. The valley of La Chartreuse was abandoned for twenty-four years. Not until 1816, when France "returned to normal," could the Carthusians come back to La Grande Chartreuse. They found it virtually in ruins. Now desperately in need of money to restore the buildings, they launched immediately into a larger scale production

of their green liqueur. Its success was inconceivable. By 1900 it was
being shipped to almost every country in the world. It made the name
of the Valley, the name of the Carthusians, the name of its green
color famous everywhere. There was more traffic in and out of the
Valley than ever before. Flagons of brandy and sacks of sugar were
delivered almost every day. More and more people drove up the
Valley to buy and carry away the liqueur. The entrance road was
widened by blasting.

Yet all this bustle and noise in the Valley—all this commercial
traffic—seemed somehow to be bringing the Carthusians nearer to
their fundamental objective. They had security. They could train
employees to distill the liqueur. To restore some semblance of peace
and quiet to La Grande Chartreuse, the Carthusians built a separate
distillery near the entrance to the Valley. The traffic no longer came
up the mountain road. Now perhaps there would be a life of silence
and solitude. Indeed, there would not.

In 1903 the French government, in a renewal of the persecutions
of the Revolution, again ordered the seizure of La Grande Chartreuse
and the expulsion of its residents. This time their exile lasted for
thirty-seven years. In 1940, with the German armies invading France
and the Paris government collapsing, the Carthusians came back
across the Swiss border and home to the Valley. They restored La
Grande Chartreuse. They did not restore the distillery for their green
liqueur. They decided that it was, in reality, an industrial operation and
should not be in the Valley. They built a new distillery in the town
of Voiron, beyond Saint-Laurent-du-Pont. The Valley of La Chartreuse
has returned almost to its original isolation—a place of peace and
solitude. The Carthusians discourage its development as a tourist
center. They are fundamentally opposed to the idea that it should
be easily accessible to the world.

Monsieur Michel was still talking as the sun set and the light
began to fade. The water still bubbled from the spring near us.
There was no other sound. It was growing dark and the stars began
to pour down their light, outlining the wild and lonely shapes of the
distant ridges. I sensed the menace of the approaching night. I
seemed to feel beneath my feet the ancient, unconcerned heart of
the earth. This did indeed seem to be the most inaccessible place in the
world.

As we walked down the rocky path in the cool evening air,
feeling very far indeed from the tense anxieties of the world, with the

lights of Saint-Pierre-de-Chartreuse shining in the valley below, I seemed to recapture an older reality, a more remote flavor of simple peasant life.

We reached the car and drove back to the Auberge. We were chilled by the night air of the mountains, and the blazing hearth was a roaring welcome. We sat in low rattan chairs and stretched out our legs towards the flames. In front of the fire the spit was turning with six partridges. Beneath each bird was a metal plate with *le canapé* (a slice of toast spread with the liver mashed with pounded juniper) where it would catch the dripping juices from the turning birds. The bouquet that teased my nostrils was almost unbearable—until Mademoiselle Vivette brought out the apéritifs and then conducted us into the dining room.

This room had a feeling of airy lightness, with long French windows looking towards the garden and the mountains. One might have been in the deckhouse of a ship, floating on a rolling starlit sea. There was even a ship's bell quality to the chimes of the tall old grandfather clock. In seagoing style, the ceiling and walls were paneled in polished wood and the corner bar was backed with dark green ships' canvas. But there was no tang of the salt sea about the earthy aromas of roasting game birds wafting in from the open hearth, where the fire was roaring and snapping as the dinner began.

MENU OF
The First Dinner

APÉRITIF: WAGON BYRRH

Coussin de Faisan Sauvage de la Diane du Grand Som
(Cushion-Terrine of Wild Pheasant)

WHITE BORDEAUX, SAUTERNES,
LA BERGERIE, BARON PHILIPPE DE ROTHSCHILD

Truite-Saumonée du Lac Paladru à la Genevoise
(Salmon-Trout in Red Wine as They Do It in Geneva)

PINOT ROSÉ D'ALSACE, LORENTZ, BERGHEIM

Perdreaux à la Broche
(Spitted or Grilled Partridge)

Gratin Dauphinois

RED BURGUNDY, 1959 POMMARD, LES EPENOTS

Fromages:
Champoléon des Alpes   Gaperon d'Auvergne
Gex Bleu du Haut Jura

Neige à la Chartreuse
(Snowy Soufflé with Green Chartreuse)

Café

KIRSCH DE CERISES SAUVAGES D'ALLEVARD

When Mademoiselle Vivette suggested that we start with a Byrrh, one of the other guests said smilingly: "Fine, I'd love a tall glass of Würzburger." But Byrrh is one of the tonic wines of France, fortified with brandy, made on the Mediterranean coast near the Spanish border. Mademoiselle served four ounces in each ice-cold glass, stirred with two ounces of dry Sherry.

Mademoiselle Ray's terrine of pheasant (brought to table in the shape of a cushion) was one of the finest I had ever tasted—made magnificently rich and strongly textured with the addition of the liver, smoky bacon, pork, wild mountain mushrooms, all marinated in Cognac and Madeira (recipe, page 172). Its name, of course, refers to the mythical huntress Diana, whose white-clad figure, with bow and arrow, is sometimes imagined during snowstorms on the mountain. The balance of the terrine with the lightly sweet wine was superb.

The fish had been brought in that morning by an old fisherman, a retired farmer of the Valley, Jean Morand, who had caught it in the emerald green waters of Paladru, the lovely mountain lake near Grenoble. Since we were only about ninety miles from Geneva, Mademoiselle chose to prepare it by the classic method of that city, in red wine (recipe, page 261).

The accompanying wine, one of the best French rosés, managed to be a link, both in color and in taste, between the red sauce and the pinkish fish.

Each diner got one whole partridge resting on its flavorful canapé and some of the gratin of sliced potatoes baked with garlic, nutmeg and cream, which is one of the glories of the Alpine region (recipes, pages 287 and 348).

The red wine with the main course was from the great Burgundy village of Pommard, from one of its great vineyards, Les Epenots, and of a great vintage year. The total effect with the aromatic flesh of the partridges was magnificent.

The local cheeses were especially planned to complement the local red wine. The small, round Champoléon, one of the most admired cheeses of the Dauphiné, is named for the high mountain village, where it is made from skimmed cows' milk flavored with wild herbs and wine.

The Gaperon is the most garlicky cheese of France, shaped like a tennis ball cut in half, with a thick, brownish, chewy crust. It is affectionately known (among those who like it) as "kill-fly," on the theory that when a fly lands on it and takes a deep breath . . . boom!

The blue Gex is from the district of that name in the Jura mountains—a rare cheese produced by local farmers in small quantities and much prized by connoisseurs. It had the shape of a medium-size grindstone, with a chewy, reddish yellow crust, and the inside flesh criss-crossed with natural blue veins developed during aging in mountain chalet storerooms. The yeast spores, which cause the blue mold, float in the air of these sheds, settle on the shelved cheeses and bore into them. One wishes one could say the same of all those mass-produced, "industrial" cheeses in which the blue mold is artificially inseminated by mechanical needles to speed production. This natural *bleu* had a homemade quality of reality never matched by the others.

The dessert was one of the greatest of all alcoholic sweet soufflés I have ever had. It was not more than two inches high, served in an au gratin dish, and more heavily laced with Green Chartreuse than I would have believed possible without preventing it from rising. The secret is in the very quick cooking in an extremely hot oven (recipe, page 404).

The *eau-de-vie* with the coffee was the famous clear cherry brandy from the resort town on the Isère River about twenty miles from the Auberge. It is one of the most beautifully perfumed of all distillations from wild cherries.

FIVE

The Art of the Perfectly Balanced Menu—Learning the Rules

At the end of this extraordinary dinner, we moved into *Le Salon* —on the opposite side of the open hearth. It was an extremely comfortable and very French room in a country style. Its walls and rough-woven curtains were in fall shades of brown and gold. Its carpet and easy chairs were spring green. These restful colors were set off by the vivid brightness of fresh flowers. In one corner there was an antique *scourtin,* a wooden cylindrical press for squeezing the oil out of olives or walnuts. On this side of the fireplace you could control the heat by lowering a large sheet of insulating glass. It hung from steel wires running over hand-wrought iron pulleys to copper-covered counterweights. With the glass down, the flames still dominated the darkened room.

When their work was done and most of the guests had gone to bed, Mesdemoiselles Vivette and Ray brought cups of hot *infusion de menthe,* perfumed fresh-mint tea, and we talked in front of the fire. I was excited by the discovery of such high gastronomic skill in this isolated place, so far from all the normal routes of tourism.

How had they come together to form this efficient team—this balance between, on the one hand, a composer of menus, a judge of wines and, on the other, a master technician in the precise control of aromatic herbs and cooking fires? What had brought them to this valley and this house?

"The house is more than two hundred years old," said Mademoiselle Vivette. "Originally, it was one of the farmhouses on the Brevard estate. The family has been in the Valley for many centuries. Generation after generation, they have been the notaries recording the transfers of land. Madame Brevard, who lives in the big house across the way, is now eighty-six. She decided, about fifty years ago, no longer to use this house as a farm and to allow it to be converted into a small auberge. When I first visited the Valley, in 1934, I stayed in this house and immediately dreamed of taking it over. But many things intervened, and I did not realize my dream until September 1948. It was then called the Auberge of the Charming Sound. We at once debaptized it. What we loved about it was the silence."

"What sort of experiences have led to your love of food and wine? And your flair for presenting them at table? How does one master this art?"

"I come from Provence," said Mademoiselle Vivette, "and that almost answers your question. In Provence, one is born a gourmet. At home, food and wine were the principal interests of my family."

"Where was your home?"

"Both my father's and my mother's families for generations have lived in the small village of Le-Puy-Saint-Réparade on the Durance River about twelve miles from Aix-en-Provence. My grandfather was mayor of the village for more than fifty years. My father was trained as a technical expert in agriculture. He was a nationally recognized specialist on the problems of growing food. He was an advisor to the farmers of the region. Then, for a while, my father's technical work took us to live in Arles—that lovely sunny town made vivid for so many people by the paintings of Van Gogh. There, my father was technical consultant on a large project for growing high-quality fruits and tomatoes. You see, I was learning about food from almost the first moment I can remember."

"Who did the cooking in your house?"

"Although at that time it was easy to find servants, my father never allowed my mother to hire a cook. He believed that a man married a woman for her cooking and that, at his own table, he should never be required to face a meal prepared by anyone else."

"Did he forbid your mother ever to be ill?"

"That was why she taught me to cook—that and the universal Provençal conviction that no girl had a chance for a man unless she was brilliant, both in the kitchen and at the table. My parents considered me a promising student, and eventually, after my father had begun to add a knowledge of wine to my knowledge of food, he quite approved of me as an alternate cook."

"Did your father have strict rules as to the proper marriage of food and wine? Do you still follow them?"

"I regard my father as one of the greatest wine connoisseurs I have ever known. But he was never a wine snob. He always questioned every oversimplified rule—every thoughtless tradition. He considered it the purest nonsense to marry wine and food by colors: red wine with red flesh, white wine with white flesh. . . . The key to success is not in the color, but in the balance between the dominance and power of the wine and the dominance and power of the food. A great, strong wine can completely kill a light, subtle dish. Highly aromatic food can overwhelm a light, subtle wine. There are some white wines so great and dominant that they go perfectly with the reddest of red meats. Some red wines are so delicately gentle that they would be perfect with almost any fish. My father also felt strongly that it was wrong to banish the sweet wines to the end of the meal. He believed—and so do I—that, as for example in our dinner tonight, very rich and strongly flavored terrine of game can be perfectly balanced by one of the lighter, slightly less sweet Sauternes of Bordeaux. The richness of the wine is needed to frame and set off the richness of the aromatic meat."

"When your father fully approved of your cooking and menu planning, did you start competing with your mother?"

"Absolutely not! He never looked to me when my mother was available. Alors—feeling that I was not really needed at home, I went off to the university at Aix-en-Provence. Then, quite suddenly, my mother died. My father—who hardly approved of the liberation of women—expected me, without question, to come home and run the house. At that moment my gastronomic education began in earnest. I was surrounded by a seemingly innumerable crowd of relatives—grandmothers, aunts, great-aunts, cousins . . . all making sure that I did not let my father down—gastronomically, at least! My grandmother used to tell me, in the Provençal dialect: 'Lou burre es cousinie!'" Butter is the best of all cooks. And, believe me, that was quite a statement in Provence, where olive oil had been king for a thousand years."

"I am very impressed by your art in balancing the menus," I said. "Do you owe that skill to your mother and your family?"

"I owe most to my mother," said Mademoiselle Vivette. "I still follow her rules precisely. She went much further than merely saying that, for example, a filling and solid first course should be followed by an airy and light second course; or that, say, an oily rich dish with a cream sauce should be balanced by something simple in natural juices; or that a very complicated preparation with a combination of many flavors should be balanced by something uncomplicated with only one dominant flavor; or that something acid should be balanced by something sweet. . . . These are the nursery rules. We all know them by heart. My mother went much further. She said that each dish on a menu must complement and enhance *all* the other dishes. Clearly, if the dishes are to be truly complementary, their flavors must not clash with or kill each other. A highly spiced dish will so deaden one's taste buds that a light subtle following dish will seem to be bland and dull. Serve them in the reverse order and the light dish will be a delicately lovely experience. After one's senses have been attacked by something aggressively strong, one should be soothed by something gentle and soft. A menu is the script of a dramatic performance. It builds, step by step, to a climax. Then it quiets down, before rising again to a secondary, smaller climax. Finally it closes in peaceful relaxation. I learned from my mother that harmony is the key to a great meal."

"You must have been *a treasure* at home. How did you finally break away from your family servitude?"

"I persuaded them to let me go to Paris. No loyal French family dares to deny a child the cultural inspiration of living for a while in Paris. Then came the war. I volunteered as a nurse's aide and was sent, eventually, to a military hospital in the Alps. There I found Ray, who was a registered nurse. We became close friends. On our days off we climbed the nearby peaks. We decided that we would like to stay among these mountains and work together, once the war was over. After all, this is a land of marvelous pastures for magnificent meats, of the cream and cheeses of the Savoy, of the flowery honeys and rich fruits and nuts of the Dauphiné. . . ."

"Did your father approve of your becoming an innkeeper?"

"*Mon Dieu,* yes! It didn't worry him the least bit that we were so isolated here. He was absolutely sure that people would come running from all over France to taste my dinners. So—I suppose, subconsciously, I have always organized the meals here as if I were still at home, trying to please my father. He came to stay with us here several times before he died."

Before going to bed on this first evening, I decided to ask Mesdemoiselles Vivette and Ray to allow me to explore in depth the cuisine of the Auberge of the Flowering Hearth. When they readily agreed, the idea for this book was conceived. Next morning, I asked for my breakfast to be sent up to my room so that I could work there on the organization of my first pages of notes and plans. I did not even notice the time until noon, when Mademoiselle Vivette called me to say that lunch was ready. . . .

MENU OF
A Provincial Lunch

APÉRITIF: CHAMBRAISE DE CHAMBÉRY

Tapenado Provençale Garni Rouge et Vert avec
Crudités du Jardin
(Three-Colored Canapé of Black Pâté, Red Caviar and Green Eggplant,
with Tidbits from the Garden)

WHITE, SEYSSEL DE SAVOIE,
BLANC DE BLANCS, VARICHON ET CLERC

Hochepot de Poule du Prince d'Orange
(Shake-Pot of Chicken in Creamed Wine, Orange-Style)

RED RHÔNE, CÔTE RÔTIE, CÔTE BRUNE

Fromages:
Beaufort du Haut Jura　　　　　　　Fourme du Cantal des Montagnes
Bleu de Bresse

Tarte aux Pommes des Belles Demoiselles Tatin
(Upside-Down Apple Tart, Baked in a Wood Fire)

Café

EAU-DE-VIE D'ALIZIER D'ALSACE

Starting lunch with the Chambraise was a neighborly gesture. Chambéry, the vermouth capital of France, is only about twenty miles over the mountains from the Auberge. This new vermouth, from Boissière in Chambéry, is made from tiny wild forest strawberries, *les fraises des bois.* We drank it with a dash of soda and a twist of lemon.

For the first course at table, there was a large platter with a varied and colorful array of hors d'oeuvres. There were slices of Russet apple, baby carrots, cherry tomatoes, Grenoble walnuts, sprigs of watercress, and, in the center, small mounds of the famous Mediterranean black pâté. (*Tapenado* is from the Provençal dialect—a *tapeno* being a caper.) I find it one of the most habit forming of aromatic mixtures —a smooth blend of anchovies, capers, black olives, tuna and Cognac. Mademoiselle Ray added two garnishing colors to the black pâté: red caviar and green eggplant (recipe, page 202).

The wine was the light, flint-dry, slightly crackling-on-the-tongue mountain white of Savoy, from the small town of Seyssel in the upper Rhône valley close to the Swiss border.

The name of the chicken dish is a part of European history. The original recipe came from the town of Orange, near Avignon. Before the sixteenth century, Orange was an independent principality belonging, not to France, but to the kings of Holland. (The Dutch royal family still calls itself the "House of Orange.") The original "hochepot" of Orange was transferred to Holland, and today the Dutch national dish is "Hutspot." The word "Hochepot" is Old French for a pot which is shaken every few minutes to prevent the contents from sticking. This is also the origin of "hodgepodge," meaning a mixture of many ingredients in one pot (recipe, page 334). The red wine was one of the lightest and loveliest from the slopes on the west bank of the Rhône just south of Lyon.

As to the cheeses, especially chosen by Mademoiselle Vivette to complement the finish of this particular red wine, the Beaufort (which might be called the Gruyère of the French side of the Alps) is made from cows' milk but does not develop the holes of its Swiss cousin. It is also much richer, more buttery, than the Swiss. It was made originally in high mountain chalets, above the village of Beaufortin, during the late summer when the cows are moved up to the high pastures. I found this natural Beaufort to have an astonishing bouquet, an attractively sharp flavor and a creamy, velvety texture.

The word *fourme* is from the ancient Auvergnat dialect and was originally used to define any round cheese shaped in a water-willow basket lined with oak leaves. Cantal is one of the Departements of the mountainous Auvergne region. Many of these cheeses are now *industriels*—made by mass-production methods in small, valley factories. A few (and Mademoiselle Vivette takes care to buy only these) are still *artisanals,* made by farmers and their wives at home, then aged in ventilated mountain caves. The yellow inside flesh has something in the character of English Cheddar and can be quite bland when young, but sharp and strong when properly aged.

The third cheese, the Bleu de Bresse, is generally considered to be the second best French *bleu* after Roquefort. The rich agricultural region of Bresse (famous also for its *poulardes*) is northeast of Lyon, between the Saône River and the Jura mountains. The cheese is made from full-cream cows' milk and has a strong bouquet, rich with vague overtones of cream and honey. Its flavor is piquant and its character seems to me to make it the nearest thing, on the French side of the border, to my beloved Italian Gorgonzola.

The dessert is claimed by the French to be the original version of an upside-down tart. Here at the Auberge it was baked in a covered pan under the glowing embers of the open hearth. The Tatin sisters were the owners of the small Hôtel de la Croix Blanche in the wild region of Sologne in central France. The story is that one day the younger sister was carrying an apple tart into the dining room when it slipped off the platter and fell on the floor upside down. She managed to scoop it up, but couldn't turn it over, because the crust had cracked. So she rushed it back to the kitchen and glazed it with caramel to hide the crack. It was such a success with the customers that it has become one of the classic recipes of France (page 378).

The clear Alsatian brandy served with the coffee was one of that marvelous multitude distilled from the various wild fruits of the Vosges mountains. *Aliziers* are the dark purple berries (with a taste rather like huckleberries) of what is called the service bush in some parts of the United States, the Juneberry in others, and sometimes the shadberry (because the white flowers of the bush bloom just as the shad are running).

SIX

The Techniques of the Kitchen—
The Making of a Cook

After lunch, I asked permission to visit Mademoïselle Ray in her kitchen. As I walked in, there was a noise as if someone were tap dancing on a stone floor. Her sleeves rolled up to her elbows, she was vigorously slapping a mound of dough on the marble top of her work table. On the chopping block, at the far side, the white-fleshed carcass of a baby kid goat gave off the warm smells of garlic and fresh tarragon.

A fair-sized kitchen had been made by combining two rooms of the original farmhouse. A wide window faced the mountains; another, on the west side, had been adapted as an indoor-outdoor greenhouse for potted herb plants. On sunny days the outer window could be opened. Mademoiselle Ray said: "In summer, of course, I step outside the kitchen door into our herb garden. But in winter it is my chief secret of good cooking to be able to reach out my hand and pick the fresh green leaves at the last moment before using them. Also, I always try to avoid overheating the herbs so that their oils do not evaporate. I may cut them into a sauce a few seconds before it is served. Or they may be added to the garnish of a dish just as it goes into the dining room."

Now she was kneading the dough, with firm and self-assured movements. The grey-veined slab (it must have been five feet by four and weighed a ton!) was supported by an iron frame and legs painted a bright red. When she wanted to use it for cutting, she covered the marble with a fitted sheet of thick zinc. For heavy chopping, of course, there was the large wooden block.

There was a professional cooking stove run on bottled gas. On the right of the cooker, at top-of-the-stove height, there was the *salamandre,* one of the essential tools of the French cuisine. A dish could be placed on an iron plate a few inches below a "hood" which reflected downward the heat from a powerful grill flame. The surface of the food could, within a few seconds, be made brown and bubbly, just before being served. My attention was diverted from the *salamandre* by a wild, scrabbling noise from one of the four sinks. It was half-full of water, with a few dozen crayfish crawling and swimming around. They had just been brought in from the garden tank.

On the opposite wall, there was a kitchen wine rack with more than two dozen bottles of reds and whites, dry and sweet Madeiras, Sherries and vermouths; various Armagnacs, Calvados, Cognacs, and dark Martinique rums; as well as a range of fruit brandies and liqueurs. Mademoiselle Ray said that the dry spirits could be used to add subtle touches to main dishes (even, sometimes, fish), while the liqueurs were mainly for desserts and for marinating fruits.

There were four professional refrigerators, deep and high, but there was no freezer, apart from a small box used solely for storing ice cream. Mademoiselle Ray said: "We do not believe in *les conserves industrielles*—our French name for anything canned, dehydrated, frozen, etc. All of us, of course, use some *conserves*. My own bottled fruits, jars of pickles, and marinated wild mushrooms, for example, are in fact *conserves*. Coffee beans and rice grains are in reality dehydrated. But whenever I have natural foods directly from earth or water, they are incomparably better."

Yet there was plenty of "conserving" going on in the kitchen and adjoining pantry. There was a marvelous array of pottery marmites of every size and conceivable shape. Some of them (large, lidded "berthes," or "cruches") were standing on the stone floor of the pantry, filled with mysterious pieces of this or that, soaking in marinating liquids, or preserved from the air under layers of white goose fat. Still, with all its equipment and stores, this room had none of the coldly impersonal feeling of a professional hotel kitchen. It was *La Cuisine*—the beautifully organized and much-loved heart of a French country home.

I asked Mademoiselle Ray: "How did you learn to be a chef? Did Mademoiselle Vivette teach you her techniques from Provence? What has been *your* gastronomic experience?"

"The first thing that will shock you," said Mademoiselle Ray, "is to know that I am half British. My mother came to the South of France from Manchester for a short vacation. She met my father in Marseille and never went home. My two sisters and I were born there. So you see, I am almost as much a Provençale as Vivette."

"Was the food in your home Manchester or Marseillais?"

"Totally English. Totally garlicless. Except when my mother went away for a few days, then my father fried Mediterranean fresh sardines in garlic-soaked olive oil and I helped him, almost before I could reach the top of the stove. My mother just couldn't bear the smell! Then, when my mother died, we three girls took turns cooking for my father. We competed fiercely for his approval. I learned one thing that my sisters missed. They tried to keep up my mother's traditions and prepared English food for him. I sensed that he was longing to go back to the Provençal cuisine of his childhood. I switched from butter to olive oil. I flooded everything with garlic. I garnished everything with olives. I sauced everything with tomatoes. I used a heavy hand with the herbs and spices. My father demanded more and more of my cooking. I basked in the sunshine of his approval. I was terribly shy. Cooking for me became the key to being loved."

"How did you finally get away?"

"I decided to become a nurse and went to Monaco for my training. Then came the war and I joined the Army Nurse Service. I was sent to a military hospital in the Alps, where I found Vivette."

Listening to the soft voice of Mademoiselle Ray and breathing in the perfumed aromas of her kitchen—the faint odors of earthy juices, the same essences one smelled in the breezes of the Valley—I felt I was discovering the secret of the extraordinary cuisine of the Auberge of the Flowering Hearth. Its heart was the combination of the strong and colorful techniques of the country cooking of Provence with the broad character of the Mediterranean internationalism—the subtle influences of the Arab world of North Africa, of Greece, Italy, Spain and the Middle East—that flowed into the great port city of Marseille, all gently restrained by the careful conservatism of England. Then, when the blend of these skills and traditions was transplanted to this Alpine valley, where Nature is still so completely in command, Mesdemoiselles Vivette and Ray were influenced by a new force. Among these mountains, there remains an irresistible regional unity in the products of a particular soil in a particular place. The earth of each valley, of each mountain slope, has its own peculiar balance of minerals and salts. They seep up through the roots of the grasses, the trees, the vegetables and vines, The cows eat the grasses. The minerals and salts control the character of the meat and the milk. The milk makes the cheese, which has a slightly different character in every valley. As soon as we try to mass-produce cheese, by mixing many milks from many valleys, this character is lost.

The minerals and salts are in the grapes, which control the character of the wines. The wine from one vineyard in one place is slightly different from every other. The earth is the unity between the products. The wines of the Savoy are the perfect complement to the cheeses of the Savoy. As soon as we try to manufacture mass wines by blending among many vineyards, the character is lost.

The cuisine of this Auberge is built on the foundation of the local products from the surrounding countryside. The meats are from animals which roam on these slopes and birds which fly among these trees. The fish are from these mountain lakes. The fruits and vegetables, from these farms. . . . This is the source of the sense of unity one feels flowing through each meal—and from one meal to the next.

There is one other Golden Rule in Mademoiselle Ray's kitchen. She follows (and does not try to overthrow) Nature's natural and perfect feeding cycle. She accepts the fundamental law that the right food always comes at the right time. By submitting to this natural cycle of the seasons, she revels in a cornucopia of delicacy and variety. She joyously prepares the first wild mushrooms after the snows. The first spring lamb, the first bright-green asparagus. . . . She happily revels in the rich flood of summer fruits . . . each month has its special meaning in her kitchen. June brings the crayfish from the rivers in the high valleys. October, the game birds and venison. December, the geese. The cycle of the year is a feast for every season.

Neither Mademoiselle Ray nor any other French cook demands soggy canned asparagus or mushy frozen strawberries in December. She does not defrost a venison steak in July. The reliance on out-of-season foods, she feels, makes the gastronomic year an endlessly boring repetition. She said: "If we try to overthrow the natural cycle, we are left with nothing more than dull and tasteless foods. But if we co-operate with Nature, if we follow instead of trying to lead, the reward is one marvelous meal after another."

This seemed to be the moment to leave Mademoiselle Ray to the preparation of, one was sure, a marvelous dinner. . . .

MENU OF
A Mountain Dinner

APÉRITIF: PERNOD SUISSESSE

Poireaux de Meyrargues
(Leeks with Purée of Tomatoes)

MACONNAIS BLANC, DOMAINE BURRIER

Brochet Braisé au Champagne
(Lake Pike in Champagne)

Caneton Glacé aux Pêches à l'Armagnac
(Duckling Garnished with Fresh Peaches and Flamed with Armagnac)

Tian de Courgettes au Riz
(Tian of Zucchini with Rice)

MAGNUM OF RED BURGUNDY, 1964 CHAMBERTIN, CLOS DE BÈZE

Fromages:
St. Félicien de Savoie   Berrichon de Valençay
Fort aux Poireaux de Dauphiné

Croquettes de Marrons
(Fried Chestnut Croquettes)

Café

MARC DE POMMARD

Since the "deadliest of all drinks," absinthe, has been banned in France (and almost everywhere else in the world), Frenchmen now consume enormous quantities of its anise-flavored substitutes: Pernod and Ricard. At her miniature copper-covered bar, Mademoiselle Vivette mixed the Pernod Suissesses with one egg white per person, two jiggers of Pernod and a tiny teaspoon of sugar. It was all furiously shaken with ice until it was the lightest of foams, then served in tall chilled glasses.

The method of preparing the local white baby leeks is from the valley of Meyrargues in Provence, which an American publicist might call "The Leek Capital of France." They were lightly poached in a sauce which included green, virgin olive oil, puréed tomatoes, chopped lemon pulp, fresh bay leaves and garlic. It was served at room temperature (recipe, page 185).

This strong sauce was well matched by the strong white wine from the Burgundian region just north of Beaujolais.

The handsome large river pike, weighing about three and one-half pounds, was first larded by Mademoiselle Ray with Cognac-marinated lardoons of salt pork, as if it were a piece of meat. Then it was lightly poached with butter, shallots, and wild forest mushrooms in brut Champagne. After the fish was done and removed, the liquid was reduced, slightly thickened with heavy cream and served as the sauce. Finally, the fish was decorated with flowerets of flaky pastry and carved mushroom caps (recipe, page 256).

The main entrée was one of Mademoiselle Ray's masterpieces—the brilliant combination of the rich juiciness of a lean young duckling, fresh from a farm near Grenoble, with the accent of brandied peaches and an extraordinary sweet and sour sauce of maple syrup (a gift sent by a Canadian friend) and tarragon wine vinegar. The duck was braised on an aromatic bed of carrots, shallots and fresh tarragon, lightly moistened with dry white wine. Meanwhile, the peach halves were quickly sautéed in butter and flamed with a mixture of Armagnac and orange Curaçao. Finally, the juices of the duck were converted into the sauce with the addition of miniscule amounts of the maple syrup and vinegar before being reduced, concentrated and slightly thickened. The duck was served garnished with the peach halves, with the sauce poured over and everything beautifully glazed under the *salamandre* (recipe, page 335).

The accompanying dish of zucchini and aromatic rice was baked and served in an earthenware *tian,* the classic shallow square baking dish of Provence. As with the word "casserole," the cooking pot gives its name to the entire dish. The chopped zucchini was folded into the rice, with cheese, onions, garlic and herbs, then baked with an enrichment of cream and beaten eggs (recipe, page 357).

Clearly, all this was worthy of one of the finest bottles from the cellar of the Auberge: a magnum from the great Clos de Bèze vineyard of Gevrey-Chambertin. Although it was still somewhat young, we all agreed that it was a very fine wine—potentially noble.

To finish such an outstanding red, Mademoiselle Vivette offered three farm-made cheeses of interesting and strong character. The Saint Félicien is an extremely rich double-cream, originally from the High Savoy village of Saint Félix but now made in several local valleys. It is shaped rather like a thin Camembert, with a bluish yellow crust and a wonderfully aromatic flavor.

The Berrichon is the most famous goat cheese of the village of Valençay, on the road from Lyon to the Loire valley. The cheese is shaped like the base of a pyramid and its crust is covered with finely powdered beechwood ash. When fresh, it is creamy and soft, but as it ages it becomes progressively harder and, finally, smells a bit like the menagerie at the circus. It was a favorite cheese of the great French statesman Talleyrand, who once owned the Château de Valençay and placed the Berrichon near the top in his "hierarchy of cheeses."

There was also the white cheese of the Dauphiné mountains, *Le Fort*, of cows' milk, perhaps given its name because it is speckled with bits of chopped leek and green peppercorns, giving it a strongly oniony, peppery flavor.

For the unusual and attractive dessert, shelled and skinned chestnuts were cooked in vanilla-flavored milk, then mashed. Next, this purée was molded into balls, each with a glacéed chestnut at its center. The balls were then rolled in fine breadcrumbs, deep-fried until crisp on the outside, sweetly luscious on the inside, and served sprinkled with powdered sugar. Each was a single luxurious mouthful (see page 384).

Sensing our warm appreciation of the entire dinner, Mademoiselle Vivette was in a mood to share her greatest treasures. She brought up from the cellar a dusty unlabeled bottle which had been given her as a Christmas present by one of her Pommard suppliers in 1948, the year she took over the Auberge. She guessed that it must have been about thirty years old when she got it and was now more than fifty. Most Burgundian vignerons distill their own private brandy (called *marc*) from the mash of grape pulp and skins (also called *marc*) left in the press after the liquid wine has run off. When this *eau-de-vie de marc* is aged, it can be extraordinary. We opened this bottle with considerable anticipation. It glub-glubbed heavily into the snifters. It was deep purple. Its bouquet was superb, and it went down the throat as a pure combination of dynamite and velvet. We tottered to bed.

SEVEN

The Marché des Maraîchers in Grenoble—A Frenchwoman Shops by Her Own Rules

Next morning, it was still dark when Mademoiselle Vivette called me. I had asked to be awakened in time to go with her to market. Now, at this uncivilized hour before dawn, the idea seemed preposterous. I threw open the wide casement windows. The air was fresh, sharp, sweet. . . . It had the shock of a cold shower.

Most of the raw materials used at the Auberge come from local farmers and suppliers. Fresh eggs are delivered almost every day, from the Carthusians in their Grande Chartreuse at the top of the Valley. Cream and milk are supplied from the farm of Joseph Mollaret, about fifty yards up the hill above the Auberge. Salad greens and vegetables come from the garden of an old lady who lives alone a little way down the hill—Madame Lucie Rey seems to have no other interest but the tender care of her garden, except on days when she goes frog hunting on the marsh. Seasonal cheeses and fruits are picked up from other farmers, and some older, retired men, with legs still strong enough to climb the mountains, gather the seasonal mushrooms and wild herbs. Village schoolchildren, on weekends, pick wild

45

summer berries and *fraises des bois.* As for bread, the village baker
Roger Cloitre of Saint-Pierre-de-Chartreuse is at the center of its
gastronomic life—supplying brioches, croissants, long loaves still hot
out of his ovens at the back of the shop, or large balls of unbaked
yeast dough to be molded to every purpose in Mademoiselle Ray's
kitchen. And Robert Goudard butchers the fresh meat.

But, of course, the Auberge cannot be totally self-sufficient from
the Valley. For the things from wider regions—for the rice from the
marshes of the Camargue—for the fish from the Mediterranean—for
the coffee from Martinique—for the dates from North Africa and the
figs from Istanbul—and for the oranges from California—Mademoiselle Vivette shops three times a week in the extraordinary markets
of Grenoble.

"We'll take 'La Route de Sappey,'" she said, "the mountain road
walked by Bruno and his companions when they first came to the
valley nine hundred years ago." As we left the Auberge in her Simca
wagon, the Valley was a pale pink, reflecting the bright glow behind
the peak of Le Grand Som. We climbed steeply and plunged into the
gloom of the forest, where night seemed still to be lingering. We
wound through the narrow pass of Le Col de Porte. Mademoiselle
Vivette drove with the daring and dash of a racer who knows every
inch of the course. Her performance was impressive, but a shade too
dazzling for complete comfort. The road was a series of giant switch-
backs. Every few seconds, Mademoiselle Vivette would snap out *"Attention, tournons!"* or *"Tenez bien, virage!"*—Gallic warnings to hang
on for a blind turn or a hairpin bend at high speed, above sheer drops
into thousand-foot gorges. Her high-pitched horn beat a tattoo. Her
brakes rumbled and squealed. Her snow tires twittered. Her voice—in
between the sharp warnings and the oaths under her breath at the
unimaginable stupidity of all other drivers—calmly described the
magnificent scenery. Since she made this journey at least three times a
week, she knew every change of light on the mountains, every sound
and rustle of the morning.

The miniature hamlet of Les Revols was so tightly hemmed in by
cliffs it seemed as if at any moment it might be crushed. Towering up
to the right was the mile-high peak of Le Charmant Som. We raced
through the village that has given its name to the road for more than a
thousand years, Le Sappey-en-Chartreuse. It was dominated by the sheer
granite cliff of Le Fort du Saint-Eynard. The road was riding the
mountain chain, called Le Massif de la Chartreuse, which runs rather
like the spoke of a wheel toward the central hub of Grenoble. Another

peak-studded spoke, marching in from the east, was La Chaîne de Belledonne. Wherever the cliffs broke into manageable slopes, there were the brilliant colors of the beech forests. The valleys below were a red sweep of wild cherry trees. There was so much variety in every slope—so many intricate patterns of colors, rocks and trees. We mounted higher. The view widened. The distant mountains were pale violet in a patchwork of haze and sunshine. More chains of much higher peaks—more spokes to Grenoble's wheel—were rising, step by step, each higher than the other: La Chaîne des Grandes Rousses, Le Massif de l'Oisans, Le Massif de la Vanoise.... Finally, far away to the northeast, there was a glimpse of the massive white spire, rising as from a cathedral among the surrounding peaks, of Mont Blanc.

We surmounted the last rise in the road. Laid out in the valley below, in a haze of trembling light, was the winding Isère River and the city of Grenoble. It is the San Francisco of France. It is built around, between and on hills. There is no street corner in Grenoble where one cannot see, above the roof tops and at the end of the road, a guardian peak looking down.

It was now about 7 A.M., and as Mademoiselle Vivette raced down towards the river and the city, she discussed her shopping plans for the morning. There is a public square in Grenoble where, for centuries, it has been the tradition for *les maraîchers*, the small farmers of the region, to come into town and operate their own open air market, *Le Marché des Maraîchers*. In the square, appropriately called *La Place des Herbes*, the city provides, without charge to the farmers, every Tuesday, Thursday and Saturday morning, benches, booths and display tables.

All traffic had been diverted from the square. It was jammed with people and riotous with noise. The sellers were shouting their wares. Shrill-voiced housewives were arguing about prices. Rude jokes were being shot from one booth to another. Mademoiselle Vivette squared her shoulders and plunged in, forcefully cutting a path to the center of the melee. I grimly hung on behind her.

But there was nothing grim about her shopping. She knew almost every farmer by name. She asked questions about the children. The talk was all very gay, good natured, full of jocular badinage. Yet, everyone knew that she was deadly serious about quality and value. No one ever tried to fool her. They offered her, at once, the best they had. I believe that Mademoiselle Vivette is the most skillful food shopper I have ever known. The first thing I learned from her was the importance of building one's reputation as a knowledgeable, sharp and tough buyer. To each farmer from whom she bought regularly, week after week, she proved that she knew as much about his products as he did. She blended her sharp criticisms with warm praise. Her judgment was so much admired and respected by each farmer that he saved the best things of the day for her.

She moved along the line of stalls, inspecting, touching, smelling, tasting. . . . "Those frogs are too big—they're not from this region." "Rub your finger over the slightly loose skin of that apple—it has been too long in storage." "Stick your little finger up the backside of that chicken—it has been frozen and defrosted." We reached one of her most regular suppliers, Serge Alibe, who had come in with his wife and his mother from the famous cheese village of Saint-Marcellin, about twenty-five miles down the Isère Valley. He had only three products from his tiny farm: a creamy fresh, soft white goat cheese, which he dug out of small wooden tubs, walnuts from his trees and his own pressing of fresh walnut oil.

As we continued along the line of display tables, the impression of care and quality was nothing short of exquisite. There were orderly arrangements of *poils et plumes* ("feather and fur"): hares, rabbits, pheasants, partridge, mounds of baby thrush. . . . One wizened old lady, who must surely have been eighty, displayed at least twenty varieties of wild mushrooms, all of which, she said, she had herself picked in the woods. She had orange brown *chanterelles*, chestnut brown *bolets*, various types of *lactaires* (so called because, when they are cut, they ooze a milk in shades of red, yellow or white), dark brown *trompettes des morts* and forest *cèpes* as large as saucers.

At the next stand, Madame Chapuis sold nothing but the day-old eggs from her own chickens on her farm in the mountain village of Quaix. After greeting her warmly Mademoiselle Vivette whispered to me: "I buy my best cooking eggs from her, not only because they are always fresh from the nest, but because the yolks are really a deep yellow. They add a beautiful color to our custards, ice creams and sauces."

Some of the finest vegetables were on the stall of Jean Raymond, whose farm is at Meylan, about two miles out of the city. He had white leeks of every size, from babies to giants. There were large, thistle-spiked grey cardoons—a vegetable comparatively little known, even in France. There were strange large green pods mottled with black, the inside rows of peas dark brown. Monsieur Raymond called them *Coco de Savoie*. I suspected that they were a kind of *pois chiches*, chick peas.

Suddenly, there was a sweet perfume on the air. Round the corner, a snowy-haired old lady was sitting, smiling, behind the most beautiful display of roses, all cultivated in her own garden.

Mademoiselle Vivette dashed here and there, making final purchases. She inspected the fruits and vegetables from the farm of Germain Foglians, also from Meylan, and bought bunches of long bright green sorrel for an *Omelette de Mon Curé* (recipe, page 189) —also, some tiny green artichokes called *Les Violets de Provence*, tender enough to be eaten raw in a salad—miniature pale mauve aubergines, so small that I could hold four in one hand, and some peaches as ripe as honey. . . . Then, she felt she had culled all the perfection she could from the *Marché des Maraîchers* and we walked towards the Place Sainte-Claire and *Le Grand Marché*. This was the covered market—still strictly regional, retail and *artisanal*—the producer selling directly to the consumer—where the butchers, the *charcutiers*, the poultrymen, the tripe men and the larger farmers rented from the city their permanent stands, to which they brought their produce every day. There was also of course, near the railroad terminal, *Les Halles*, the wholesale market, which Mademoiselle Vivette considered *industrielles*, mass-production, to which she went only as a last resort. Among the larger farmers and cattlemen, she seemed as much at home and as much respected as she had been with the *Maraîchers*.

From "Monsieur le Boucher," Georges Charrat, she bought various larger cuts of fresh meat which she knew she could not get in her valley. Since it is legally forbidden for a butcher in France to sell any form of salted or smoked meat, she went next to "Monsieur le Charcutier," Michel Rouge, for *le lard* ("bacon"), *la poitrine fumée* ("smoked brisket") and *le salé* ("salt pork"). She might have been tempted by at least fifty other specialties from the dazzling display on the marble counters and shelves. The charcutier (as everywhere in France) was half a chef, and he had prepared dozens of kinds of pâtés, sausages, *terrines en croûte*, including some specialties for which he was famous throughout the region.

But Mademoiselle Vivette moved on to "Madame la Tripière," Annie Cherigni, who sold not only seventeen different kinds of tripe (I counted them!), but also all the other "variety meats" which cannot legally be sold by either the butcher or the charcutier. She was looking, especially, for tripe and small feet from very young lambs. She wanted to prepare for me a Provençal specialty, *Pieds Paquets*

Marseillaise ("Packaged Feet," believe it or not!) (page 300). She also bought whole veal heads, lambs' tongues and *joues de boeuf* ("ox cheeks").

Mademoiselle Vivette's final chores of the morning were quick visits to some of the small, family run shops in the Old Quarter of Grenoble. (She never shopped for food in the midtown department stores. "Everything you buy there," she said, "has a kind of standard-ized taste, whether you buy the package in Grenoble, Paris, or Bordeaux. I want our cooking to be special to our region.") From Jean-Paul Dessertine, the coffee merchant, she picked up five kilos of a two-to-one blend of whole beans of Martinique and Arabia. From Henri Vachon, *le quincaillier* ("the ironmonger"), she bought one of his own hand-forged-and-hammered black iron "witches' cauldrons" to hang over the fire in the open hearth. Next she went to "Monsieur le Poissonnier," Vincent Terraillon, who specialized in fish, both from local lakes and rivers and from the Mediterranean fishing ports of Agay, Fréjus and Saint-Tropez. From one of his saltwater tanks she picked a live sole and a large *lotte de mer,* the latter for a *bourride* (page 248)—the rich and garlicky fish stew that is Nice's answer to Marseilles' *Bouillabaisse.* In other fresh or salt tanks there were *chien-de-mer* (Mediterranean dogfish); *bogue* (porgie); *merlan* (whiting); *julienne* (ling); *raie* (skate); *lingue* (hake); *lieu noir* (black pollock). . . . There were two freshwater tanks side by side, and in one a male rainbow trout was ogling a female in the other. The gentleman then rose to the surface, took a great leap and, with much splashing and water spilled on the floor, neatly dived into the second tank with his girl friend.

The last stop of the morning was, to me, the most dramatic. There had been a lot of cheese on display at the various markets, but Mademoiselle Vivette had refused to consider any except the fresh white *chèvre fermière* of Serge Alibe. Now we reached a most hand-some shop in the Old Quarter, La Fromagerie, owned and run by Monsieur and Madame Pierre Coulon and their daughter, Madeleine. "There are plenty of cheese shops in Grenoble," said Mademoiselle Vivette, "run by merchants and salesmen—here we have a family of cheese technicians and, most important of all, true lovers of cheese." The Coulons are the top specialists on the mountain cheeses of south-eastern France. They also stock, of course, almost all the cheeses of the rest of the country. But the most dramatic point about the Coulons is that, before they sell any cheese, they take the responsibility of bringing it up to the point of ripeness which they call *parfaitement fait* ("perfectly done").

Madeleine showed me how this result was achieved. In the warehouse behind the shop, there are ten separate storage rooms, each automatically maintained at a precise humidity and temperature. If, say, a Reblochon arrives unripe from the Col-des-Aravis in the Savoy, it goes at once into one of the damper, hotter rooms. An overripe cheese can be cooled down and slightly dried out.

In the shop, the *parfaitement faits* cheeses were displayed, each on its own wooden cutting board, on large marble-topped tables. One's freedom to taste was unlimited. The various tables were labeled by regions and cheese types: *les bleus du Dauphiné, les crèmes de la Savoie, les fromages fermiers de l'Auvergne, les double-crèmes de la Normandie. . . .* Mademoiselle Vivette knew exactly what she wanted. Madeleine explained for me.

On the table of local goat cheeses (almost all called simply *chèvre fermière*) there were twenty-three types, each with a different taste because it came from a different region or valley. Testing my way around the various *bleu* tables, I realized that the cows' milk cheeses, the Bleu d'Auvergne, Bleu de Bresse, Bleu des Causses and the local Sassenage, were all creamier, richer, softer, more buttery, in sharp contrast to the dry and salty, almost ascetic quality of the sheep's-milk Roquefort. The rarely available local blue, Lavazein, made half-and-half of cows' and goats' milk, was less rich than the others but strongly aromatic with mountain herbs. There was a whole table of *crottins*— small ball-shaped cheeses. I tasted Crottin Sancerrois, Crottin de Bresse, Crottin de Chavignol. . . .

Perhaps I was getting drunk on cheese. I tasted wildly from table to table. A Chaource from Champagne. Two creamy marvels: a Caprice des Dieux from Normandy and a Savoureux de Neige from the Savoie. A memorable Tome de la Valleé de Queyras from the mountains southeast of Grenoble. A Camembert-shaped Chambarand from the Dauphiné. . . .

Madeleine explained why there are always so many different cheeses from a mountain region where there is a great deal of snow. In late summer the cows are taken up *en alpage* to graze on the lush grasses on the higher slopes. It would be heavy and messy to carry the liquid milk down to the valley. Far better to build cheese-making chalets on the mountains, since cheese is, basically, hardened milk without the weight of its water. Then, when the snows come, the cheeses are carried down in baskets on the backs of the herdsmen. To prevent these creamy soft cheeses from sticking together when they are packed, they are wrapped with strange coverings. Madeleine showed me a goats' milk Valençay covered with the ash of burnt beechwood. A Pithiviers from Orléans was wrapped in straw. A Vacherin from the local valley of the Joux was completely covered in birch bark. Other cheeses were wrapped in chestnut and oak leaves.

We left Grenoble and started climbing towards the mountains. By noon we were unloading our precious packages at the kitchen door of the Auberge, eager to fit some of these treasures into our next meal....

MENU OF
The Lunch on Market Day

APÉRITIF: SUZE DES ALPES

Coeurs d'Artichauts Violets de Provence à la Grecque
(Hearts of Artichokes in a Vinaigrette Sauce)

WHITE BORDEAUX, CHÂTEAU LOUDENNE, MÉDOC

Bourride à l'Aïoli Provençal
(Mediterranean Fish Stew with Garlic Mayonnaise)

RED BEAUJOLAIS, CHIROUBLES

Fromages:
Chèvre Frais de Serge Alibe en Petit Panier

Tome de Queyras   Pithiviers au Foin de Gatîne

Tarte à la Crème aux Framboises
(Creamed Raspberry Tart)

Café

EAU-DE-VIE DE MIRABELLES DE LORRAINE

Mademoiselle Ray planned this menu, so far as she could in the short time before lunch, around the fresh foods we had brought back from Grenoble. We waited in *Le Hall*, sitting before the roaring log fire, sipping the apéritif, which was strictly Alpine. Suze is the lightly fortified cocktail version of the Enzian which we had had at the end of the first lunch. It also is fermented with the roots of the mountain gentian and served undiluted, ice cold.

Since we had brought back the tiny artichokes called *les Violets de Provence*, Mademoiselle Ray quickly stripped them to their hearts and cooked them in the classic, *à la Grecque*, mixture of oil and vinegar (recipe, 178). They were served at room temperature—a delicately light *amuse-gueule* (which means, literally, "amuse-throat") before the solidly rich nutrition of the *bourride*.

The charming white wine was from one of the less well known châteaux of the Bas-Médoc. Since the French government does not want to do anything to diminish the worldwide fame of the Médoc as a red wine region, the phrase "White Médoc" is not permitted by law. Yet there are delightful white wines made there and they are now beginning to be more widely distributed in the United States. (See Index.)

Next to *La Bouillabaisse, La Bourride* is the best known fish stew of the Mediterranean coast. Down there, it can be a great blowout of unlimited garlic. But Mademoiselle Ray's English conservatism kept the garlic down to manageable proportions. A *bourride* is often made with a mixture of several kinds of fish, but she proved that it could be simplified by using only the *lotte de mer* we had brought back from Grenoble. She cut it into large chunks and poached them in aromatic *court-bouillon*. She made a standard mayonnaise and worked into it the required amount of mashed garlic to convert it into a Provençal *aïoli*. When the fish was done, it was served resting on chunks of fried bread in a soup plate, and the bouillon, thickened with the *aïoli*, was poured over the fish until the plate was full of the gorgeously yellow soup. In Provence, this dish is called "sunshine in a plate" (recipe, page 248).

With the choice of a very light Beaujolais to go with this rich dish, Mademoiselle Vivette again showed her remarkable ability to achieve a precise gastronomic balance. The fruitiness of the very young red wine perfectly cut the unctuous richness of the fish stew.

As we unpacked the cheeses, we wondered whether our choices in Grenoble, under the pressure of so many alternatives, had been good. Serge Alibe's homemade fresh white goat cheese was so creamy and smooth that it was best eaten with a spoon. So Mademoiselle Ray served it on large lettuce leaves in a little wicker basket. On our plates we ground over it plenty of fresh Indian Tellicherry black pepper and consumed it with hot-from-the-oven walnut bread (recipe, page 142).

The Tome from the village of Queyras, near the Italian border, was made from cows' milk. It had a rather chewy grey crust, but inside, it was soft and smooth and had a very satisfying aromatic flavor.

After the Pithiviers (from the village of that name, northeast of Orléans) had been unwrapped from its straw covering, we found a soft crust and creamy texture. It was an excellent complement to the last of the Beaujolais.

The beauty of Mademoiselle Ray's raspberry tart was that the fruit was almost entirely uncooked and so held its marvelous mountain freshness under the smooth custard cream. She baked a special yeast-raised tart shell, filled it with the raspberries, poured over the custard and set it in the oven for five minutes (recipe, page 401).

We ended the meal with one of the clear fruit brandies of Lorraine. The mirabelle is the sweet golden plum of that rich agricultural region. The best variety is *La Petite de Metz*, which has such a strong flavor and perfume that it makes an outstanding brandy—the name "Lorraine" on the label being the legal guarantee of quality.

MENU OF
The Dinner with the Foods from Grenoble

———————

APÉRITIF: PICON GRENADINE

Omelette de Mon Curé
(French Omelette with Creamed Sorrel)

WHITE BURGUNDY, MEURSAULT, LES CHARMES

Potage aux Poireaux Grenobloise
(Cream of Grenoble Leeks)

Filets de Sole à l'Etouffée
(Fillets of Sole Braised on the Hearth)

Aloyau de Boeuf à la Méridionale
(Spit-Roasted Sirloin with Aromatic Herbs)

Cardons à la Moelle
(Cardoons with Beef Marrow)
Gratin Savoyard
(Potatoes with Cheese Baked in Consommé)

RED BORDEAUX, 1961 CHÂTEAU PALMER, MÉDOC

Fromages:
Caprice des Dieux de Normandie   Bleu de Sassenage
Crottin Sancerrois de Chavignol

Glacé aux Noisettes
(Homemade Filbert Ice Cream)

Café

EAU-DE-VIE GRATTE-CUL D'ALSACE

In France, more than in the United States, people seem to enjoy prefacing their meals with the bitter-sweet brandy-based mahogany-colored apéritif spirit called *Picon*. Mademoiselle Vivette used one jigger per person in a very cold old-fashioned glass, with a little less than a teaspoon of grenadine, a dash of soda and a twist of lemon.

Some of the long leaves of the fresh sorrel we had brought from Grenoble were snipped into half-inch lengths, briefly sautéed in butter and incorporated into the omelette. Finally, it was garnished with warm heavy cream and Cognac and brought, still bubbling, to table (recipe, page 189).

For the rich cream soup Mademoiselle Ray used the wonderfully sweet baby leeks we had brought back from Grenoble. She chopped them, sautéed them in butter, poached them in light cream, then slightly thickened the soup with yolks of eggs (recipe, page 212).

The wine with the omelette and the fish was from one of the finest vineyards in the famous white wine Burgundian village of Meursault on the slopes of the Côte de Beaune in the superb area known as *La Côte d'Or* ("the Golden Slope").

Mademoiselle Ray boned the sole which we had brought back in the morning and steamed the fillets in their own juices in a tightly covered iron pot. (This is the classic meaning of the word *étouffée*, literally "suffocation" in its own steam.) In the pot, she laid the fillets on a bed of aromatic herbs and vegetables, then tightly sealed the pot and placed it under the glowing wood embers in the open hearth. After about thirty minutes, the fish was exactly *à point,* and the oils of the herbs had injected a dramatic and subtle flavoring so that no other sauce was needed beyond the natural juices (recipe, page 263).

The word *aloyau* is simply the French name for our "sirloin." But for this dish, which involved turning it on a spit, the meat was cut to the shape of a long rectangle, with both sides of roughly equal width. This was covered all over with a highly aromatic, typically Provençal mixture of chopped anchovies, diced beef marrow, chopped shallots, melted butter and olive oil. Then the whole messy business was tightly wrapped with long wide strips of dark-smoked bacon, tied with string and spit-roasted before a blazing wood fire until everything was a gorgeously smoky and tasty brown. The sauce was the natural juice that dripped off the meat as it turned (recipe, page 268).

The cardoons we brought from Grenoble were skinned and sliced, then slowly cooked in oil and lemon juice, put into an au gratin dish with cream sauce and slices of beef marrow, covered with grated Parmesan and grilled until brown (recipe, page 366).

A *Gratin Savoyard* is basically the same casserole of aromatic sliced potatoes as a *Gratin Dauphinois,* but with two differences. First, the sliced potatoes are interleaved with cheese, and second, the cream is replaced by a concentrated chicken consommé. After the slow baking in the oven, the taste and texture were slightly different, but the eating was equally satisfying (recipe, page 349).

The vineyard of Château Palmer is one of the most consistently underrated of all the "classified" wines of the Médoc district. According to the now-largely-out-of-date Classification of 1855, it should be a "third-classed growth." In fact, it now runs, consistently year after year, slightly above the average standard of the "second-classed growths." The 1961 vintage of this and other great châteaux of the Médoc will, in my opinion, eventually be regarded as one of the great vintages of the last fifty years—perhaps, by the year 2000, one of the greatest of the century!

We finished the wine, of course, with more of our Grenoble cheeses. The *crottin* came from the famous wine town of Sancerre in the Loire Valley and its satellite village of Chavignol. Only this district in France is permitted to call its small round cheeses *crottins* because of their quality. This version was a medium-hard goat cheese, brown-grey in color and fairly mild in taste.

The Caprice des Dieux was an extremely rich, smooth and soft cows' milk cheese from Normandy, which is still the butter and cream capital of France. Why a cheese as good as this should be associated with the "capriciousness of the gods" escapes me. Obviously, it is a most carefully planned and extremely successful creation.

The village of Sassenage is about five miles west of Grenoble, but its famous blue cheese is now also made in various other villages of the district. The cheese can be of cows', goats', or sheep's milk (or a mixture of two or three of them) and the inside paste is heavily blue-veined, with a creamy rich texture.

The ice cream was another of Mademoiselle Ray's masterpieces—rich, velvety smooth, and with a strongly nutty flavor. She made it, quite simply, from a classic egg custard base (recipe, page 407).

We ended the dinner with the clear Alsatian fruit brandy affectionately named (and this is officially printed in all the reference books) "Scratch Arse." It is distilled from the hips of the wild eglantine rose, or dog rose, which grows in the woods on the slopes of the Vosges mountains. The stalks are so heavily thorned that presumably the name of the brandy refers to the condition of the backsides of the pickers as they return from the woods. There is a "second theory."

Some distillers use the rose's astringent fruit which is shaped like a tiny elongated red egg. It is hard to handle. At its center it has a mass of stiff, spiny hairs, all of which must be carefully removed before it is used. If you should unwisely eat the fruit before it is cleaned out, you will have a big pain, and later, in the bathroom, you will have a *cul* quite badly *gratt*ed.

EIGHT

Menus for the Winter Season— Fire Burns and Cauldron Bubbles

We were talking, again, in *Le Salon,* after everyone else had gone to bed. We were nibbling Mademoiselle Ray's small cream-and-liqueur-filled pastry puffs, which she called *Les Petits Choux à la Chartreuse.* I wanted to know what it was like to live and eat at the Auberge for the full cycle of the year. What was it like here on New Year's Day? How deep was the snow? When did the first snow usually fall?

"It usually comes in the first part of November," said Mademoiselle Vivette, "and almost always at night. In the morning, even before I open my eyes, I know from the silence. From end to end of our valley the silence is total. It's palpable. Oh, of course, it brings many practical problems with it, but what it brings, above all, is the peace of that silence. So one welcomes it, with a secret gladness—knowing that it will be with us until the end of March.

"By the time the first snow falls, the beeches are already bare," Mademoiselle Vivette continued, "and the only green is the dark of the pines. On the first day of snow, Ray and I always try to take a walk through the beech forests, late in the afternoon, as the light is just beginning to fade. The snow is still powdery. The forest is pure fairyland. Every branch, every blade of grass, every leaf of every growing thing is outlined in the lightest of white fluff. The path has disappeared. One is overcome by the mystic beauty of the scene. One cannot speak a word.

"But, of course, this is only the first touch of snow. Next day, the great flakes are falling, always straight down in completely still air, steadily, day and night, for many days and nights. Soon there is five feet of it around our Auberge. Almost to the tops of our ground floor windows. Much more, of course, up near the monastery and on the high passes. There the snow is often fifteen to twenty feet deep."

"So the skiers come to the Valley.... Are you usually full on New Year's Day?"

"Oh, yes. We are always full for all the school and university holidays."

"And what do you serve to these hungry boys and girls? What rich, solid and, as we Americans say, rib-sticking cold-weather dishes?"

"From morning to night," said Mademoiselle Ray, "my largest black iron 'witch's cauldron' hangs from the hook above the huge log fire. We ladle the food out of it hour after hour. One day it may be filled with our Spécialité de la Maison, *Le Hochepot de Poule du Prince d'Orange,* made with chicken, veal, celery, leeks, onions and so on, gently simmering in veal stock and white wine. Or it might be a Mediterranean dish from my home, *Les Pieds Paquets Marseillaise,* with lambs' feet and aromatic little packages of tripe bubbling in a bouillon. Or a pot roast of *Boeuf à la Mode Marseillaise* with blackberry brandy and olives. Or our Grande Spécialité, *La Marmite de Lesdiguières,* with every kind of meat, chicken and vegetables, and the sauce laced with Cognac."

"This last dish, what does its name mean? Was there a chef called Lesdiguières?"

"No. During the reign of King Henry IV, at the end of the sixteenth century," said Mademoiselle Vivette, "Lieutenant-Général de Lesdiguières was the *Connétable,* the Constable—you might say the Governor—of our ancient province here of the Dauphiné. He was a great man for organizing public dinners. He traveled continuously from one end of the province to the other, and whenever he wanted to talk something over with the leaders of a particular town or village, he would find the largest available hall, organize a menu, and invite perhaps a hundred people to dinner. His menus were

famous throughout southern France. For a celebration in Grenoble
he gave a dinner for two hundred guests, and the main dish was this
marvelous 'marmite,' for which de Lesdiguières wrote out the recipe
for the cooks in his own hand. That piece of paper has been preserved
through the centuries and is now in the historic archives of the University of Grenoble. The amounts are for two hundred servings and
it begins like this:

" 'Line a big-bellied iron pot with 120 slices of bacon. Put in 160
pigs' feet, 200 pounds of best beef, 320 large carrots, 200 tomatoes,
50 onions stuck with 200 cloves and 60 bay leaves. Then pour in
40 bottles of red wine, 24 bottles of white and a gallon of best Cognac. Later, add 32 whole chickens and 50 pounds of mushrooms. . . .'
And that was only the beginning of what had to go into that Gar-
gantuan marmite! So Ray copied this famous recipe, brought it down
to manageable proportions and started experimenting with it. Now
we have our version of *La Marmite de Lesdiguières*, in our specially
made pot for about twelve people."

So far, we had been discussing the specialties of this region of
the Dauphiné; its cuisine naturally dominated by the physical char-
acteristics of mountains, of impenetrable snows, the need to conserve
summer supplies for winter eating. But these two ladies had come
from the eternally sunlit land of Provence, where the olives grow the
year round, where there is no snow and not much fear of a shortage
of winter supplies. I asked whether they had brought any of their
original Provençal recipes with them and had succeeded in adapting
them to the way of life of the Alps. Mademoiselle Vivette told me
the story of her *Grande Terrine de Canard à la Grand-mère Artaud*. . . .

"For all the years that I was a young girl in my father's house
in Provence, always, at our Christmas and New Year feasts, my
grandmother prepared a simply magnificent terrine with which to
open the menu. It was famous in our village and for miles around.
It was my grandmother's secret. She walked out into the hills, where
the sage, the savory, the thyme and other herbs grew wild, and I am
sure she selected the leaves almost one by one. Nor did we ever find
out what kind of meats went into that famous terrine: whether it was
a mixture of chicken, duck, goose, wild game birds. . . . As she grew
very old, we begged her to write out the recipe. She always refused.
When she died, she took her secret with her.

"It was a family crisis, so to speak. As I told you, my father was
a 'grand gourmet,' and he was increasingly happy about my cooking.
He asked me if I would be willing to try to replace *La Terrine de*

Grand-mère. It was the most terrifying assignment of my young life! The only saving grace was that there were still nine months until Christmas. I was determined not to try merely to imitate the famous terrine. I would develop something entirely different and new. After several months of research among ancient cookbooks in the library at Aix-en-Provence and of experimenting with recipe after recipe in the kitchen, I decided to concentrate on a terrine of duck. I worked at it for endless hours. I must have made at least thirty advance terrines for private tasting by my father. He was a severe but constructive critic. Finally, at Christmas, he wisely made the rule that no one should compare my terrine with his mother's— that each diner should judge it as harshly as he wished, but standing on its own. It was my great victory. Everyone agreed that it was magnificent. My father made a speech and said that I had proved that I had the true gastronomic blood of the Artaud family in my veins.

"Then came the war and the German occupation of France. All food stuffs were in very short supply. There was no problem about the ducks. One could go out and shoot them. Nor about the truffles. They were dug up at night and sold on the black market. But my recipe also required an exceedingly rich and unctuous white stock to make the marvelous aspic, and for this I had to have veal bones and knuckles. I also needed the white meat of very young veal to lighten the dark meat of my duck. There was absolutely no veal in the market. The first week of August, with tears in my eyes, I told my father that I could not possibly make a terrine for Christmas that year. Next morning, he went off very early by himself to the agricultural market. He returned a few hours later, walking along the dusty road leading a live cow. She was a pregnant cow. Her calf was due to be born the first week in December. My terrine was saved. When my father told the story at Christmas dinner, I saw one of the guests wink at the lady on his right and heard him whisper: 'I always told you that when it comes to food, old Papa Artaud is crazy.' "

MENU OF
A Winter Lunch

APÉRITIF: PUNT E MES

Lactaires Délicieux Sanguins Vinaigrette
(*Wild Mushrooms Vinaigrette*)

Potée Montagnarde
(*Winter Vegetable Soup*)

ROSÉ D'ANJOU, VIEUX CHÂTEAU DE TIGNÉ, LOIRE

Pieds Paquets Marseillaise
(*Lambs' Feet with Tripe Surprise Packets*)

RED RHÔNE, 1964 CHÂTEAUNEUF-DU-PAPE,
DOMAINE DU MONT-REDON

Fromages:

Vacherin des Bauges   Tome de Savoie

Lavaldens Bleu de La Mure

Crêpes Surprises

Café

EAU-DE-VIE DE MYRTILLES

The name Punt e Mes means, technically, "point and a half," an expression much used on the Turin stock exchange, whose members consume vast quantities of this Italian bitter vermouth. After all, Turin is the vermouth capital of Italy. To maintain good relations between the two countries, Mademoiselle Vivette, for the Americano, teams the Italian with the sweet Dolin, a French vermouth of Chambéry. Half a jigger of each, with a dash of soda and a twist of lemon peel.

In September, when the bright orange Lactaire mushrooms appear in the woods, Mademoiselle Ray picks them and then preserves them in oil and vinegar. Then she brings them out in winter as a sharply savory hors d'oeuvre. No wine is served with them, since it would clash with the vinegar (recipe, page 425).

In virtually every mountain region of the world, there is at least one kind of "rib-sticking" winter mixed-vegetable soup based on a rich meat bouillon. They are all completely flexible and can be made light or solid, according to the amount of potatoes involved. The ultimate test of solidarity is whether the ladle will stand up straight in the serving pot! Mademoiselle Ray makes hers fairly light, with red cabbage, onions, smoked pork and red wine, all simmered slowly for hours (recipe, page 224).

The rosé (considered to be one of the finest of France) properly met the requirement of a light wine to go with the *potée*. At the Auberge, we all followed the Dauphiné tradition of *faire chabrot* with the wine. As the large bowls of soup were served, absolutely piping hot, each guest added a little wine from his glass and stirred it in for the dual purpose of cooling the soup and sharpening its flavor. Then, when all the solid vegetables had been eaten and nothing remained in the bowl but bouillon, one added a little more wine and it was permissible to lift one's bowl to the lips to drink the last few delicious mouthfuls.

The *Pieds Paquets* were a winter *Spécialité de la Maison* from a regional recipe of Mademoiselle Ray's birthplace, Marseille. She cut squares of lambs' tripe and folded them so as to form Christmas-card-size envelopes. She filled these with a highly aromatic garlic and pork stuffing. She simmered them in a huge iron pot already half-filled with smoky bacon, vegetables, baby lambs' feet and white wine (recipe, page 300). The very light rosé accompanying the *potée* was properly followed by a much more solid red from one of the finest vineyards in Châteauneuf-du-Pape.

The cheeses with which to finish the wine were some of the best of the winter Dauphiné and Savoy types. The Vacherin is probably the most admired cheese from the region, made from cows' milk in small huts high in the mountains during the late summer when the cows graze on the upper slopes. It's at its creamiest when the cows chew grass that is stiff with frost. The small whole cheeses come to table still tightly wrapped in birch bark. When it is peeled off, the crust of the cheese is almost unbelievably bright yellow. In each valley the taste is slightly different, and the one of the Bauges district, which Mademoiselle Vivette buys directly from farms only a few miles from the Auberge, is considered to be among the best.

The Tome de Savoie is also a universal cheese of the Savoy mountains, made from fermented buttermilk, each type varying slightly in flavor and texture. The one served by Mademoiselle Vivette was a round wheel, about eight inches across and perhaps five inches high. The crust was colored with patches of brownish grey and reddish yellow, with a chewy texture and aromatic flavor. The inside flesh was yellow, with tiny Gruyère-style eyes, with a smooth, semi-soft texture and a rich creaminess on the tongue. It was quite wonderful in bringing out the fruitiness of the wine.

There was also a fine and rather rare local blue, a Lavaldens (sometimes spelled Lavazein) from the mountain village of Lavaldens. It had a firm crust, but the inside paste was velvety and wonderfully perfumed with mountain herbs.

The surprise about Mademoiselle Ray's crêpes was her whipped sugar-cream filling and topping very strongly flavored with the marvelous local Allevard Kirsch. The hot topping was textured with delicately burnt almonds (recipe, page 387).

As to the *eau-de-vie*, it was a clear brandy distilled from the bluish-black fruit variously called, in different parts of the world, bilberries, huckleberries or whortleberries.

MENU OF
A Winter Dinner

APÉRITIF: SAINT RAPHAEL CHANTECLAIR

Le Feuilleté au Roquefort
(*Roquefort Cheese Flaky Pastry Pie*)

WHITE RHÔNE, CHÂTEAUNEUF-DU-PAPE BLANC,
DOMAINE DE BEAU RENARD

Consommé Florentine aux Oeufs Pochés
(*Consommé Florentine with Poached Eggs*)

La Grande Marmite de Lesdiguières
(*The Grand Feasting Pot of Governor General de Lesdiguières*)

Riz au Safran	Griottes au Vinaigre
(*Saffron Rice*)	(*Pickled Sour Griotte Cherries*)

RED BORDEAUX, 1961 CHÂTEAU PETRUS, POMEROL

Fromages:

Beaumont des Alpes		Chambarand du Dauphiné
	Bleu des Causses	

Tarte au Citron à l'Atre Fleuri
(*Lemon Cream Tart*)

Café

EAU-DE-VIE DE PRUNELLES

Although Saint Raphael has an Italian name, it is an extremely French delicate red bittersweet apéritif tonic wine fortified with brandy. Mademoiselle Vivette converted it into a *Chanteclair* by mixing two jiggers of Saint Raphael with one jigger of the equally French Marie Brizzard "Old Ladies" aromatic gin, then icing them and serving in a chilled glass.

The hors d'oeuvre was a large flaky pastry shell filled with a mixture of Roquefort cheese, butter, cream and eggs and cut into piping hot wedges just before serving (recipe on page 197).

With this first course, the dry white wine of strong character was from the Rhône village of Châteauneuf-du-Pape, most famous for its red wines. Many of the younger producers, including Paul Coulon, the owner of the fairly small Domaine of Beau Renard, are now also growing white grapes and producing excellent, refreshing white wines. This one was an outstanding example of this relatively new trend.

The classic *Consommé Florentine* involves, first, a highly aromatic, rich and strong chicken bouillon, which Mademoiselle Ray prepared the day before. In this superb broth, she then poached an egg for each person and set it on a canapé round of fried toast, in the soup plate. Finally, she lightly sprinkled the surface with grated Parmesan cheese (recipe, page 211).

The great festive marmite of the famous de Lesdiguières family (see page 61) is unquestionably the most historic dish of the Dauphiné region. And this modern version, adapted from the ancient recipe by Mademoiselle Ray, is certainly the top specialty of the Auberge. Its appearance at table is dramatic. It comes in an enormous, specially made heavy ceramic dish divided into seven compartments. In the first is the impressive slab of poached beef. In the second, the veal. In the third, the pork. In the fourth, the chicken. In the center, a huge pile of saffron rice. At the two ends, the two accompaniments: one a hot and peppery sauce; the other the tiny pickled sour cherries—the *griottes* of the mountain slopes, the perfect foil to all this richness. And over all is the superbly unctuous broth, laced with red and white wines and unbelievable quantities of Cognac (recipe for the marmite and its sauce, page 276; for the pickling of the cherries, page 423).

A great dish of such complexity of flavors and textures demanded to be balanced by a dominant and powerful wine. It has been said that the district of Pomerol is the "Burgundy" of Bordeaux. And the finest of all the Pomerols is Château Pétrus, of which the greatest recent vintage is the 1961.

The first of the cheeses with which to finish the wine was the Beaumont, of cows' milk from the small region of that name along the valley of the Drac. It was rich and soft. It converted the wine into velvet.

The Chambarand, also of cows' milk, came from the village of Roybon in the Dauphiné. It had a reddish yellow crust and a firmly chewy texture. It had something of the taste of a Reblochon and was shaped like a quite small Camembert.

The Bleu des Causses is from the central mountains of the region of the Auvergne and is made from unskimmed cows' milk. It is not to be confused with the original Bleu d'Auvergne (page 76). Variations of the Bleu des Causses are also made in the Bordeaux region and in the ancient province of Gascony. The type set before us at this dinner had been aged in natural caves and was beautifully dry and crumbly, with bluish green veins and a fine, medium-strong flavor.

Mademoiselle Ray's lemon cream tart is highly original. She bakes a pastry shell and then fills it with a creamed mixture of eggs, sugar, lemon juice and grated rind, and melted butter. All this goes into the oven until it is delicately golden brown. The final result is extraordinary (recipe, page 394).

The clear *prunelle* brandy was distilled from sloe berries, bluish-black small wild plums from the blackthorn bush which grows as well in the mountains of Kentucky as it does on the Alsatian slopes of the Vosges. What sloe gin is to the American South, *prunelle* is to France.

NINE

*Menus for the Spring Season—
The Leaves Climb up the Mountain
and the Garlic-Flavored Lambs
Come Gamboling Down*

I asked Mademoiselle Vivette what was usually the first sign of spring at the Auberge. She answered: "In this Valley, people always say that they know it is spring when 'the leaves start climbing up the mountain.' When I came here, I didn't understand what they meant. But it's true. When the first tiny new leaves appear on the beech trees, they are a marvelously delicate green, but they are only on the lowest trees, at the edge of the fields around the village. Higher up, the beeches are still bare and dark. Then, day by day, you watch the green climbing up in the brilliant sunlight. Every morning it has moved up, perhaps ten meters. It's one of the most exciting times of the year, to see that lovely, light and tender green climbing, climbing, until it meets, on the highest slopes, the somber dark green of the pines.

"Ray and I often climb with it. We go out into the woods early in the morning. When the sun is bright and it shimmers through those young leaves, the effect is magical. It is as if one is walking

70

under water. One is immersed in a trembling, unearthly light. I have
never found this strange light anywhere else in the world. Perhaps
it's the extreme brightness of the sunlight at this high altitude? Perhaps the beech trees in these forests are shaped in a special way, or
are closer together or wider apart? It is something quite unique to
this valley of La Chartreuse."

"Every year in the sparkling springtime," said Mademoiselle Ray,
"it is almost as if we have a bright, clean, new valley to explore.
Every year, as the snow recedes, there are changes—some things are
different. As we walk up the wooded slopes, there are new views of
airy hillsides suddenly and unexpectedly visible through the trees—
always new shapes in the early morning wisps of white fog drifting
across the valley below us. We look down to our own house, and the
checkered patterns of fields and walls and woods rising up behind
it also seem to be changing. On spring mornings there is a coolness
in the air and, sometimes, a briny feeling, as if the breezes were
coming straight from the Mediterranean and mingling with the earthy
vapors of our own soil. In the sunrise stillness, the crowing of a cock
seems to come from a great distance as it echoes and reverberates
among the high rocks. Then, in the burnished stillness, the whole
scene is like a stained-glass window, shimmering with a new restless-
ness, shining with new hope."

"In virtually every part of the world," I said, "there seems to be
one particular food delicacy which is the special harbinger of spring.
In England it is the wonderfully fine first asparagus. Even in New
York, hemmed in as we are by concrete and steel, we know it's
spring when the shad start running up the Hudson River. What is
your first spring food at the Auberge?"

"Here, it is our *hygrophore de neige*," said Mademoiselle Ray,
"our wild 'snow mushroom,' which is creamy white and pushes its
way up underneath the snow just as it is thinning out and receding
in the warm sunlight during April and May. It is as if the earth is
releasing the spring and this little mushroom is too impatient to hold
back its desire to come up and meet the sun. One sees the little bumps
in the thin snow over the soft mosses around the trunks of the trees
in sheltered hollows. We dig with our fingers and bring the mushrooms quickly to the kitchen. Their perfume is marvelously delicate,
and, before they fade, we sauté them and serve them with the lightest
of sauces. Also, during April and May, there are the dark morels,
which are more difficult to find."

"And dangerous, too," said Mademoiselle Vivette, "because the poisonous snakes like them and are usually near the beds where the morels are growing. But the prize is worth the danger."

"And then, at the end of April or the beginning of May," said Mademoiselle Ray, "in the fields at the bottom of the Valley, there are the mysterious 'Roses of St. George,' so-called because they are usually there in profusion on St. George's Day, April 23. The mystery about them is that they always grow in fairy rings: perfectly rounded small white circles here and there among the patterns of the darker grasses on the pastures. At the same time, in other parts of the fields, we pick up the little beige *mousserons*. They go perfectly with our spring lamb."

"I suppose there are different mushrooms, here around the Auberge, to announce every season?"

"Our Valley seems to be an ideal place," said Mademoiselle Vivette, "for every kind and type, from the moment the snows melt until winter returns. Our temperatures are mild, the winds soft; there is moisture in the air—all the right conditions for the mushrooms. Different varieties grow at different heights. There are flavor essences in the rich earth distilled from the roots of the trees. It is all a complex balance of Nature.

"Among the hundreds of varieties, there are strange names and even stranger colors and shapes: the 'golden orange,' the flamboyantly red 'bleeding latex,' the 'sparassis,' which grows and is colored like clumps of coral, and the pink 'pigs' ears' along the banks of forest streams. In an ideal year, with damp and soft weather, there may be more than five hundred varieties—all deliciously edible. We have sometimes been able to pick more than two hundred kinds in a single morning, without even walking very far."

"What else announces the spring?" I asked.

"The croaking of the frogs," said Mademoiselle Vivette. "Just below the Auberge there is a small piece of marshland called La Martinière, at the bottom of the Valley. There, as the snows melt and the marsh fills with water, the frogs breed. Following the sounds of their enraged croakings, Ray and I track them down and net them.

"And as to main dishes," Mademoiselle Vivette went on, "when the fresh supply of young spring garlic arrives, we like to make an *aïoli* —the marvelous garlic-flavored egg mayonnaise which goes so perfectly as the sauce for fish or for young vegetables, either hot or cold."

"You use a lot of garlic?"

"Not as much as all that," said Mademoiselle Vivette, "because after all, Ray is still a little bit English! Once I remember that a friend of my brother came to stay with us from Provence. You know, of course, that there they make their *aïoli* almost solid with garlic! It was a warm spring day and this friend, Madame Ricard, said that she just felt she would love an *aïoli* for lunch. We happened to have some cold poached cod, some freshly boiled spring potatoes and quite an array of fresh spring vegetables. So naturally Ray assembled them all on a handsome platter and prepared her *aïoli*, beginning, of course, with the raw yolks of eggs and the best Provençal olive oil. Then she began adding, bit by bit, her mashed garlic, and, to sharpen the flavor, spritz after spritz of lemon juice until she thought she had it right. I didn't taste it before carrying it into the dining room, but an instant later Madame Ricard cried out: 'This isn't an *aïoli*! This is a Parisian mayonnaise. I don't even taste the garlic! What did Ray think she was making? A lemonade? In Provence, we wouldn't dream of diluting our beloved garlic with lemon.' "

MENU OF
A Spring Lunch

APÉRITIF: VERMOUTH-CASSIS, BOISSIÈRE DE CHAMBÉRY

Cuisses de Grenouilles à la Poulette
(Sautéed Frogs' Legs in Cream and White Wine Sauce)

WHITE SAVOY, ROUSSETTE DE SEYSSEL, VARICHON ET CLERC

Hygrophores de Neige à la Paysanne
(Wild Snow Mushrooms, Peasant Style)

Agneau de Printemps Grillé
(Grilled Spring Lamb)

Les Asperges au Vin Rouge   Le Farçon de Pommes de Terre
(Asparagus with Red Wine Sauce)   *(Potato Pancakes, Alpine Style)*

RED, GAMAY DE SAVOIE, FICHARD

Fromages:
Pouligny-Saint-Pierre de Berry   Bleu d'Auvergne
Savoureux de Neige de la Savoie

Gâteau de Savoie
(Cake of Savoy)

Café

EAU-DE-VIE DE SUREAU D'ALSACE

At the Auberge, a vermouth-cassis is virtually a local drink. The fine dry vermouth of Boissière comes from the nearby Savoyarde town of Chambéry. The fortified black-currant syrup of cassis is the great specialty of Dijon, where Mademoiselle Vivette buys it from local small producers on her tasting trips to Burgundy. With such exceptional ingredients, her proportions are one ounce of Crème de Cassis, mixed over ice cubes with four ounces of dry vermouth in an eight-ounce tumbler, then filled up with soda and vigorously stirred.

When there is a good harvest of frogs from the marsh at the bottom of the Valley below the Auberge, Mademoiselle Ray sautés the legs in butter with chopped shallots, then covers them with a sauce of spiced white wine, thickened with egg yolks and faintly acidulated with lemon juice (recipe, page 247).

What she does with her wild *hygrophores* would be equally effective in bringing out the best flavor from any good fresh mushrooms anywhere in the world. She lightly sautés them in butter until their water has been expelled and they begin to absorb the butter. She very lightly seasons them, sprinkles them with a few drops of lemon juice and covers them with a sauce of slightly thickened aromatic chicken broth (recipe, page 397).

Nothing goes so perfectly with a bright spring day as the light, wonderfully fruity and refreshing red and white wines from the mountain vineyards of Savoy. The first, on this menu, was the dry and slightly *pétillant* Roussette from the small town of Seyssel in the upper Rhône Valley, where the great river comes in from Switzerland. The second, the red wine, had many of the qualities of a fine Beaujolais, made from the Gamay grapes which grow on the French slopes looking down on the Lake of Geneva. Both of these wines are now being imported into the United States.

The whole baby lamb was, of course, turned on the spit in front of a roaring log fire in the open hearth, but it could also be *rôtissed* over charcoal. At the same time, spring green beans and young tomatoes were lightly sautéed. Slender spears of asparagus were steamed and sauced with a homemade mayonnaise, colored and flavored with red wine. The feather-light potato crêpes were browned and puffed in butter. Finally the beautifully browned lamb was laid on a huge pottery platter and made a brave show, surrounded by the bright colors of the garnishing pancakes and vegetables (recipe for the lamb, page 298; for the asparagus with red wine sauce, page 361; for *Le Farçon*, the potato crêpes, page 351).

Of the cheeses with which to finish the wine, the Savoureux de

Neige (which comes to market as soon as the snows begin to melt on the mountains) gets its especially creamy and rich quality from the fact that it is made, in the late summer, when the cows are browsing in the high Alpine pastures on grasses which are tipped with frost in the early morning. This "frosted food" seems to give the cows' milk a quality ideal for this particular cheese. It is aged and cured through the winter and is ready to be eaten in the spring.

The Pouligny-Saint-Pierre is a creamy, brown-crusted goats' milk cheese made in the form of a tall pyramid (it is locally called "The Eiffel Tower") and is named after the village of Pouligny-Saint-Pierre, near the city of Poitiers, in the agricultural region of Berry.

The Bleu d'Auvergne, with firm, crumbly flesh, is one of the most famous of French "blues," made from cows' milk. Like the wild valleys of the central region of the Auvergne from which it comes, it is full of character and strength—aggressive, pungent on the tongue.

The *Gâteau de Savoie* is made in a buttered and sugared tube pan with a mixture of beaten egg yolks and whites, with cake flour and sugar, all slowly baked until the cake rises to such lightness that it virtually floats to table.

The clear brandy with the coffee was another of those powerful fruit distillations for which the Alsatians are famous. The *sureau* is a variety of wild elderberry which grows on the slopes of the Vosges mountains.

MENU OF
A Spring Dinner

APÉRITIF: BLANC DE SAVOIE À LA CRÈME DE FRAMBOISE

Flan de Bifteck et de Foies de Volailles aux
Écrevisses, Sauce Nantua
(Steak and Chicken Liver Pie, Garnished with Crayfish)

SPARKLING WHITE OF SAVOY, SEYSSEL,
BLANC DE BLANCS BRUT, LE DUC, VARICHON ET CLERC

Crème de Laitue Printanière
(Cream Soup of Bibb or Boston Lettuce)

Jeune Chevreau de Printemps aux Morilles
(Young Spring Kid, Stewed with Wild Mushrooms)

RED BORDEAUX, 1961 CHÂTEAU MARGAUX

Salade de Pissenlit aux Lardons
(Wilted Dandelion Salad)

Fromages:

Saint-Marcellin de l'Isère   Reblochon de la Savoie

Tignard Bleu

Clafouti Limousin
(Cherry Batter Pie, Limousin Style)

Café

GRAND ARMAGNAC, DOMAINE DE NOACES

Whenever a dinner menu included subtle complications of flavors and textures, it was Mademoiselle Vivette's rule to begin with an extremely simple apéritif. She opened a bottle of the dryly unpretentious blended white *vin du pays* of Savoy, poured it, ice cold, into fairly narrow and tall glasses, then gently dropped into each a bright red blob of heavy raspberry syrup. It rested at the bottom of the glass like a tiny pulsing heart before being stirred up to give a pretty pink color to this most refreshing of apéritifs.

The first course was an extraordinary invention of Mademoiselle Ray's. As described on the menu, it seemed to be an incompatible mixture of fish and meat ingredients, but in the eating it was an entirely successful combination. It was served as a flat, round baked pie of chopped sirloin and chicken livers bound with cream, eggs and Cognac, and garnished with poached crayfish tails and mushrooms. The sauce was a classic pink *Nantua* made from the pounded crayfish shells. At the table, the pie was flamed with more Cognac (recipe, page 235).

The wine was the famous sparkling white of Seyssel in the upper Rhône Valley which many French connoisseurs consider to be a close second-best to Champagne—better, in fact, than some of the lower-quality Champagnes. This sparkling Savoy had a fine body and flavor. It is now being imported into the United States.

For the cream soup, baby spring lettuces were whirled in an electric blender with an aromatic chicken bouillon with milk and cream (recipe, page 213).

The young kid was cut into large chunks, simmered slowly in white wine, shallots and onions and garnished with wild black mushrooms. It was served, tender and savory, from its heavy iron pot (recipe, page 294).

This dish, naturally, demanded a great wine. The demand was met by the 1961 vintage of the *Premier Crû,* Château Margaux of the Haut-Médoc. It is becoming unquestionably one of the most important wines of this century. Already, it is a superb drinking experience.

For the salad, young dandelion leaves were garnished with garlic croûtons and crisp dice of salt pork, then dressed with hot pork fat and tarragon wine vinegar (recipe, page 367).

The drinking of the wine was, of course, suspended during the consumption of the vinegary salad, but we returned to the remainder of the superb bottle with the cheeses. The first, the Saint-Marcellin (from the village of that name near Grenoble), was made, as the local saying goes, of "one-cow-one-goat," a mixture of the two milks. This particular version, a typical *fromage de montagne,* had a firm-textured crust, a creamy soft flesh of strong character and the shape of a half-size Camembert. It came from our friend of the Grenoble Farmers' Market, Serge Alibe, whose small farm is in the village of Saint-Marcellin.

The second cheese was the famous Reblochon of Savoy. The word *reblocher* means, in the local dialect, to milk the cow a second time within the same hour. It is this second milk, with a slightly stronger flavor than the first, which is used to make the Reblochon. The cheese looks like an extra-large Camembert, and the best examples come (as did this one) from the Col des Aravis, above Annecy. The crust was reddish yellow, and the inside the color of saffron, with a vague perfume and taste of mountain flowers.

The third cheese was an extremely rare type—a farm-made blue from the Tigne Valley of Savoy—small, made from cows' milk, with good blue veins, a speckled green crust and a crumbly dry texture. Exceedingly good.

The *clafouti* of sweet cherries is an irresistibly habit-forming dessert. It is a square pie, heavily loaded with cherries, but made from fluffy light crêpe batter which surrounds the cherries, holding in their flavors and juices, while it bakes in the oven to a deep gold (recipe, page 382).

This grand dinner ended in the grand manner with one of the finest of Armagnac brandies.

TEN

Menus for the Summer Season—Butter and Cream Taste of Mountain Flowers

"This valley is so tightly enclosed by the mountains," I said, "it must be a veritable sun trap. Does a savage sun beat down here in summer?"

"When I go shopping in Grenoble on a midsummer day," said Mademoiselle Vivette, "it seems as if the sky above the city is bleached by the immense and unbearable heat. Then I come back to our valley, and at once I am in a cool vault of lacy green under the trees. Here one never senses a sultry stillness of high noon heat. This earth always seems to be humming and trembling with its inner secret life. One knows it is noon, during the peak of the summer, because, almost every day, a single thick white cloud drifts slowly across the clear blue sky. Almost exactly at noon. When it has passed, the breezes return and the day begins to cool."

"Does it rain much in summer?"

"Does it rain!" exclaimed Mademoiselle Vivette. "Our valley of La Chartreuse is generally called, throughout the entire Alpine region, 'the piss-pot of the Dauphiné'! I am not a Dauphinoise, as you know, but I defend our Valley. It is not that we have more rainy days here. It is simply that when it starts to come down, it pours ten times as hard as anywhere else. It's nothing at all for us to have three inches of rain in a few hours. When I lived in Normandy, it used to rain there for fifteen days in a row. Here, it only has to rain one day to get the same amount of water."

"You are so proud of your valley that you even boast about its rain," I said. They shouted with laughter.

Visions of fruits, vegetables and vines drawing nourishment from the rain-soaked earth led me to my next question: "Which is the food that heralds the arrival of summer?"

"It is the flower-scented butter," said Mademoiselle Vivette, "with the special flavor that comes from our mountains in summer. At the end of June or the beginning of July, depending on the weather, the dairy farmers of our valley lead their cows up *en alpage,* as we say. They are taken to graze on the high slopes of Le Charmant Som, the mountain that dominates La Chartreuse. There, for several weeks the cows crop the lush new grass mixed with dozens of mountain flowers. Every day, the milk is taken at once to the dairy chalets right there, high on the mountain, where it is churned into butter. Although it is a lot of trouble to go up there to fetch the butter, I drive almost every other day as high as I can on the rough mountain road, then climb to the chalet. The butter seems to be filled with the perfume of the mountain—a taste entirely special to this region—one of the most exquisite gastronomic experiences of the year."

"But summer also brings the harvest for which the Dauphiné region is famous everywhere," said Mademoiselle Ray. "The thousands of walnut trees which grow on the lower slopes and on the Isère plain are ready to give their fruits. You have already tasted my walnut ice cream. I also bake walnut bread in a coarsely textured country style, very simple and strong in character, with the chewiness of the whole nuts. Lightly buttered slices make an excellent combination with the farm-made Tome de Savoie cheese which is just in perfect condition at this time and which Vivette fetches from the cheese-aging barn at Paulette's farm at Sappey."

"If you have a large summer party here at the Auberge," I said, "what kind of magnificently showy desserts do you serve?"

"Our biggest 'spectacle' is our flaming *Chamechaude* of mixed fruit ices, sugared sponge cake, sweet cherry liqueur, whipped cream with *glacé* fruits and . . ."

"*Chamechaude?*" I interrupted. "Isn't that the mountain over there that dominates the Valley, and this dining room too?"

"Yes," continued Mademoiselle Ray, "and we fashion our dessert as a miniature model of the mountain, complete with green slopes, jagged rocks, ice and snow—even bright flowers, mosses and trees. . . ."

"But it is not so miniature at times," added Mademoiselle Vivette. "If the party were large enough, we could make our Chamechaude stand three feet high!"

"I can't bear the suspense," I said. "How do you do it?"

"I begin with a foundation of butter-sponge cake—our French *Genoise*," said Mademoiselle Ray. "I glaze it with a mixture of sugar syrup and our local mountain-cherry liqueur. Next comes an irregularly shaped layer of bright green pistachio ice cream. . . ."

"As I help in sculpturing it," added Mademoiselle Vivette, "I look out of the window at the mountain, so as to copy exactly the sweeping curves of the grass-covered lower slopes. . . ."

"Then, a layer of brownish hazelnut ice cream," continued Mademoiselle Ray, "very jagged and rough, to represent the lower masses of rock. Next, the snow—masses of whipped cream rising and narrowing towards the peak—with glistening ice of spun sugar."

"Don't forget the pine trees," said Mademoiselle Vivette, "of *glacéed* green sticks of angelica."

"Near the very top," said Mademoiselle Ray, "where the wind blows the snow away, we build more rocks of hazelnut ice cream, and the final peak, the sharp tooth pointing up at the sky, is carved from *nougatine,* or praline-speckled almond paste."

"How do you serve this unwieldy monster?" I hardly dared to ask.

"At table," said Mademoiselle Vivette, "I pour over it a cup of warmed *génépi* (our local brandy, distilled from various mountain plants) and set the whole thing on fire."

In a state of slight shock, I went up to bed. Before going to sleep, I checked the fire escape outside my bedroom window.

MENU OF
A Summer Lunch

APÉRITIF: AMERICANO ITALO-FRANÇAIS

La Soupe au Pistou
(The Summer Meat and Vegetable Soup of Southern France)

PROVENÇAL WHITE, ESTANDON, BAGNIS, CUERS

La Chartreuse de Thon Frais à la Provençale
(Chartreuse of Fresh Tuna in the Style of Provence)
Les Cornichons et Les Lactaires Délicieux Sanguins Vinaigrette
(Pickled Cucumbers and Wild Mushrooms)

PROVENÇAL WHITE, CHÂTEAU SAINT MARTIN,
COUNT DE ROHAN CHABOT

Fromages:

Vendôme de la Loire   Rigotte de Condrieu

Bleu du Velay

Tarte aux Groseilles
(Gooseberry Tart)

Café

EAU-DE-VIE DE MÛRE DES BOIS

An Americano is normally an all-Italian mixture, but Mademoiselle Vivette, in honor of the "Entente Cordiale," mixes the usual one ounce of bitter Campari with an equal amount of the local sweet French vermouth of Dolin from Chambéry (or the sweet Noilly-Prat from Marseille). To each ice-cold glass, she adds a twist of lemon rind and a dash or two of soda.

The soup (more a stew than a soup) is the fine summer specialty of the Auberge. It is a glorified form of minestrone, which came, originally, from Genoa and must have crossed the Italian border at Nice, before spreading through southern France. Mademoiselle Ray's version includes her homemade noodles and the local Alpine Comté, Gruyère-style cheese (recipe, page 219).

With such a strongly Provençal dish, it was perfectly right to have one of the dry and refreshing white wines from the countryside, near Nice. The Estandon, which is drunk all along that hot and thirsty coast, is beginning to be imported into the United States. It is now recognized by the French government as a "controlled appellation" and given the designation of "V.D.Q.S.," which means a "Vin" from a specifically Delimited area of a Quality that is Superior. This designation enforces strict controls on the growing of the grapes and the making of the wine.

The main dish, a highly perfumed cold salad of fresh Mediterranean tuna, was prepared by Mademoiselle Vivette from one of the family recipes of her home in Provence. Earlier in the day, we had seen the black iron pot resting in the open hearth under the glowing embers of the wood fire. Then, when the food was being cooked, we had been allowed to sniff as the lid was lifted. We wanted to dig in right away and were permitted to taste it. It was superb. But there were still several hours to go before lunch time, and in any case the decision had already been made to serve it to us cold. It was equally good (recipe, page 265). The pickled tiny cucumbers (*les cornichons*) and wild mushrooms (*Les Lactaires Délicieux Sanguins Vinaigrette*) provided a contrast of textures (recipes on page 424 and 425).

So far this was a Provençal meal, and there followed another wine of the region. The Count Edmé de Rohan Chabot until his recent death had been president of the Winegrowers of Provence and was one of the region's best *vignerons*. His Château Saint Martin produces a dry, rich and strong white wine.

The cheeses with which to finish the wine were irresistibly uncomplicated. The Vendôme came from the village of that name in the Loire Valley about halfway between Tours and Orléans. It is made from cows' milk, with a white-mold crust and a soft, sometimes runny interior, rather like Camembert, but with a quite different shape. Vendôme is a cylinder about five inches across and four inches high. After it has first solidified, it is rubbed with salt and then aged in cool, moist cellars, buried in powdered wood ash. The taste is strong, more aromatic than Camembert, with a richly creamy texture.

The round, small Rigotte de Condrieu, from the lovely wine village on the Upper Rhône, is one of the finest of the half-cream cheeses. If you like a strongish flavor, you eat the chewy reddish crust. If you prefer something blander, you cut out only the inside, which has an attractive flavor of nuts, with a refreshing aftertaste as of the savor and scent of a tropical lemon grove. Exceedingly good!

The blue was from the Velay in the high central mountains of France, the Massif Central. It is made of cows' milk, and the natural blue mold is started by covering the cheese with breadcrumbs, then leaving it to develop in coolly ventilated mountain caves. This natural blue had a homemade quality of reality never matched by the factory-made types.

The dessert was Mademoiselle Ray's entirely superb gooseberry tart, in which the fruit was hardly cooked at all and was poured with its syrup, which jelled almost at once, into a fully prebaked buttery and crumbly tart shell (recipe, page 389).

The delightful brandy with the coffee was distilled from wild mountain blackberries.

MENU OF
A Summer Dinner

APÉRITIF: PIKINA

Chanterelles Jaunes d'Été à la Savoyarde
(*Wild Summer Mushrooms à la Savoyarde*)

ROSÉ RHÔNE, TAVEL, DOMAINE DE LA GENESTIÈRE

Rognons de Veau Grillés à la Broche, Sauce Diable
(*Spit-Roasted Veal Kidneys with Deviled Sauce*)

La Timbale Épicurienne de Curnonsky
(*The Epicure's Supreme Shellfish Casserole of Curnonsky*)

WHITE BURGUNDY, LE MONTRACHET, JACQUES PRIEUR

Fromages:

Banon de Provence   Chambarand du Dauphiné

Bleu de Devoluy

Soufflé de Framboises
(*Hot Soufflé of Raspberries*)

Café

CALVADOS DE NORMANDIE, PAYS D'AUGE, BUSNEL

The apéritif, a fortified wine informed with the flavor of bitter oranges, is a twin brother of Amer Picon, both from Levallois in the Perret district and drunk all over France. Mademoiselle Vivette served it ice cold, with dashes of sweet French vermouth and soda, plus a twist of lemon rind.

That morning, the lush green fields around the Auberge had been dotted bright yellow with the overnight wild *chanterelle* mushrooms. Mademoiselle Ray had been out at dawn to pick them. Now, she had lightly sautéed them to extract their water, had impregnated them with fresh butter and completed their sauce with a touch of sour cream and cheese. There could never be a more perfect hors d'oeuvre (recipe, page 372).

Since the main course tonight was to be fish, there was, with a fine sense of menu balance, a light dish of highly aromatic meat for the second course. The young veal kidneys had been spit-roasted in front of the open fire while Mademoiselle Ray prepared her special *Sauce Diable* by combining chopped shallots and wine vinegar with *Sauce Velouté*, the whole highly seasoned with horseradish and plenty of red Cayenne pepper (recipe, page 325).

To link these strongly contrasting first two courses, Mademoiselle Vivette chose a rosé—one of the best of that extraordinary group of pink wines from the hot, dry slopes around Tavel in the Rhône Valley opposite Avignon.

Until tonight, the cuisine of the Auberge had been, generally, of a "country-style." Now Mademoiselle Ray produced a dish of haute cuisine complications—her adaptation of a recipe from the great master Curnonsky, a lengthy preparation, but of a final magnificence that justified the effort. An enormous earthenware casserole was filled with crayfish, lobsters, oysters, wild mushrooms, black truffles, shallots, tomatoes, butter, cream, white wine, Cognac and a whole range of herbs including bunches of fresh tarragon. The tightly fitting lid was never once lifted during the cooking but only after the great dish had been placed before us on the table. I will always remember the marvel of the bouquet (recipe, page 238).

Such a dish could be adequately framed only by a truly great and powerful white wine—from one of the best *parcelles* of what is probably the finest white vineyard in the world, the great hill of Montrachet in the Côte d'Or of Burgundy. I rated it among the greatest I have ever tasted.

To finish such a wine, Mademoiselle Vivette chose three quite special cheeses. The Banon was farm-made from goats' milk in Provence. Each small round cheese is first wrapped in savory leaves and sprinkled with Armagnac. After a few weeks of aging, it gets a second wrapping of chestnut leaves, sprinkled with red wine and marc brandy. Then the cheese is allowed to ferment in earthenware jars, and the final result is a soft, winy crust, with the flavor of the inside flesh—almost impossible to describe—having something of the ambiance of the wild region of Les Alpilles, the rocky hills covered with wild lavender, rosemary, savory and thyme, shaded by lime and olive trees. (The word *banon*, incidentally, refers to the ancient right of the goatherdsmen to pasture their animals on the lands of the seigneurs.)

The second cheese, the Chambarand is from the village of that name in the forests of the lower Isère. It is made from cows' milk and is about the size of a Camembert, with a firm, chewy, light yellow crust and a creamy soft, spicy inside flesh.

The blue was another local Alpine cheese from cows' milk, with a reddish crust and natural blue veining. Its flavor reminded me vaguely of Roquefort but was slightly coarser and less sophisticated.

The dessert was a magnificent fruit soufflé prepared by a method perfected by Mademoiselle Ray. She first sealed in the flavor and freshness of the raspberries by quickly poaching them in a sugar syrup. Then, still bubbling hot, they were folded into the beaten egg whites and instantly put into an extremely hot oven, where they puffed and rose. Finally, in less than fifteen minutes the soufflé was rushed to table. (Recipe, page 399.)

A magnificent meal ended with the great and powerful apple brandy of Normandy.

ELEVEN

*Menus for the Autumn Season—
Snapping Fire and Turning Spit:
The Hunter Comes Home
for Dinner*

After dinner, Mademoiselle Vivette was remembering the seasonal cycles of almost forty years since she first came to the Valley of La Chartreuse: "There are certain special times of each year when Ray and I could not bear to be away from here. Perhaps the most magnificent weeks usually come between the middle of September and the beginning of November. It is the brilliant time of color when we watch the splendid shadings of browns, golds, greens, reds, yellows changing from day to day—even between the early morning and the late afternoon."

"It's also the time when there's great excitement in the air," interrupted Mademoiselle Ray, "in every valley of our Alpine region. Everywhere one sees the farmers with their wives out together working in the fields, the orchards and the vineyards. Against almost every fruit and walnut tree, one sees a small ladder. Our Valley is filled with laughter and shouting from early morning until late evening. . . ."

"Also, punctuated, surely," I said, "by the shots of the hunters from the mountain slopes? It's the open season for the big game animals, isn't it?"

"Hunting is permitted for only three weeks," said Mademoiselle Vivette. "Our French conservation laws are extremely strict. You see, during the war years, from 1940 to 1945, when the German armies occupied this part of France, we were so short of meat that all the strong men of our Valley spent most of their time doggedly tracking down our big game. They were so successful that, by 1945, our big animals were almost extinct."

"But, today," said Mademoiselle Ray, "we have brought them back to normal numbers by sharply controlling the hunting, and also by restocking the mountains with imported breeding animals."

"The prince of these mountains," said Mademoiselle Vivette, "is our local breed of Carthusian chamois, one of the most beautiful of antelopes. We find him, most often, on the high rock ledges of the Chartroussette and the Valombré. He is hard to track. He can climb even the most precipitous rock faces and leap across wide crevasses, where the hunters cannot follow. But when we get him, he makes the most magnificent feast."

"I would have thought him to be so muscular that his flesh would be exceedingly tough."

"On the contrary," said Mademoiselle Vivette, "the meat of the young chamois is as tender as lamb. But his flesh is dark red, with a superbly strong flavor. When my brother visits us from Provence, he always says that a feast of chamois gives him a furious energy— the meat seems to him so full of power."

"If the chamois is the prince, who is the king?"

"Our *grand cerf,* the great stag," said Mademoiselle Ray, "but he is seldom seen nowadays. Partly to replace him (and to give a better chance to our hunters), we have, since the war, restocked our mountains with the *chevreuil,* the smaller mountain deer, the Würtemberg type from the Black Forest of Germany. He has taken to our Alpine heights as if they were his paradise. He is breeding happily and his numbers are increasing. He, too, makes superb eating."

"And in our deep forests of the Cucheron, the Génieux or La Petite Vache," said Mademoiselle Vivette, "the hunters track the *marcassin,* our young wild boar, or the *sanglier,* the larger and older beast. Also the *lièvre,* the big mountain hare, with wonderfully gamy meat. Then there are all our birds—first among them (but now rather rare) the *coq de bruyère,* the Alpine grouse."

"The chance to feast on all these marvelous meats," said Mademoiselle Ray, "comes, of course, only rarely. Not more than thirty chamois may be taken in the season by all the hunters combined, and the law forbids any of the meat (and this ban includes the *coq de bruyère*) from being bought or sold. So we have to rely on gifts from hunters."

"Our friends Jean Combalot and Pierre Morand can sometimes bring down a *coq de bruyère* when his stomach is full of undigested blueberries. Then, quickly, we grill him on the turning spit in front of the wood fire, and he is absolutely delicious. We do the same with the *grive*, the thrush, when he has eaten his fill of juniper berries. The taste goes right through the meat. Then there are partridge, pheasant, quail—and so many others . . . it's a splendid time!"

It was past midnight. Our discussions of the menus of the seasons were coming to an end. Mademoiselle Vivette spoke softly: "So, you see, we have come around the full circle of the year and are back on the Eve of Christmas. This Auberge of ours—here among these snow white mountains—sometimes seems a very long way from my sunny childhood in Provence. But on the night before Christmas I like to bring Provence into this house with the ceremony of 'The Thirteen Desserts of Reveillon.' "

She noticed my questioning look and added: "To understand this ancient custom, one must know about the family traditions at the time when I was a child."

I said: "Would I get the feel of it, if your words could take me there?"

"On Christmas Eve in my home in Provence," she said, "the huge dining table was laid with a snow white cloth for what we call, in the Provençal language, *Lou Gros Soupa*. But before we could start eating, there had to be the ceremonial relighting of the great log fire in the hearth, beginning with the partly burned log which had been kept from Christmas Eve the year before. In every home the head of the house, called in Provençal *Lou Maistre,* went to fetch the log from the closet where it had been stored, placed it in the hearth and, while rekindling it, spoke in Provençal these traditional words:

> 'Fire, Beautiful Fire,
> Log, Beautiful Log,
> Gather us around you for this feast,
> And warm us from the hearth.
> And if, next year, there are not more of us,
> Then, at least, let us not be fewer.'

"Then new logs were added to the old, and when the fire was burning brightly, our family took its place at table for *Lou Gros Soupa*. It was, of course, a meal for a day of fasting, because of the coming Midnight Mass and the huge feasting of Christmas Day. We ate, first, white sticks of raw celery dipped into the famous Provençal *Anchouiado*, a thick, warm sauce of pounded anchovies, with garlic, parsley and shallots. A little of this was ladled onto each plate, and we dipped into it with our celery sticks. Next, there was served a dish of poached salt cod, flaked into a hot purée of spinach and garnished with hard-boiled eggs. Finally, our table was set with the Thirteen Desserts (for the thirteen days from Christmas Day through Epiphany), all extremely simple, all exactly the same every year: Tunisian dates, Smyrna figs, muscat raisins, whole walnuts, soft almonds, hazelnuts, boiled candies inside tiny Christmas crackers for the children, *marrons glacés,* black nougat, white nougat, bright red apples, sweet grapes slightly sun-dried on straw mats, and small knobby cakes called *Pompes* or *Gibassiers* (*gibes* in Provençal means 'lumpy'). We stayed a long time at table, nibbling, talking and watching the flaming logs. We always drank the local sweet wine from the village of Palette, near our city-with-the-fountains, Aix-en-Provence. When it was time to leave for the village church, my father, *Lou Maistre,* put out the now-dying fire by pouring on the remaining wine. Again he asked a blessing on the house and then set aside the log to be kept for the next year. The Thirteen Desserts would remain on the dining table for the thirteen days so that if a hungry beggar came to our door, he could be offered food to eat."

MENU OF
A Fall Lunch

APÉRITIF: PINEAU DES CHARENTES

Salade des Haricots Verts aux Champignons
(Salad of Green Beans with Raw Mushrooms)

WHITE SAVOY, APREMONT, FICHARD

Billi-Bi
(Cream of Mussel Soup with Sorrel)

Gigot de Mouton de Sept Heures
*(Leg of Mutton Poached in White Wine and
Garnished with Fall Vegetables)*
Haricots de Soissons au Cresson
(White Haricot Beans of Soissons in Watercress Cream)

RED BORDEAUX, 1966 CHÂTEAU BOUSCAUT, GRAVES

Fromages:
Charolais   Chaource de Champagne
Fourme d'Ambert

Poires Bartlett au Vin Rouge
(Bartlett Pears Poached in Red Wine)

Café

Les Bouffettes

EAU-DE-VIE D'ABRICOTS D'ALSACE

The apéritif was the unusual and relatively unknown fortified wine which is regularly drunk before dinner by the residents of Cognac. It is a soft wine, fermented from the white pineau grape (the grape which also provides the basic alcoholic liquid from which the famous brandy is distilled), and then slightly fortified with Cognac. It is a charming, hungry-making drink with a distinct Cognac character. Incidentally, the name Pineau des Charentes is a legal *appellation contrôlée,* which guarantees the regional quality of the wine and may be used by any maker. Several brands are now beginning to be imported into the United States.

The opening salad consisted of bright green, crisply fresh, cut string beans mixed with slices of raw mushroom, marinated in a light *vinaigrette* and garnished with chopped chives (recipe, page 363).

The first wine was another of the delightfully dry, thirst-quenching small whites from the mountain vineyards of the Savoy. Apremont is a village that looks down on the Lake of Geneva, from the French side. Its wine is now available in the United States.

The mussel soup with the un-French name *Billi-Bi* is in fact a classic bourgeois dish of France, claimed by both Normandy and Périgord. Since it does *not* contain truffles and *is* a specialty of some of the best restaurants of Rouen, perhaps we should award the palm to Normandy. The mussels are first poached in spiced white wine. Then this winy juice is converted into a delicately aromatic cream soup, flavored with sorrel and slightly thickened with beaten egg yolks, into which the mussels are dropped at the last moment before serving (recipe, page 208).

The specialty of this fall lunch was not so much the main dish as the vegetable, the giant white beans of Soissons, which came fresh at this time of the year and which Mademoiselle Ray prepared simmered in an aromatic stock, then garnished with a rich sauce of creamed watercress. She thinks that this is the ideal accompaniment to a boned leg of mutton, stuffed with smoky bacon, gently poached with white wine in a tightly covered *cocotte* for seven hours, with more smoked bacon, carrots, eggplant, onions, green peppers, tomatoes, plus a knuckle of veal to enrich the sauce; everything, finally, is flamed with Armagnac. The meat came to the table on an open platter, surrounded by the bright colors of its garnishing vegetables (recipe, page 304).

The wine could only have been a light, fruity red, one of the good recent vintages of the third growth Graves Châteaux, which produce excellent reds and whites.

The cheeses were chosen to complement the remainder of this wine. The first comes, of course, from one of the best-known villages in France. Charolles is at the heart of the rich, rolling pasture country which produces the white Charolais beef cattle, generally considered to be the finest beef in every corner of France. The native cheese is made of mixed cows' and goats' milk and is a small cylinder with a chewy crust and a very creamy inside flesh.

The second cheese, the Chaource, is made in the country around Troyes in Champagne. It looks a bit like a large Camembert, is made in farmhouses, eaten either young and bland or aged and strong—or even very old and exceedingly stinky!

The word *fourme* usually means a cheese "formed" in a rush basket. This one is a natural blue from the central mountains of the Auvergne. The crust is reddish yellow and the inside marbling is a bright deep blue. The cows' milk gradually dries out in the cool mountain caves, and the ripe cheese is dry and crumbly. Marvelous with the wine!

The dessert was as supremely simple to prepare as it was supremely good, but it must be ready at least three hours before the meal, so that the spices can blend together and soak through. Perfectly ripe Bartlett pears (or, later in the year, it could be winter Anjou or Comice pears) are skinned and very lightly simmered in a good red wine, with lemon juice, cinnamon, cloves, vanilla and sugar, then allowed to cool in the wine, which slightly thickens and forms the sauce (recipe, page 398).

The *bouffettes* are cream-filled cakes. The *eau-de-vie*, with the coffee, was a clear, very fruity and strong apricot brandy.

MENU OF
A Fall Game Dinner

APÉRITIF: LILLET-COGNAC GOLD

Terrine de Lièvre à la Grande Chartreuse
(Terrine of Wild Hare)

WHITE BURGUNDY, BÂTARD-MONTRACHET, PRUDHON

Potage Chasseur
(Soup of the Hunter with Pheasant and Cream of Lentils)

Coq de Bruyère Grillé à la Broche
(Spit-Roasted Alpine Grouse)
Chanterelles d'Automne Sautées à la Crème
(Wild Autumn Mushrooms Sautéed with Cream)

RED BURGUNDY, 1957 VOSNE-ROMANÉE, LES RICHEBOURG

Artichauts à la Barigoule
(Artichokes Poached in Aromatic Wine)

Fromages:
Chabichou de Poitou   Marcigny de la Loire
Bleu de Laqueuille d'Auvergne

Bananes Flambées au Rhum
(Bananas Flamed with Rum)

Café

Les Fourrées

EAU-DE-VIE DE POIRE WILLIAMS DE LA VALLÉE DU RHÔNE

The apéritif was an invention of Mademoiselle Vivette's. In an ice-cold old-fashioned glass, she mixed one jigger of the golden Lillet vermouth of Bordeaux (a fortified wine based on Sauternes) with half a jigger of Cognac, a dash of soda and a twist of lemon peel. She served it with a silver straw.

Mademoiselle Ray's terrine of wild hare was nothing short of magnificent. Apart from the strong, gamy meat, it was rich with ground liver, pork, Cognac and gin. Its texture was chewy, its aura was fortifying, its character was irresistible (recipe, page 170).

It demanded a rich wine, and the demand was met by one of the great whites of the Côte d'Or of Burgundy in a fine if not an outstanding vintage.

The Hunter's Soup was an excellent combination of the meat of a roasted pheasant with carrots, onions, leeks, butter, herbs and a not-too-thick purée of lentils. It was, finally, a creamy soup with a slightly gamy flavor, garnished with garlic croûtons (recipe, page 217).

The *coq de bruyère* is the great fall specialty of La Vallée de la Grande Chartreuse. This magnificent bird flies very high, is very fast on the wing and extremely difficult to shoot. The great trick is to get it at the precise moment when its belly is gorged full of blueberries and raspberries. Then Mademoiselle Ray cleaned out the intestines but left the stomach intact, so that the flavor of the berries permeated the flesh. The birds turned slowly on the spit in front of the roaring, open wood fire. Under each bird was the *lèchefrite* ("lickfry"), the metal platter with *le canapé*, the slice of buttered toast catching the drippings from the bird. Finally, the bird was served with *le canapé* as the base on which it rests. The flesh was so juicy and perfumed that no sauce was necessary. The perfect accompaniment was the wild fall mushrooms, sautéed in butter, and then creamed (recipes for *coq de bruyère* and *chanterelles*, pages 285 and 370).

The red Burgundy was from the great vineyard of the village of Vosne-Romanée, considered by many connoisseurs to be the greatest single wine village in Burgundy. The wine was spicy, velvety—the perfect partner to the grandeur of the flesh of the game bird.

The vegetable, in true French peasant style, was served as a refreshing and separate course. Small young artichokes were slowly poached with carrots, garlic and onions in olive oil and white wine, then served with the aromatic juices poured over them (recipe, page 360).

The cheeses with which to finish the wine were, first, the Chabichou of goats' milk from the region of Poitou, in the hills south of the Loire.

It looked rather like a Camembert, but its flavor was much stronger and beautifully creamy. Its crust was very dark, but the inside flesh was almost pure white. It is aged in what are called *coffins*, forms made of wicker basketwork.

The beautiful Romanesque village of Marcigny in the upper Rhône Valley northwest of Lyon produces a small goats' milk cheese which can be all things to all cheese lovers. About one week old, it is like a bland, soft cream cheese, ready to be sprinkled with salt and pepper, then eaten with a fork. At a month old, it is firm, chewy, strong, and has to be cut with a sharp knife. At three months, it is positively stinky. At six months, it is hard as a rock, but fine for grating over spaghetti. Take your pick.

The third cheese, the Bleu de Laqueuille, is made from cows' milk in the mountain village of Laqueuille and was sold in the market of the nearby town of Rochefort as a plain white cheese. Then, around the year 1850, a local farmer named Antoine Roussel discovered that if he mixed stale breadcrumbs with the paste before it set, a mold would develop which would turn the cheese blue. Today, in the village of Laqueuille, which is in the mountains of the Auvergne, there is a statue to Roussel. His blue cheese has brought a lot of fame and a good deal of profit to the region. I found it aromatic, crumbly dry, extremely attractive with the end of the wine. One can judge the age (and thus, the strength) of the cheese by the varying colors of its crust. When it is young, it is red ochre on top, whitish around the sides. Then, as it ages, it develops bright, cardinal red spots all over. The more there are, the stronger the cheese. If I ever found one solid red, I'd run a mile!

For the dessert, there were bananas baked with lemon juice and sugar, then flamed at table with the excellent French rum of Martinique. There was a fine affinity between the tropical fruit and the tropical spirit of the Caribbean Islands (recipe, page 381).

With the coffee, we had local petits-fours called *les fourrées* and small snifters of one of the greatest of all non-grape fruit brandies. I regard the clear spirit, distilled from the brown Williams pear—whether it be made in Germany as "Williams Birnen Brantwein," or in Switzerland as "Williamine," or in France as "Eau-de-vie de Poire Williams"—to be the almost-perfect translation of the flavor of a fresh fruit into a clear alcoholic spirit.

TWELVE

A Proud Wine Cellar on a Low Budget

Just to the left of the entrance to the dining room, there was the heavy oak door that opened onto the long steep flight of stone steps down to the wine cellar of the Auberge of the Flowering Hearth. I spent many hours among its cool and silent racks with Mademoiselle Vivette (usually at midmorning or midafternoon, when she did her cellar management) checking and discussing the dusty bottles which she has been lovingly collecting and assembling for more than thirty-five years. This was her province—she was in charge here—just as Mademoiselle Ray was in charge in the kitchen. In terms of an inn, it was quite a small cellar. In fact, it was more like the cellar that might be assembled in a home by an intelligently knowledgeable connoisseur. There were some great and noble wines for the occasional visit of an important and demanding guest. There were many fine wines in the middle ranges of quality—perfectly good enough to accompany even the most outstanding dinner menu. And there were simple, inexpensive, "gulping wines" to add pleasure to a country-style lunch or Sunday night supper—or just to quench a summer thirst in an easy chair by the fountain in the garden.

In one way, though, Mademoiselle Vivette made it clear from the first that there was a special quality about her cellar. She had never had a great deal of capital to lay down in wine. "If you have unlimited money to spend," she often said, "then there is no particular skill about building a magnificent cellar. You just go out and buy the *Grands Crûs*, the greatest vintages of the greatest châteaux and domaines at any price—and there you are! Even a simpleton could do that."

Her cellar, by contrast, had been gradually built, always on a low budget. Instead of money, she had used know-how, careful study, intelligent planning, and certain basic rules and tricks to find ways of beating the immutable laws of supply and demand that rule the world of wine.

In the course of my long talks with her, she told me many of her practical secrets. I have since discovered that they work as well for me in the United States as they do for her in France. . . .

Basic Rules for Buying Good-Value Wines

"Here at the Auberge, we are only about seventy-five miles from Burgundy," Mademoiselle Vivette said, "so I drive there in my big Simca station wagon and go shopping around for wine among the *négotiants* and *producteurs*, just as I did, years ago, among the little corner wine shops of Paris, when I lived there—or as I would in any city, whether I was in Brussels, or Rome, or New York, or San Francisco. . . . The basic principles for buying the best possible wine at the fairest possible price are the same everywhere." She was, of course, absolutely right. In these days of spiraling wine inflation, one can hardly expect to find "good buys" without moving around.

Her first lesson, then, is to get to know as many as possible of one's local suppliers. It is almost ridiculous—except when buying a standard bottle of gin—to expect to get all one's wines from the nearest liquor store on the next corner. Each shop, after all, is a reflection of the personal opinions of its owner or manager. Each, in his way, has a special slant on his buying of wine. One may be especially interested in Bordeaux, and his shop will always show a far better selection of Bordelais wines than any other shop in town. Another dealer may shrug off the German wines and just keep a few on hand, uncared for and unloved, simply because he feels he has to. One must get to know not one but at least half a dozen of one's local dealers. One will soon learn where, for each category and type of wine, are the best selections and most frequent bargains.

The problem is the same with food. If you are even half a gourmet, you will shop around for your fancy foods. You will buy your olives from the Greek grocer. You will prefer the long French loaf of one baker over another. You will buy your veal from one butcher, your pork from another. It is just as important to shop around for your wine. No single dealer can possibly give you the best of everything.

Mademoiselle Vivette also proved to me a vital second point. She had in her cellar many labels of so-called unfashionable years—years in which the vintages were generally considered poor; and yet, because she had learned to know and trust her suppliers, she had bought, at bargain prices, some particular bottles from these off-years. She knew the basic truth that in every generally poor year there are some producers who are lucky and finish up with an excellent wine, which of course remains relatively inexpensive because there is no strong demand for the wines of that year. Again, this is a matter of knowing and trusting the word of the supplier, of being secure in one's own tasting judgment of a relatively unknown wine and, as soon as one finds a potential bargain, of jumping in with both feet and investing a small amount of capital toward future drinking pleasure.

The True Meaning of a Vintage Chart

"You must always understand what a vintage chart does not do," Mademoiselle Vivette said. "It does not simply grade wines—giving some of them in some years a 100 percent best and, in other years, a zero worst, with every grade in between." Mademoiselle Vivette's point is especially true in the United States, where, because of the extra aging caused by the rigors of the transatlantic voyage, it is absolutely essential to interpret intelligently the vintage charts. If, for example, a certain wine of a particular year is given the highest possible rating (perhaps ten points, or twenty, or whatever the scale of the chart happens to be), this does not mean that that particular wine was "great" from the moment when the grapes were pressed. No. The chart is saying that, potentially, if that wine is given the chance to develop to its fullest potential, it will become "great." But if you drink it, say, when it is only a couple of years old, you are not drinking it at its full potential, and at that point it is almost certainly not as good as another wine of a much lower rating but more fully developed and in a more ready state to be consumed. It was Baron Philippe de Rothschild, I believe, who once said that anyone who drank his marvelous Château Mouton wines before they had reached their full potential was guilty of committing infanticide.

Let us take a specific example. Most experts are now agreed that the 1961 vintage, especially in Bordeaux, will in time be very great indeed—probably the greatest, so far, of the century. It is, shall we say, destined to climb to the top of a very high mountain of quality, and when it reaches its peak, the view will be magnificent! But because of its internal chemical makeup, it is developing extremely slowly—it is taking its time to climb its mountain. Against this potential giant, the vintages of 1964, 1966, and especially 1967, all have, according to their ratings on the vintage charts, a lesser potential. They were destined from their birth to climb much smaller hills. Yet during the past few years, people who do not understand the true meaning of a vintage chart have been steadily buying and drinking the 1961 vintage (at extremely high prices), simply because the numbers on the charts appeared to be saying that it was a better wine than all the others. The 1961, until now, has been much less pleasurable to drink than the 1964, 1966 and 1967 (the latter, often, at half the price). They have already reached the tops of their smaller hills and are presenting excellent views—though of course not so sublime as that, eventually, from the great mountain. Yet it is much better to be standing on the top of a smaller hill and surveying the smaller view than to be standing at the base of a mighty mountain with hardly any view at all. In fact one could go even a step further and say that a lesser wine, with a delicate charm and lightness which the bigger wine will never have, may be much more right for some foods and some less formal occasions. Vintage charts can help us to make these important decisions, but we must learn to interpret their true meaning.

The Reds and Whites of Burgundy

The oldest red Burgundy I found in Mademoiselle Vivette's cellar was the 1946 Pommard, Hospice de Beaune, Dames de la Charité, which was a perfect example of her cost-saving technique. The year 1946, especially in Pommard, was definitely "unfashionable." The wines were considered to be hard and tannic. Yet this particular wine, which

Mademoiselle Vivette had been advised to buy in the early fifties and which she had judged by her own tasting to be above the average, had developed magnificently and had proved to be an outstanding investment. For conservative guests of the Auberge who demanded famous names on their wine labels, she also had some of the great vintages of the past decades—the 1957 and 1961 vintages of the Clos Vougeot of Morin and the Musigny of Count de Vogüé; the 1959 vintages of Le Corton, Les Grands Echézeaux, and the Volnay of Thénard; the 1964 vintages of Chambertin-Clos de Bèze and Les Richebourg. Also, for guests with slimmer pocketbooks, there were various vintages by various producers of the almost always excellent Côtes de Beaune-Villages.

The basic problem in buying Burgundy, of course, is that the famous village and vineyard names, on the basis of their worldwide prestige, always command relatively high prices. In order to reduce the cost one must begin exploring the less well known names, which include many of the wines from Fixin, Morey-Saint-Denis, Savigny-les-Beaune. . . . These are wines which can often represent outstanding value, because they have not yet been overwhelmed by an irresistible demand. Also, quite apart from cost, these not-yet-so-fashionable wines have their own special qualities to recommend them. They are fruity, elegant, gentle and lovely to drink, as against the big, chewy, dramatically exciting, velvety wines of the famous vineyards.

"As to white Burgundies to drink with our various preparations of Alpine fish," Mademoiselle Vivette told me, "there is still, as always, the strongest demand for Chablis. Personally, I think it is a pity, because the very word '*Chablis*' has gained such magical prestige that the price of any bottle is bound to be exceptionally high. Yet there are ways of at least ensuring that one gets the best possible value." Translated into United States terms, her advice is to steer away from the topmost grade, *Grand Cru* labels (always relatively expensive), and to look for the next, only slightly lower grade, the *Premier Cru*—remembering that these label definitions of quality are legally controlled. Below these quality levels, the wine is simply labeled *Chablis* and often without the specific name of any particular vineyard. Still lower down the quality ladder, the label reads *Petit Chablis*.

The difference in price between a *Premier Cru* and a plain *Chablis* is relatively small; yet the higher grade more or less guarantees a "selected quality" with much more careful bottling and handling by an individual producer and vintner determined to protect the prestige of his name. One must remember, though, that there are differences in character and personality between different labels of *Premier Crû* Chablis, even within the same range of prices. The point to remember about Chablis is that, while it is always a dry wine, it is softly, tenderly dry, with different degrees of acidity, according to the positions of the vineyards on the hillsides. For example, the famous vineyard of Montée de Tonnerre is always particularly low in acidity and, therefore, especially good and ready to drink when it is quite young. On the other hand, the vineyard of Fourchaume produces wines with substantially more acid, which are better to drink when they are two or three years old and have developed a certain aromatic quality. Thus, by gradually learning the significance of each name and definitive word on the label, you can get precisely the best quality and value for your taste.

To find the other white Burgundies, Mademoiselle Vivette regularly drives to Beaune, to Meursault and to Puligny-Montrachet to consult her favorite merchants and, in the more southerly district of the Côte, to taste. The cellar of the Auberge includes the current vintages of Corton-Charlemagne, the Beaune, Clos des Mouches, the Meursault, Les Charmes, as well as the Bâtard-Montrachet, the Puligny-Montrachet and the incomparable Le Montrachets of the Marquis de Laguiche, Jacques Prieur and Baron Thénard. The eternal problem, though, even about the whites of Burgundy, is that wines are produced in such small quantities and against such an enormous worldwide demand that there is in reality no such thing as a truly inexpensive label. There is just no such thing as a "little" Burgundy—either red or white. For these lesser wines at the lower prices (but still within the larger framework of Burgundy), one must look farther south to the wines labeled with the names of the larger districts of the Maconnais and the Chalonnais, which are always well represented in Mademoiselle Vivette's cellar, as they are now also in mine. There is the refreshing, soft (and less expensive) red of Mercurey, which is, one might say, both in geography and in personality, about halfway between the power of the big Burgundies and the lightness of the Beaujolais.

As to the whites of Pouilly-Fuissé, I feel forced to say, quite frankly, that for a dry, light, simple white wine of such relatively unpretentious character, it is absurdly too fashionable at prices that are absurdly too high. I think it has had its head turned by being taken, like Cinderella, too young to the Prince's ball! On the other hand, from the Maconnais communes all around Pouilly-Fuissé (including Pouilly-Loché, Pouilly-Vinzelles and Saint-Véran), there come quite excellent wines at very fair prices. Some reach the United States under the labels of these villages; others are simply labeled by the name of the grape, *Pinot Chardonnay de Macon*. They are all well worth exploring.

The Problem of Beaujolais

"Here at the Auberge we face, every day, the increasingly difficult problem of finding a fair Beaujolais at a fair price," Mademoselle Vivette said. "Most of our guests are devoted to Beaujolais. Yet most of them—even French aficionados—hardly know the difference between a quite poor Beaujolais and a very fair one. So I always try to make sure that we are in a position to surprise and delight them with a whole range of exceptional Beaujolais at exceptionally reasonable prices. In my opinion, no cellar is properly balanced unless it excludes completely that most useless of wines, a bad Beaujolais; and includes an important selection of that most all-purpose of wines, the best of Beaujolais." You cannot find in Mademoiselle Vivette's cellar any general, nondescript, undefined bottles simply labeled *Beaujolais* or *Beaujolais Supérieur*. She visits, tastes and selects in the famous Beaujolais villages of which the names on the labels are an immediate guarantee of a certain character, quality and personality. She goes (as I go in my local New York wine store) to Brouilly, Chénas, Chiroubles, Fleurie, Juliénas, Morgon, Moulin-à-Vent and Saint-Amour. (Mademoiselle Vivette is lucky. She can buy her less expensive Beaujolais in 60-liter *containeurs*, which she loads into the back of her large Simca station wagon. These wines are then served at her tables *en carafe* as the quite inexpensive *vins de la maison*.) Among the better, estate-bottled Beaujolais, the cellar includes from Brouilly the exceptional Château de La-Chaize and Château Thivin, with also the Château de Chénas and the Château de Juliénas.

The essential point to remember about Beaujolais, of course, is that most of it is made to be drunk young and should not be left lying around. Only a very few Beaujolais are deliberately made by their producers to be aged, perhaps, for two or three years. One must learn to read the signals on the labels. If a Beaujolais is called *Primeur* (and this is a legal definition), it will almost certainly have been bottled immediately after the fifteenth of November of the year of its harvest —that is, within less than eight weeks after the grapes were picked. If the label defines it (again, a legal term) as *Beaujolais de l'année*, it will have been aged in the barrel three or four months longer and have been bottled, usually, in the following spring. These wines are meant to be enjoyed in the bloom and blush of youth.

Mademoiselle Vivette also provides one more surprise for her guests with that oddity among wines, the *Beaujolais blanc*—quite dry, very light, always refreshingly tart. As she showed me the row upon row of Beaujolais bottles, she said: "Our cellar is bursting with the best of Beaujolais!"

The Reds and Whites of Bordeaux

When Mademoiselle Vivette showed me the Bordeaux section of her cellar, she began her discussion by saying: "Our Auberge, as does every hotel and inn in France, has to be able to offer, simply for the sake of prestige, a reasonably broad selection of the *Grands Crûs*—the great château-bottled reds of Bordeaux." Then, with a slightly satiric smile she added that, at the prices which these old bottles now command, *"tout le monde les a, mais personne n'en vend"*—everybody has them, but nobody sells them. In fact some restaurants seem to want to discourage their customers from even thinking about buying them. After all, it looks marvelous on a wine list to be able to show a 1937 Château Latour at three hundred dollars for a magnum, but there may be only one bottle left in the cellar and when that bottle goes, the wine list will have to be rewritten!

Realizing that most of the great vintages of the famous Bordeaux châteaux vineyards are now virtually priced out of reach of the average diner, I asked Mademoiselle Vivette which, of all her red Bordeaux wines, she considered to be the one that offered the best balance between a noble quality and, not necessarily a very low, but a reasonably fair price. She hesitated only a few seconds before answering: "Out of the top dozen or so of the red Bordeaux labels that are always in our cellar, the consistent, exclamatory praise of our guests, when they see their bills, seems to award the palm for good value to the Château La Mission Haut Brion of Graves, of which we are currently offering the vintages of 1955, 1961, 1964 and 1966. Another excellent value, in our opinion, is provided by the red 1966 Château Bouscaut, also of Graves."

Yet of course these and all others of the outstanding "classified" red wines of Bordeaux can never, because of the universal demand for them, be really inexpensive. For any substantial reduction of cost, one must begin to explore the unclassified, relatively unknown vineyards. There are almost ten thousand names in the Bordeaux region, of which only about sixty are the famous "classified growths." This, obviously, leaves 9,940 labels waiting for intelligent exploration. (Incidentally, even in the two topmost districts of Bordeaux, the Médoc and the Graves, where most of the great classified châteaux lie, there remain more than nineteen hundred smaller, unclassified vineyards eminently worthy of trial by tasting.) Admittedly some are almost as well known (and as expensive) as their classified neighbors. A majority of the others never reach the United States. Some are not altogether worthy of exploration. But this still leaves thousands of wines, many of them rating from superior to fine, with relatively unknown names, unable to command anything more than relatively low prices.

The most basic of all rules for this irresistibly fascinating kind of exploration is that one will always find more pleasure in drinking a fully matured, fruity and ripe, relatively small wine from a more or less little-known district, such as, say, the Côtes de Bourg, than in trying to drink a still thoroughly green wine from a famous and classified château long before it is ready, while it is still stiff with tannin and only just beginning to flex its muscles.

As well as the Côtes de Bourg, Mademoiselle Vivette suggested that I should explore the less well known châteaux vineyards of the districts of the Côtes-Canon-Fronsac and Entre-Deux-Mers—not forgetting also the Médoc, the Graves, Saint-Emilion and Pomerol. I have found many of these charming and often fine wines in the United States, including, from the Côtes de Bourg: Château des Arras, Château de La Grave and Château Gullaud-Cheval Blanc; from the Côtes-Canon-Fronsac: Château Bodet and Château Canon; from Entre-Deux-Mers: Château Bonnet and Château Jonqueyres; from the Médoc: Château Le Boscq, Château Greysac, Château Loudenne and Château Les-Ormes-de-Pez; from the Graves: Château Picque-Caillou and Château La Vieille France; from Saint-Emilion: Château Figeac; and finally, from Pomerol: Château Trotanoy and the noble Château Petit-Village.

When Mademoiselle Vivette first poured some of these wines for me, she said: "It is ridiculous to know Bordeaux only through its great wines. That is like owning a beautiful piano and trying to make music on it by using only the five notes on either side of middle C."

As to the white and golden wines of Bordeaux, Mademoiselle Vivette said: "We are always trying to find the best values in the dry white wines, but I believe, as my father taught me, there should also be a place in proper menu planning for the superb golden sweet wines."

Mademoiselle Vivette continued: "The secret in choosing dry Bordeaux whites is to have the clearest and most precise idea as to what kind of wine we want. If we are looking for a wine that is clean, fresh and fruity, we would do better to go to Alsace or the Loire. If we want a big, full, luscious, rich and powerful wine to go with strong food, better choose from Burgundy. What Bordeaux has among its finest whites that cannot come from anywhere else is the marvelously aromatic and spicy quality of the wines made from the Semillon grape, after they have been aged in the bottle for several years. This is why our cellar offers the noble Château Laville Haut Brion and the Domaine de Chevalier. As to the golden, sweet wines, our cellar offers La Bergerie of Baron Philippe de Rothschild, the Château Suduiraut and the Château d'Yquem."

The Whites of Alsace

When I discussed with Mademoiselle Vivette the question of inexpensive white wines, she expressed her firm opinion that the vintners of Alsace are now offering some of the best values in all the world of wine. She said: "At prices that are quite extraordinarily low, we can find wines that are clean, crisp, delicious, grapey, lovely and refreshing to drink—perfect with so many foods—even, because of their aromatic quality, as an accompaniment to the lighter meats." Following Mademoiselle Vivette's advice, I have thoroughly explored the Alsatian wines that come to the United States and, indeed, they provide extraordinary pleasure at extraordinary values.

The basic buying rules are few and simple. The Alsatians use the varietal system of labeling, and the name of the grape indicates the character of the wine. If it is from the Sylvaner grape, it is almost always very dry, light, uncomplicated, and the least expensive type for everyday quenching of inevitable thirsts.

If it is Riesling, it is more luscious, richer, slightly softer, a more luxurious grade to accompany one's fancier culinary efforts. If it is Gewürztraminer, it is (as its German name implies) more aromatic, more dominant, spicier, for the richer foods and the special dining occasions. There are also some other grape (and blend) names on Alsatian labels, but relatively few of them reach the United States.

Mademoiselle Vivette proved to me—by comparative tasting of the bottles in her cellar—that within each basic type of wine there are various grades of price, quality and style, clearly signaled by the names on the labels. The least expensive wines are blended from the grapes of many small vineyards whose owners work together in regional or village cooperatives. The slightly more expensive grades (often representing the best possible values) show the names of the famous family firms, and it is really quite essential when buying Alsatian wines to learn these names and to relate them in one's mind to the style of wine one most enjoys. There is in Alsace a "family style" of making wine which has been followed for centuries by such families as Beyer, Blanc, Dopff, Hugel, Jux, Klipfel, Lorentz, Schlumberger, Trimbach and Willm.

Finally, at the top of the Alsatian tree, there are three famous vineyards which make, so to speak, "château-bottled" wines, which are the finest in Alsace and among the best in France: the Clos Sainte Hune, the Clos Les Murailles and the Clos de Zisser.

The Reds and Whites of the Loire

Among the dry whites of the lovely Loire Valley, the Pouilly-Fumé of the village of Pouilly-sur-Loire and those of the beautiful hilltop village of Sancerre have now become virtually too fashionable for the hunter of exceptional values. The third village of this upper-Loire trio, Quincy, is less well known, has a considerably larger production than the other two, and is therefore more modest in its prices for some beautifully refreshing, roundly balanced and subtle wines. Those of the famous village of Vouvray may be dry, slightly sweet, very sweet, or sparkling, but they are now generally too fashionable ever to be really inexpensive.

As to the best known Loire reds—those from the two villages of Bourgueil and Chinon—they are now being imported into the United States at extremely fair prices for wines of such an attractive and charming bouquet, lightness and quality of refreshment.

Finally there is the ubiquitous Muscadet, where the problem is mainly to find exceptional quality by concentrating either on the estate-bottled labels of individual growers, or on the best grades of wine that are labeled as being from the famous and fine district of Sèvre-et-Maine.

The Reds and Whites of the Rhône

Mademoiselle Vivette felt that the vineyards along both banks of the River Rhône, from just south of Lyon to the districts around Avignon, were among the happiest of hunting grounds for the wine lover in search of excellent quality at fine values. She regularly drives to the Rhône to taste and buy the attractive and charming light reds from the "roasted slope," the Côte Rôtie; some of the excellent reds from the districts of Crozes-Hermitage, Cornas, and Saint-Joseph. Also, she will try the fruity and exceptionally light reds of the Domaine du Beau Renard in Châteauneuf-du-Pape.

Among the whites, she had chosen for her cellar some excellent labels from Châteauneuf-du-Pape, from Hermitage, from Laudun and also from Saint-Joseph.

There are some important points to remember when looking for relatively inexpensive, good value Rhône wines. The name of the village of Châteauneuf-du-Pape has become extremely fashionable (in much the same way as the name "Pommard" in Burgundy), and most of its wines are now commanding fashionable prices. Some of its very best vineyards, in very good years, may produce such superlative wines that they are worth the high cost. But one should remember the warning that the less successful wines (especially those labeled with fancy made up brand names instead of legitimate château or vineyard names) are generally overpriced. Châteauneuf-du-Pape, in short, is slightly dangerous territory for explorers in search of value. They would do better to turn toward the less fashionable districts of the Côtes du Rhône, especially the labels which include the names of the best of the village communes, including Cairanne, Gigondas, Vacqueyras and Vinsobres.

The "Local" Wines of the Auberge from Provence and the High Savoy

Whenever Mademoiselle Vivette drives southward to visit her family in Provence, she loads her large station wagon for the return trip with the feathery light, almost grapejuicy white wines from the far south (most of them now imported into the United States at extraordinarily fair prices), including the dry white V.D.Q.S. (the indication of government supervision of quality) from the village of

Rognac in the district of Aix-en-Provence, the Bellet from the vine-yards around Nice, with the Bandol and Estandon from the Mediter-ranean coast. All are worth a serious exploration in terms of charming, light, everyday wines.

As to the crackly crisp red and white wines from the lower slopes of the High Alps (which might reasonably be called the *vins du pays* of the Auberge), Mademoiselle Vivette said, "We like to buy and serve the wines of the vineyard villages of our mountains, not only because they are our good neighbors, but also because they make ex-cellent wines. The names of the districts, the grapes and the villages are the lilting names of the wines: Apremont, Crépy, Gamay de Savoie, Roussette de Savoie, with the sparkling and still Seyssel." Al-most all of these charming wines are now being imported into the United States.

The Rosés of the Auberge

"I am convinced, of course, that our cellar will gain prestige," Mademoiselle Vivette said, "if we offer our guests the incomparable Tavel, which is surely the most attractive and unique rosé of all. It is now, of course, very fashionable everywhere and its price is high. Fortunately, however, when cost is a factor, it can be replaced by the almost equally attractive and certainly less expensive rosés bearing the name of its neighboring village of Lirac. We also propose another extraordinary pink wine, the magnificent Pinot Rosé d'Alsace, made from an unusual planting of Pinot Noir grapes near the Alsatian village of Bergheim. Then there is the noble Château de Tigné from grapes growing along the banks of the River Loire. Finally, the lesser (but still excellent) rosés made from the Cabernet grape in our provinces of Anjou, Provence and Touraine. I do not agree that a rosé wine goes with any and every kind of food, but these special rosés from our cellar have their important place in the planning of our informal and light menus."

The Sparkling Whites of Champagne and the High Alps

The cellar of the Auberge listed at least a few bottles of the finest *cuvées*, names and vintages of Champagne, but when a guest was less concerned with the prestige of the label and more with the matter of cost, Mademoiselle Vivette served (as I do at home) the sparkling *vin du pays* of her own region—the charming, light-as-a-mountain breeze, dry and sparkling wines of the High Savoy, the Seyssel *Blanc de Blancs* from the little mountain town of that name above the Valley of the Rhône, near the point where the great river enters France from Switzerland. Seyssel sparklers always seem to be among the best of "bubbly" values.

Cognacs, Armagnacs, Calvados and Other Eaux-de-Vie

"Our cellar book lists all the major labels of Cognac," said Mademoiselle Vivette, "which remains, perhaps, the ideal *digéstif*, but we can also offer three important labels of the gay and robust brandies of Armagnac: the Marquis de Caussade, the Larressingle, and the Domaine de Noaces. We also have a Calvados, the remarkable apple brandy of Normandy, that has been aged for fifteen years and has the smoothness of velvet. Then, I often surprise our guests by offering them an almost complete spectrum of the extraordinary fruit brandies of Alsace, which seem to capture, in a brilliant clear spirit, the pure essences of the wild fruits of the Vosges Mountains. Our list includes apricot, *alizier* (made from the service berry), *cassis* (from black currants), *fraise des bois* (from miniature wild strawberries), *framboise* (raspberries), *marc de gewürztraminer* (distilled from the famous Alsatian wine grape), *gratte cul* (from the hips of the eglantine rose), Cherry Kirsch, *mirabelle de Lorraine* (from golden plums), *mûre des bois* (from wild mulberries), *myrtilles* (from huckleberries), *prunelle* (from sloe berries), *prune sauvage* (wild plums), *quetsch* (Alsatian miniature purple plums), Queen Claude greengage plum, *sorbier* (from rowanberries), and *sureau* (from elderberries)."

Mademoiselle Vivette continued: "Also, when we have guests at Christmas, they are often quite shocked and certainly surprised when I offer them the *eau-de-vie* called *baies de houx*, which, believe it or not, is distilled from the red berries of the holly." Finally, Mademoiselle Vivette put on a slightly conspiratorial air and almost whispered: "And for our special friends, we have, in unlabeled bottles, an *eau-de-vie* distilled privately by one of our friends in this Valley from the plums which I pick from the tree in our own garden." Somehow, I felt I was back in Kentucky in the days of Prohibition.

The Sweet Liqueurs

"We feel that we should offer to our guests," Mademoiselle Vivette said, "some of the *spécialités* of our Dauphiné and Savoy regions and so we buy, as much as possible, the products of local distillers. First, naturally, there are the extraordinary liqueurs which have carried the name of our Valley to every corner of the world, our Green Chartreuse and Yellow Chartreuse, made for more than two hundred and fifty years from the secret recipe of Les Pères Chartreux, who live in the monastery at the peak of our Valley. Their green liqueur also comes in a more aromatic and luxurious version under a V.E.P. label, which means that the *vieillissement*, the aging, has been extra-prolonged. Then, our cellar also proposes the famous cherry liqueur distilled in the mountain valley where the best cherries grow, at the Côte Saint-André, near the village of Roybon. There are also liqueurs made from the brown Williams pear in our Isère Valley. There is the specialty of our city of Grenoble, the cherry Ratafia. We also buy, in the small town of Voiron, just about five miles outside our Valley, a series of locally distilled sweet spirits of which I approve because they are strongly characteristic of our region. They include a walnut liqueur, a hazelnut liqueur, a wild Alpine raspberry, a sweet *génépi* made from the long yellow roots of the mountain gentian, and a concoction known as 'Spirit of the Glaciers'—flavored with mint and with a fine blue color, exactly as we see it among our highest mountains in the early morning light. There is also a local gin with bits of gold leaf floating in it—an obvious imitation of the German *Goldwasser*. We do not think that gold leaf adds very much to the bouquet or flavor, but we keep it in our cellar for guests to whom appearance means everything. Last of all, in the village of Saint-Laurent-du-Pont which guards the gateway to our Valley there is a local distillation called Le Bonal which, one might say, is a locally acquired taste."

MENU OF
A Wine-Tasting Lunch

APÉRITIF: AN ICE-COLD GLASS OF WHITE ALSATIAN SYLVANER, HÜGEL, RIQUEWIHR

Jambon de Montagne Flambé
(*Flaming Canapés of Mountain Ham*)

A TASTING OF THREE NOBLE ALSATIAN WHITE WINES:
RIESLING, LES MURAILLES, DOPF & IRION, RIQUEWIHR
RIESLING, CLOS SAINT HUNE, TRIMBACH, RIBEAUVILLÉ
RIESLING, CLOS DE ZISSER, KLIPFEL, BARR

Carré de Veau à l'Aixoise
(*Boned Rack of Veal as They Prepare It in Aix-Les-Bains*)

A TASTING OF THREE LIGHT RED BURGUNDIES
FROM THE CHALONNAIS:
MERCUREY, CLOS-DU-ROI
MERCUREY, LOUIS LATOUR
MERCUREY, DOMAINE DE SUREMAIN

Fromages:

Barberey de Champagne   Bourseau de Chèvre
Bleu de Chèvre d'Aveyron

Tarte aux Reines Claudes
(*Tart of Queen Claude Plums*)

Café

LIQUEUR DE CERISES ROCHER

After spending the morning with me in her wine cellar, Mademoiselle Vivette decided to offer at lunch a tasting of some of her finest light wines. So she eliminated the normal spirituous apéritif and served instead an extremely dry, almost sharply refreshing, simple white Alsatian wine made from the Sylvaner grape. It was near to perfection on this warm day, but it would have been an ideal starter for any lunch or dinner, however complicated the menu to follow. The fruity dryness of the best Alsatian Sylvaners cleanses the palate, clears the taste buds and stimulates the appetite.

At table, the meal began with canapés of sun-dried mountain ham —each small slice on a crisply fried toast-round which was then covered with a sauce of sour cream and eggs, subtly acidulated with tarragon wine vinegar, and then flamed with Armagnac (recipe, page 184).

With these habit-forming mouthfuls there was a comparative tasting of three of the most exceptional white wines of Alsace. The majority of Alsatian wines, even when they are made from a single grape type, are blended from the production of several different vineyards. There are, however, three famous vineyards which are entirely "domaine bottled"—the wine limited to the grapes of that particular plot so that the name of the vineyard may legally be printed on the label. Since these vineyards are extremely small (the "Clos Sainte Hune," for example, in the village of Hunewihr, is only three acres), the production of these finest of Alsatian wines is restricted, and only very limited quantities can be exported to the United States.

The main course, the boned and rolled rack of veal, poached with chestnuts and garden vegetables, is a regional specialty of the famous resort town of Aix-les-Bains in the Alps of the Savoy. The recipe is on page 320.

South of the world-famous slopes of the Côte d'Or of Burgundy there are two lesser wine districts, the Chalonnais and the Maconnais, of which the best red wines are those from around the village of Mercurey. They are comparatively light, with a definite Burgundy character, but representing a compromise between the extreme delicacy of the more southerly Beaujolais and the velvety power of the more northerly great Burgundies. The village, incidentally, takes its name from a Roman temple on a nearby hilltop to the messenger god Mercury. We were offered for a comparative tasting three wines, all of the same year, from three of the best-known producers and shippers.

Each of the bottles was an excellent partner to the aromatic veal and its garniture of vegetables, but the true character in each glass—light weight, yet still Burgundian—did not come out to meet us until we were joined by the cheeses. The Barberey de Champagne comes from the village of Barberey near the town of Troyes in the southern part of the Champagne country. It is farm-made from cows' milk and aged in earthenware molds, from which it emerges in the shape of a large Camembert. In summer, while still young, it is sold as a soft, unripened cream cheese. For the winter the rounds are aged and dried, taking on a new personality: aggressive, forceful and strong. At this lunch we had both types.

The second cheese, the famous small Bourseau—about two inches across and two inches high—had a creamy brownish crust, with a strong flavor and smell (the crust, that is!). The inside flesh was a complete contrast—beautifully creamy, silky-smooth on the tongue, with the subtle pungency of goats' milk. It was an outstanding cheese that happily uplifted the wine.

The third cheese, the Bleu de Chèvre d'Aveyron, is a rare oddity regarded by many connoisseurs (including the late great André Simon) as "one of the finest blue cheeses in all of France." Aveyron is, of course, the famous region—north of Montpelier, west of Avignon—rocky and wild, its ancient hills shot through with caves, where Roquefort is the absolute monarch. Since there is very little good pasture in Aveyron, cows' milk is always in short supply (Roquefort is made from sheep's milk), but goats flourish and their milk is used for this farmhouse blue from the Millau district. Like Roquefort, it is matured in the mountain caves, but there the comparison ends. Roquefort is made in vast quantities and is a world traveler. The little goat blue is a charming shy country boy who seldom leaves home.

The dessert tart was filled with the magnificent French "Queen Claude" plums, with such a superb bouquet that the whole house was filled with a scent of the baking fruit, and with such sweetness that they virtually needed no sugar (recipe, page 404).

Where the Alpine slopes descended into the Isère plain, west of Grenoble, the two fruits-of-the-earth which dominate the agriculture are the cherries and the walnuts. Both are distilled into at least a dozen different kinds of powerfully spirituous brandies and liqueurs. On one of the lower slopes, La Côte Saint-André, near the "cherry capital" of Roybon, the famous distillery of La Maison Rocher converts sour cherries into this highly scented, strongly flavored cherry liqueur.

MENU OF
A Dinner with Four of the Greatest Wines of the Auberge's Cellar

---

APÉRITIF: DUBONNET DES ALPES

Terrine de Foies de Porc ou de Volailles
(Terrine of Herbed Pork or Chicken Livers)

WHITE BORDEAUX, 1965 CHÂTEAU SUDUIRAUT,
PREIGNAC, SAUTERNES

Velouté de Tomates à la Provençale
(Cream of Tomato in the Style of Provence)

WHITE BORDEAUX, 1964 CHÂTEAU LAVILLE HAUT BRION,
TALENCE, GRAVES

Tourte de Marcassin aux Aubergines à la Crème
(Wild Boar in a Pastry Crust with Creamed Eggplant)

RED BURGUNDY, 1961 LES MUSIGNY, DOMAINE DE VOGÜÉ,
CUVÉE VIEILLES VIGNES

Fromages:
Bouton de Culotte Maconnais   Tome au Marc de Savoie
Epoisses de Bourgogne

RED BORDEAUX, 1949 CHÂTEAU LATOUR, PAUILLAC, MÉDOC

Entremet aux Petits Suisses
(Dessert of Sugared Cream Cheese)

Café

RATAFIA DE CERISES DE GRENOBLE, TESSEIRE

Tonight's dinner was a special celebration in honor of the completion of my exploration of the wine cellar of the Auberge. In this menu, the wines took precedence over the foods—as they always should when truly great bottles are involved. These wines were chosen first, and each dish was a secondary partner planned to show off the superb liquid in the glass. The labels, naturally, are no longer listed on the *Carte des Vins* of the Auberge. Mademoiselle Vivette brought them out from the darkest and most secret recesses of her cellar—as personal treasures of which perhaps only two or three entirely irreplaceable bottles are left.

The apéritif obviously had to be light and simple. Each ice-cold glass contained two ounces of the standard dark Dubonnet, two ounces of the locally distilled cherry Kirsch of Allevard, a dash of soda water and a twist of lemon peel.

The fine chicken or pork liver terrine was lightly and subtly seasoned with chopped fresh sage leaves and then moistened with Cognac and Madeira (recipe, page 164).

The luxurious smoothness of this terrine was almost perfectly balanced by its accompanying noble wine. I have already discussed (on page 30) Mademoiselle Vivette's point of view (taught her by her connoisseur father) that very rich dishes are ideally balanced by lightly sweet wines. The romantic turreted seventeenth-century Château de Suduiraut is one of the first growth sweet wine vineyards of the village of Preignac in the great Bordeaux district of Sauternes, and in very sunny years its wine can be almost thickly honeyed. But in 1965 there was not enough sunshine and the wine was delicately light, yet still with the marvelously balanced, aromatic character of a truly noble Sauternes. It was an ideal balance to the richness of the terrine.

The soup was no ordinary cream of tomato. The "à la Provençale" took care of that! The preparation of this version began with crisply fried dice of salt pork, chopped onions, white leeks, the peeled and seeded tomatoes and a goodly supply of dry white wine. After slow simmering, *la soupe* was converted to *la crème* by being thickened with a whipped purée of rice. Finally—and unsurprisingly—the typical ambiance of Provence was added in the form of a small mash of garlic —more or less to taste (recipe, page 223).

The second wine was a dramatic contrast to the first. It was also a product of the soil of Bordeaux—from the village of Talence in the Graves, only a few miles from Sauternes; yet the dominant dryness of the white Graves completely swept away the aftertaste of the Sauternes. In my opinion, the vineyard of the Château Laville Haut Brion produces one of the supreme dry whites of Bordeaux. It is a powerful, full-bodied, at times almost glutinous wine, made largely from the Semillon grape—a wine often so masculine and muscular that it keeps to perfection for many years. The vintage of 1964 was very great, and the wine, as we tasted it with this dinner, had developed an aroma, a spiciness, a personality of such dominant character that its consumption was a memorable exprience.

The "tart" of wild boar was an extraordinary and brilliantly successful composition. Mademoiselle Ray cut thin strips from the filet—the tenderest part of the lean sirloin back meat—of a young animal, marinated the strips in Cognac with fresh chervil, then briefly sautéed them in butter. Next, the meat strips were enclosed in a flaky pastry that was beautifully decorated as a double-crust pie, with a small chimney at its center. After it was baked to a golden brown, the spaces inside the pie were filled (by pouring in through the chimney) with a rich *velouté* of cream and eggs. A few more minutes in the oven brought everything to a perfect harmony of textures before being served accompanied by a *Sauce Bordelaise,* with a dish of sliced young eggplant, first browned in butter, then baked in sour cream (recipes for the wild boar on page 289; for the eggplant, page 368).

Mademoiselle Vivette's "greatest" red Burgundy turned out to be very great indeed. It was from one of the supreme vineyards, Les Musigny, in the commune of Chambolle—of the supreme vintage year, 1961—from the supreme part of the vineyard, the *parcelle* owned by Count Georges de Vogüé, and it was the "best of his best," the specially selected wine which he labels *Cuvée Vieilles Vignes,* because, in any vineyard, the oldest vines give the finest fruit. This wine, challenged and yet lifted by the strong flavor of the game meat, had a delicate distinction, a gentle femininity, a soft savoriness, all united by the smooth velvet that is the hallmark of a truly great Burgundy.

With the arrival of the cheeses, Mademoiselle Vivette departed from her usual dinner sequence. Tonight she served a fourth bottle of wine—a red Bordeaux, unexpectedly supported by Burgundian cheeses. But how, I wondered, could she possibly meet the classic menu rule that the last wine must top all the others. We were already on such a rarefied peak of perfection. Yet she produced a higher peak with a supremely great Château Latour. What is there left to say of this vineyard—one of the two or three noblest in the world? Its great wines are so big that they seem almost to last forever. I tasted the 1865 vintage when it was a hundred years old. It still had breed and dignity. The 1893 is still a *grande dame,* in retirement, but unfailingly reflecting her former beauty and dominance. This century has been studded with supreme Latour vintages: 1928, 1929, 1934, 1945—but the one which is, perhaps, now at its peak of development is the 1949, presented tonight by Mademoiselle Vivette with its greatness highlighted by her brilliant choice of cheeses.

The first came in tiny round cones so small that their French name on the menu means "trouser buttons." They are made from goats' milk by farmers around the village of Tournus, in the Maconnais district of southern Burgundy. They looked like nothing so much as small marshmallows, some of them toasted brown, others with a red crust.

The second cheese, the Tome au Marc, is the original version of all the cheeses with a crust of grape pits. This, now quite rare, authentic type was dipped at the time of the grape harvest in the *marc*, the mush of grape skins and pits left at the bottom of the fermenting vat after the new wine had been drawn off. The *marc*, as it dried around the cheeses, formed a highly perfumed blackish crust which not only protected the cheese but gradually injected its delicately winy flavor into the flesh. This was a slow process, unsuited to *la production industrielle.* So many of the cheeses are now made in factories and, instead of being dipped and aged, are simply pounded with dried grape pits. This way, no one has to wait for the grape harvest. Nor should anyone mistake such cheeses for the real thing: the true Tome au Marc, with its blackish crust and winy flavor.

The third cheese, the Epoisses de Bourgogne, is generally considered to be the best blue of Burgundy, made from whole cows' milk by farmers around the village of Epoisses and shaped into small cylinders. Its flesh is creamy, rich and soft, sometimes punctuated inside with black specks of coarsely ground pepper, bits of clove, or fennel seeds. Some of these cheeses, also, are dipped in the *marc*, in the fermenting vats at harvest time, then dried on beds of rye straw, until an orange red crust develops.

The dessert was an interesting variation of the classic *Pot de Crème*, made, of course, in France with the ubiquitous Petits Suisses —the small, cylindrical cream cheeses rolled in wax paper. (They are now available in some United States fancy food shops, but can reasonably be replaced by our standard foil-wrapped cream cheese.) The yolks of very fresh eggs were lightly beaten with sugar, then worked into the soft cream cheese, with some cream and several good dashes of cherry Kirsch brandy. When the mixture had been worked to a velvety mousse, it was lightened to an airy fluff by the incorporation of the beaten whites. Finally, the mixture was put into individual small hand-pottery serving bowls and refrigerated until the cream was absolutely ice cold (recipe, page 386).

As a link with the faintly cherry-flavored dessert, we accompanied the coffee with the famous local cherry liqueur, the Ratafia of Grenoble. What does this strange name mean? No one seems to be sure. One theory is that this drink was always sipped when any kind of business or political agreement was reached between two people or two groups. The drink was the symbol of ratification—and everyone knows, or ought to know, the origin of that Latin-rooted word: "res," or "ras," meaning "the thing"—"ata" meaning "agreed"—"fiat" meaning "under contract of law." I find this explanation so delicious in its fantasy that it deserves to be true!

THIRTEEN

Travelers Sheltering From the Storm
—"Le Snack" Is Also an Art

The first sudden thunderclap seemed to shake the Auberge to its foundations. We were in the dining room, in the middle of lunch. It had grown so dark that Mademoiselle Vivette had come in to turn on the lights and announce that we were about to experience "*la grande tempête des Alpes.*" Each rolling boom, multiplied by the echoing reverberations of the valley, seemed to envelop us from every direction. One sensed the vibrations beating down on houses, pastures, trees. . . . As boom followed boom in rapid fire, the bright copper pots and utensils which decorate the rooms of the Auberge began vibrating in a buzzing harmony: the long *poissonière,* the "fish boiler" on the old oaken bread-chest, the tall *bidon,* the ancient five-gallon "milkcan" standing in the corner.

The rain came down in almost solid sheets. The windows shook with a steady rhythm. I went up to my room and opened my casement window. Through all the noise and roar there was a sense of solitude, of isolation, of the relaxation of pent-up force and tension. I could hear the water rumbling in the Valley. I imagined the flooded and steaming landscape, the river swelling and overflowing, the roots of plants laid bare, the most private cracks and gullies of the earth penetrated and violated. Then the storm rolled on and away.

I went out into the garden. Shouts were coming up from the village. There was a frothy wind in my face. Overhead, rosy clouds were galloping. There was a damp, rich smell, perhaps from bared roots, sap oozing from broken branches, the nectar of crushed flowers. . . . I breathed deeply. Soon, I was sure, the crushed flowers would slowly lift up their heads again, the thick blood of the earth would revive everything. Mademoiselle Vivette was loudly announcing that tomorrow morning the woods would be thick with wild mushrooms.

During the storm, the Auberge had filled up with passing motorists, unable to see ahead through the sheets of falling water and afraid of the hairpin bends. The smaller mountain roads, in fact, immediately became impassable—turning into rushing streams a foot deep, with large, rounded, weather-polished pebbles rolling down under water. Alpine storms make no allowances for automobiles.

So the low rattan chairs in *Le Hall* were filled with gossiping guests, drying and warming themselves before the crackling logs in the open hearth. Listening to their voices one could place the people by their reactions to the storm. The middle-aged husband and wife in the corner had obviously discovered the Valley years ago and had come back again and again. They were joyously uplifted by the dominant roar of Nature in command. The couple with the three young children had, it appeared, stumbled into the Valley by accident this morning. They were awed and overwhelmed. They spoke in whispers. With some guests there was a sense of fear. One man asked about possible rockfalls on the high Sappey road. A young mother discussed the danger of poisonous snakes if the children went for a walk. The leather-jacketed couple who had come in the noisy sports car were asking whether it was safe to leave the Valley after dark by the narrow twisting Porte de la Fourvoirie. . . .

Mademoiselle Vivette bustled among them, handing out her *Carte du Jour,* taking orders for *le snack,* or pouring drinks behind her small copper-covered bar with its back wall of dark green canvas and its striped canopy of apricot yellow and tulip green behind the wrought iron screen. One could tell more about the guests by what they ordered. The simplest commitment was to that most ubiquitous of all French soft drinks, Pshitt. (The first time I tasted it, I decided its name was precisely right.) Thirstier throats called for tall glasses of beer: the selection ranging from the simple, unsophisticated, locally brewed Kronenberger *Blonde ou Brune,* up to the luxuriously smooth, world-traveling Carlsberg. Those who had been chilled by the ice-cold rain demanded doubtful French vodka, or safe-and-sound "le Scotch." But the couple who took delight in the storm were celebrating with one of Mademoiselle Vivette's house-label bottles of *le Champagne, Blanc de Blancs.*" An English family, of course, ordered a pot of tea, and Mademoiselle Ray converted it into something quite French with a piled-up dish of her home-baked *petits-fours.*

For guests who claimed they were starving at this midway point between lunch and dinner, Mademoiselle Vivette would serve, at a table in the dining room, her basic snack meal—available, in an emergency, at almost any hour of the day or night—*Le Gouteron pour le Motoriste.* It consisted of home-baked rustic-style walnut bread, locally churned butter, a platter of paper-thin slices of mountain-cured sun-dried ham, locally made fresh white goats' milk cheese, some of Mademoiselle Ray's superbly light miniature fresh fruit tartlets, a carafe of the house white wine, and coffee. (Incidentally, I have been able to reproduce the imaginatively balanced simplicity of *Le Gouteron* in New York, with Smithfield ham, my own walnut bread baked from Mademoiselle Ray's recipe, page 412, imported French goat cheese, etc.)

Other guests were more demanding. They were willing to wait while Mademoiselle Ray prepared a hot version of *le snack.* Listening to their discussions as they studied the *Carte du Jour,* I realized how seldom the French think in terms of "le sondvitch," "le homburger," or "le hottdog." (The two latter, of course, are considered merely as variations of "le sondvitch" and thus have to accept their share of the contempt which all Frenchmen feel for all gastronomic things British and all inventions of the Earl of Sandwich.) Instead, these demanding guests wanted something altogether more imaginative. To them *le snack* was a special branch of the culinary art, involving very little compromise from a fancy dinner dish, except that it had to be prepared quickly. I discovered that in this department of the kitchen Mademoiselle Ray was as much the gastronomic master as she was in every other. She has taught me, with her recipes for L'Aligot Dauphinois, Crêpes de Chèvre aux Oeufs Rouges, Croque Monsieur, Oeufs aux Champignons Farcis, Le Bifteck de Gruyère des Alpes, and Tôt-Fait des Cerises d'Allevard (see recipes beginning on page 178), that the French *les snacks* are dramatic, practical and relatively simple.

MENU OF
A Quick Lunch on a Thunderously Busy Day

APÉRITIF: LE BONAL DE SAINT-LAURENT-DU-PONT

Crêpes de Chèvre aux Oeufs Rouges
(Crêpes Filled with Goat Cheese and Red Caviar)

WHITE BURGUNDY, POUILLY-FUISSÉ, CHÂTEAU DE FUISSÉ

Le Bifteck de Gruyère des Alpes
(Grilled Cheese Steak of Alpine Gruyère)

RED BEAUJOLAIS, CHÂTEAU DE JULIÉNAS

Fromages:

Selles-sur-Cher   Macquelines des Vosges

Grièges de l'Ain

Pets de Nonne de Chamonix
(Puffs of a Chamonix Nun)

Café

LIQUEUR DE NOISETTE DES ALPES

The apéritif—a local product well known throughout the Dauphiné and Savoy regions—is made in Saint-Laurent-du-Pont, the village which guards the gateway to the Valley. Mademoiselle Vivette said: "We serve it because the people of Saint-Laurent-du-Pont are our good friends and neighbors."

The crêpes filled with cheese and red salmon roe were a slightly enlarged version of one of les snacks served earlier in the day by Mademoiselle Ray to stormbound guests in a hurry (recipe, page 193).

This very light and simple lunch was at once made memorable by the outstanding quality of the first wine. The Pouilly-Fuissé whites of southern Burgundy have become almost as popular everywhere in the world as Beaujolais. Inevitably, this means—as the volume of production is forced up and up—that many wines are called, but only a few should have been chosen. Of the few which deserve the highest accolades year after year, consistently among the best are the wines of the great vigneron family of Marcel Vincent. At his lovely fifteenth-century Château de Fuissé (which has been owned by the family for four generations), he produces wines of crystal clarity, never aggressive or dominant, but calmly and gently refreshing and reviving.

The main course—the luxuriously nourishing "steak" of eggs and cheese—was another of Mademoiselle Ray's stormy-day specialties (recipe, page 179).

Of all the variations of Beaujolais in the wine cellar of the Auberge, those from the important wine village of Juliénas are usually among the best—and especially those produced and bottled by the Château of the village. I found this one to have a strongly individual character, a fine balance of flavors and a firm texture in the mouth.

The first of the cheeses with which to finish the wine takes its name from the village of Selles-sur-Cher, on the small river which flows into the Loire just above the city of Tours. The cheese is of goats' milk, with the shape of a small truncated pyramid. The aging process involves rolling the cheese in salt and wood ash, which gives it a blackish crust. It has the strong taste and slightly runny softness of a very ripe Camembert, but with a nutty saltiness that makes it, in my opinion, one of the most unusual goat cheeses of France.

The second cheese, the Macquelines des Vosges, is a variation of the famous Coulommiers, made in the farmhouses around the village of Rouvres in the northeastern Vosges mountains. Because it is made

from partially skimmed cows' milk, it is much less rich than either
Camembert or Coulommiers and is a pleasant change from the multi-
plicity of very creamy cheeses which nowadays seem to flood the
market.

The third cheese, the Grièges de l'Ain, comes from the rich agricultural region just northeast of Lyon. This cheese was an exquisitely
delicate blue, shaped like a long cylinder, with the basic color of its
inside flesh a deep yellow instead of the near white of, say, a Roquefort. The color comes from its high content of cream. When it was
cut, it broke into soft, glistening pieces, almost like large curds of
a fresh cream cheese, but with blue mottling and a gentle version
of the *bleu* taste.

The dessert with the irreverent name is a French classic specialty,
listed in all the most important reference and cook books. The cream
puff pastry is made by blending together, in a hot saucepan, butter,
flour, grated lemon peel, sugar and eggs. This dough is then shaped
into tiny puff balls and deep-fried until golden brown. Each was, indeed, as light as a feather, and the slightest wind could have blown
them off the plate (recipe, page 416).

The concluding liqueur of Alpine hazelnuts was another local and
regional product bought by Mademoiselle Vivette in the nearby
town of Voiron, from its principal distilling firm with the charming
and intensely French name, La Maison Meunier, Mère et Fils.

MENU OF
A Relaxing Dinner After the Storm

APÉRITIF: KIR DE CHABLIS

Soufflé aux Épinards
(Soufflé of Creamed Spinach)

ROSÉ RHÔNE, LIRAC

Moules Pochées au Vin Rouge
(Mussels Poached in Red Wine)

Boeuf à la Mode de la Famille Artaud
(Pot Roast of Beef in the Style of Mademoiselle Vivette's Family)

Gratinée Savoyarde
(Casserole of Potatoes and Mushrooms as They Do It in Savoy)

RED BURGUNDY, 1959 CLOS VOUGEOT, MORIN

Fromages:

Marolles de la Loire   Tête de Moine du Jura

Bleu de Bassilac Limousin

Mousse aux Abricots
(Mousse of Fresh Apricots)

Café

SUC DES GLACIERS, MEUNIER

Instead of her usual Kir de Provence—made with the white Provençal wine of Rognac—Mademoiselle Vivette tonight mixed a classic Kir de Chablis. The comparison proved one important point: the extraordinary variety that can easily be achieved, with the classic apéritifs, by simply varying the base ingredients. The sprightly young wine of Provence produced a Kir that was attractive, energetic, stimulating, like a gay giddy girl. The Kir of the Chablis was more beautiful, gentler, more relaxing, more seductive, like a mature and lovely lady.

The first course, Soufflé of Creamed Spinach, was a typically French beginning—effective and unusual. Mademoiselle Vivette teamed it, not with the expected white wine, but with a light pink Lirac of the Rhône, which related superbly to the Alpine Tome cheese that Mademoiselle Ray had used subtly to flavor the spinach (recipe, page 201).

The classic Moules Pochées was slightly varied from the norm by the fact that Mademoiselle Ray steamed the mussels in light red wine instead of the usual dry white. After being flavored with celery, garlic, onions, then combined with the juices of the mussels, the red *bouilli* was buttered and thickened into a bright pink sauce. It made the blue-shelled mussels look particularly attractive and linked up ideally with the continuation of the pink Lirac (recipe, page 254).

The main entrée was a Provençal version of a pot roast of beef. Its simmering liquid drew its body from a piece of veal and its flavor from fresh mountain herbs, white wine and Armagnac—but, surprisingly for Provence, not from any garlic (recipe, page 270).

The beef was accompanied by the feminine version of the famous Savoy specialty of potatoes and mushrooms. The potatoes were thinly sliced, layered with wild *bolets*, Alpine Gruyère cheese and onions, soaked with butter and cream, then baked to an exhilarating richness (recipe, page 350).

The wine was from one of the very great vineyards of Burgundy, the Clos Vougeot, which, however, can vary considerably in quality. The 124 vineyard acres within the high grey stone walls of the former Cistercian monastery are divided among about one hundred different owners, each of whom has different ideas and a varying degree of skill in terms of making his wine. Also, one *parcelle,* or "plot of earth" —even within the limits of the great vineyard—may simply not be as good as many of the others. So it is always important, when choosing a Clos Vougeot, to know the name of the individual owner-producer. This wine, from the Domaine of Jean Morin, was entirely satisfactory.

The first of the cheeses with which to finish the wine was "The Marvel of Marolles," made originally by the monks of the Abbey of that name on the plains of Flanders in northeastern France not far from the border of Belgium. It is one of the most vehemently smelly of French cheeses—of the family of the Limburger, or of our American Liederkranz!—and the authentic version can be recognized by its reddish crust and white cows'-milk inside flesh. Other versions are mass-produced in factories in various places, including Belgium and Germany, but are much less good and strong. At Marolles, the cheeses are aged and dried in caves that face towards the sea, since the faintly briny winds add a special flavor and quality to the crust. The great gastronome Curnonsky once called Marolles "the King of the strong cheeses of France."

The second cheese, "The Monk's Head of the Jura," was originally invented by the monks of a fifteenth-century abbey in the mountains of the Bernese Oberland of Switzerland but is also now produced in the French mountains on the Swiss border. It is made from cows' milk and shaped in smallish balls, with dark brown crusts and an inside flesh that is dry and crumbly, with a dominant flavor and strong character.

The third cheese, the "Blue of Bassilac," comes from the central region of France around the city of Limoges. It is made on farms also all over the famous truffle district of Périgord—but no truffles, unfortunately, get into the cheese. The blue mold forms naturally as the cheeses are aged in caves or damp cellars.

For the dessert, fresh apricots were cooked, mashed and finely puréed, then flavored with lemon juice and made fluffy light by being folded into a mixture of whipped cream, beaten egg whites and vanilla sugar. Finally, the ice-cold fluff was garnished with sections of more apricots, previously marinated in orange Curaçao liqueur (recipe, page 380).

With the coffee, the spirituous ending of the meal was the locally distilled "Spirit of the Glaciers," a strong drink with a brilliant blue color, claimed to be exactly the shade of a real glacier when seen by mountain climbers in the first light of sunrise. The informing flavor was, obviously, a faint touch of white mint.

FOURTEEN

The Past—
Stendhal Came and Dined Well

On stormy nights at the Auberge of the Flowering Hearth,
when the furious winds made the old stone house shudder
and the rain pounded on the windows, we would gather after dinner
in front of the crackling log fire in *Le Salon* and browse among the
bookshelves that lined one wall of the room. There were a good
many volumes on the history of La Vallée de la Grande Chartreuse.
Dipping into their pages, I soon realized that many of the visitors
who had "discovered" the Valley over the centuries (including the
famous world leaders, kings and queens, generals and statesmen, explorers and scientists . . .) had all felt—as I had—that one's first
entry into this Valley is an extraordinary personal experience—an
adventure into an overwhelming sense of peace, a withdrawal from
the fears and tensions of the aggressive world of men.

On 27 April 1887 when Queen Victoria of England came
through the narrow and twisting pass of La Porte de la Fourvoirie, her
carriage drawn by eight white horses straining up the steep grade,
it was reported that the generally talkative queen was absolutely

silent and apparently deeply impressed by the scene. Three hundred years earlier the effect had been the same on Catherine de Médici. Later, there would be silence also for Queen Wilhelmina of the Netherlands, for the Empress of Brazil, for the Duchess of Berry and others.

Many painters, photographers, poets, writers, have come to this Valley to try to recapture the essence of its beauty and power in their pictures and words. On 7 April 1805 the great French writer Chateaubriand rode up into the Valley on horseback; later, in his memoirs, he described his feelings of joyous solitude and his agony of fear when his wife's horse bolted during the immense thunderstorm that rolled over them. The poet Alphonse de Lamartine longed to stay in these mountains for the rest of his life. The novelist Honoré de Balzac, after his visit, decided to write *The Country Doctor* and set the scenes of the novel in this region.

Yet it seemed to me that one writer succeeded better than all the others in transforming into words not only the power but also the gaiety and simplicity of the Valley of La Grande Chartreuse. It is hardly surprising, considering that the great French novelist Stendhal was born in Grenoble and, in his youth, explored almost every path and track of the High Alps of his native Dauphiné region. All his life, from his literary struggles in Paris, from his military service under Napoleon, from his diplomatic posts in Italy, he felt the need to return to the Alps, as if to renew his strength. I heard of the existence of the original manuscript of Stendhal's notes on his last visit to the Valley from another guest at the Auberge, a professor of literature at the University of Grenoble. When Stendhal returned to Paris he rewrote and expanded his original notes as part of his book, *Memoirs of a Tourist,* published in 1838; in various cut and edited versions it has since been translated into many languages.

Stendhal's letters and personal papers are now housed partly in the Stendhal Museum in Grenoble and partly in the Library of Historic Archives at the University of Grenoble. Going back to his handwritten notes, I did my own translation of his French words.

> The 1st of September 1837. . . . I started out from Grenoble yesterday at four in the morning, as soon as the gates of the City were opened, with two horses—one for me, the other for my guide.
> Now, we began to climb out of this beautiful valley of the Isère on the mountain track leading to the hamlet of Corenc. It rises

through the vineyards on the slopes of the mountain that dominates the Valley on the north. . . .

When the River Isère and the floor of the valley are at last out of sight, the view ahead becomes at once magnificent. One faces the famous peak, Taillefer. Behind and beyond it are the great chains of the High Alps. The higher one climbs, the more crowded is the horizon, with new peaks crossing and criss-crossing each other. Even with only my small opera glasses, I could clearly see the granite "needles" at the summits of the peaks, where the angle of the rocks is so steep that the snow cannot rest, but slides back and piles up at the foot of the cliff.

As I looked down upon the simple agriculture in the valleys between the mountains, I could not help comparing them with other, more highly developed regions which I have seen and studied: for example, the Lowlands of Scotland, or the Plains of Belgium. In those areas of sophisticated farming, where one often sees forty ploughs working at the same time in the same field, there is the feeling of a great mass-manufacturing process. There is no feeling of solitude, of the simple joys of the countryside. It is nothing but a gross vanity for those mass-farmers to apply to their work the terms that Vergil, Rousseau, or other philosophers . . . used about the simple life of the fields. Worst of all, mass-agriculture involves a virtually continuous struggle between the owners of the land and the hired peasants who, because of their servitude, become increasingly poor, increasingly greedy and increasingly dishonest.

There is no such tension as this in the high valleys of the Alps. Here one feels only the pure joy of the open land in a setting of the most sublime beauty—with serried rows of vines on the slopes and, below them, the lush green of the pastures. . . .

As we continued to climb toward the village of Le-Sappey-en-Chartreuse, at the entrance to La Vallée de La Grande Chartreuse, the land became wilder and the vegetation poorer. The trees were stunted by storms. We passed peasants yelling at their two cows, but calling each by its name . . . others were drawing loads of wood towards the market in Grenoble—an essential source of revenue, so that the farmers can pay their taxes—monies used by the government in Paris to build useless palaces like the Quai d'Orsay. . . .

Approaching Sappey, I overtook a group of tourists from Grenoble, also on their way to the Valley. . . . There were six young ladies on horseback. It must take courage for a girl to undertake this wild ride. . . . I introduced myself to one of these ladies and her husband. Since the "desert" through which we were now passing was almost depressingly wild, they seemed eager to invite me to join their company. Just as we reached the highest point and were about to enter the magnificent gorge which led to La Grande Chartreuse, one of the husbands called out: "Listen, I hear a hissing at the cork of one of our bottles of Champagne. At any moment, all the bottles may explode!" As soon as I realized that they had food and drink with them, I pretended to be an expert on the problems of travel at high altitudes. I said that, in this thin air, we would all soon suffer from terrible headaches if we did not eat something immediately. They believed me. We stopped under a huge beech tree, and a few moments later I was attacking a superb cold *pâté*. It was, nevertheless, a brilliant idea of mine; the general nervous tension diminished. After our brief rest for refreshment the girls were again bubbling with the joy of youth. Everyone was very gay as we remounted our horses. We were all talking at once.

The path now became extremely narrow and difficult. It was covered by stones, partly rounded by friction. Obviously, during great storms, this small road became a torrent of water and the stones rolled down. Now, they made the horses slip and slither. The girls were quite terrified—much too afraid to taste the utter sublimity of the view.

Now, quite suddenly, we saw the great buildings of La Grande Chartreuse. . . . As we entered the wild Valley, I remembered the words of Pierre Dorlande, one of the first historians of these hermits: "A frightful place, cold, covered with snow, mountainous, surrounded by awful precipices, darkened by towering pines. . . . A more suitable place for wild animals than for men . . . with immense rocks covering the sterile and unfruitful earth. . . ."

Below the grey stone hermitage, on the floor of this high valley, runs the small River Guiers, at the foot of a towering mountain called "Le Grand Som" . . . such is the somber and terrible menace of its cliffs that one's soul is overwhelmed. . . .

These were my thoughts as we advanced slowly into the Valley. But before we could do so, there came running toward us one of the Brother Servants of the hermits, a young man, looking quite terrified. He said his name was Jean-Marie and he begged the ladies to come no farther. He had obviously heard their joyous laughter. We all stopped. . . . Apparently, the Chartreuse hermits are horrified by the sight and sounds of women. . . . Now, one of the hermits came towards us, also looking quite terrified by the sight of six beautiful young women. He said at once that, if they insisted on coming into this valley, they would not be permitted to approach the hermitage but would be lodged in the infirmary some distance away. He added, rather pointedly, that in ancient times women were forbidden to enter the Valley. But the revolution had changed all that.

The hermit who told us all this was a handsome man of between forty-five and fifty, wearing a cloak of white wool, and since there was a cold wind, he kept the white hood firmly over his head.

I admit that at that moment I thought our entire journey to be a ridiculous mistake. . . . Why should these hermits, trying to escape from the world of men, trying to find peace and solitude in this wild place, be disturbed by our curiosity, which was both cruel and indiscreet? . . . Perhaps our coming would revive some intense pain which they sought to forget. I could not resist crying out: "Ladies, believe me, it would be far better if you would take the side road and wait for us in the Auberge at Saint-Laurent-du-Pont. The younger and more beautiful you are, the more your presence in this Valley is a lack of delicacy and tact. . . ." But of course the husbands objected. "Monsieur," one of them replied, "you forget the one important word of our era: money . . . these hermits are poor . . . they rely on travelers to buy their eggs and their milk, during the few summer months when courageous climbers can enter the Valley, thus providing a small income. . . . Each of us will pay them five francs a day for as long as we stay here." I must say that his attitude greatly annoyed me. . . .

So Jean-Marie led us to the infirmary building in which there were three large, almost bare rooms. We did not yet settle into them, as we wanted first to explore the Valley. . . . But soon we were dying of hunger and returned to the good news that our meal was ready. It had the first essential merit of being abundant. There were fried carp, potatoes, eggs and other simple things. We sat at a long pinewood table in one of the large infirmary rooms. . . . Jean-Marie served us and treated me with special attention. . . .

As we were finishing our meal, the hermit came back to see us. He overheard one of the ladies asking Jean-Marie for coffee and said, rather pompously, that coffee was not permitted, because it was not a necessity of life. To which the girl who had asked for the coffee replied: "But it seems to me, Father, that you are smoking." To which the hermit answered: "That is quite different, madame. Tobacco has been ordered for me as a cure for my terrible headaches." I must say that I was slightly shocked by the girl's tone of voice. She was too right.

Jean-Marie then led us up the hill to the spring where the original hermitage had been built, about 750 years ago. . . . I felt, again, overwhelmed by the wildness of the place, by its somber and terrible solitude, which completely overshadowed all the buildings of man. . . . Suddenly a blustering wind began blowing, and black storm clouds rolled overhead, so we hurried down. Just as we entered the infirmary, a dreadful thunderclap shook the rocks and the forests. I think I have never before heard such a great noise. The ladies were terrified. The wind now redoubled its fury, slashing the rain against the windows as if it were trying to smash them. "What will happen to us if the glass breaks?" they cried. For me, the spectacle was sublime. It was as if the great pine trees were moaning, while the storm tried to break them. The whole valley was lit up by an extraordinary glow. The ladies became even more frightened. The approaching night heightened the terrifying view. The thunderclaps were more and more magnificent. I wanted to go out and be alone with the storm. The ladies would not let me go.

Jean-Marie came in and made the shocking announcement . . . that, according to the Chartreuse rules, the gentlemen, even the husbands, would not be permitted to remain with the ladies during the night. The ladies must remain alone. Their terror was now uncontrollable. "What will happen if robbers attack us?" Jean-Marie said that even if there were cries in the night or pistol shots, the men would not be permitted to return. . . .

At the words "pistol shots" one of the girls almost fainted, and her husband asked me in a whisper whether I could not possibly bribe Jean-Marie. I tried, but he refused. I offered him ten Napoleons and suggested that he could give them to the poor if he did not want them for himself. I got nowhere with him. Someone suggested that we should all go back to Sappey and stay in the Auberge there. Jean-Marie said that it would be impossible to get through the gorge, which would now be a small torrent of water. . . . Two of the men threatened to refuse to leave. Jean-Marie said: "You force me to tell you, messieurs, that according to our rules I would then be required to bring twenty men and lock up the infirmary, after having forcibly put these ladies outside. Why did you have to bring these ladies into *our* Valley?"

At last, since Jean-Marie remained sincerely firm, we were forced to abandon our poor companions. We left one of our pistols with them. I felt very sad. . . . At the moment we left, there was a series of really deafening thunderclaps. We thought of what they must be suffering at the infirmary. We were to be lodged in the main building, and each of us was shown to a narrow cell with a hard bed of rough pine wood. In spite of the continuing tempest, we were so overcome with fatigue that we fell asleep almost instantly. I was awakened in the middle of the night by the terrifying clanging of a great bell and by more thunderclaps that literally shook the building. I have seldom had a more fearful awakening. It was as if the last judgment were upon me. . . . Although the season was still summer, at this altitude the night was already piercingly cold. . . . As morning approached, the storm departed and the night sky was filled with stars. The next day dawned superbly, but it remained extremely cold. I found it very hard to force myself out of my warm bed. The husbands had long since returned to their wives.

I soon learned that the ladies had had a most alarming night. At about two in the morning, while the storm still continued, the ladies became convinced that thieves were trying to force open the front door. One of them had pushed her bed across the door, and perhaps while she was asleep had knocked against the wood with her elbow. Then, one of the more courageous of the ladies—the one who, I thought, had the most beautiful eyes—called out in a trembling voice to demand who was there. No answer. There was then a quarter of an hour of silent terror. . . . Is it possible to believe that during this terrible storm there was a group of young men camping in the woods? As soon as the storm passed, they came and stood outside the windows of the infirmary, serenading our ladies. But the girls were still much too frightened to enjoy this flattery. At least, that is what they told us. You see, before these young gentlemen started singing, their approaching footsteps were heard from a long way off among the trees, as sinister sounds against the background of the vast silence.

At about seven in the morning, Jean-Marie had come to unlock the front door but had hastily retreated without looking inside. One of the girls had then thrown a pile of logs on the fire, which had been kept burning all night. The other ladies were just beginning to wake up and to discuss the events of the night when they heard strange voices in the hallway. An instant later, the door of their room was violently thrown open, and in a flash they all dived under their bedcovers. To their amazement, they heard the voices of strange men and women congratulating each other on having discovered such a good fire. These strangers did not even notice the hats of the ladies hanging on hooks around the room, or the bodies under the bedcovers. The new arrivals concentrated all their attention on the fire. Then Jean-Marie came in to scold them and point out that each of the beds they saw around the room was, in fact, inhabited. So the ladies, at last, were able to get up and dress themselves.

By the time I arrived, an excellent breakfast was being served. Again, there were potatoes, fried carp, eggs, etc. . . . Each lady found, as she unfolded her napkin, a small piece of paper with a poem. They were not bad poems, either. . . . The ladies thought—or perhaps hoped —that the poems had been placed there by the young serenaders of the night. . . . The ladies were now extremely gay, flattered by so much attention and, after the terrors of the night, revived by such a good breakfast. For the rest of their lives, they said, they would never forget this night in La Vallée de La Grande Chartreuse. One of the husbands— the one who was still very much in love with his wife—had had the excellent idea of sending someone down to the village to bring back some coffee. Out of politeness to our hosts, the Chartreux hermits, we did not serve this coffee in the infirmary; we built a campfire at a spot out of sight of the hermitage and heated the coffee there. Jean-Marie brought us fine fresh milk and served us with charming hospitality. Again, he treated me is if I were an important personality. . . .

Later in the morning, I continued my exploration of the Valley. I would like to have climbed Le Grand Som but was told it would take at least three hours to reach the summit, where there is a cross of wood. I could see it clearly. It has to be continually replaced, since it is so often shattered by lightning. What would people say if, for example, a memorial tree were so frequently struck by lightning? Would they not soon begin to believe that the Divine Providence disapproved of their memorial? . . .

Since I am always full of evil ideas—and am a thoroughly immoral person—I thought it would be nice if our ladies could finally meet the young men who had serenaded them. So I deliberately announced that I was going to hear the service in the church inside La Grande Chartreuse and that it would be extremely interesting, etc. I added an admirable description of what the service would be and invited the husbands to accompany me. Only two accepted my invitation. . . .

Our friend the hermit showed me their excellent library. I could see, from the dust on the shelves, that no one ever touched the books. I was sufficiently simple-minded to say: "You should place here some books on botany or agriculture. You could surely grow, in this place, all the useful mountain plants of Scandinavia. Surely such a study would amuse and interest many of you." He drew himself up and said: "But, m'sieur, we do not wish to be interested, or amused. . . ."

Before leaving, we paid five francs per head per day for our food and lodging. We also discovered, happily, that the Chartreux sell a green liqueur, and we all bought a few bottles. It is extremely expensive but very powerful. . . .

Jean-Marie brought me the guest book. He told me that he would not present it for signature to those who had brought with them the rich *pâtés*. The Chartreux consider it an insult that anyone should bring luxuriously rich foods into their mountain valley. This is a pleasant conceit and reminds me of the resentments of some women against others who have weaknesses. The book will not be presented, either, to the young serenaders with the romantic beards. They might write improper words, or trace unsuitable drawings, on the pages of the book. I found in this book some very big names and some very poor ideas signed by those big names. . . .

At last, having relaxed for a long time in these magnificent pine woods, we decided, with deep regret, to remount our horses, which were calmly cropping the grass while waiting for us. We took the track down to La Fourvoirie and Saint-Laurent-du-Pont. Soon we came to the small River Guiers. Along its banks are the most majestic of trees. There are oaks, ash, beeches, elms at least eighty feet high, and the rocks on the skyline above have strange and wonderful shapes. . . .

Just as we entered the narrow pass, there was a single great rock which seemed completely to bar our way. However, between it and the edge of the precipice falling down to the river's torrent, there was a space of hardly more than three feet. At this point, one of the ladies almost had a terrible accident. In fear of the precipice, she pulled her horse up against the wall of rock. Her umbrella, which was strapped to her saddle, caught its point on the rock. Luckily, the stick broke instantly. If it had not, the horse might have been jerked so violently that it could have stumbled and thrown the girl over the precipice into the river. . . .

Before leaving the Valley through the narrow pass, I stopped and looked back up towards La Grande Chartreuse. There is a tall pyramid of rock which seems to stand guard across the path, and precisely at its summit, a single pine tree rises against the sky. There is, perhaps, no other valley in the world as beautiful as this. . . .

MENU OF
Breakfast as It Might Have Been Served to Stendhal

———

Les Cerises et Les Noix du Dauphiné
(Fresh Cherries and Walnuts of the Dauphiné)

Omelette à la Savoyarde
Aligot de Fromage et de Pommes de Terre Dauphinois
(Aligot of Cheesed Potatoes in the Style of the Dauphiné)

Les Brioches du Four
(Freshly Baked Brioches)

Les Confitures de Framboise, de Groseille et de Myrtille
(Homemade Jams and Jellies of Raspberry, Gooseberry and Blueberry)

Le Café de Saint-Pierre-de-Chartreuse

Since the Dauphine region is famous for its cherry and walnut trees, the combination of these two marvelous fruits of the earth is an ideal beginning to a Chartreuse breakfast. In September, when Stendhal was in the Valley, both fruit and nuts would still be fresh from the harvest. At other seasons, the cherries might be preserved in one of several ways, but the walnuts would always be in their shells—Nature's perfect packaging.

The omelette in the style of the Savoy region would have a strongly nutty flavor from its filling of finely grated Alpine Beaufort cheese and would be speckled pink with slivers of sun-dried mountain ham, all smoothed by the addition of cream, plus the sharpening accent of nutmeg and coarsely ground black pepper (recipe, page 189).

The extraordinary *aligot* of cheese and potatoes whipped together until they come out almost like a mixture of chewy, *al dente,* noodles and spaghetti seems to work best when the cheese is the creamy-yellow, medium-soft, slightly rubbery Beaumont des Alpes (recipe, page 195).

Add to these regional delights a basket of soft brioches still hot from the oven, little ceramic pots of homemade jams and jellies of the local wild fruits, and one has a superb breakfast which would be highly approved by Stendhal if he were to return to this world, at any time, for, let us say, a flirtatiously relaxed Sunday brunch. (Recipes for the brioches, page 410).

When Stendhal visited the Valley almost 150 years ago, coffee was somewhat disapproved by the Chartreux hermits on the top of their hill, as if it were some sort of unnecessary and vaguely dangerous drug. But Stendhal insisted on his morning coffee and sent down to the village of Saint-Pierre-de-Chartreuse for a supply to be brought up in a large pottery jug. The local rumor is that he also had it nicely laced with cherry brandy.

MENU OF
A Dinner in Memory of Stendhal's Visit

Le Matefaim au Jambon des Montagnes
(Pancakes with Mountain Ham and Alpine Cheese Sauce)

SPARKLING WHITE SAVOY, SEYSSEL, BLANC DE BLANCS,
CAVES DES MOINES

La Carpe à la Broche ou Grillée
(Grilled or Spitted Whole Fresh Carp)

Le Farçon de Pommes de Terre
(Potato Fritters of the Valley)

Fromages:

Valençay de la Loire   Comté de la Haute Savoie

Olivet Bleu

Le Tôt-Fait aux Cerises d'Allevard
(Cherry Egg Custard of Allevard)

Café

LA CHARTREUSE VERTE, V.E.P.

The first course, the local specialty, Le Matefaim, came to table looking rather like a pile of Mexican-American tortillas, with chili con carne in between. But, in this French version, the yellow pancakes were of egg batter and the pink meat in between was mountain ham, all covered with a sauce made with grated Alpine Gruyère (recipe, page 194).

When Stendhal paid his famous visit to the Valley in 1837 (see page 132), he and his friends brought their own supply of wine— a commodity of which the Chartreux hermits rather strongly disapproved—in the form of bottles of the light, dry, sparkling Mountain Whites from the Savoy village of Seyssel in the upper Rhône Valley almost at the spot where the great river first enters France from Switzerland. Fortunately for all of us, this lovely wine—considered by many French connoisseurs to be second only to the better Champagnes—is still being produced and imported into the United States. It is so dry and refreshingly light that it goes perfectly as the single wine throughout a simple meal.

In Stendhal's time, carp was caught every day in one or other of the ninety-two mountain lakes within reasonable hiking distance of La Grande Chartreuse. Today, neither the lakes nor the carp seem to have changed. Fresh whole carp (or any other whole fish of similar size and type of flesh), after being properly cleaned and scaled, can be made into a memorable main dish by being dipped into and sealed with Mademoiselle Ray's feather-light frying batter. As the great French gastronome Brillat-Savarin once explained, the batter is like a glove which holds in and protects the flavor juices. This batter was made with egg yolks, olive oil, flour, milk and sugar, all then brought to the consistency of fluff by the folding in of the stiffly beaten whites. Finally, the lightly encrusted fish was served with a butter-lemon sauce and the famous *Le Farçon*, the potato fritters of the region. (Recipes for the frying batter are on page 180; for the preparation of the carp, page 230; for the potato fritters, page 351.)

The first of the light cheeses (chosen to go with the sparkling wine) was the goats' milk, Valençay, from the village of that name near the city of Nevers in the region of the Central Valley of the Loire. The cheese is shaped like a small cut-off pyramid and dipped in light grey wood ash. It has a strong bouquet, a firm and chewy crust, an unctuously runny inside texture, with a nutty flavor and a faintly lemony aftertaste.

The second cheese, the Comté (the word originally meant a cheese from the region of the Franche-Comté), was developed in the

Burgundian city of Dijon and has now spread to farms all across the mountains of the High Savoy. It is sometimes called "The Gruyère of France," but its holes are smaller and it is strongly challenged for that title by various other French cheeses, including the Beaufort of the Dauphiné. Comté is made from cows' milk, and after proper aging the color of the inside flesh can vary from ivory to pale yellow.

The blue Olivet also comes from the Loire Valley, from the village of that name in the region around the city of Orléans. It is made from partly skimmed cows' milk, inoculated as it sets with the blue penicillium mold, then rubbed with salt and aged on straw mats in cool damp caves or cellars. After a few days, the crust begins to form with a pale reddish hue, which soon turns to a very light, pastel blue. At this stage, many of the cheeses are rolled in the charcoal grey ash of burnt vine stocks and wrapped in walnut leaves. The cheese has a soft flavor and texture, with the *maigre* ("fat-free") quality that comes from the skimmed milk.

The dessert was the *Tôt-Fait* (the word means, in the local dialect, "all done quickly") which Mademoiselle Ray served to her unexpected guests on the day of the storm. It is basically a Spanish-style egg *flan,* or custard, enriched with lusciously preserved cherries of the region, and strongly laced with cherry brandy (recipe, page 383).

When Stendhal came he discovered the Green Chartreuse liqueur which has made the name of the Valley known all over the world, and he took several bottles with him in the saddlebag of his horse (see page 138). In his honor, this dinner ended with the V.E.P. version of the liqueur—the letters on the label meaning, *Vieillissement Exceptionnellement Prolongé,* Aging Exceptionally Prolonged. The extra years in cask and bottle bring a quality of smooth velvet that is always a memorable experience.

FIFTEEN

The Future—Cécile Is in Love But Will Not Stay the Night

Below the Auberge, down the steep hill to the bottom of the Valley, was the village of Saint-Pierre-de-Chartreuse. I went down there almost every day for razor blades or toothpaste or for the three-day-old Paris papers. . . . The village was hardly more than a single street from which courtyards opened between the clustering stone houses with brightly painted balconies and window shutters. The predominant colors were stone grey and ochre yellow, with brown slate roofs, steeply sloping, so that the snow would slide off. Yellow also dominated the gardens, set off by shades of scarlet among the dahlias, geraniums, zinnias. . . . There were chicken coops in shady corners of the courtyards. Narrow stairways led up to some of the balconies, with old peasant women sunning themselves on the lowest steps.

The tiny central square, *La Place,* with its old stone and wrought iron fountain next to the bridge across the river, always gave the impression of being crowded. People had business at *La Mairie* (the miniature equivalent of "City Hall") and the *Bureau de Poste.* Here, twice every day, was the end of the run from Grenoble of the small trans-mountain bus which seemed to be part passenger service, part delivery truck. In fact, the arrival of essential goods from the outside world seemed generally to be the main business of Saint-Pierre-de-Chartreuse.

Mademoiselle Vivette came down to buy fresh bread and unbaked dough from *monsieur le boulanger*. When I was with her I was usually on my way to the other principal shop, the general store —L'Épicerie Brun—which had a fantastically haphazard medley of everything from everywhere. One had the impression that when a box of something-or-other arrived on the bus, it was opened up at once and the items were simply stacked at any vacant spot on any shelf. The ski wax was mixed in with the sunglasses. My razor blades were among the books: children's coloring cutouts, mountaineering maps, novels, text books on skiing, tourist guides. . . . Slightly sticky candies were entangled with skeins of knitting wool. Sun-dried *jambon crû* (mountain hams) were hanging from the ceiling alongside huge, double-handled tree saws. Brightly patterned ski sweaters were resting on top of large wheels of Alpine Gruyère cheese. With the cans of Tunisian sardines, the bottles of Crépy, Gamay and Seyssel wines, the jugs of homemade rosemary vinegar, the local fruits and vegetables, there were (a bit too close, I thought) drums of kerosene for mountainside homes without electricity or gas. Yet the local *reinettes*, the russet apples in the barrel, were some of the best I have ever bitten into while gossiping with the owner of a country store. The instant Mademoiselle Vivette saw them she weighed out three kilos and promised us *La Tarte des Desmoiselles Tatin*, an upside-down apple pie, within a matter of hours.

Grandfather Brun, who owned the store, was a delicate, gentle, thin little man—a typical Dauphinois—with a wind-chiseled face, lips that never smiled and eyes that always seemed to be looking past you, up to the mountains. He was helped by his widowed daughter, a buxom, dark-haired, lively woman. Her daughter, Cécile, joined them on weekends. She was a lovely, tall, athletic, highly intelligent girl, obviously in her early twenties, with long brunette hair—a fourth-year student majoring in the social sciences at the University of Grenoble. She spoke excellent English and had worked the previous summer in Australia. At moments when the store was not busy I gossiped with Cécile, asking her questions about the young people of La Vallée de La Grande Chartreuse who, as everyone knew, were steadily leaving the Valley. During the ten years from

1960 to 1970, the population had fallen by half—from about fourteen hundred to about seven hundred. Would it be three hundred and fifty in 1980? Was there no future for this valley?

Cécile said that she had already broken many of her ties with the Valley. She came home early on Saturdays from a sense of duty to her grandfather and her mother, who were struggling to keep the store open about fourteen hours every day, but she went back to Grenoble at night to be with her university friends. She would spend Sunday with her family, but again would return to Grenoble at night. She did still have emotional ties here in the village with her friends and, yes, also with the mountains. Yet she knew without question that when she gained her university degree she would have to find her career somewhere else. She was aware that the world outside was an aggressive and polluted place, but she could not shrink from facing it.

Was there, then, any future for a valley as isolated as this? Could it survive at all without being opened up to the business of tourism? Cécile said that there were already a few small ski lodges, and on the main slope of the mountain there was a minor ski-lift, but other nearby valleys had much longer, steeper, more exciting ski runs. Perhaps there could be an increase in tourism, but most of the established families were against it. A large tourist crowd would mean a nightlife in Saint-Pierre-de-Chartreuse. There would have to be bars—perhaps even a *club de nuit*. No one wanted that. People—even young people—loved the peace of the Valley. Usually, each year, when the snow lay thick, the serious skiing started, and the rooms were reserved at the ski lodges by the fifteenth of December. In some years the heavy snow fell early, and skiing conditions were ideal by the first of December. Yet no one would think of trying to earn extra money by encouraging the tourists to come earlier. No ski lodge sent out letters or made telephone calls to its customers trying to promote extra business. Everyone was agreed about the advantages of enjoying two more weeks of peace.

I asked about the possibility of bringing in outside capital for a much larger development of tourism. Perhaps a helicopter strip could be built on the floor of the Valley to serve a large luxury resort hotel which could give employment to almost everyone in the Valley? Cécile laughed at the pure nonsense of my question. "Let me tell you," she said, "about the airstrip in another valley—much larger than this one. The mayor of that valley married a rich American woman and they dreamed of bringing in planes—perhaps in order to fly direct to New York. The airstrip is still there—never used—

now overgrown with grass. The downdraughts from the mountains, the turbulence around the peaks, the bad visibility, the fogs and sudden storms, made it all so impossibly dangerous that the project was abandoned. Nature was against it.

"As for building a huge hotel here," she said, "not one of the old families who have owned the fields and the forests for centuries would sell. People here believe that one has no right to own land unless one loves it, sweats over it, works it oneself. To hand it over to others, to become an employee, is thought of as a form of slavery. No, I am sure that things will stay as they are."

She continued: "One of the great things about our Valley is that almost everything here—the shops, the farms, the small businesses, the restaurants, the ski lodges—still belong to local families, or at least to people who live here because they love our Valley—people like Mademoiselle Vivette and Mademoiselle Ray. They all agree with Les Pères Chartreux that there should not be any great or sudden change in the life of the Valley. If a family has been happy here for five hundred years, its members feel no need for change. I do not want it to change, although obviously I must go away and make my life and my work somewhere else. I shall always want to feel that I can come back to the same place."

It was my last evening in the village. I had been the final customer of the day. Cécile had closed the shop, and while she waited for the last bus back to Grenoble, we sat on the parapet of the bridge above the tumbling waters of the River Guiers. The sun was setting. The air was gentle, limpid. Puffs of wind, the rustlings of trees, tired voices echoed around the Valley. Across the river the mountain slopes rose, etched by the low sunlight, curving and sweeping, like the flanks of giant, resting cattle. I breathed the scent of the exhaling warmth of the earth. The day was ending in a fragrant stillness.

"You're in love with this valley, aren't you?" I asked Cécile.

"Yes—in a way. I feel a gentleness here. The mountains tower above us, but they never seem menacing or ruthless. In other valleys of the Alps, one senses a fierce, invincible harshness. In the Pass of La Morienne, for example, or among the needle peaks of La Tarentaise, the walls of granite seem to lean over you, as if ready to crush you. Those chains of peaks are like bared teeth, or like rows of bayonets. Our mountains seem more like guards, facing outward, protecting the warm security of our Valley. Perhaps, because of that security, I always feel a dominant sense of life here.

"Do you know about the growth of our forests? We are so sheltered and the air is normally so still here that the seeds from the trees fall straight to the ground and the forests replant themselves, and continuously expand. At the edge of the fields that surround our village, if the forest were left to itself, it would advance about twenty-five feet each year. If you own a field at the edge of the forest and you do not cut it for three years, you will no longer be able to cut it. The stumps of the baby new trees will already be strong enough to break your cutting blade. If you then want to save your field, you will first have to pull up the roots one by one. The forest already rules three quarters of this valley. If we were to stop resisting, it would take over an extra one hundred acres every year. You see, in this Valley of La Grande Chartreuse, Nature is still the king. Here, man has not yet become the invincible master."

The sun had set. The moon was bright—thinning out the stars. I invited Cécile to my farewell buffet party the following day, saw her onto the Grenoble bus and walked up the hill toward the Auberge. The trees on the open slopes made a thousand patterns in the moonlight. I felt the expectant night silence of the forests. The Valley seemed virgin, wild. The sound of my footsteps did not even touch it as I climbed the hill for the last time.

MENU OF
An Au Revoir Buffet Lunch
for Friends From Saint-Pierre-de-Chartreuse

APÉRITIF: SPARKLING WHITE SEYSSEL BLANC DE BLANCS
À LA CRÈME DE FRAISE

Panade à l'Ail au Gruyère des Alpes
(Bread and Garlic Soup with French Alpine Gruyère)

DRY WHITE LOIRE, VOUVRAY, CLOS DU HAUT-LIEU

Escalopes de Dinde à la Savoyarde
(Escallops of Turkey Breasts in the Style of Savoy)

Dodine de Canard au Cognac et au Madère
(Boned Stuffed Duck with Cognac and Madeira)

Noix de Veau en Gelée
(Boned and Rolled Galantine of Veal in Its Own Aspic)

Boeuf en Daube à la Saint-Tulle
(Stewed Beef of Saint-Tulle)

Salade de Ratatouille à la Niçoise
(Cold Vegetable Salad of Nice)

RED BORDEAUX, 1966 CHÂTEAU LES ORMES-DE-PEZ,
SAINT-ESTÈPHE, MÉDOC

Fromages:
St. Nectaire d'Auvergne   Romme de Belley
Bleu de Mont Cenis de la Savoie

Parfait Mocha au Rhum de Martinique
(Mocha Ice Cream with Martinique Rum)

Café

MARC DE GEWÜRZTRAMINER D'ALSACE

Mademoiselle Vivette offered each arriving guest a charming and pretty apéritif conceit. The local sparkling *Blanc de Blancs* was served in tall tulip glasses and into each one she gently dropped about half a teaspoon of sweet strawberry liqueur. Since it was heavy with sugar, it sank to the bottom of the glass, where it rested as a palpitating red globule. Each guest, then, had the choice: either of stirring it up so as to make the wine a gay pink, or of leaving the globule at the bottom and consuming its sweetness as the last sip.

The first course was a hot, thick bread and garlic soup, served (so as to be easy to hold) in large double-handled cups. The word "panade" means thickened with *pain*, bread. Cloves of garlic were boiled in a mixture of bouillon and crustless white bread, accented with bay leaves. When exactly the desired degree of garlickiness had been achieved, the soup was enriched with butter and cream, plus a pinch of nutmeg. It was served sprinkled with grated, nutty French Alpine Gruyère (recipe, page 210).

A powerful soup needed a wine of strong character. The need was met by a dry Vouvray from the most famous white wine village in the region of Touraine in the Valley of the Loire. It produces wine of an extraordinary variety: some dry, some semi-sweet, some almost honeyed, some still, some *pétillant* (slightly bubbly), some fully sparkling. The dry wine of this menu was produced by the mayor of the village, Gaston Huet, whose family has, for generations, owned the topmost vineyard of the hill; the wine is properly called "the Clos of the High Place."

Each of the four main dishes—all placed on the table at once— had some special and unusual quality, involving some degree of historical background, which gave a rare interest to the meal. Only the breasts of the turkey were used, cut into thin, escallop slices. Obviously the idea originated with the Italians of Nice and their veal scallopine, but the Savoy preparation is entirely different. Slices were cut from a local Reblochon cheese and each was wrapped in a thin envelope of mountain ham. This was then placed between two turkey escallops, neatly tied with string, dipped in egg and breadcrumbs, then quickly gilded in hot butter in a sauté pan. The string was cut away and each "sandwich" was crisp on the outside, but filled with a luxuriously unctuous hot cream of melted cheese (recipe, page 344).

The *dodine* of duck is an ancient fourteenth-century way of boning, stuffing and garnishing the bird. After every bone had been neatly removed, the duck was reshaped around the stuffing: a mixture of strips of veal, slices of pork, chicken and duck livers, eggs and shallots, mushrooms and truffles—all moistened with Cognac and dry Madeira. When the duck looked as good as new and was neatly sewn at the seams, it was gently roasted, beautifully glazed with Port and served cold. The guests were amazed to find that they could slice the boned duck straight through, as if it were a terrine! (Recipe, page 342.)

For the magnificent galantine of jellied veal, Mademoiselle Ray had stuffed the veal, then gently poached it in a mixture of bouillon and dry white wine with a veal knuckle (for natural jelly), butter, shallots and mountain herbs. It had then been molded and cooled in its own jelly (recipe, page 322).

The beef was a specialty of the Périgord village of Saint-Tulle, deep in the truffle region. Solid chunks of beef sirloin were first marinated overnight in red wine, with a small measure of vinegar and the essential wild herbs and truffles. The following day, the beef chunks were browned in smoky bacon fat, then gently poached in wine with carrots, garlic and onions. It could, finally, be served hot or cold (recipe, page 274).

The universal salad with all these main dishes was that great Mediterranean specialty of Nice, the *ratatouille*. In Mademoiselle Ray's version, the salad was lightly gilded in virgin Provençal olive oil, a mixture of sliced eggplant, onions, green peppers, tomatoes and baby zucchini, with the inevitable Provençal touch of garlic. After slow simmering, until all the flavors were refreshingly combined, the *ratatouille* was served cold on this occasion, although it would be equally good hot (recipe, page 373).

The white Vouvray was dominant enough to be continued through the turkey and the duck; with the meats, however, Mademoiselle Vivette served one of the simple and informal *crû bourgeois* reds from the famous Médoc district of Bordeaux. The Médoc is so well known for the supremely great châteaux at its southern end (of which such names as Latour, Lafite, Margaux, Mouton are household words everywhere) that relatively few people are aware that it also produces, especially at its northern end, many small, inexpensive, pleasantly aromatic red wines (as well as some charming whites). The main reason for this difference is the gradual change of the soil as the land narrows toward the ocean, from the perfect balance of gravel to a mixture with an increasing content of clay, marl and sand—not as good for the noble grapes. The village of Saint-Estèphe is just about on the borderline between these two wine worlds. It has some well-known classified growths (Châteaux Beauséjour, Beau-site, Calon-Ségur, Cos d'Estournel, Montrose, etc.) and some much larger vineyards producing excellent everyday wines, of which the Château Les Ormes-de-Pez is highly regarded. At this meal I found its 1966 vintage to be a big wine with a distinctively fruity bouquet and a warm generous flavor—ideal for an informal lunch.

The cheeses, of strong character, were also ideal—for the happy purpose of finishing the wine. The first, the famous Saint Nectaire, was a cows' milk cheese from the central mountains of the Auvergne. The best types are still farm-made, but all too many factories are now beginning to dot the valleys and turn out mass quantities of *le Saint Nectaire industriel.* The best cheeses are matured on rye mats in cool, damp caves. They are best eaten before they are four months old and begin to harden. The young inside flesh is very smooth and creamy—in my opinion, this is one of the best soft cheeses of France.

The goats' milk Romme de Belley is from the small town of Belley in the Ain region to the northeast of Lyon. It was said to be the favorite cheese of the greatest of all French gastronomes, Brillat-Savarin, who was born in 1755 in the house which is still proudly shown to visitors at 62 Main Street in Belley. I am not sure that I altogether agree with Brillat-Savarin's taste in cheese.

The third cheese, the blue of Mont Cenis, is an extraordinary mixture of cows', goats' and sheep's milk, so that the cheese seems to share some of the qualities of Roquefort, Gorgonzola and the pure cow cheeses, such as, for example, the Bleu de Bresse. Whether this blend of styles makes the Mont Cenis better than the others is seriously questionable. But it does have an interesting quality of its own. Its original home is the high valley of the Mont Cenis mountains east of Grenoble. There, in a magnificent landscape of forested slopes, of small glittering lakes, of lush green pastures, the cheeses are still made by hand and the blue mold is encouraged by mixing the paste with stale breadcrumbs.

The dessert was the classic French ice cream of egg yolks beaten with coffee, cream and vanilla sugar, then smoothly frozen and served in narrow, tall glasses—with a final garnish of golden rum (recipe, page 397).

The fruit brandy with the coffee was an unusual experience. One of the best-known of the Alsatian wine grapes is the originally German Gewürztraminer (the German word *gewürz* means "spicy") used to make one of the most superbly aromatic of Alsatian wines. A few producers then take the remaining must, or mash, from the fermenting vats and distill from it a fine *eau-de-vie*—a kind of alcoholic essence which magnifies all the attractive qualities of the best of Gewürztraminer wine. This particular version came from the famous cellars of the Trimbach family of the Alsatian village of Ribeauville.

MENU OF
The Grand Farewell Dinner
Before the Return to New York

APÉRITIF: CHAMPAGNE, LAURENT PERRIER, CUVÉE DU GRAND SIÈCLE

La Grande Terrine de Canard à la Grand-mère Artaud
*(The Great Terrine of Duck in Honor of
Mademoiselle Vivette's Grandmother)*

WHITE BORDEAUX, SAUTERNES, JOHNSTON ET FILS

Soupe à l'Oseille
(Sorrel Soup)

WHITE SAVOY, CRÉPY, MERCIER ET FILS, DOUVAINE

Truite-Saumonée au Crépy sur Croûtes
(Salmon-Trout in Crépy on Pastry Crusts)

Selle de Chamois à la Cartusienne
(Saddle of Alpine Chamois à la Carusienne)

Haricots Verts à la Crème   Grand Gratin Dauphinois

RED BURGUNDY, 1959 VOLNAY, LE CLOS DES CHÊNES,
ROPITEAU-MIGNON

Fromages:
Brie de Meaux   Camembert Fermier de Camembert
Roquefort de la Société B

RED BURGUNDY, 1945 LE CORTON-BRESSANDES, PRINCE DE MERODE

Neige à la Grande Chartreuse
(Snowy Soufflé with Green Chartreuse)

Café

COGNAC, 1911 GASTON BRIAND

For the final grand feast before the return to New York, Mademoiselle Vivette set before us the finest of everything she had, with some repetitions (for which I had especially asked) of superbly successful food and wine combinations from previous menus. The ambitious objective tonight was to try to construct the almost perfect dinner. We considered, first, the question of the ideal apéritif and decided that, after all, a great Champagne, unadorned and unmixed, was the unmatchable starter. But which? All the great houses of Epernay and Reims, these days, put out a "special top label" with a fancy name, with the claim that supreme quality has taken precedence over cost. Between these most luxurious of labels, I believe the choice is a matter of personal taste. Instead of our selection for tonight, the Laurent Perrier *Cuvée du Grand Siècle,* we might equally as well have opened the Heidsieck *Cuvée Royale,* the Mercier *Réserve de l'Empéreur,* the Moët *Dom Pérignon,* the Piper *Floren-Louis,* the Roederer *Cristal Brut,* the Taittinger *Cuvée des Comtes de Champagne* or the Veuve Clicquot *La Grande Dame.* Each would have made the finest of beginnings for a great dinner.

For the first course, Mademoiselle Vivette had been working in the kitchen for the previous three days preparing (as she does only two or three times a year) her magnificently festive terrine of duck, which she invented in honor of her grandmother, years ago, in the family home in Provence. The story of its creation is on page 62. Her recipe is on page 165.

Once again, tonight, Mademoiselle Vivette proved her point that the ideal complement to a rich terrine is a lightly sweet and interestingly aromatic wine. She chose the delicately blended regional Sauternes of the ancient Bordeaux firm, Nathaniel Johnston and Sons, which was already shipping its wines to England when Lord Nelson was fighting the Battle of Trafalgar and which, in 1807, received a recommendation from the Marquis de Lafayette to the office of General George Washington as the producers of "the best wines of France." Tonight's Sauternes excellently served its purpose of cutting the richness of the great terrine.

Mademoiselle Ray prepared her soup by first melting the chopped sorrel leaves in hot butter, then adding thinly sliced new potatoes and a delicate bouillon, with a thickening of whipped cream and eggs (recipe, page 222).

For the accompaniment to this subtle soup, we turned back to our day of arrival at the Auberge and our delight in the gaily refreshing local white wine of Savoy, the Crépy, from grapes which grow on the French slopes, looking down across the border to the Swiss Lake of Geneva. This alternative label was as strongly *bouqueté*, as firm in body and flavor, as crackling on the tongue, as entirely enjoyable as the first bottle on the day of our arrival.

There had arrived at the Auberge this morning from the clear waters of Lac Paladru a large and beautiful salmon-trout. This time, it was boned and divided into fillets, which were gently poached on a bed of butter and chopped shallots in some of the Crépy wine. Meanwhile, individual shells of flaky pastry of exactly the size to hold one of the fillets were rolled out and baked. The sauce was made from the poaching liquid enriched with cream and eggs, then poured over each fillet and decorated with slivers of black and white truffles (recipe, page 259).

The dramatic climax of the dinner—perhaps of our entire stay at the Auberge—was the appearance of a whole saddle of the great game animal of the region, the Carthusian chamois. It had been shot the previous week by our huntsman friend, Jean Combalot. It had been hung for three days and marinated for three more. (A description of the hunting of the chamois in the mountains is on page 90.) Mademoiselle Ray had first larded the meat, then prepared the marinade by lightly sautéing carrots, onions and shallots in the purest virgin olive oil, then adding bay leaves, rosemary, thyme, a small quantity of wine vinegar and several bottles of dry white wine. In this regal bath, the chamois was drowned for seventy-two hours, but brought up for air and turned over four or five times each day. Finally the saddle was rubbed with more olive oil and grilled on a turning spit before a roaring wood fire in the open hearth. A metal tray was placed on the firebricks below the spit to catch the irresistibly odorous drippings, the *lèchefrite,* which, after being deglazed with Green Chartreuse, would be the key ingredient of the sauce. Its preparation began with chopped onions and shallots melted in walnut oil, then moistened with some of the marinade, spiced with fresh green peppercorns and juniper berries, then, finally, worked into the red-blooded meat drippings (recipe, page 282).

The accompanying French-cut green beans were briefly sautéed in a hot mixture of butter and cream, then richly coated with egg yolks beaten with chopped chives and brought to table crisply fresh (recipe, page 362).

I had also asked for an encore of the great regional potato specialty, Le Gratin Dauphinois. It was, again, a magnificent combination of sliced potatoes soaked in butter, cream and garlic (recipe. page 348).

The wine to go with all these superbly balanced flavors and textures was an almost perfect choice, one of the great lighter Burgundies, the 1959 Volnay from the vineyard that is among the finest of that celebrated village, Le Clos des Chênes, of the Domaine of the famous wine family of Ropiteau-Mignon. The Volnays of great years are always, to me, well above even the best of Pommard. Tonight's Volnay was among the most attractive of all red Burgundies—wonderfully fine and gay—with a superb bouquet and the feel of soft velvet in the mouth and down the throat. This wine played a perfect second fiddle to the subtle strength of the red meat of the chamois. A bigger wine might have tried to play a duet!

For tonight's cheeses, Mademoiselle Vivette simply chose the three that are generally considered to be the finest of France—the kings of cheeses and the cheeses of kings. They were considered worthy of having their own bottle of wine—a Burgundian contrast to the Volnay. One of the biggest, most dominant, longest lived of all the great wines is of the Côte de Beaune, the 1945 Le Corton-Bressandes from the vineyard of the Prince de Merode, part of the commune appellation of Aloxe-Corton. It had a magnificent texture, a majestic balance, a silkiness on the tongue, with, in the nose, a distant wisp of wild woodland violets.

The first cheese was a fitting partner to this supreme wine—Le Brie Fermier de Meaux. Even cheese fanciers who may eat Brie every day often fail to realize that there is Brie and then there is Brie. All of it comes from the province of La Brie, immediately to the east of Paris, along the lower valley of the River Marne. The chief town of La Brie is Meaux, where two kinds of Brie are made—the *industriel* in factories and the handmade on surrounding farms. The latter always carry on their labels the magic word *fermier*.

The story is just about the same with Camembert. All the authentic cheeses come from the district around the village of Camembert in Normandy, but most of it is *industriel,* made from pasteurized milk in factories in the nearby town of Vimoutiers. The finest Camembert ripens perfectly by the growth of bacteria in the unpasteurized milk. These are handmade on farms from unpasteurized milk close to the village of Camembert: *Le Vrai Camembert Fermier de Camembert.*

Neither is every Roquefort the same. An individual producer may have his own herd of sheep, but the operation of converting his milk into the cheese is undertaken by one or another of several cooperatives. They work differently and have different objectives. One cooperative, for example, produces Roqueforts which are particularly strong in flavor and are destined entirely for the Paris market, where experience has shown that the consumer wants strong cheeses. Each cooperative is called a *Société* and is given an identifying letter. My favorite Roqueforts are made by *Société B*, which dramatizes its name by having honey bees pictured all over its silver wrapping paper. This is in addition to the "red sheep seal," which is on every authentic Roquefort, not as a commercial trademark but to identify every cheese made within the legally delimited Roquefort area. As my Aveyron friends keep telling me: "Every Roquefort is blue, but not every blue is Roquefort."

The dessert was also an encore "by request." Mademoiselle Ray's masterpiece is a variation of the classic Oeufs à la Neige, heavily laced with the powerful Green Chartreuse of the Valley—to me, the best dessert of the Auberge and one of the best liqueur desserts I have ever tasted. (Description on page 27; recipe, page 404.)

The last *digestif* of the last evening had to be something outstanding. One of our friends in the Valley, a man who maintains a magnificent cellar, had sent, in honor of this occasion, a bottle of the 1911 vintage of an unblended single-vat Cognac of Gaston Briand from the Charente village of Ambleville. The soft velvet, the delicate power, the aromatic excitement of this ancient spirit are almost beyond description. It was a climactic curtain.

PART II

The Recipes

SECTION I

The Great Game Pâtés and Terrines of the Valley

TERRINE OF CHICKEN OR PORK LIVERS
(*La Terrine de Foie de Volailles ou de Porc*)

FOR ABOUT 8 PEOPLE, BUT KEEPS WELL

A terrine does not have to be a big production. Here is one of the simplest—fine as an hors d'oeuvre for family meals, or as the main course of an informal supper—that is still quite good to give a fine start to an unexpected party. This recipe involves only about 30 minutes of preparatory work, plus about 1 hour in the oven.

Staple Items	*Shopping List*
Butter (about 3 Tb)	Chicken or pork livers (1 lb.)
	White pork fat (1 lb.)
Flavorings	Caul skin, to wrap the terrine
Crystal salt, freshly ground	(about ½ lb.)
black pepper, rosemary, sage	Cognac (¼ cup)
leaf, thyme	Madeira, dry Sercial (¼ cup)

*Active Preparation About 30 Minutes—Unsupervised Baking 1 Hour
—Must Be Refrigerated 24 Hours*

Melt 2 tablespoons of the butter in a sauté pan and quickly sauté the livers, for hardly more than 3 or 4 minutes, after sprinkling them with salt and pepper. They should remain quite rare inside. If necessary, add the other tablespoon of butter. Cut the pork fat into medium chunks. Using the coarse cutting disk of a meat grinder, pass through the livers and the fat. Add to the mixture 2 tablespoons of crumbled sage leaf, 1 tablespoon of rosemary, 1 teaspoon of thyme, the ¼ cup each of Cognac and Madeira, plus more salt and pepper, if necessary, to taste. Mix everything thoroughly, using light, lifting strokes, rather than pressing and stirring. Preheat the oven to 350 degrees. Line a rectangular terrine pan with 2 or 3 thicknesses of the caul skin, leaving some hanging over the edges for the final enclosure of the terrine. Now pack in the liver mixture, firmly but lightly, gently pressing it into the corners and leveling the top surface. Fold over the caul skin.

If the terrine pan does not have its own lid, cover it with foil, then place it in a *bain-marie* tray of boiling water about 2 inches deep. Put everything into the center of the oven and bake for 1 hour. As soon as the terrine comes out of the oven, remove its covering and place directly on the terrine a board or flat plate, weighted down, so that the terrine will be squeezed into a tighter texture as it cools. As soon as it has cooled enough, put it, with its weights, into the refrigerator and leave it there for at least 24 hours. Before serving, unmold it and remove any last traces of the caul skin, most of which will already have melted away. Decorate the terrine in any way that suits your fancy and serve it in ⅜-inch-thick slices.

THE GREAT TERRINE OF DUCK IN HONOR OF MADEMOISELLE VIVETTE'S GRANDMOTHER
(*La Grande Terrine de Canard à la Grand-mère Artaud*)

HORS D'OEUVRES FOR ABOUT 25, BUT KEEPS ALMOST INDEFINITELY

The story of this famous terrine of Mademoiselle Vivette's family in Provence is told on page 62. It would be ridiculous, of course, to claim that the recipe below is the one that was used by Grandmother Artaud more than fifty years ago. For one thing, she went out into the hills and woods of Provence and gathered the perfumed wild herbs that scent the air of southern France. For another, she died without writing down the secrets of her terrine. Her granddaughter, Mademoiselle Vivette, had to re-create the recipe, partly by analyzing her memories of the taste of the original terrine, partly by indefatigable experimentation. Then the new recipe passed through various transformations. Mademoiselle Vivette carried it with her to the Auberge in the Alps, where the qualities of the ingredients were entirely different from those of Provence. Finally, I made the duck terrine in New York of American ingredients with the equipment of an American kitchen. The moral is that a recipe is basically a regional document, and that in each new place it becomes something new. Yet if the heart of its concept is right (and if, each time, it is "made with love"), something of its original character and personality remains within each new version. This recipe is not easy or simple. You must prepare it at least 2 days in advance and be ready, on the first day, to devote at least 3 hours to its active preparation. It was said to be *un grand plat*, "a grand dish," when Grandmother Artaud made it. I still find my New York version a magnificent starter for the most luxurious of party dinners—especially for the great holiday feasts of the year (suggested menu and wines on page 155).

Staple Items
Butter (5 ½ ounces, or 11 Tb)
Eggs (2 large)
Lemon (1)
Carrots (2 medium)
Yellow onions (2 medium)
Unflavored gelatin (2 envelopes)
Sugar (2 to 3 tsp)

Flavorings
Crystal salt, freshly ground black pepper, whole bay leaves, sage, savory, tarragon, thyme

Shopping List
Duck, domestic (1 at about 5 lbs.)
Duck livers (2 lbs.)

Veal, very white meat, boneless and fatless (1 lb.)
Veal knuckle, sawed in half (1)
Fresh white pork fatback, thinly sliced (¾ lb.)
Tart cooking apples (4 large)
Leeks, white part only (2 medium)
Parsley (1 small bunch)
Shallots (4)
Tomato juice (¼ cup)
Black truffles (1 or 2, as pocketbook permits)
Cognac, best-quality *Fine Champagne* (¼ cup)
Madeira, dry Sercial (⅜ cup)
Port, ruby (¼ cup)
Sherry, dry *fine* (2 Tb)
Dry vermouth (2 Tb)
Dry white wine (¼ cup)

2 Days Before Serving—Active Preparation About 3 Hours—Followed by 1½ Hours Unsupervised Baking

With a very sharp, small knife remove the skin from the duck, but keep it in one piece. First make a lengthwise cut from neck to tail, along the top edge of the breast. Make a single cut, the length of each leg and thigh. Disregard the skin of the wings. It does not matter if there are a few holes in the peeled-off skin. The job may seem a bit difficult the first time. From the second time onwards it will be easy. Soak the skin in lightly salted cold water to keep it flexible until it is needed.

Remove all the underskin fat from around the duck and discard it. Neatly carve off all the breast meat, then cut it lengthwise into narrow thin strips and put them in a bowl to be marinated. Finely mince the 4 shallots and sprinkle them over the breast strips. Also sprinkle on 2 crumbled bay leaves, ½ teaspoon salt, 1 teaspoon thyme and 2 or 3 good grinds of pepper. Sprinkle on ¼ cup each of the Cognac and the Madeira. Toss everything gently with a wooden spoon to mix thoroughly. Cover and reserve.

Cut off legs from duck and remove all meat. Since this will be ground, you need not worry about the irregular shapes of the pieces. Sauté them lightly in about 4 tablespoons of the butter and reserve them.

Using a chopper, crack duck carcass into 5 or 6 pieces and put them with the veal knuckle into a 3-quart stewpan. Add the 2 carrots, peeled and thinly sliced, the 2 onions, chopped, the 2 leeks, washed and chopped, a small handful of the parsley and about ½ teaspoon of salt. Pour in 1 quart of freshly drawn cold water. Simmer very gently, uncovered, for 2 hours, more or less, to make a strong duck broth for the aspic. The liquid will reduce slowly. When it is down to about half, stop further reduction by covering the pan. Taste occasionally and adjust seasonings. Broth should become ducky, glutinous and rich.

Season the 2 pounds of duck livers with salt and pepper. Adding more butter, as needed, to the sauté pan previously used for the leg and thigh pieces, quickly sauté the livers for hardly more than 2 or 3 minutes, keeping them quite rare at the centers. Then reserve them in the sauté pan, covered and off the fire.

Peel, core and quarter the 4 apples. Put them in a saucepan with a teaspoon or 2 of sugar, according to their tartness, 2 tablespoons of butter and the juice of half the lemon and cook them gently, covered, stirring occasionally, until apples are mushy—usually in 8 to 10 minutes.

Cut the 1 pound of lean veal into chunks. Using the finest cutting disk of a meat grinder, put through the sautéed duck livers, the sautéed pieces of leg and thigh meat and the chunks of veal. Now as soon as apples are soft, thoroughly mash them and add to the ground meats. Also add 1 of the eggs, then, lightly and vigorously, work everything thoroughly together—lifting and turning it over, rather than pressing or stirring it. If necessary to bring out flavors, add a little more salt. Preheat oven to 350 degrees.

Now we are ready to begin filling our lidded oval earthenware terrine. It should be a handsome affair, since it will be used as the serving dish. You can judge the size required by remembering that it should be large enough just to hold the original duck. Line the inside completely with slices of the white fatback. Now take the duck skin out of its soaking water, shake and pat it dry, then carefully spread it inside the terrine, like a bag, with its main opening upward. Now begin filling every corner and across the bottom with half of the ground meat mixture. On top of this layer, place 3 or 4 thin slices of black truffle, each one lightly wrapped in a slice of white fatback. Next, neatly and evenly lay in the marinated strips of breast meat, with all their marinade, each strip running the length of the terrine. If you have enough black truffles, lay in 2 or 3 more slices, each, again, wrapped in the fatback. Finally, put in the remaining half of the ground mixture. Now, close the duck-skin bag, overlapping the flaps as much as possible and making everything thoroughly tidy. Completely cover the top with slightly overlapping slices of fatback and top with 4 or 5 whole bay leaves. Put the lid on the terrine. Stand the terrine in a *bain-marie* tray of boiling water about 2 inches deep, then slide the whole arrangement into the center of the oven and bake for 1½ hours. When the terrine is perfectly done, the fat which cooks out and rises to the top will be crystal clear.

While the terrine is baking, deal with the duck broth for the aspic. Strain the liquid out of the stewpan. It should now measure about 1½ or 2 cups and is ready to be clarified. Take a clean 1-quart saucepan. Separate the remaining egg, and put away the yolk for some other use. Crush the shell in your hand and drop it into the saucepan. Lightly beat the white with a few strokes of a fork and add to the saucepan, with a few spritzes of lemon juice, ½ teaspoon each of sage, savory and tarragon, and the ¼ cup of Port. Pour this into the duck broth, stir around, then bring rapidly to a boil. Turn down heat and let it gently bubble, covered, while you prepare the strainer. Line a colander or sieve with a piece of thickish flannel that has been soaked in cold water and lightly wrung out. Turn off heat and let the duck broth cool slightly; then pass the broth through the flannel, twice if necessary, until it is crystal clear. All the impurities will stick to the eggshell and white. Let this clear broth come to room temperature, then refrigerate, covered, overnight.

When the terrine is perfectly done, remove the lid, place a small wooden board or flat plate directly on it and weight it down, so that the terrine will be squeezed into a tight mass as it cools. As soon as it is cool enough, put the whole arrangement, including the weights, into the refrigerator overnight. Here endeth the work of the first day.

The Day Before Serving—Sealing the Terrine With the Aspic in About 40 Minutes of Work

Remove the weights from the terrine and, most carefully, using a thin, blunt spatula to loosen the side, turn out the entire duck-skin bag (which will now be firmly solid), so that you can remove (and put away for some other use) every scrap of the white fatback and all other bits of fat from outside the skin bag. Now put the bag back into the terrine, but the opposite way around, so that the overlapped opening is now at the bottom. If you have any black truffle left, dice and slice it into pretty shapes and decorate the top of the terrine. Re-cover it and put it back into the refrigerator until you have made the aspic.

Into a 1½- or 2-quart saucepan put 1¼ cups of the clear duck broth and heat it. Empty the 2 envelopes of gelatin into a small mixing bowl and dilute them with ¼ cup each of the tomato juice and white wine. Stir until it forms a smooth paste, then spoon this mixture into the now-simmering duck broth, stirring in each spoonful until it is melted. When all the gelatin is thoroughly dissolved and the broth has come just back to the boil, turn off the heat, stir in ½ teaspoon of the sugar, then taste and, if necessary, adjust seasonings. When liquid has cooled enough so that it no longer burns the tip of your finger, stir in 2 tablespoons each of the Madeira, Sherry and vermouth.

While the aspic is still warm and liquid, pour as much of it as possible into the terrine, filling up all the odd corners and forming a smooth top surface. Re-cover and put back in refrigerator, so that aspic can thoroughly set overnight. If you want to be ambitious about the decoration of the terrine, you might add any remaining clear duck broth to the aspic liquid, reheating to mix thoroughly and adding more gelatin, if necessary, at the rate of one extra envelope for each extra cup of liquid. This extra aspic can then be poured into a shallow square cake pan to make a layer not more than ¼ inch deep. After this has been set in the refrigerator, the thin layer of aspic can be cut with the point of a knife into neat dice which can be used for the final decoration of the top of the terrine.

Serving the Terrine

Never try to unmold the terrine. Serve it from its earthenware home. Cut it into ⅜-inch-thick slices and garnish on the plate with *cornichons*, olives, sprigs of green watercress, etc. The ideal accompaniment is a delicately sweet wine—say, a light regional Sauternes. As you taste and sip, remember Grandmother Artaud in Provence.

TERRINE OF HARE À LA GRANDE CHARTREUSE
(*Terrine de Lièvre à la Grande Chartreuse*)

FOR 4 TO 8 PEOPLE

In La Vallée de La Grande Chartreuse, of course, Mademoiselle Ray has local hares brought to her as gifts by hunters in the surrounding mountains. She cleans and skins them herself, then hangs them for several days to develop the gamy flavor. We city folks cannot do as well as that, but I can often get a Canadian hare, which allows me to make at least a fair imitation of the original of this magnificent terrine—rich, fortifying and irresistible with ground liver, pork, Cognac and gin. (See discussion on page 97; menu and wine suggestions on page 96.)

Flavorings
Crystal salt, freshly ground
    black pepper, whole bay
    leaves, whole nutmeg,
    thyme

Shopping List
Young hare, with liver (1)
Pork, lean (¾ lb.)
Pork fat, white (¾ lb.)
Thin, wide slices of pork fat,
    or fat salt pork, or fatback
    (¾ lb.)
Cognac (½ cup)
Aromatic Holland gin (¼
    cup)

Prepare at Least 1 Day Before Serving—Working Time About 1 Hour—Unsupervised Baking About 1½ Hours

If your hare happens to be frozen, it must first be slowly and completely defrosted. Now, using a fairly small, extremely sharp boning knife, carefully slice off all the best parts of the meat—slices about ⅛ inch thick and roughly the length of your index finger—from the fleshy parts along the back, from the haunch, the thighs and the legs. Put all these first-grade slices into a bowl and marinate them with the ½ cup of Cognac, the ¼ cup of gin, and salt and pepper. Stir them around and turn them over, making sure that they are all thoroughly moistened. Next, cut off all the rest of the hare's meat, but since this will be ground up, just get it all off in chunky pieces of any convenient shape and size. (Incidentally, the remaining carcass of the hare should later be boiled with vegetables for a wonderful soup.) Using the meat grinder with its fine cutter, put through all the chunks of hare, with the liver and the ¾ pound each of lean pork and white pork fat. Mix thoroughly, adding about 2 teaspoons of freshly ground nutmeg, about 3 teaspoons of thyme, plus salt and pepper to taste.

Choose a long, narrow, tightly lidded terrine pan about 14 inches long, preferably of enameled iron, then completely line it with the slices of pork fat. Divide the ground meats exactly in half and put the first half into the terrine pan, gently pushing it into all the corners and nicely leveling it off. Next, make an even, neat layer of all the marinated slices, placing them lengthwise and thoroughly moistening them by dribbling over a good part of the marinade. Then fill up with the rest of the ground meat. Preheat the oven to 325 degrees. Place 3 whole bay leaves on top of the meat and cover the meat with more slices of pork fat. Put the lid on the terrine and stand it in a *bain-marie*, a baking pan about 2 inches deep filled about 1 inch deep with boiling water. Place the entire contraption in the center of the oven and bake for 1½ hours.

As soon as the terrine comes out of the oven, remove its lid and place on top of the meat a wooden board or piece of metal of a size just to fit inside the terrine pan so that weights can be placed on it to press down and solidify the meat while it is cooling.

When the meat is down to roughly room temperature, put it in the refrigerator, still with the weights on top of it. The weights can be removed and the lid put back on as soon as the meat is completely cold. When the weights are finally removed, also discard the fat slices and bay leaves from the top. Finally, the terrine may be sliced and served from its pan, or turned out onto a platter (discard all the pork slices) and handsomely garnished. The remaining part keeps best if it is put back into the terrine pan and refrigerated, tightly covered, to avoid any drying out.

CUSHION-TERRINE OF PHEASANT
(Coussin de Faisan de la Diane du Grand Som)

ENOUGH FOR 30 SERVINGS, BUT KEEPS FOR 2 WEEKS OR MORE

The Grand Som is the highest peak that dominates the Valley of La Grande Chartreuse, and the reference to Diana, the mythical goddess of the hunt, means, naturally, that this dish might be made in the fall hunting season with wild pheasant and wild thrush from the mountain forests. (See menu and wine suggestions on page 25.) Mademoiselle Ray's version has always seemed to be better than the average game terrine, even in three-star French restaurants. Her secret is that she takes into account the fact that pheasant alone can often be bland and dry—so she interlayers the bird's meat with a rich and aromatic stuffing. I have prepared a most excellent version in my New York kitchen, using domestic pheasant and squab. This dish is called a *coussin* because when it comes to table in its golden crust it is square-shaped, like a cushion. Yet it is a true "terrine" (the word comes from *terre*, earth) since it is baked in a square earthenware dish about 12 inches by 12 and about 3 inches deep.

Staple Items	*Shopping List*
Eggs (3)	Pheasant (1, about 2½ lbs.)
	Squabs (2, medium-sized)
Flavorings	Chicken livers (½ lb.)
Freshly ground nutmeg, crystal salt, freshly ground black pepper	Bacon, lean rashers, dark-smoked (1 lb.)
	Pork, lean (1 lb.)
	Mushrooms (¼ lb.)
Also one batch of Pastry Dough for the crust (see recipe below), one batch of Clarified Aspic (see recipe below)	Black truffle, large, optional (1)
	Cognac (¼ cup)
	Dry Madeira (¼ cup)

First Day—Active Preparation of the Meats in About 1 Hour for Marination Overnight

With a not-too-large and very sharp knife, cut all the useful meat off the uncooked pheasant. Most of the meat should be, as far as possible, in not very thick or large slices. The odd-shaped pieces will be cut into large dice. Put all this meat into a fair-sized mixing bowl. Add the ½ pound whole chicken livers, the sliced truffle (if you have one), the ¼ cup Cognac, the ¼ cup Madeira, and salt and pepper to taste. Stir it all around with a wooden spoon and let it marinate, covered, in the refrigerator overnight. For the stuffing, also cut all the uncooked meat off the squabs, and put the pieces through a meat grinder with its coarse cutter in position. Put the ground flesh into a medium-sized mixing bowl. Next, put through the grinder the 1 pound bacon and the 1 pound pork. Add both to the squabs. Also add ¼ pound mushrooms, wiped clean and sliced, 2 of the eggs, with ½ teaspoon nutmeg, 1 teaspoon crystal salt and pepper to taste. Then, thoroughly blend everything, cover and place in the refrigerator to ripen overnight. Prepare aspic according to recipe below. Make a batch of pastry for the crust according to recipe below; wrap it in wax paper and set to rest in the refrigerator overnight.

Second Day—Filling the Terrine in About 45 Minutes—With 2 Hours of Unsupervised Baking

Take both bowls of meats out of the refrigerator and let come to room temperature. Remove chicken livers and truffle from bowl of pheasant mixture. Roll out pastry dough according to recipe below. Lightly butter the inside of the square terrine (see above) and line it with the pastry, leaving about ½ inch hanging over top edge of pan all around. In the bottom of the pan, put a ½-inch layer of the squab stuffing. Next, a slightly thinner layer of the pheasant meat. Then a second layer of squab stuffing. Cut the chicken livers into ½-inch pieces and put them as the next layer. Then a thin layer of truffle and the rest of the pheasant meat. Finally, fill up the pan to within about ¼ inch from the top with the remainder of the squab stuffing. From the remaining pastry cut a piece to fit the top of the terrine. Fold over the hanging flaps of pastry, moistening the edges with water, then roll them and press them into the edges of the top piece, so that the terrine is completely sealed. Turn on oven to 330 degrees. Cut three ¼-inch holes in the pastry top of the terrine and stick into each a miniature metal funnel (from the front end of a pastry bag, or make little chimneys from aluminum foil). Separate the third egg and lightly brush the pastry top with egg yolk. Carefully cover top with aluminum foil and place the terrine on a shelf so that it is exactly at the center of the oven. Let it bake with the foil for one hour, then remove the foil and continue baking until golden brown, usually about another hour. During the baking time, complete the clarification of the aspic, according to the recipe below.

When baking of terrine is completed, let it cool slightly. Reheat the aspic just until it is thoroughly liquid. Using a glass funnel carefully held, in turn, in each of the three chimneys on the terrine, slowly pour in the aspic until all the internal spaces in the terrine have been filled. Finally, refrigerate terrine for at least 24 hours, to give the aspic a chance to set and the flavors to blend before serving. It may be carefully unmolded, or left in the terrine pan for storage (covered, of course) and then cut into roughly ⅜-inch-thick slices as an hors d'oeuvre, or, with a salad, as the main dish of a light supper.

PREPARING AND CLARIFYING ASPIC FOR A TERRINE

Staple Items
Bones of pheasant and squabs, from above recipe
Egg whites (4)
Lemon (1)
Carrots (2 medium)
Yellow onion (1 medium)

Flavorings
Thyme, crystal salt, freshly ground black pepper

Shopping List
Knuckle of veal, cut in half (1)
Calf's (or pig's) foot, cut in half lengthwise (1)
Oxtail, small, cut in pieces (1)
Ground beef, top round (6 ounces)
Dry white wine (4 cups)
Dry Madeira (¼ cup)

Preparation in About 15 Minutes—Unsupervised Simmering for About 4 Hours

One can, of course, lazily use a can of jellied consommé, but part of the extraordinary quality of this terrine comes from the magnificent flavor of properly preparing Mademoiselle Ray's aspic. It is well worth the not-too-much trouble.

Put into a 6- to 8-quart soup kettle with a lid: the veal knuckle, the calf's (or pig's) foot, the oxtail, the pheasant and squab bones, the onion and carrots, chunked, 1 teaspoon of thyme, the 4 cups of wine, 8 cups of cold water, and 2 teaspoons of salt and pepper to taste. Bring to a boil, skimming off the rising scum, and then cover and simmer gently for about 4 hours. Let it cool slightly. Strain off liquid into bowl; cover and store in refrigerator overnight.

Clarification of the Aspic in About 20 Minutes—Unsupervised Simmering for About 1 Hour

Take the now-jellied aspic out of the refrigerator and carefully lift off all surface fat. Into a 4-quart saucepan put the 4 egg whites, lightly beaten, the ground beef, the ¼ cup Madeira, and the juice of the lemon. Place saucepan on high heat and quickly ladle in the jellied aspic, stirring it around. Continue stirring until liquid boils. Then turn down heat to gentle simmering and cook, uncovered, for one hour. Let liquid cool slightly, then strain through a muslin-lined sieve. Aspic is now ready.

PASTRY CRUST FOR A TERRINE
(*Pâté à Foncer*)

Staple Items

Sweet butter (½ lb.)	Sugar (¼ tsp)
Egg yolks (4)	Salt (2 tsp)
All-purpose flour (1 lb., or 4 cups after sifting; 3½ before sifting)	Ice water (⅔ cup)

Mixing and Kneading Dough in About 15 Minutes

Pour flour into pile in center of heavy board or marble top. Make well in center of pile and put in the ½ pound of butter cut into small bits, the 4 yolks, the 2 teaspoons of salt and ¼ teaspoon of sugar dissolved in the ⅔ cup of ice water. Using tips of fingers, quickly and lightly blend central ingredients first, and then begin at once combining with flour. As more liquid is needed, add small dashes of ice water, but keep to minimum, never allowing dough to become wet. As soon as dough will stick together, roll into ball, set it aside, clean and lightly flour the top and begin kneading ball. Using heel of your hand, push and stretch dough into a flat round, then roll up again, then push and stretch again. After repeating this process firmly and quickly three times, roll dough once more into ball, wrap in wax paper and refrigerate for at least 3 hours or overnight.

Rolling Out Crust for Terrine in About 5 Minutes

Again, lightly flour board or marble top. Using tapered French rolling pin, begin rolling out dough, first into a thick round slab, then into a sheet ⅜ inch thick. Line cushion-terrine as described in main recipe above.

SECTION II

Hors d'Oeuvres,
Including
Light Luncheon Dishes
of Cheese and Eggs

COLD ARTICHOKE HEARTS À LA GRECQUE
(Les Artichauts Violets de Provence à la Grecque)

FOR 4 PEOPLE

In the language of French menus, a vegetable served as a cold appetizer *à la Grecque* means that it has been cooked in a sharply aromatic oil and vinegar marinade. Perhaps it was so called because, throughout the Middle Ages, the Greeks were famous for their olive oil. (Notes on buying the miniature "violet" artichokes of Provence are on page 49; suggested menu and wine list on page 53.) Use fresh artichokes during their season from September to June. At other times, use ready-preserved artichoke hearts. The *à la Grecque* preparation can be done days in advance —they keep for weeks in tightly capped jars in the refrigerator.

Staple Items
Lemon (1)
Olive oil (¾ to 1 cup)
Tarragon white wine vinegar
  (¼ to ½ cup)

Shopping List
Artichoke hearts (about 12,
  according to size)
Fresh parsley (3 or 4 sprigs)
Fresh watercress (1 bunch)

Flavorings
Bay leaves, whole fennel
  seeds, thyme, crystal salt,
  whole black peppercorns

Active Preparation About 15 Minutes—Unsupervised Simmering About 20 Minutes

If using fresh artichokes, wash them thoroughly, pull off all outer leaves, cut away chokes and cut off stems. In a 2-quart saucepan, preferably enameled iron or tinned copper to avoid interaction with the acid, mix: 1 cup cold water, ½ cup olive oil and ¼ cup vinegar. Bring up to simmering while adding aromatics: 2 whole bay leaves, 1 teaspoon whole fennel seed, ½ teaspoon thyme, 1 teaspoon crystal salt, 12 whole peppercorns and 3 or 4 whole sprigs of parsley with

178

stems. Simmer, covered, for about 10 minutes to develop flavors. Then drop in artichoke hearts, making sure there is enough liquid to cover them. If not, add more oil, vinegar and water in same proportions as above. Continue gently simmering, covered, until artichokes are cooked through—usually in 15 to 20 minutes. Then, let everything cool and pour artichokes and marinade into wide-mouthed screwtop storage jars and refrigerate until needed. If they are to be kept for many days, it is best to strain out and discard the aromatic spices, since they tend to keep on strengthening the flavor.

Serving at Table

Serve artichoke hearts at room temperature with lemon wedges on a bed of chopped watercress leaves. (Incidentally, after using up all the artichoke hearts, save the marinade. It can be reheated with a new batch of artichokes, mushrooms, or other vegetables.)

LE BIFTECK DE GRUYÈRE DES ALPES

FOR 4 PEOPLE

This is another classic French cheese snack dish. It takes its name from the fact that it is, in reality, a *bifteck* of French Alpine Gruyère cheese cut in the shape of a ½-inch-thick slab about the size of a filet mignon, covered with a fritter batter and baked, fried or grilled until the cheese is almost melting, so that it is rich and unctuous in the mouth. Finally, the *bifteck* is topped with eggs and aromatic herbs. (See menu and wine suggestions on page 125.)

Staple Items
Butter (about ¼ lb.)
Eggs (8 large)

Flavorings
Crystal salt, freshly ground
    black pepper

Shopping List
French Alpine Gruyère cheese
    cut into ½-inch-thick slabs,
    each about 5 by 3 inches
    (4 slabs, each weighing
    5 to 6 ounces)
Light cream (½ cup)
Parsley (a few Tb, chopped)

Plus ingredients for 1 batch of Fritter Batter to coat the cheese:

Butter (2 Tb)   Flour, all-purpose (1 cup, or a
Eggs (2 large)   bit more)
Milk (½ cup)   Superfine sugar (3 Tb)
Baking powder (1 tsp)   Armagnac brandy (1 ounce)

*About 45 Minutes Before Serving—Active Preparation in About 25
Minutes—Unsupervised Frying and Baking for About 20 Minutes*

BASIC RULE FOR FRITTER BATTER: Prepare the fritter batter in a
large mixing bowl. Break into it the 2 eggs and beat them lightly
with a fork. Then mix in the ½ cup of milk and the 1 ounce of
Armagnac. Put into a flour sifter the 1 cup of flour, the 3 tablespoons
of sugar, the 1 teaspoon of baking powder and sift into the egg mixture, pausing in the sifting to stir in the flour every couple of minutes.
The finished batter should be quite thick, so that it will solidly coat
each cheese slab. If at first it is not thick enough, sift in more flour
until exactly the right consistency is achieved.

In a large sauté or crêpe pan, over medium frying heat, melt the
first 4 tablespoons of butter. Dip each slab of cheese thoroughly into
the fritter batter, so that it is very well coated, then quickly fry until
golden in the hot pan, turning once with a large spatula. Preheat
the oven to 375 degrees. Choose a low, open baking pan, just
large enough to hold the four cheese steaks but not leaving too much
space around them, to avoid unnecessary spreading of the following
egg mixture.

Break the 8 eggs into a mixing bowl and beat them and the ½
cup cream very lightly with a fork. Season them with salt and pepper,
to taste. Then when all four now-batter-covered cheese steaks are
safely in the baking pan, pour the eggs over them. Place them in the
center of the oven and bake them until the eggs are set, with the top
surface brown and puffy—usually in 20 to 25 minutes. At this point,
the cheese, while still holding its *bifteck* shape, should be just about
at the point of melting. With a little practice you can achieve this
precisely every time. Needless to say, you must now serve the *bif-
tecks* instantly, on very hot plates, the tops sprinkled with the chopped
parsley.

LE CROQUE-MONSIEUR

FOR 4 PEOPLE

There is really no adequate English translation of this classic and universal French snack. It means, literally, "A Crackly Tidbit For Mister." The French, however, with a refreshing absence of male chauvinism, also have a slightly more luscious, more sensuous, softer version called Croque-Madame. Perhaps, in truth, this very French version of fried bread is the original of that all-American breakfast specialty with the inexplicable name of "French toast."

Staple Items
Bread slices, fairly thin (8)
Butter (about 6 Tb)
Eggs (4 large)
Milk (¼ cup)
Baking powder (½ tsp)
Flour (2 Tb)

Flavorings
Crystal salt, freshly ground
  black pepper, sweet
  Hungarian paprika, Tabasco

Shopping List
French Alpine Gruyère cheese,
  grated (½ lb.)
Ham, reasonably thick slices
  cut to fit the bread (4
  slices)
Cognac (1 ounce)
Dry white wine (¼ cup)

About 25 Minutes Before Serving—the Cheese Sauce May Be Prepared in Advance and Held

First prepare the aromatic cheese sauce. Put together into a mixing bowl the ¼ cup of milk, the 2 tablespoons of flour, the ½ teaspoon of baking powder, then mix thoroughly. Break the 4 eggs into a separate bowl, beat them lightly with a few strokes of a fork, then blend them into the milk mixture, with the ½ pound of grated cheese, the 1 ounce of Cognac, ½ teaspoon of the paprika, with salt, pepper and a drop or two of Tabasco to taste. Again, mix thoroughly. At this point, the sauce may be held for a couple of hours.

About 15 Minutes Before Serving

The bread slices should be about ⅓ inch thick. You may, if you wish, cut off the crusts. Mademoiselle Ray does not. Butter each slice fairly thickly on both sides. In a sauté or crêpe pan, over medium-high frying heat, quickly fry the bread slices until they are golden and nicely crisp. They must provide the *croque* of the title of the recipe. Hold the bread slices warm while you lightly brown the ham slices in the same sauté pan, adding a bit more butter, if necessary. While this is in progress, gently heat up the cheese sauce in a saucepan, stirring almost continuously, until it smooths out and thickens—usually in hardly more than 5 minutes. As it begins to thicken, work in, tablespoon by tablespoon, as much of the wine as is required to prevent the sauce from overthickening and to give it a nice, faintly tart flavor. It should finish up as thick as possible while still being pourable from the pan.

Now spread four of the bread slices fairly thickly with the cheese sauce, place a ham slice on top, then another spread of cheese and, finally, a second slice of fried bread. Cut each "sandwich" diagonally into quarters and serve at once, very hot, on well-warmed plates.

EGGPLANT APPETIZER OF THE IMAM BAYALDI
(*Aubergine de l'Imam Bayaldi*)

ENOUGH FOR 12 PEOPLE, BUT WILL KEEP REFRIGERATED FOR
SEVERAL DAYS

This is a delicate French version of the classic Middle Eastern baked cold eggplant. *Imam Bayaldi* means "The Swooning Imam" and the story goes that when the Imam was offered this dish by his wife for the first time, he found the smell and taste of it so unbearably marvelous that he fainted dead away. I have eaten authentic versions in some of the best restaurants of Beirut and Istanbul, but none was quite as dramatic as Mademoiselle Ray's. For one thing, she adds her unique new dimension to the texture by putting in slivered, browned almonds. It is well worthwhile to bake about a dozen eggplants at a time, since they keep, covered, in the refrigerator for days. Each is an irresistible hors d'oeuvre or midnight snack.

Staple Items	*Shopping List*
Butter (1 to 2 Tb)	Tiny Italian eggplants (12—
Yellow onions (6 medium)	best supplies available in
Virgin olive oil (1 cup)	summer months)
	Slivered almonds (8 ounces)
Flavorings	Pitted black olives (4 ounces)
2 cloves garlic, thyme,	White raisins (½ lb.)
crystal salt, freshly ground	Peeled Italian plum tomatoes
black pepper	(two 2-lb. cans)

Preparation Before Baking About ½ Hour

Preheat oven to 425 degrees. Wash the 12 eggplants, cut off the green tops, then make a single deep lengthwise slit in each, being careful not to go right through. Sprinkle salt inside each to help bring out moisture, then put all the eggplants directly onto the shelf in the center of the oven and leave to sweat for about 7 minutes. Meanwhile, sauté the 8 ounces of slivered almonds in 1 to 2 teaspoons of butter until brown. Then, using several thicknesses of paper towel to avoid burning the fingers, take out each eggplant and firmly squeeze it over the sink, so that as much internal juice as possible runs out of the slit.

Turn oven temperature down to 250 degrees. In a mixing bowl, combine the 6 onions, finely chopped, the 2 cloves of garlic, minced, the ½ pound white raisins, 2 ounces of the olives, sliced, 4 ounces of the sautéed almonds, 3 teaspoons dried thyme and pepper, to taste. Choose an ovenproof dish just large enough to hold the eggplants, closely touching, in a single layer and arrange them slit-side up. Drain the canned tomatoes (reserving the juice for some other use) and put about 2 tablespoons solid tomato into each eggplant. Now, fill the slits with the aromatic vegetable-raisin-nut mixture and spoon the rest of the tomatoes in and around the eggplants. Slice the remaining 2 ounces black olives and sprinkle over the eggplants with the remaining 4 ounces browned almonds.

Pour the 1 cup olive oil into the baking dish, adding more if necessary, so that the level reaches about halfway up the sides of the eggplants. Using a small ladle or a bulb baster, baste each eggplant with the oil.

Baking the Eggplants in 3 to 4 Hours

Set the dish, uncovered, in the center of the oven and bake very slowly until the eggplants collapse and are very soft, usually in 3 to 4 hours. Throughout the baking period, every 30 minutes or so, thoroughly baste the eggplants with hot olive oil from the baking dish. When they are done, drain off the oil and, after cooling, store them, covered, in the refrigerator.

Serving at Table

The eggplants should be served ice cold. Open up the slits slightly with a smallish wooden spatula and pile on the cooked purée from the bottom of the dish. The insides of the eggplants are then dug out and eaten with a spoon.

FLAMING CANAPÉS OF MOUNTAIN HAM
(Jambon de Montagne Flambé)

FOR 4 PEOPLE

These are classic French-style canapés, each small slice of ham resting on a crisply fried round of toast, covered with a sauce of sour cream and eggs, touched with the tartness of tarragon wine vinegar and flamed with the robust brandy of Armagnac. (See menu and wine suggestions on page 114.)

Staple Items	Flavorings
Butter (about 4 Tb)	Crystal salt, freshly ground
Egg yolks (2 large)	black pepper
Tarragon white wine	
vinegar (2 Tb)	Shopping List
Neat crustless rounds of	Slices of dry-cured, dark-
bread to be fried in	smoked ham, cut to fit the
butter (12)	bread rounds (24)
	Sour cream (1 cup)
	Armagnac (⅓ cup)

Total Working Time From Start to Serving About 20 Minutes—
May Be Prepared About an Hour or So Before Serving

In a sauté pan over medium frying heat melt 2 tablespoons of the butter and lightly brown on both sides the 12 bread rounds. Lay them out at once on a warm serving platter and hold them in a keep-warm oven. Add more butter, as needed, to the sauté pan and quickly brown the 24 slices of ham. Place two slices on each bread round. Hiss the 2 tablespoons of vinegar into the sauté pan and bubble it hard for 2 to 3 minutes to reduce it and concentrate its flavor. Then, work in the cup of sour cream, stirring thoroughly and scraping the bottom of the pan. Lightly beat the 2 egg yolks with a few strokes of a fork and blend them into the pan. Now turn down the heat to quite low and, using a wire whisk, vigorously beat the sauce to incorporate air and lightness, until you have almost a fluff —usually in 3 or 4 minutes. While continuing to beat, add salt and pepper to taste. Spoon this sauce, in equal parts, over the 12 canapés. Heat the ⅓ cup of Armagnac to just above blood heat and, in front of your guests, spoon it over the canapés and flame them.

LEEKS IN TOMATO SAUCE IN THE STYLE OF MEYRARGUES
(*Poireaux de Meyrargues*)

FOR 4 PEOPLE

French cooks, more often than Americans, have the courage to start a dinner with an utterly simple, cold cooked vegetable in a subtly spiced sauce which seems to titillate the appetite and clean the palate while providing only a minimum of filling bulk. This way of cooking leeks whenever they are in season (usually the year round, with peak supplies in the spring and fall) is, to my mind, one of the very best examples of this kind of light hors d'oeuvre. (A suggested menu and wine list to follow this dish is on page 41.)

Staple Items
Lemon (½)
Olive oil (4 Tb)
Yellow onion (1 medium)

Shopping List
White leeks (2 lb.)
Tomato paste (6-ounce can)

Flavorings
Bay leaves, 2 cloves garlic,
   crystal salt, freshly ground
   black pepper

*Active Preparation About 10 Minutes—Unsupervised Cooking
About 20 Minutes*

The leeks should, of course, be prepared several hours or the day before the meal. It is very important for this dish to use the finest green virgin olive oil. Gently heat 4 tablespoons in a fair-sized sauté pan. Finely chop the onion and gild it in the hot oil. With a small, sharp knife, dig out the pulp from the ½ lemon, chop finely and add to sauté pan. Also add, working everything together smoothly, the 5 tablespoons of tomato paste, the 2 finely minced cloves garlic, 2 crumbled bay leaves, with salt and pepper to taste. Cover and simmer very gently, to blend and develop flavors, for as long as it takes to prepare the leeks.

Carefully wash and chunk them into ⅜-inch cross sections and drop them, for not more than 15 seconds, into rapidly boiling water. Drain them at once, dry them in a towel and add them to the sauté pan. Make sure that each chunk is well incorporated into the sauce, then let everything gently simmer until leeks are perfectly soft— usually in about 20 minutes. Taste and adjust seasonings. If you think the tomato taste should be stronger, add a few more teaspoons of tomato paste. Then, the entire contents of the sauté pan can be refrigerated, tightly covered, for several days. Always serve at room temperature.

AROMATIC EGGS STUFFED INTO MUSHROOMS
(*Les Oeufs aux Champignons Farcis*)

FOR 4 PEOPLE

When large mushrooms with reasonably rounded and fairly deep caps are available, they can be used as "boats" in which to bake eggs with bits of smoky bacon, anchovy butter and aromatic herbs, for breakfast, as dinner table hors d'oeuvres, or as a main luncheon or supper dish. The preparation is simple and extremely quick. (See menu and wine suggestions on page 124.)

Staple Items
Bacon, thick-sliced, dark-smoked (3 rashers)
Eggs (5 large)
Breadcrumbs (about ¼ cup)
Yellow onion (1 medium)
Olive oil (about 2 Tb)

Flavorings
Crystal salt, freshly ground black pepper, red Cayenne pepper, chives, garlic (2 cloves), tarragon, paprika

Shopping List
Large mushrooms, with nicely rounded and deep caps (4)
Parmesan cheese, grated (¼ cup)
Parsley, minced (2 Tb)
Italian peeled tomatoes (1-lb. can)
Italian tomato paste (6-ounce can)

Plus ingredients for Anchovy Butter:
Butter (4 Tb)   Anchovy fillets (8)
Lemon juice

About 1 Hour Before Serving—Active Preparation in About 20 Minutes—Unsupervised Baking for About 40 Minutes

BASIC RULE FOR ANCHOVY BUTTER. Let the 4 tablespoons of butter soften. Cut up the 8 anchovy fillets, pound in a mortar to a fairly coarse paste, then work in butter with a few drops of lemon juice.

Hard-boil 1 of the eggs. Remove the stems from the 4 mushroom caps, wipe them thoroughly clean and hold them. Assemble the stuffing in a mixing bowl: the hard-boiled egg and the cleaned mushroom stems, both finely diced, the 2 peeled garlic cloves, mashed, the onion, finely chopped, about 1 tablespoon each of snipped chives and minced parsley, 1 teaspoon of tarragon, the ¼ cup of breadcrumbs, the 3 rashers of bacon, finely diced, plus very little salt, paprika, black pepper and Cayenne, to taste. As you thoroughly mix all this, moisten it with 2 or 3 teaspoons of the olive oil. Preheat the oven to 325 degrees. Choose an open au gratin dish large enough to take the 4 mushrooms and rub it thoroughly inside with olive oil. Fill each mushroom cap with the stuffing, pressing it down firmly, so that each cap is completely filled and the top surface of the stuffing is level. At the center of this surface, place a heaped teaspoon of anchovy butter. Put the mushroom caps into the au gratin dish and bake them for 30 minutes, basting them 2 or 3 times with the pan juices.

About 15 Minutes Before Serving

Take the mushrooms out of the oven and, using the rounded back of a kitchen spoon, make a depression in the top surface of the stuffing. Into each of these depressions break a raw egg. Lightly cover each egg with the ¼ cup grated Parmesan and a pinch or two of paprika for color. Carefully set everything back in the oven for just long enough to bake the eggs—usually in just about 10 minutes. Meanwhile, whip up a very simple tomato sauce by puréeing in an electric blender the 1 pound of Italian tomatoes and the 6 ounces of tomato paste, with a teaspoon or two more olive oil, plus salt and pepper to taste. Then quickly heat it up to boiling in a smallish saucepan. Serve the mushrooms the moment the eggs are set, with the tomato sauce poured over.

OMELETTE IN THE STYLE OF SAVOY
(L'Omelette à la Savoyarde)

FOR 4 PEOPLE

Staple Items
Butter (6 Tb)
Eggs (8 large)

Flavorings
Crystal salt, freshly ground
   black pepper, freshly grated
   nutmeg

Shopping List
Alpine Gruyère cheese,
   grated (½ lb.)
Ham, slivered (¼ lb.)
Heavy cream (¼ cup)

About 15 Minutes Before Serving

Make the omelette in the usual way, but just before pouring the eggs into the hot pan, lightly beat into them the ¼ pound of slivered ham, with salt and pepper, to taste, plus 1 or 2 grinds of nutmeg. In a small saucepan over low heat, set the cream to get warm but never to be near boiling. Melt the 6 tablespoons of butter in the omelette pan, make the omelette, and just before folding it, sprinkle on the ½ pound of Gruyère cheese, dribble on the hot cream, then fold and serve at once on very hot plates. (See discussion on page 141; menu and wine suggestions, page 140.)

OMELETTE OF CREAMED FRESH SOURGRASS
(Omelette de Mon Curé)

FOR 4 PEOPLE

The lemon-flavored wild grass, sorrel (in French, *oseille*), is much better known and adds its refreshingly sharp flavor to many more dishes in France than it does in the United States. This most unusual omelette is an excellent way to get to know it during its spring season in our markets. (See menu and wine suggestions on page 56.) The strange French name of this dish, "Omelette of My Priest," probably originated when it was invented by the greatest of French gastronomes, Brillat-Savarin, who served it for Sunday lunch to his local priest, Chanoine Chevrier, in the small Jura district town of Belley.

Staple Items	*Shopping List*
Sweet butter (3 Tb)	Sourgrass (small bunch,
Eggs (6)	enough coarsely chopped
	leaves to fill about 1 cup)
Flavorings	Heavy cream (¼ cup)
Crystal salt, freshly ground	French Cognac (about 1 Tb)
black pepper	

About 20 Minutes Before Serving

Break the 6 eggs into a mixing bowl, add about ½ teaspoon salt and a few grinds of pepper, then beat with small wire whisk just enough to blend whites and yolks. Wash the sourgrass and, using kitchen scissors, snip enough leaves into ½-inch lengths to fill 1 cup. Heat 2 tablespoons of the butter in a sauté pan and gently "melt" the sourgrass for 3 or 4 minutes. Then blend it, with its butter, into the eggs, giving everything a final whip.

About 10 Minutes Before Serving

Gently heat the ¼ cup of cream to just above blood heat, so that it feels hot to the tip of the finger. At the last moment before starting to make the omelette, add the 1 tablespoon of Cognac to the cream.

About 5 Minutes Before Serving

Make a French-style omelette in the usual way. Heat remaining 1 tablespoon of butter in an omelette pan, lightly stir the eggs once more, then pour, all at once, into the pan. There is no separate filling inside this classic omelette. As soon as it is folded onto its hot platter, make a fairly deep incision down almost the full length of the thickest part of the omelette and dribble into it the Cognac-cream. Pour remainder over top of omelette and serve instantly.

PANCAKES WITH CHEESE AND MOUNTAIN HAM
(Pannequets au Fromage et au Jambon Montagnard)

FOR 4 PEOPLE

These light, small filled crêpes are equally excellent served as the hors d'oeuvre of a party dinner, or as the main course of a lunch or supper. The ideal cheese is the firm, nutty Beaufort of Savoy, but a fine imported Switzerland Gruyère or Appenzeller will do as well. (See menu and wine suggestions on page 142.)

Staple Items

For the Pancakes:

Butter (about 6 Tb)
Eggs (3 large)
Milk (1½ cups)
Double-acting baking powder
 (3 tsp)
All-purpose flour (2 cups)
Salt (1 tsp)

For the Béchamel Sauce:

Butter (3 Tb)
Milk (1½ cups)
All-purpose flour (3 Tb)

For the Filling and Garnish:

Butter (about 4 Tb)

Flavorings
Crystal salt, freshly ground
 black pepper, freshly
 ground nutmeg

Shopping List
Cheese, either Beaufort of
 Savoy, or Switzerland
 Gruyère (6 ounces)
Boiled ham (12 small slices)
Sour cream (1 cup)

About 1 Hour Before Serving—Preparing Pancake Batter in About 5 Minutes

After first sifting flour to measure it correctly, sift it a second time with the 3 teaspoons baking powder and the 1 teaspoon salt into a mixing bowl. In a separate bowl, break the 3 eggs and beat them with a fork just enough to mix yolks and whites. Just melt the

6 tablespoons of butter and measure exactly ⅓ cup. Do not let it get too hot. Using a wire whisk in the main bowl, lightly beat in the 3 eggs and the melted butter. Now, beating all the time, gradually dribble in the milk, until batter has the consistency of thin custard, so that finished pancakes will be very thin. Do not necessarily use all the milk—or, if batter remains too thick, add an extra dash or two of milk. Continue beating until bubbles appear, then let batter rest to develop lightness and texture.

About 55 Minutes Before Serving—Preparing Béchamel Sauce in About 15 Minutes

In a 1-quart saucepan, over medium heat, melt the 3 tablespoons of butter and blend in the 3 tablespoons of flour. Stir until fully blended and very smooth. Then leave on low heat to cook the flour while you heat up the 1½ cups of milk in another saucepan. Now again, stirring continuously, begin gradually blending the milk into the butter-flour *roux,* continuing to stir until it all thickens and is very smooth. Leave it to bubble very gently while you grate the 6 ounces of cheese. Work half of this cheese into the white sauce, adding a few grinds of nutmeg and salt and pepper to taste. Sauce should finally be fairly thick. If it ·is not thick enough, continue bubbling and stirring it until it reaches the right consistency. Then turn off heat and cover the saucepan.

About 40 Minutes Before Serving—Griddling and Filling the Pancakes

Heat up and lightly butter the pancake griddle. Give the batter a final beat or two and spoon it onto the griddle in amounts to give you about a dozen thin pancakes, each about 2½ inches across. Cook until brown on both sides. Spread each with the Béchamel sauce, lay on a slice of ham cut to fit, then roll up each pancake and place in a single layer in a buttered grill pan. When all pancakes are lined up side by side, dribble the sour cream over them, sprinkle over the remaining grated cheese and liberally dot them with butter. They may now be held until . . .

About 10 Minutes Before Serving—Gratinée the Pancakes Under the Grill

Turn on the grill. When it is hot, place the pan of pancakes under it and leave them until the cheese is browned and the sour cream is bubbling hot. Serve at once.

CRÊPES FILLED WITH GOAT CHEESE
AND RED CAVIAR
(*Crêpes de Chèvre aux Oeufs Rouges*)

At the Auberge in the Valley, the cheese with which to stuff these crêpes is the Père Ernest, a soft, unctuous cream cheese of goats' milk. On this side of the Atlantic there are now some good, soft goat cheeses in the fancy cheese shops—or, as a somewhat blander compromise, one could use the standard cream cheese. A good part of the attractive flavor comes from the grated Alpine Gruyère and the red caviar. These filled crêpes make an excellent hot hors d'oeuvre, served as the first course at table, or, in larger quantities per person, as a luncheon or supper main course. (See menu and wine suggestions on page 125.)

Staple Items
One batch of about 2 cups
    of Crêpe Batter as
    described in Pancakes
    with Cheese and Mountain
    Ham on page 191
Butter (about ¼ lb.)

Flavorings
Crystal salt, freshly ground
    black pepper

Shopping List
Red caviar, salmon eggs or
    roe (8 ounces, about 1 cup)
Goat cheese, creamy soft (6
    ounces), shaped into 12
    small (1 x ¼ inch)
    medallions
French Alpine Gruyère
    cheese, grated (½ cup)
Heavy cream (½ cup)
Parsley, minced (about 2 Tb)

*Preparation in Less Than 15 Minutes—Make a Fine Show
in a Crêpe Pan Over a Spirit Stove at Table*

Prepare a crêpe batter, making it quite a bit thicker than usual, as described in Pancakes with Cheese and Mountain Ham on page 191. Set your crêpe pan (or alternative) over fairly high frying heat and quickly melt 4 tablespoons of the butter. At the same moment, set the oven to a keep-warm temperature (about 175 degrees) and put in it, to warm up, a serving platter large enough to hold the 12 crêpes. When the butter is thoroughly hot and sizzling, ladle in as many crêpes as the pan will hold, each fairly thick and about 2 inches across. Place at the center of each 1 tablespoon of red caviar. Cover it with a small, not too thick medallion of the creamed goat cheese. Then, sprinkle on 1 teaspoon of the grated Gruyère, 2 teaspoons of the cream and a grind or two of salt and pepper, according to the saltiness of the goat cheese. Now, at once, cover this construction with another ladle or two of crêpe batter, so that you have a kind of sandwich. Flip each crêpe over and quickly brown the second side. The moment each crêpe is lightly golden on both sides, set it on the serving platter in the keep-warm oven and repeat the frying operation with more butter, as needed. If you are doing this at table, you don't really need a keep-warm oven or a serving platter— far better to serve each guest directly from the pan onto very hot plates.

A PILE OF PANCAKES AND HAM

(*Le Matefaim*)

FOR 4 PEOPLE

This is not even a regional dish of the Alps. It is virtually a unique specialty of the tiny Valley of La Grande Chartreuse. In the local dialect, *matefaim* means "cut hunger," and it is the food most often served for a kind of brunch on Sunday or for a simple supper at any time. You make a batch of crêpes and quickly fry each one in very hot walnut oil, so that it puffs up and absorbs the nuttiness. Then you pile up the crêpes (more or less as if they were Mexican tortillas) between slices of grilled mountain ham, cover the pile with a creamy-white cheese sauce, and at the last moment put everything into a hot oven to get brown and bubbly. The traditional accompaniment is a tossed green salad. (See menu and wine suggestions on page 142.)

Staple Items
Butter (4 Tb)
One batch of crêpe batter
One batch of cheesed
  Béchamel sauce
(Recipes for both the batter
and the sauce can be found
with Pancakes With Cheese

and Mountain Ham, page
191.)

Shopping List
Dark-smoked ham, cut into
  fairly thick 2½-inch
  rounds (8)
Walnut oil (about ½ cup)

About 40 Minutes Before Serving

Mix and beat up a batch of crêpe batter as described on page 191 and let it rest. Prepare a batch of cheesed white sauce as described on page 192 and keep it warm, but not bubbling. In a pan over medium frying heat, melt the 4 tablespoons of butter; nicely sauté the 8 slices of ham and hold them, warm. Preheat the oven to 400 degrees. Turn up the heat under the sauté pan to fairly high temperature, pour in the ½ cup of walnut oil, and when it is thoroughly hot but certainly not smoking, fry the crêpes, pouring in just enough batter so that you get a puffy disk about 2½ inches across. As each is done, set it on a heatproof serving platter with a slice of ham on top—then another crêpe, then another slice of ham, until you top the pile with the last crêpe. Dribble over this pile a plenitude of the cheesed white sauce, so that it dribbles down the sides and forms luscious pools on the platter. Heat everything in the center of the oven until the pile is dotted with brown specks and the sauce is bubbling—usually in about 10 minutes. Serve at once, extremely hot, on very hot plates. The traditional way is to cut downward, with a very sharp knife, as if you were dividing a pie into wedges.

ALIGOT OF CHEESED POTATOES IN THE STYLE OF THE DAUPHINÉ
(*L'Aligot Dauphinois*)

FOR 4 PEOPLE

The word *aligot* comes from the Provençal dialect word *aliquot*, meaning a ragout. In this particular version, a hot mash of potatoes is whipped up with butter, cream and slivered cheese, until the latter melts and, quite suddenly and almost magically, the whole thing becomes stringy, like strands or ribbons of nicely chewy spaghetti or noodles. To achieve the maximum effect, one must use a slightly rubbery medium-soft cheese, and the best, unquestionably, is either the Beaufort or the Beaumont des Alpes, made on Dauphiné mountain farms and both now widely available in fancy cheese shops across the United States. (See note on page 141; menu suggestion on page 140.)

Staple Items	*Shopping List*
Butter (6 Tb)	Potatoes, baked or boiled, then lightly mashed (4 cups)
Flavorings	
Crystal salt, freshly ground black pepper, garlic (1 or 2 cloves, peeled and mashed)	Medium-soft cheese, see above, or it could also be Comtal or Tome of central France, thinly slivered or coarsely grated (2 cups)
	Heavy cream (½ cup)

Preparation in Less Than 10 Minutes—Makes a Fine Show
Prepared at Table in a Chafing Dish or Electric Frypan

Put the lightly mashed and well-seasoned potatoes into a sauté pan over low frying heat (or prepare the dish at table, as suggested above) and heat them up while moving them around, not so much by stirring as by lightly lifting and folding. At the same time, work in the 6 tablespoons of butter and the ½ cup of cream. As soon as the potatoes are thoroughly hot, begin, spoonful by spoonful, working in the slivers of cheese, continuing to lift and fold dexterously. At first, you hardly do more than lift and turn over. Then, after all the cheese is in and it is beginning to melt, your strokes should become faster and faster, and at the same time higher and wider. Suddenly, quite dramatically and almost without warning, the mixture becomes slightly rubbery and begins to hang together in thick strands. Now, using two wooden forks, lift the strands and pull them apart, so that they become longer and thinner. When you have thus converted everything into what looks like a pile of mixed spaghetti and noodles, quickly work in a little mashed garlic (according to your taste) and recheck the seasonings. Serve extremely hot, directly from the pan, onto very hot plates. Eat at once—the *aligot,* which is irresistibly chewy and tasty when hot, tends to become slightly leathery as it cools.

ROQUEFORT CHEESE FLAKY PASTRY PIE

(*Le Feuilleté au Roquefort*)

FOR 4 PEOPLE

This recipe seems to be unique to Mademoiselle Ray. I have never found anywhere else precisely this kind of aromatic hot cheese pie, to be cut into oozy wedges at the table and served as an hors d'oeuvre. It could easily be adapted, of course, to be served as individual tartlets, baked in small pans—in the style of the Swiss Ramequins au Fromage. After all, the Swiss border is only a few kilometers from the Auberge. (See discussion on page 68; menu and wine suggestions on page 67.)

For the Flaky Pastry Shell and Top:

Staple Items	*Flavorings*
Sweet butter, chilled (10 ounces—2½ cups)	Hungarian sweet paprika, freshly ground black pepper
Egg yolk (1, for glazing)	
All-purpose flour (1½ cups)	
High-gluten flour (½ cup)	
Salt (1 tsp)	

For the Filling:

Staple Items	*Shopping List*
Butter (4 Tb)	Roquefort cheese (¼ lb.)
Egg (1 large)	Heavy cream (about ¾ cup)
Arrowroot or cornstarch (about 2 tsp)	

At Least 5½ Hours Before Serving—Preparation of Dough up to
Baking About 4½ Hours—Initial Mixing and Kneading About 15
Minutes—First Chilling 40 Minutes

Lightly but thoroughly blend the two flours in a mixing bowl.
Make a well in the center and put in 4 tablespoons of the butter,
cut into bits, and the 1 teaspoon salt. Using the tips of the fingers,
work the butter into the flour until you have the consistency of whole
kernels of corn. (The technique for working these things together
with the tips of the fingers is described in detail at the very end of
the recipe for Cushion-Terrine of Pheasant, page 175—the section
of the method subtitled Mixing and Kneading Dough in About 15
Minutes.) Add dashes of ice water, as needed, so that dough gathers
into a ball without ever becoming wet. Place on marble or on a
floured board and knead thoroughly. Then, gather again into a ball,
wrap in wax paper, and leave to chill in refrigerator about 40 minutes.

The 6 Turns and the Resting in About 3¾ Hours

Remove chilled dough from refrigerator and roll out into a rough
circle about 10 inches in diameter. Place the remaining butter in the
center of the dough and pull up the edges to enclose it completely,
pressing with the fingers to seal the top. Working quickly, roll out
the dough to a rectangle 8 by 16 inches in length. Fold the dough
up by thirds, as if it were a letter. Turn it so that the fold is away
from you, with two edges facing you, and roll again into a similar
rectangle 8 by 16 inches. Again fold by thirds, then wrap in wax
paper and refrigerate another 40 minutes.

After the period of chilling and resting, repeat the sequence of
twice rolling the dough into a rectangle and folding it into thirds.
Then, again wrap and chill, this time for 1 hour.

After the hour is up, repeat the rolling and folding ritual twice
before returning dough to refrigerator for a final chilling of 2 hours
or longer—until you are ready for it.

About 1 Hour Before Serving—Active Preparation About 30 Minutes With Unsupervised Baking for 30 Minutes More

In a 1-quart saucepan, over quite low heat, slowly melt the ¼
pound Roquefort with the 4 tablespoons of butter, stirring often.
Work in a fair amount of pepper and paprika—enough to give a

pleasantly aromatic taste and a good, reddish glow. Turn off the heat and quickly work in the single egg. Measure ¼ cup of the cream and blend into it 1 teaspoon of the arrowroot or cornstarch, then work into the cheese mixture. Put the saucepan back on medium heat and, stirring continuously, let the mixture cook and thicken. It should be quite firm—so that it does not run when the pie is cut and served in wedges at table. If it is too thin, work in the second teaspoon of arrowroot or cornstarch, diluted with another ¼ cup of the cream. If it becomes too thick, blend in more cream alone. When it is exactly right, keep it nicely warm, covered, but not so hot that it goes on cooking.

Take the pastry out of the refrigerator, divide it into two equal halves and roll them out into two rounds, each about ⅛ to ¼ inch thick and about 10 inches across. With the first, line a lightly buttered French-style 9-inch tart pan, preferably with a removable bottom. When the pastry is neatly in place in the pan, spread it with the cheese filling, but leave about ¾ inch of space around the edge, then cover it with the second pastry round. Using a pastry brush, paint the bottom and top edges with the egg yolk, lightly beaten with a teaspoon of cold water, then roll and press the two pastry edges together to make a reasonably airtight seal. Preheat the oven to 450 degrees. With the point of a knife, make several slits in the top of the pie to release steam, then paint the top with the remaining egg yolk to give a handsome glaze during the baking. Place pie at lower-middle level in oven and bake until pastry is just beginning to puff and brown—usually in about 20 minutes—then turn oven down to 400 degrees. Continue baking until pie is fully puffed —usually in about 20 minutes more. If the top shows signs of darkening too much, cover pie loosely with aluminum foil or wax paper. Rush pie to table and serve on very hot plates.

SOUFFLÉ OF ALPINE CHEESES
(*Soufflé aux Fromages des Alpes*)

FOR 4 PEOPLE

With this basic soufflé, dozens of variations of flavors and textures are possible, simply by changing the combinations of the cheeses (see menu and notes on pages 16 and 17). French cooks generally serve this as a first course, filled with various fresh cheeses as they are at their seasonal peaks of quality. In France there is much awareness of the seasonal cycles of the hundreds of different cheeses.

Staple Items	Shopping List
Sweet Butter (4 Tb)	Gruyère cheese, French or
Eggs (5)	Swiss (¼ lb.)
Milk (1 cup)	Alpine Tome of Savoy, or a
Lemon (½)	sharp-flavored alternative
All-purpose flour (½ cup)	(¼ lb.)

Flavorings
Ground mace, crystal salt,
    freshly ground black pepper

About 1 Hour Before Serving—Active Preparation About 30 Minutes—Unsupervised Cooking About 30 Minutes

Grate both the cheeses and measure precisely ⅓ cup of each, then mix them and hold. Separate the 5 eggs, placing each yolk in a separate cup. The whites should preferably be assembled for later hand-beating in a round copper bowl that has been lightly rubbed with the ½ lemon to eliminate any slight film of fat. In a 1½-quart saucepan, melt the 4 tablespoons of butter and smoothly work in the ½ cup of flour. Heat gently, stirring continuously. At the same time, in another saucepan, heat the 1 cup of milk until it is just too hot to touch, then gradually blend into the butter-flour *roux*. Continue heating gently, still stirring, until it thickens. Then turn off heat and let cool, until it can again be touched. Blend in egg yolks, one at a time. Again, gently reheat, still stirring and carefully scraping bottom and sides, until mixture thickens to consistency of custard and drips lazily from spoon. Blend in combined cheeses, continuing to heat and stir until they are melted. Add ¼ teaspoon mace, 1 teaspoon salt and pepper to taste. Turn off heat and let cool while you beat egg whites.

Turn on oven to 325 degrees, setting lower shelf about two inches from bottom of oven and upper shelf near the top. Beat whites until they first glisten, then stand up in stiff peaks on balloon whisk. Using a rubber spatula, lightly and quickly fold ⅓ of whites into cheese mixture, then pour all of it back into the remaining whites in the beating bowl. Lightly and quickly continue folding—do not overdo it—do not worry about a few remaining white streaks. Pour instantly into a 1-quart unbuttered soufflé dish and put on lowest shelf of oven. Adjust upper shelf so that it is about 3 inches above top of still-unrisen soufflé, then invert a shiny cookie sheet on this upper shelf to reflect heat downwards onto the top surface. Gently close oven door—never slam—and do not open for the first 25 minutes. Then check every 5 minutes. Soufflé is ready when top is golden brown, probably with large crack, and is springy to the touch—usually in about 30 minutes. Rush it to table and serve instantly on very hot plates.

APPETIZER SOUFFLÉ OF AROMATIC SPINACH
(*Le Soufflé aux Épinards*)

FOR 4 PEOPLE

It is a typically French country tradition to serve a spinach soufflé, not as a vegetable, but as an hors d'oeuvre first course. The "secret trick" here is to add an aromatic tang to the creamed spinach by working into it some grated sharp Tome de Savoie cheese. (See menu and wine suggestions on page 128.)

Staple Items
Butter (about 2 Tb)
Eggs (5 large)

Flavorings
Crystal salt, freshly ground
    black pepper

Shopping List
Young spinach leaves (1 lb.)
Tome de Savoie cheese, or
    other firm, sharp types,
    grated (¼ lb.)

Plus 1 batch of about 2 cups of white Béchamel sauce as described in the recipe of Pancakes with Cheese and Mountain Ham on page 192.

About 1 Hour Before Serving—Active Preparation of Sauce and Soufflé in About 30 Minutes—Unsupervised Baking for About 30 Minutes

Thoroughly wash the pound of spinach and at once cook it in a large covered pot over high heat with only the water that sticks to the leaves, plus a little salt. Then squeeze out any remaining water, finely chop the leaves and cream them through a sieve, or use an electric blender. Prepare the 2 cups of Béchamel sauce as described on page 192. Separate the 5 eggs and beat the whites, preferably by hand, until they are very stiff. Preheat the oven to 375 degrees. Now work into the creamed spinach, first, the 2 cups of white sauce; second, the 5 egg yolks; and third, the ¼ pound of grated cheese, plus salt and pepper, to taste. Now carefully and lightly fold in the whites, lifting rather than stirring and not trying to mix everything completely. Have ready a well-buttered soufflé dish, large enough so that the soufflé mixture will fill it only ¾ full. Place it at once in the center of the oven and bake it, without opening the oven door for the first 10 minutes, until it has risen above the edge of the dish and the top is firm and springy to the touch— usually in 20 to 30 minutes.

THE BLACK PÂTÉ OF PROVENCE
(*Tapenado*)

FOR 4 PEOPLE

This famous hors d'oeuvre from the Mediterranean coast is in season throughout the year. (See menu and wine suggestions on page 33.) Mademoiselle Ray serves it as a three-colored canapé platter, garnishing the black mound of pâté with concoctions of red—salmon-roe caviar—and green—mashed eggplant. The two principal ingredients of the *Tapenado* are anchovies and black Morocco olives, and if you can get both of them fresh from Greek or Italian groceries you will have the finest possible flavor and texture. If not, use the 2-ounce cans of flat anchovy fillets and the best available quality of preserved black olives. For the red and green garnishes, see separate recipes below. Instead of serving only slices of bread on which to spread the pâté, Mademoiselle Ray produced a handsome platter of what the French call *crudités du jardin*, best translated as "raw tidbits from the garden" (see list below).

Staple Items	Shopping List
Olive oil (½ cup)	Black olives, pitted (½ lb.)
	Anchovies, whole fresh in
Flavorings	brine (¼ lb.), or flat fillets
English dry mustard,	(½-ounce can)
freshly ground	Tuna fish (2-ounce can)
black pepper	Capers (3 ounces)
	French Cognac (¼ cup)

Preparation in 20 Minutes or Less

If you are using fresh whole anchovies, first behead, clean and bone them. Then put them into the jug of an electric blender, with ¼ cup of the olive oil, 1 tablespoon of the Cognac, 1 teaspoon of the mustard, a few grinds of pepper and all other ingredients. Set the blender on a medium-high speed and at once start dribbling in more olive oil and Cognac. (But do not necessarily use entire amount.) Stop blender frequently and push down ingredients. As soon as everything is completely mixed and has the texture of a coarse, spreadable paste, stop the blending. Check seasoning and texture. If paste is too thick, work in more olive oil. If flavor is not sharp enough, add a tablespoon more or so of Cognac, mustard and/or pepper. The anchovies, of course, supply the salt. Mold pâté into a neat pyramid on serving platter.

RED CAVIAR GARNISH FOR TAPENADO

This can be made with the normal salmon roe available in jars at most supermarkets. If, however, you are near a Greek grocery and can get the *tarama*, reddish yellow carp roe, it makes a superb variation of flavor and texture.

Staple Items	Shopping List
Lemon (1)	Red salmon-roe caviar (4
Olive oil (about ½ cup)	ounces), or Greek *tarama*,
Breadcrumbs (½ cup)	carp roe (4 ounces)
	Tomato paste (1½ Tb)

Preparation in 5 Minutes, or Less

Squeeze juice from lemon and put it in the jug of an electric blender with ¼ cup of the olive oil, plus the 4 ounces of roe and the 1½ tablespoons of tomato paste. Blend at medium-high speed. The entire mixture should have the consistency of a stiff mayonnaise. If it does not thicken enough, add breadcrumbs, 1 tablespoon at a time. If it thickens too much, add more olive oil. Serve in piles alongside the *Tapenado*.

GREEN EGGPLANT GARNISH FOR TAPENADO

Staple Items	*Shopping List*
Lemon (1)	Eggplant (2 medium)
Olive oil (¾ cup)	

Flavorings
Marjoram,
crystal salt, freshly ground
  black pepper

Preferably Made the Day Before—Active Preparation About 10 Minutes—Unsupervised Baking of Eggplant About 1 Hour

Preheat oven to 400 degrees. Prick each eggplant with fork in about a dozen places, rub with olive oil and place in open baking dish in center of oven. Eggplant will be done when skins begin to crisp and split, while inside pulp feels soft—usually in about 1 hour. Open up eggplant, dig out inside pulp with a spoon and put into a saucepan over medium heat. Mash down pulp and stir continually to evaporate water and thicken. At the same time, work in ½ cup of the olive oil, the juice of the lemon, about 1 teaspoon of dried marjoram, plus salt and pepper, to taste. When mixture has achieved stiffness and texture of mayonnaise, turn out into storage bowl and chill thoroughly in refrigerator. Check seasonings once more when it is cold and adjust if necessary. Arrange and serve alongside black *Tapenado* and red caviar.

RAW "TIDBITS FROM THE GARDEN" TO GO WITH TAPENADO

The most dramatic way of serving the *Tapenado* is to mound it as a black pile in the center of a serving platter, and then surround it with two shallower circles of the red caviar and green eggplant. Finally, the remaining space on the platter can be filled with neatly arranged tidbits, including all or some of the following: slices of crisp apples, inch-long slices cut lengthwise from young carrots, cherry tomatoes, shelled walnut halves, sprigs of watercress, small celery sticks, cucumber slices, etc. There should also, of course, be French bread for mopping up.

SECTION III

Bisques, Consommés, Crèmes,
Panades, Potées,
Soupes and Veloutés

BILLI-BI OF CREAM OF MUSSELS WITH SORREL
(*Le Billi-Bi*)

FOR 4 PEOPLE

There is a somewhat questionable story as to the strange name of this very French rich seafood soup with the unusual flavor. It is said to have been invented for, and affectionately named after, the American scientist, explorer and gastronome William Beebe. Somewhere in France. But where? I have found it in country bistros (including the Auberge) in virtually every part of France that is within a reasonable distance of the sea. But nowhere more regularly than in Normandy, and especially in the restaurants of the principal Norman city, Rouen. Although this is officially a soup, it is so filling and nourishing that it should be served in small portions or followed by a light course; or, it could be the main dish of a lunch or supper. Again, it makes use of the refreshing, lemon-tart flavor of the wild sorrel, or sourgrass. (See menu and wine suggestions on page 93.)

Staple Items
Salt butter (2 or 3 Tb)
Eggs (4 large)
Shallots (4 or 5 cloves)
Parsley (small bunch)
All-purpose flour

Flavorings
Crystal salt, freshly ground black pepper, red Cayenne pepper

Extra Items for the Advance Preparation of Mussels
Yellow onion (1)
Whole bay leaf (1), garlic (1 to 2 cloves, to taste), thyme (1 tsp)

Shopping List
Fresh mussels in their shells (3 lbs.)
Heavy cream (1 pint)
Sorrel, the *oseille* of so many fine French recipes (enough to fill ½ cup, chopped)
A dry Muscadet wine from the Loire Valley (1 bottle)
The leaves from 1 heart of white celery
Parsley (3 whole sprigs)
Dry white wine (2 cups)

The Day Before

Clean and fatten the mussels.

BASIC RULE FOR CLEANING AND FATTENING MUSSELS: Pile the mussels in the sink under cold running water and arm yourself with a stiff wire brush and an old oyster knife. Scrape off all the clinging seaweed and barnacles until the shells "shine." Discard any half-open shells (indicating that their owners are in a poor state of health) or any that are suspiciously heavy from internal sand. Then put them into a large bowl, cover with water, and salt to the taste of the sea. Having made the mussels feel at home, give them a Roman feast with the food that is their caviar. Throw in 3 or 4 handfuls of flour and stir around to distribute evenly. Within a few minutes there will be a gentle stirring and scraping as the mussels open up to gorge on the flour. Set the bowl in the refrigerator, where the feast continues all night, until the mussels have glutted themselves to a fat whiteness, at the same time throwing out all excrement and dirt. In the morning the water is black, and when the mussels have once more been thoroughly rinsed under cold running water they are ready for cooking.

About 40 Minutes Before Serving

Steam the mussels.

BASIC RULE FOR STEAMING MUSSELS AND OTHER SHELL FISH: Into a tall soup pot with a tightly fitting lid pour the 2 cups of white wine and begin heating gently. Add the 1 onion, finely chopped; the leaves of the celery, finely chopped; the 3 whole sprigs of parsley; the garlic, finely minced; the bay leaf, crumbled; the teaspoon thyme; plus salt and pepper. Turn heat up high and bring liquid to a rolling boil. When pot is filled with steam, put in mussels and cover tightly, leaving the heat on high for about 4 minutes. When lid is lifted, disclosing mussels enveloped in boiling foam, some are seen to have opened, and these are picked out with tongs and put into a bowl to cool. For the more obstinate mussels, replace the lid for 1 or 2 minutes longer, at the same time lifting the pot and shaking it. When all mussels are out of pot, turn off heat.

About 30 Minutes Before Serving

Preheat oven to keep-warm temperature (about 150 degrees), then set in it a large serving platter. As soon as each is cool enough to be handled, remove mussels from shells and hold, throwing away shells. Strain wine in which mussels were steamed (now rich with their juices) through a double thickness of cheesecloth and hold. These are the foundation ingredients of the dish. Finely shred the sorrel and let it simmer, covered, in a small saucepan with about 1 tablespoon of the butter until it is quite soft, usually in 5 to 10 minutes. Stir it once or twice and add more butter if it gets dry. Separate the 4 eggs, storing the whites for some other use, then beat yolks into the pint of cream. Combine this with the mussel liquor in a 2-quart saucepan and heat slowly, stirring continuously and scraping sides and bottom with a wooden spoon, until it all thickens. Do not under any circumstances let it boil. Now blend in the cooked sorrel, together with any butter surrounding it, then taste and season, as needed, with salt and black pepper and a very little Cayenne. While soup is kept hot but well below boiling, quickly pick through mussels and, with kitchen scissors, trim off any dark edges, and drop mussels into the soup. Allow them to heat for 1 or 2 minutes, but no longer, or they will toughen. At the same time, check the thickness of the soup and, if needed, thin with a dash or two more wine. The Billi-Bi may now be served at once, piping hot, or allowed to cool, then refrigerated and served cold later.

COUNTRY SOUP OF BREAD AND GARLIC WITH FRENCH ALPINE GRUYÈRE
(*La Panade à l'Ail au Gruyère des Alpes*)

FOR 4 PEOPLE

The word *panade,* of course, comes from *pain* and generally means any kind of soup, stuffing or other mixture thickened with bread-crumbs. This soup seems to be so simple that at first glance one's snobbish instincts can hardly accept the fact that, eventually, on the tongue, it can be so extraordinarily good. There is a kind of strength and sustaining power about it. Remember, as you lift the first spoonful to your mouth, that probably at that very moment ten thousand French families are doing the same—sharing your pleasure in garlic soup. (See menu and wine suggestions on page 150.)

Staple Items
Butter (5 Tb)
Dry breadcrumbs (about 1½
  cups)

Shopping List
French Alpine Gruyère,
  grated (1 cup)
Heavy cream (½ cup)

Flavorings
Crystal salt, freshly ground
  black pepper, whole bay
  leaves, garlic (4 cloves),
  whole nutmeg

Prepare It in 5 Minutes—Simmer It for 30 Minutes

Do not ever be tempted to "gild" this dish by using beef or chicken bouillon as the base instead of plain water. It requires the simplicity of the water to allow the other flavors to dominate. Put 6 cups of freshly drawn cold water into your soup kettle and, as it comes up to boiling, add the 4 cloves of garlic, finely minced, 2 whole bay leaves, plus 1¼ cups of the dry breadcrumbs. (These can be the packaged kind, but it is better to use your own stale slices of any good loaf with the crust removed.) Simmer gently, covered, for about ½ hour.

Just Before Serving

Salt and pepper the soup to your taste. Turn off the heat under it and thoroughly stir in the ½ cup of cream, the 5 tablespoons of butter and 2 or 3 grinds of nutmeg. Now adjust the thickness. It should have the consistency of a light cream soup. If necessary, add a tablespoon or two more breadcrumbs. Now reheat the soup, but do not let it boil. Serve the grated Gruyère separately at table and encourage your guests to sprinkle on plenty of it.

CONSOMMÉ FLORENTINE WITH POACHED EGGS
(*Consommé Florentine aux Oeufs Pochés*)
FOR 4 PEOPLE

The French are devoted to the idea of starting a dinner with an egg in one form or another. Here, a richly aromatic chicken consommé (usually made the day before) is converted into a hearty, nourishing first course with a perfectly poached egg in each bowl (menu and wine suggestions on page 67).

Staple Items	*Flavorings*
Clear chicken consommé, ready ahead (1 quart)	Crystal salt, freshly ground black pepper
Eggs (4)	
Canapé rounds of butter-fried bread, each large enough to support a poached egg (4)	*Shopping List*
	Parmesan cheese, grated (½ lb.)

About 15 Minutes Before Serving

Heat up the chicken consommé in a wide saucepan or sauté pan, so that you can poach the 4 eggs in it. Remove them with a slotted skimmer and let them drain on a towel, while you quickly strain out any egg bits from the consommé and reheat it, just to boiling.

Serving at Table

Into each soup bowl or plate, put a round of fried bread, with a poached egg on top. Gently pour in the consommé and sprinkle its top surface with plenty of grated Parmesan. Each diner uses his spoon to blend the egg into his soup.

CREAM OF LEEK SOUP IN THE STYLE OF GRENOBLE
(*Potage aux Poireaux à la Grenobloise*)

FOR 4 PEOPLE

A rich and velvety soup—fine whenever fresh leeks are available, usually year round, with best supplies in the fall and spring. (Menu and wine suggestions on page 56.) I usually prefer to begin the preparation of a rich soup with a previously prepared aromatic beef or chicken bouillon, but this one is an exception. The leeks have so much flavor to give out, and flavor of such strong character and attractive personality, that the only liquid added to them should properly be pure water.

Staple Items
Sweet butter (¼ lb.)
Egg yolks (4)
Breadcrumbs (1 cup)
Fried croûtons, for garnish-
　ing (1½ cups)

Flavorings
Crystal salt, freshly ground
　black pepper

Shopping List
White leeks (12)
Heavy cream (1 cup)

*About 1 Hour Before Serving—Active Preparation About 15 Minutes
—Unsupervised Simmering 45 Minutes*

Carefully wash and finely chop the 12 white leeks, then lightly sauté them in 4 tablespoons of the butter in the bottom of a 4-quart tightly lidded soup pot. As soon as leeks show signs of gilding, add 2 quarts cold water, bring rapidly to boiling, then bring down to gentle simmering, cover and continue for 45 minutes. Turn off heat, taste and add salt and pepper as necessary. Put 1 cup of this hot liquid into the jug of an electric blender and add the 1 cup of breadcrumbs, then turn on to high speed for about ½ minute, until you have a smooth, thickish mixture. In a separate mixing bowl, beat the 4 egg yolks until smooth, blend into them the 1 cup of heavy cream and then work in the thickish mixture from the blender jug. When everything is perfectly smooth, gradually work this thickening mix into the cooling liquid in the main stewpot, stirring vigorously to avoid lumping. Then reheat soup, still stirring continuously, until it thickens to the consistency of heavy cream.

CREAM SOUP OF BIBB OR BOSTON LETTUCE
(*Crème de Laitue Printanière*)

FOR 4 PEOPLE

Mademoiselle Ray prepares this delicately creamy soup mainly in the spring, when she can get the local baby lettuces of the Valley. In the United States, however, we can do better. We can get small, soft young Bibb or Boston heads at almost any time of the year. Incidentally, the kitchen of the Auberge is quite modern in terms of having a good old American electric blender standing in one corner of the work counter. It helps to prepare this irresistibly delicious country soup in virtually a few seconds. (See menu and wine suggestions on page 77.)

Staple Items	*Shopping List*
Butter (2 Tb)	Bibb or Boston lettuce, small
Milk (1 cup)	and soft, all fibrous and
Flour (2 Tb)	tough outer leaves removed
	(2 medium heads, or 3 or
Flavorings	4 small)
Crystal salt, freshly ground	Clear chicken bouillon (1
black pepper	cup)
	Sour cream (1 cup)

Complete Preparation in About 15 Minutes or Less

Bring the 1 cup of chicken bouillon up to the boil in a saucepan just large enough to hold it and the lettuce, but do not put in the lettuce yet. Tear apart the leaves, wash and dry them thoroughly, then boil for 5 minutes in the chicken bouillon, pushing them down so that they are well covered. (Or, you can do this operation in two batches, putting half the leaves into the bouillon at a time.) Put the 1 cup of milk into another saucepan and warm it up gently, but do not let it get anywhere near to boiling. In a third saucepan, prepare, in the normal way, a Béchamel white sauce, melting the 2 tablespoons of butter and working in the 2 tablespoons of flour, then gradually stirring in the warm milk. Let it bubble very gently, stirring often, to cook the flour, for 2 or 3 minutes. It should finally have the consistency of heavy cream. If it becomes too thick, work in a tablespoon or two of the boiling chicken bouillon; if too thin, continue bubbling for a minute or two longer. Finally, add salt and pepper, to taste.

Lift out the briefly boiled lettuce leaves with a slotted spoon—it does not matter if they remain dripping wet—and lightly push them down into the jug of the electric blender. Add the Béchamel and the 1 cup of sour cream. Whirl everything at high speed until the lettuce has been just pulverized, but do not go on too long, or the soup will become oversmooth and sticky—usually 30 seconds is enough. Return soup to a saucepan and gently reheat (without, of course, boiling) while you finally adjust flavor and thickness. Stir in as much more of the chicken bouillon, tablespoon by tablespoon, as you feel you need for your personal taste. Add more salt and pepper, if required. Serve at once, very hot. This soup should be accompanied by slices of crunchy dry toast.

THE MAGNIFICENT MUSSEL SOUP OF JEAN AND PIERRE TROISGROS

(*La Soupe de Moules des Frères Troisgros*)

FOR 4 PEOPLE

Sometimes, while I was staying at the Auberge, either Mademoiselle Ray or Mademoiselle Vivette would take the day off. (One of them, of course, would always stay home to "mind the store.") Then, it would give me a special pleasure to take one of them to lunch or dine at a great restaurant of the central provinces in the area around Lyons. One Sunday we drove as far as Roanne to explore the marvelous menu of the Brothers Troisgros (whom I consider to be among the top half-dozen chefs of France) at their extraordinary three-star restaurant. We were overwhelmed by the magnificence of the mussel soup, and Jean Troisgros, with charming grace, wrote down the recipe for us. Now, whenever Mademoiselle Vivette can find fresh mussels in the fish markets of Grenoble (see Chapter Seven), she joyously brings them home, and Mademoiselle Ray prepares this, one of the great soups of the world.

Staple Items
1 batch of 2 quarts of fish *fumet* as described in the recipe for the Epicure's Supreme Shellfish Casserole of Curnónsky, the Prince of Gourmets, on page 238
Flour (2 or 3 handfuls)
Carrots (3 medium)
Yellow onions (2 medium)
Tomatoes (5 medium)
Olive oil (2 Tb)

Flavorings
Crystal salt, freshly ground black pepper, garlic (2 cloves), filaments of saffron, thyme

Shopping List
Mussels in shells (about 4½ lbs.)
Heavy cream (1 cup)
Leeks, white part (3 medium)
Shallots (2 cloves)
Dry white wine (5 ounces)

The Day Before—Active Preparation of Fish Fumet and Mussels in About 40 Minutes—Unsupervised Simmering About 2 Hours With Overnight Soaking

Prepare 2 quarts of fish *fumet* as described on page 239. Let it simmer gently, covered, for a couple of hours, then strain it and reserve it. If it is to be held overnight, refrigerate it, letting it return to room temperature well before the final preparation of the soup.

While *fumet* is simmering, wash and scrub the mussel shells according to the BASIC RULE FOR CLEANING AND FATTENING MUSSELS, from the recipe for Billi-Bi of Cream of Mussels with Sorrel, page 208.

About 1¼ Hours Before Serving—Active Preparation in About 30 Minutes—Uusupervised Simmering for About 40 Minutes

Put 1 teaspoon of the saffron filaments into a tiny saucepan with 2 tablespoons of the wine, then heat it up and let it simmer gently while you complete the other operations, so that the bright yellow oils and pigments of the saffron are dissolved into the wine. Finely mince the 3 carrots, the 2 onions, the 3 leek whites (previously thoroughly washed) and sauté all of them lightly in the bottom of a 4-quart soup kettle with the 2 tablespoons of olive oil. Do not let the vegetables brown. Then add the 2 cloves of garlic, finely minced, the 5 tomatoes, peeled and chopped, the saffron with its wine (carefully rinsing out the tiny saucepan with a tablespoon of fish *fumet*), 1 teaspoon thyme and the 2 quarts of fish *fumet*. Let it all gently bubble, uncovered, for about 40 minutes.

Meanwhile, deal with the mussels. Drain them and wash them thoroughly under running cold water, finally removing any barnacles and/or hanging "beards." Put them into a lidded pot large enough to hold them all, then sprinkle over them the 2 cloves of shallot, finely minced, plus the remaining ½ cup of wine. Over highest heat, bring it to a rolling boil, so that the pot is filled with steam, then clamp on the lid tightly and, occasionally shaking the pot vigorously to encourage the mussels to open, leave it over highest heat for about 5 to 7 minutes. As each mussel opens, take it out with pincers and let it cool. Continue boiling and shaking the pot until every last mussel has opened. Then, turn off heat and carefully strain the cooking liquor (which is now marvelously flavored by the juices of the mussels) to get rid of all sand. Reserve the strained liquor in a warm bowl. As soon as the mussels are cool enough to handle, remove the meats and drop them back into the warm cooking liquor, discarding all the shells.

About 5 Minutes Before Serving

Add the mussels and their cooking liquor to the main soup pot. Carefully stir into it the ½ cup of heavy cream. Taste and rectify the seasonings, as needed, then serve at once, extremely hot.

FALL SOUP OF THE HUNTER WITH PHEASANT AND CREAM OF LENTILS
(*Potage Chasseur*)

FOR 4 TO 6 PEOPLE

This is a magnificently rich and hearty soup—almost a main course in itself—certainly a dramatic centerpiece for an informal buffet or supper. It is creamy and gamy at the same time and should be accompanied by a big, full-bodied, aromatic white wine, say, a Bâtard-Montrachet from the Côte d'Or of Burgundy. (See discussion on page 97; menu and wine suggestions on page 96.)

Staple Items
Sweet butter (6 ounces)
Lemon (1)
Carrots (2 medium)
Yellow onion (1 medium)
Fried garlic croûtons

Flavorings
Crystal salt, freshly ground black pepper, rosemary, thyme

Shopping List
Pheasant, can be a fairly old bird (about 3½ to 4 lbs.)
Clear chicken broth (2 quarts)
Lentils, fancy large (½ lb.)
Leeks, white part only (2 medium)
Parsley (small bunch)
Dry white wine (½ bottle)

About 2½ Hours Before Serving—Active Work at the Start and the End About 45 Minutes—Unsupervised Baking and Simmering About 1¾ Hours

Rub the pheasant inside and out, first with the cut side of half the lemon; second with salt and pepper; third with 2 or 3 table-spoons of the butter. Preheat the oven to 325 degrees. Scrape and chunk the 2 carrots, peel and chunk the onion, carefully wash and chunk the 2 leeks, then place all these vegetables inside the pheas-ant. Balance it on a roasting rack, breast up, then roast it in the center of the oven for 45 minutes.

Meanwhile, wash, drain and pick over the ½ pound of lentils. Choose a large, perhaps 8-quart, soup kettle and in it bring up just to the boiling point the 2 quarts of chicken broth. Cover it and keep it hot until the pheasant is ready.

About 1½ Hours Before Serving

As soon as the pheasant has completed its oven time, lower it, with its vegetables still inside, into the hot broth and sprinkle the lentils over and around it. Adjust the amount of liquid by adding a little of the wine, if necessary, so that everything is well covered and the lentils are swimming around with plenty of room for expansion. Check seasonings and adjust, if necessary. Now gently simmer the *potage* until the lentils are perfectly soft—usually in 1 hour.

About 30 Minutes Before Serving

Now take the *potage* apart and then put it back together again. Lift out the pheasant, cut or tear all its meat off the bones, pass through the fine cutter of a meat grinder and hold for the moment. Strain the lentils and other vegetables, reserving their liquid and putting it at once back into the kettle; then purée the lentils in a food mill or, for only a few seconds, in an electric blender. Put the puréed lentils and the ground pheasant meat back into the liquid in the kettle. (Incidentally, the carcass of the pheasant should be saved for some other use, perhaps in the family soup pot.) Bring the *potage* back up to simmering and work in the remaining 9 tablespoons of butter. Check the seasonings once more. Serve very hot, with garlic croûtons sprinkled on top of each portion.

LA SOUPE AU PISTOU

FOR 4 PEOPLE

This is the classic one-dish meal of *Le Midi*, the entire southern region of France along the Mediterranean from Italy and Switzerland to Spain. Obviously, it is an historic variation of the Italian minestrone, which began originally in Genoa and must have crossed the French border at Nice. Then, the irresistible gastronomic influence of Provence took the dish in hand, adding garlic, green virgin olive oil and innumerable subtle touches. The name became *pistou,* from the ancient Provençal dialect words *pista* or *pisto,* for a pestle, to indicate the mash of garlic, butter, cheese and herbs pounded in a mortar. There must be a hundred versions of *pistou* all over the South of France. Mademoiselle Ray's recipe seems to incorporate ideas from many of them. Provided you stick to the basic principles, you can vary the recipe almost as you please. I have had it crispy and light, with the spring and summer vegetables. It has warmed me with its solid strength when the fire was crackling in the hearth and the winter wind was howling off the Alpine glaciers. (See discussion on page 84; menu and wine suggestions on page 83.)

Staple Items
Butter (3 Tb)
Carrots, peeled and sliced (2
    medium)
Yellow onions, chopped
    (2 medium)
Green virgin olive oil,
    preferably from Provence
    (up to 9 tsp)

Flavorings
Crystal salt, freshly ground
    black pepper, 4 cloves
    garlic, peeled, fresh or dried
    basil, dill, oregano and
    savory

Shopping List
French Alpine Comté,
    Swiss Gruyère, or
    Italian Parmesan, grated
    (½ lb.)
Chicken livers (½ lb.)
Elbow macaroni (½ lb.)
Green beans (½ lb.)
Dried white haricot, Great
    Northern, or marrowfat
    beans (½ lb.)
Leeks, white part only,
    (2 medium)
Potatoes, peeled and cubed
    (4 medium)
Tomatoes, peeled, seeded and
    chunked (4 medium)
White turnip, peeled and diced
    (1 medium)
Clear beef bouillon (about 8
    cups)

*On the Morning of the Day—Boiling the Dried Beans in 5 Minutes
—Unsupervised Soaking for 2 Hours*

Bring about 1½ quarts of freshly drawn cold water up to a
rolling boil, then dribble in, through your fingers, the ½ pound of
dried beans, slowly enough so that the water does not go off the boil.
Let them boil hard for 2 minutes. Turn off the heat and leave them to
soak for at least 2 hours, or more if you can spare the time.

*About 4 Hours Before Serving—Active Preparation About 45 Minutes
—Unsupervised Simmering About 3 Hours*

First, measure and prepare all the ingredients as indicated in the
list above. *Pistou* is truly a one-dish meal, authentically prepared
and served in a single large casserole or *cocotte*, preferably of enameled
iron, that can be used for frying on top of the stove and for baking
in the oven, and one that is handsome enough to be brought to the
table. Set this lidded pot over medium-high frying heat, melt in it the

3 tablespoons of butter, then sauté until lightly browned the 2 chopped onions and the 2 sliced leeks. Add the ½ pound of chicken livers and stir them around with a wooden spoon until they are just stiff, but. still rare inside—usually in 3 to 4 minutes. Turn down the heat to simmering. Take out the chicken livers with a slotted spoon, chunk them and put them back in the pot. Add the 4 chunked tomatoes, the 2 sliced carrots, the ½ pound of chunked green beans, the 4 cubed potatoes, the diced turnip, then let everything heat up and sweat, covered, for about 5 minutes. Next, add enough of the beef bouillon just to cover the solids (you may need to add more later) and bring up to gentle bubbling. Add and gently stir in the ½ pound of elbow macaroni. Keep the bubbling going while you drain the diced beans from their soaking water (discarding it) and add them to the main pot. Add more beef bouillon, if necessary, to cover. Adjust the heat so that everything is gently simmering—the surface of the liquid "just smiling"—and keep it going, covered, for about 3 hours. The timing is distinctly flexible, but of course must be continued until all the dried beans, macaroni and vegetables are perfectly soft. Watch carefully that there is never any heavy bubbling which would break up and mash the ingredients. Incidentally, the simmering of the soup can be done on top of the stove or in a 325-degree oven.

Meanwhile, prepare the *pistou,* the aromatic mash which will finally bind and unify all the various parts. In a large mortar, pound and crush the 4 cloves of peeled garlic to a smooth pulp. Then pound in either ¼ cup of fresh basil leaves or 2 teaspoons of dried basil, plus ½ teaspoon each of dill, oregano and savory. Now pound and stir in with the pestle, one by one, up to 9 teaspoons of the olive oil, until you have a very smooth and fairly thin *pistou* paste. Hold it in the mortar, covered with foil, until serving time.

Serving at Table

When you think the *pistou* is done, taste the various ingredients to make sure that all are soft, and check the seasonings, adding salt and pepper, as required. Finally, at the last moment before serving, thoroughly blend in the *pistou* garlic mash. Serve in the cooking casserole, or in a very hot tureen. Each diner sprinkles over his serving substantial quantities of the grated cheese. True aficionados of Provence will also stir in a few extra teaspoons of olive oil. This is surely one of the great *potages* of the world!

SORREL OR SOURGRASS SOUP
(La Soupe à l'Oseille)

In France, as in the United States, the wild sorrel, or sourgrass, is picked in the fall and can often be found among the vegetables in the local market. As its name implies, it is a form of grass with a definite lemon flavor, and it makes refreshingly tart soups and sauces. (See discussion on page 156; see also Billi-Bi on page 208; Omelette de Mon Curé on page 189. Menu and wine suggestions are on page 155.)

Staple Items	*Shopping List*
Butter (about 4 Tb)	Sorrel (about 2 lbs.)
Egg yolks (2 large)	Heavy cream (½ cup)
Potatoes, starchy (4 medium)	Chicken broth (4 cups)

Flavorings
Crystal salt, freshly ground
   black pepper

About 40 Minutes Before Serving—Active Preparation About 15 Minutes—Unsupervised Simmering About 25 Minutes

Wash the long strands of sorrel, removing the coarse root ends, then snip them into ½-inch lengths with sharp kitchen scissors. Put the bits into a lidded soup pot large enough so that the sorrel will fill it not more than half-full. Dig a hole down the center of the green bits and put in the 4 tablespoons of butter, pushing them under, so that they are on the bottom of the pot. Place it over gentle heat and melt the butter, stirring everything around, so that all the sorrel becomes butter-coated and quite soft—usually in about 5 minutes. Meanwhile, peel and very thinly slice the 4 potatoes, then add them to the sorrel with the 4 cups of chicken broth. Bring up to gentle bubbling and continue, covered, for about 20 minutes. During this cooking period, mash the potatoes with a fork, stirring them around, using them to thicken the soup. Also check the seasonings, adding salt and pepper, if required.

While the cooking is in progress, beat the 2 egg yolks with the

½ cup of heavy cream and reserve for the final thickening. Mademoiselle Ray serves this soup in the French way in a warm tureen. At the very last moment, she pours the egg-cream mixture into the tureen, then, beating furiously with a wire whisk, she pours in the hot soup, which thickens itself as its heat cooks the yolks. If you are not going to use a tureen, the alternative way is to spoon a ladle or two of the hot soup very gradually into the egg-cream mixture, beating hard all the time. Then, just as the eggs are diluted, warmed up and thickening, turn off the heat under the soup and rapidly stir in the thickening mixture. The trick is, of course, to stir so rapidly that none of the egg forms into little scrambled-egg bits. Frankly, the French way is easier and safer.

CREAM OF TOMATO IN THE STYLE OF PROVENCE
(Velouté de Tomates à la Provençale)

FOR 4 PEOPLE

This is no ordinary tomato soup. It is touched with the aromas of smoky bacon and fried salt pork, enriched with the oils of leeks and onions, the fruitiness of a soft white wine, with everything finally enveloped, in the true Provençal style, in an all-pervading mash of garlic. At the end, it is converted into a richly creamy *velouté* in a unique way—by being thickened with a whipped purée of rice. (See menu and wine suggestions on page 117.)

Staple Items
Bacon, thick-sliced, dark-
smoked, fairly fat (about
3 rashers)
Yellow onions (2 medium)

Flavorings
Crystal salt, freshly ground
black pepper, basil, garlic
(2 cloves), thyme, sugar
(1 Tb)

Shopping List
Tomatoes, peeled and seeded
(2 lbs.)
Beef bouillon (1½ cups)
Cabbage, very small, heart
only (1)
Leek, white part only (1 large,
or 2 medium)
Rice, raw (⅓ cup)
White wine, slightly sweet, say
a light regional Sauternes
(1 cup)

*At Any Time Beforehand—Active Preparation in About 15 Minutes
—Unsupervised Simmering About 1 Hour*

Mince the 3 rashers of bacon and put into a sauté pan over medium frying heat and begin melting out the fat. Meanwhile, mince the 2 onions and the well-washed leeks. Add both to the sauté pan and gently melt them, also, for about 5 minutes. If you have not already done so, now is the moment to peel and seed the 2 pounds of tomatoes. Mash them into the sauté pan and bubble them gently, uncovered, for another 10 minutes.

Meanwhile, in a 2-quart saucepan, bring up to boiling the ½ cup of wine with 1½ cups of freshly drawn cold water and 1½ cups bouillon. Discard all the tough outer leaves of the cabbage and finely mince its heart. Add to the simmering liquid. Also add the contents of the sauté pan, scraping and rinsing the pan so as not to leave behind any valuable flavorings. Season the soup with salt and pepper to taste, plus 1½ teaspoons basil, 1 teaspoon thyme and 1 tablespoon sugar. Simmer gently, covered, for 30 minutes.

Meanwhile, in another saucepan, cook the ⅓ cup of rice until it is very soft and mushy, then drain it. Finally, combine, batch by batch, the soup, the rice, and the 2 cloves of garlic, peeled and chopped, in the jug of an electric blender. Purée only briefly at high speed, so that the soup does not become too smooth. Return soup to the saucepan, stir in ½ cup wine and ¾ cup water and simmer gently, covered, for about 20 minutes.

About 10 Minutes Before Serving

Check the seasoning of the soup and adjust, if necessary. Also check the thickness, and if it is not yet thick enough for a *velouté*, bubble it a little bit harder, now uncovered, until it reduces and thickens to exactly the right consistency. Serve it extremely hot.

WINTER VEGETABLE SOUP OF THE MOUNTAINS
(*La Potée à la Montagnarde*)

FOR 4 PEOPLE

A fine, filling, hearty soup which can be made light or solid, thin or thick, simple or spicy, according to your needs and tastes of the day. The "solidity" is largely controlled by the amount of potatoes. This version is fairly light, with red cabbage, smoked pork and red wine. (See menu and wine suggestions on page 64.)

Staple Items	*Shopping List*
Butter (6 to 8 Tb, or more if necessary)	Bacon, solid piece, dark-smoked and lean, with rind if possible (about ¾ lb.)
Croûtons, fried in butter	Red cabbage (1 fairly small)
	Bermuda or Spanish onion (1 large)
Flavorings	Potatoes (between ½ and ¾ lb.)
Crystal salt, freshly ground black pepper	Robust red wine (about ½ bottle)

Best Made the Day Before—Improves With Reheating—Active Preparation About 30 Minutes With About 3 Hours Unsupervised Simmering

Remove hard outer leaves from the cabbage, mince it fairly finely, quickly sauté in the 4 tablespoons of butter and transfer it to a largish soup kettle. Mince the onion, also sauté, adding more butter if necessary, then add to cabbage. Peel the potatoes, cut into fairly thin slices, also sauté in more of the butter, then add to kettle. Place the piece of bacon, rind side down, on top of the vegetables. Add about 2 quarts of freshly drawn cold water, or a little more if necessary, just to cover everything. Stir in plenty of salt and pepper. Bring quickly to the boil over high heat, then bring down to the gentlest simmering (the surface of the liquid "just smiling") and keep it going, without any violent bubbling, covered, for between 2 and 3 hours. Then let it cool. It is hardly necessary to refrigerate it if it is going to be served the following day, but it should be refrigerated for longer storage.

On the Day—Reheating and Serving

Several hours before serving, skim all fat off the top, remove the piece of bacon and set aside, strain out all the solid vegetables and purée them in a food mill or, very briefly, in an electric blender. Then return them and the bacon to the soup.

About 40 Minutes Before Serving

Bring back to boiling and simmer, covered, for about 15 minutes, to heat through the bacon.

About 15 Minutes Before Serving

Add enough of the red wine to give a nice, winy flavor and a good red color to the *potée*. You may need only 1 cup of wine or all of the half bottle. Stir and bring back to simmering.

Serving at Table

The French way is to take out the piece of bacon and bring it to table on a hot platter. When the *potée* is ladled out, the bacon is sliced and 2 or 3 one-inch squares are put into each soup bowl. Sprinkle the top liberally with the croûtons.

SECTION IV

Aïolis, Bourrides, Flans,
Mousses, Quenelles and Timbales of
Fish and Shellfish
from "Les Lacs," "La Mer"
and "L'Océan"

THE TRUE PROVENÇAL AÏOLI OF MADAME RICARD
(*Le Véritable Aïoli Provençal de Madame Ricard*)

FOR 4 PEOPLE

The story of Madame Ricard and her dissatisfaction with the *aïoli* prepared by Mademoiselle Ray at the Auberge is on page 73. A few months after this unfortunate incident, I was in Provence and visited Madame Ricard, asking her to show me how she would prepare her "true Provençal *aïoli*," the garlic mayonnaise that is virtually the symbol of *Le Midi* of southern France. Madame Ricard invited me to what she called "an authentic Provençal lunch."

We drove along narrow, rising and falling, twisting roads, across the wild hills of western Provence called *Les Alpilles*. The slopes were covered by wild lavender, rosemary and thyme. As the hot sun bore down on the earth, it drew out the aromatic bouquet until the soft still air was soaked with the scent. Madame Ricard's lonely house, on the top of the hill, was shaded and surrounded by olives, fruit and nut trees.

Madame Ricard led me into her kitchen. The floor was of hexagonal dark red tiles. The stone walls were whitewashed. The green window shutters were closed, but still letting in narrow beams of the powerful sunlight, which threw an orange glow onto the rows of hanging copper saucepans. The kitchen was so dark that it seemed cool. Madame invited me to help her in making her *aïoli*.

When it was ready, she set the lunch table in front of the house in the shade of a vine-covered trellis. On the handwoven white cloth she placed an earthenware bowl of salad, a long loaf of crusty bread, a bottle of the white Rognac de Provence wine, several rounds of creamy-pink goat cheese, Le Banon de Provence, with a bowl of purple figs picked earlier from a tree behind the house. Then she placed the main platter in the center: a large piece of poached white salt cod surrounded by green beans, orange

228

carrots and creamy boiled potatoes. Finally, the bowl of bright yellow *aïoli*.

Following the custom of Provence, I stuck the corner of my huge napkin into my collar, while Madame cut chunks of bread, poured the wine and served the fish and vegetables. I ladled a dollop of *aïoli* onto the side of my plate. It stood up, glistening and stiff. I spread a little of it on a piece of fish, on a bean, on a carrot, on a slice of potato, on a morsel of bread . . . the garlic seemed to be the perfect companion to enhance the flavor of everything on the table. Perhaps it is the aromatic strength of the food, the hot softness of the air, the lazy beat of the sunlit hours . . . in Provence, garlic is a way of life. Here is the way Madame Ricard taught me to make her *aïoli*.

Staple Items	*Flavorings*
Egg yolks (2)	Fine salt, freshly ground
Milk (about 3 Tb)	black pepper, garlic (4
Fairly stale bread (1 thick	cloves)
slice)	
Virgin olive oil (2 cups)	
Tarragon wine vinegar (2	
tsp)	

Preparation in About 20 Minutes

The Provençal way is always to make the *aïoli* with a pestle and mortar, using the pestle instead of a spoon for stirring. (Incidentally, this also works very well for making ordinary mayonnaise.) You should have a stone or heavy glass mortar large enough to hold almost 4 cups. When you take the trouble to make *aïoli*, it is obviously best to have a supply for several days. Peel the 4 cloves of garlic, drop them into the mortar and grind and pound them into a paste. Cut the crust off a slice of stale bread, wet the center crumb thoroughly with the 3 tablespoons of milk, then squeeze it out and, taking enough of it to roll into a ball about the size of a large walnut, drop it into the mortar and grind and pound it into the garlic paste. Next, drop in the 2 egg yolks plus 1 teaspoon of the olive oil, and again combine. Work in salt and pepper to taste. Now begin dribbling in the 2 cups of olive oil, stirring, of course, all the time with the pestle. With this method, which includes the bread for added stability, it is possible to add the oil much more quickly than with an ordinary mayonnaise. Run the oil in, in fact, as fast as it is absorbed by the paste. When all the oil is safely amalgamated, work in, drop by drop, the 2 teaspoons of vinegar and continue stirring until the *aïoli* is so thick that it holds its shape when a dollop is lifted on a spoon.

FINAL NOTE: Naturally, you can vary the amount of garlic entirely to suit your taste. Start, if you wish, with only 2 cloves—or be a super-aficionado of Provence and start with 6 cloves! I have one friend, a gourmet of Aix-en-Provence, who would start with 10.

SPIT-GRILLED WHOLE CARP
(*La Carpe à la Broche ou Grillée*)

At the time when the great French writer, Stendhal, visited the Valley of La Grande Chartreuse (see page 131), the Carthusians would certainly have given him carp from their privately stocked lake and would have prepared it over the open fire, in the most direct and simple way. Nowadays, by using a spit rack and a rotisserie, we can almost exactly reproduce the excellence of that historic method. You clean the carp (or other whole fish of roughly the same size) and fill it with some herbs to add subtle flavor— fresh dill or tarragon with sprigs of parsley, plus, sometimes, slices of onion or green pepper. Then the fish is sewn up or tied, balanced in a rack or on a spit, then turned, close to the heat. There is usually no need to baste it, since the fat in the skin lubricates the flesh. But if there is insufficient natural fat, you can baste with melted butter or olive oil, with lemon juice or white wine. The skin becomes crisp and dark—a delicious part of the eating. When the flesh is perfectly done, usually in 15 to 25 minutes, serve it with melted parsley butter. (See menu and wine suggestions on page 142.)

CRAYFISH OR SHRIMP À LA BORDELAISE
(*Les Écrevisses à la Bordelaise*)

FOR 4 PEOPLE

This obviously is not a regional dish of the Alps but the classic high cuisine preparation of various forms of shellfish in dry white Bordeaux wine. It does involve the extra effort and time for the advance preparation of a classic Brown Sauce, but the final result is worth the effort. The complicated and subtle flavors of the sauce, contrasting with the crisp flesh of the shellfish, make this a party dish in the grand manner.

For the Brown Sauce:

Staple Items
Sweet butter (½ lb.)
Carrots (2 medium)
Yellow onions (2 medium)
All-purpose flour (about ½ cup)
Olive oil (about ½ cup)

Flavorings
Bay leaves, garlic (2 cloves), dried thyme, crystal salt, whole black peppercorns

Shopping List
Beef and veal bones, cut up by your butcher for roasting (2 lbs.)
Green Pascal celery (3 stalks)
Parsley (3 or 4 sprigs)
Tomatoes (3 medium)
Strong beef bouillon (6 cups)
Tomato sauce (1 cup)
Sherry, dry Fino (½ cup)

For the Shrimp à la Bordelaise:

Staple Items
Butter (7 Tb)
Brown Sauce (2 cups—see recipe below)
Arrowroot or cornstarch (a few Tb)
Olive oil (7 Tb)

Flavorings
Bay leaf, garlic (1 clove), tarragon, thyme, crystal salt, freshly ground black pepper

Shopping List
Crayfish or large shrimp in shells (16 to 24, depending on size)
Heavy cream (a few Tb)
Green Pascal celery (1 small stalk, with the leaves)
Parsley (2 sprigs)
Shallots (4)
Fresh tarragon leaves (enough to fill ¼ cup, chopped)
Italian plum tomatoes (1 lb.)
Tomato paste (1 to 2 Tb)
Dry white wine (2 cups)
Cognac (¼ cup plus 1 to 2 tsp)

The Day Before—Classic Preparation of the Basic Brown Sauce— Active Preparation About 30 Minutes—Unsupervised Simmering About 3 Hours

Preheat oven to 450 degrees. Prepare the 2 pounds of beef and veal bones by rubbing olive oil into each piece, then dipping in flour to coat on all sides. Place in open, lightly greased roasting pan in oven until bones are browned to a good dark color—usually in about 30 minutes.

Chop the 2 carrots and 2 onions and hold. Peel, seed and dice the 3 tomatoes, coarsely chop the 3 stalks green celery and 3 or 4 sprigs parsley, peel and finely mince the 2 cloves garlic. In a 3-quart sauce-pan, melt the ½ pound butter and add the carrots and onions, sauté-ing them until lightly browned. At the same time in another sauce-pan, heat up the 6 cups beef bouillon, and when it boils, pour it into the vegetables, blending it in with a wire whisk. Then whisk in the 1 cup tomato sauce, the tomatoes, celery, parsley, the 2 bay leaves, crumbled, ½ teaspoon dried thyme, the minced garlic, 1 teaspoon crystal salt and 10 whole black peppercorns. Let it all simmer, un-covered, until the bones are ready.

Put the browned bones into the sauce and keep everything simmer-ing, now covered, for about 3 hours. The bones will give a deep, rich brown color to the sauce. Before using it in the Bordelaise, check the seasoning, strain it and add the ½ cup Sherry. Any part of the sauce left over may be refrigerated, tightly covered, for a few days, or frozen into cubes and kept more or less indefinitely.

About 1 Hour Before Serving—Final Preparation of the Shellfish and Sauce

Finely dice the 3 carrots and 3 onions and set them aside. Then wash and trim the 24 crayfish or shrimp, but do not shell them yet. In a heavy frying pan over quite high heat, warm up the 7 tablespoons of olive oil and quickly sauté the shellfish, after adding salt and pepper, until they have turned a good red color. Take them out at once and reserve them, keeping them warm. In a sauté pan over medium heat, melt 4 tablespoons of the butter, add the carrots and onions, the 4 shallots and the clove of garlic, all finely minced, then put in the shellfish, stir them around, and flame with ¼ cup of the Cognac. Remove from heat.

In a second saucepan, over medium heat, combine the 2 cups white wine with the 2 cups brown sauce, then work in 1 or 2 tablespoons of tomato paste, the 1 pound Italian tomatoes, peeled, seeded and diced, the small stalk of celery with its leaves, 2 sprigs of parsley, 1 whole bay leaf, ½ teaspoon each of tarragon and thyme, with salt and pepper, to taste. Add the contents of the sauté pan and let everything simmer, covered, for not more than 10 minutes. Then, fish out the bay leaf, the stalk of celery and the parsley sprigs and discard them. Now, finally, thicken the sauce by working in, tablespoon by tablespoon, the arrowroot or cornstarch diluted with a little of the heavy cream, until it is thick enough just to coat the spoon. Check the seasonings once more, melting in the final 3 tablespoons of butter and adding a final teaspoon or two of Cognac, to your taste. At the last moment before serving, stir in about ¼ cup of finely chopped leaves of fresh tarragon. Serve very hot over rice.

THE CLASSIC GRATIN OF CRAYFISH OR SHRIMP TAILS
(*Le Gratin des Queues d'Écrevisses*)

FOR 4 PEOPLE

This is the classic French high cuisine combination of the succulence of shellfish with the richness of cheese and cream, plus the aromatic excitement of tarragon and other herbs and spices, all informed by the fruity refreshment of white wine.

Staple Items
Butter (about 5 Tb)
Breadcrumbs (½ cup)
Flour (1 Tb)
Lemon juice, or white wine vinegar (a dash)
Mustard (1 Tb)

Flavorings
Crystal salt, freshly ground black pepper, red Cayenne pepper, dried or fresh tarragon

Shopping List
Crayfish, or large shrimp (about 24, according to size)
Gruyère cheese (about ¼ cup, grated)
Heavy cream (¾ cup)
Dry white wine (¼ cup)
Armagnac (about ½ ounce)

About 40 Minutes Before Serving—Active Preparation About 25 Minutes—Unsupervised Cooking About 15 Minutes

Drop the shellfish into boiling salted water with a good dash of lemon juice or white wine vinegar, then boil for not more than 5 minutes. As soon as they are cool enough to handle, shell them and lay them side by side in a well-buttered au gratin dish. Let them rest while you prepare the sauce. If you are using crayfish and you find some coral, purée it in a small bowl with a few teaspoons of the cream and hold it.

In a 1½-pint saucepan over medium heat, melt 2 tablespoons of the butter, work in the 1 tablespoon of flour and, when it is smooth, gradually stir in, tablespoon by tablespoon, the ¼ cup of wine. Let it all bubble merrily, still stirring, for a minute or so, then work in the 1 tablespoon of mustard, the remainder of the cream and the ½ ounce of Armagnac. Let it all continue bubbling and thickening, adding a minimum of salt, a few grinds of pepper, a pinch of Cayenne and either 1 teaspoon of dried or 2 tablespoons of chopped fresh tarragon. Now, if you have some, carefully work in the creamed coral and the ¼ cup of grated Gruyère cheese. Preheat oven to 325 degrees.

Spoon this hot sauce over the shellfish, so that each tail is well covered. Sprinkle with the ½ cup of breadcrumbs, liberally dot with bits of butter, cover with foil and put in the center of the oven for the ingredients to heat up and the flavors to amalgamate—usually in about 10 minutes. Turn on the grill, remove the foil from the au gratin dish and place it about 2 inches under the heat. As soon as the breadcrumbed surface begins to brown, blister and bubble, serve the *gratin* instantly on extremely hot plates.

CRAYFISH OR SHRIMP ON A STEAK AND CHICKEN LIVER PIE

(Le Flan de Bifteck et de Foies de Volaille aux Écrevisses, Sauce Nantua)

A PARTY DISH FOR 10

This is probably the most extraordinary, the most outré, of all specialties served at the Auberge. At first description it sounded as if it were an incongruous collection of incompatible ingredients: chopped beef, chicken livers, crayfish, shrimp, all covered with a pinkish shellfish sauce. But after the flames had died down and I tasted it, I realized at once that it was a highly successful, daringly imaginative combination of tastes and textures. I have served it a number of times to friends in New York. They were put off by it if I told them in advance what it was. But if I let them taste it first, almost all of them were won over by it. If one may twist a cliché, this is a dramatic conversation dish for any dinner party. (See menu and wine suggestions on page 77.)

For the Meat Pie and Its Shellfish Garnish:

Staple Items	*Shopping List*
Butter (6 Tb plus a bit to rub on baking dish)	Beef sirloin, lean only, ground (1 lb.)
Eggs (5 large)	Chicken livers (1 lb.)
Egg yolks (5)	Crayfish or shrimp (2 lbs.)
Light cream (1 quart)	Cognac (¼ cup)

Flavorings
Crystal salt, freshly ground
   black pepper

For Mademoiselle Ray's Modified Nantua Sauce:

Staple Items	*Shopping List*
Butter (6 Tb)	Mushrooms (½ lb.)
Carrots (2 medium)	Sour cream (1 pint)
Yellow onions (2 medium)	Cognac (¼ cup)
Flour (¼ cup)	Dry white wine (2 cups)
Tomato paste (about 1 Tb)	

Flavorings
Crystal salt, freshly ground
   black pepper, red Cayenne
   pepper, thyme

About 2 Hours Before Serving—Active Preparation of the Meat Pie About 30 Minutes—Unsupervised Baking 1½ Hours

In a large sauté pan, melt the 6 tablespoons of butter and quickly sauté the 1 pound of chicken livers for hardly more than 2 or 3 minutes, after sprinkling them with salt and pepper. They should remain quite rare inside. Now, using the finest cutting disk of a meat grinder, pass through the livers and the 1 pound of beef sirloin. In a separate mixing bowl, beat together just enough to mix them thoroughly the 5 whole eggs, plus the 5 yolks, then lightly work them into the meat mixture with 3 cups of the light cream, the ¼ cup of Cognac, plus more salt and pepper if necessary to taste. Preheat the oven to 275 degrees. Now adjust the thickness of the mixture. It should not be as stiff as a stuffing or a terrine. It should be almost runny, since it is going to set in the oven as if it were a custard. To achieve this slight runniness, work in, as required, all or part of the final cup of cream. Now choose a round pie pan or shallow casserole deep and wide enough to hold 3 quarts. Butter it lightly and cut a round of wax paper exactly to fit its bottom. With this paper in place and also lightly buttered, pour and spoon in the cream-meat mixture. Stand the pan in a *bain-marie* tray of boiling water about 1 inch deep, slide the whole arrangement into the center of the oven and bake until the inside is set and the top nicely browned—usually in about 1½ hours. If the top shows signs of browning too quickly, loosely cover the pan with foil. At the end, the pie must be sufficiently set to be turned out onto the serving dish. During the baking, prepare the modified Nantua Sauce.

About 1½ Hours Before Serving—Active Preparation of the Sauce in About 1 Hour

Into a 3-quart saucepan, put the 2 cups of wine, and while it is coming up to boiling, add the 2 carrots and 2 onions, both finely chopped, 1 teaspoon of thyme, plus salt and pepper to taste. Let it bubble merrily until the crayfish or shrimp are ready to go in. Clean and trim but do not shell them, then simmer them gently in the hot wine for exactly 10 minutes. Take them out at once with a slotted spoon, reserving the wine, and let cool briefly. Meanwhile, wipe clean the ½ pound mushrooms and hold. As soon as the shellfish are cool enough to handle, shell them, set them aside, covered, and put the shells into a mortar. Grind and pound the shells until they are thoroughly broken up. Then transfer all this debris from the mortar, with the important juice that has come out, to the jug of an electric blender. Add to the jug 1 strained cup of the wine bouillon. Cover the jug and blend at top speed until the shells are completely pulverized—usually in about 30 seconds to 1 minute. Strain this powdery liquid through a muslin cloth so that all the nasty bits of shell are left behind, and carefully reserve the highly flavored liquid, which is the key to the Nantua Sauce.

Turn again to the sauté pan in which the chicken livers were fried. Melt in the 6 tablespoons of butter and quickly sauté the cleaned mushrooms. Remove them with a slotted spoon and reserve them. Quickly sauté the crayfish or shrimp, sprinkling them with the ¼ cup of flour, until they are just delicately gilded—usually in hardly more than 4 minutes—then remove them with a slotted spoon and reserve them. Now turn down the heat under the sauté pan and complete the sauce. Work into the remaining butter the 1 tablespoon of tomato paste and the juice from the electric blender. Next, work in, tablespoon by tablespoon, stirring continuously, most of the 1 pint of sour cream. As you continue blending and stirring, adjust the seasonings; adjust the pink color with more tomato paste if necessary; adjust the thickness with more sour cream if necessary; and adjust the richness by melting in, if necessary, more butter. At the end it should have the consistency of runny custard. If it becomes too thick, add a strained tablespoon or two of the remaining wine bouillon. Finally, cover and keep just warm until the meat pie comes out of the oven.

Serving and Flaming at Table

Carefully unmold the meat pie onto a hot platter. The wax paper will now be on top. Peel it off and decorate this top with the mushroom caps and the crayfish or shrimp arranged in neat circles or wedges. Dribble the pink Nantua Sauce over everything, letting it run nonchalantly down the sides of the pie. At the last moment, slightly heat up the ¼ cup of Cognac and, as the dish is set on the table, pour the spirit around, not over, the pie and set it on fire.

THE EPICURE'S SUPREME SHELLFISH CASSEROLE OF CURNONSKY, THE PRINCE OF GOURMETS
(La Timbale Épicurienne de Curnonsky)

FOR 4 PEOPLE

This is certainly the most complicated and most demanding dish in this book—perhaps one of the most challenging in all of the French high cuisine as it was set down by the incomparable gastronome, Curnonsky. Almost all of Mademoiselle Ray's recipes are in the French country style, but here she plunges into the classic cookery of the great chefs. Not that this *timbale* is particularly difficult in terms of technical skill, but it is a fairly big job in terms of time and determined effort. It is a marvelously perfumed mixture, in a huge earthenware casserole, of lobsters, crayfish or shrimp, oysters, mushrooms, truffles, all bound together in a sauce of cream, Cognac, wine, shallots, tarragon and plenty of butter. The recipe involves several different operations, covering shopping and cooking intermittently over three days. I usually start on a Friday afternoon, work through Saturday and Sunday, then hurry home from the office as early as possible on Monday and serve the *timbale* to my guests that evening. This is an adaptation of a professional recipe, involving the prior preparation of some of the basic sauces and stocks which, of course, are continuously available in a restaurant kitchen: as, for example, the fish *fumet,* the basic Brown Sauce used in the Lobster Américaine and the Crayfish or Shrimp Bordelaise. These can all be made well in advance, and if you make larger quantities, they are useful elements of dozens of other recipes. Finally, on the night of the dinner, there is little more to do than to assemble the various parts, and the concluding cooking time, just before serving, is hardly more than 45 minutes. (See menu and wine suggestions on page 86.)

Three Days Ahead—Preparing the Fumet—Active Preparation About 10 Minutes—Unsupervised Simmering About 30 Minutes

For the Fish *Fumet:*

Staple Items
Lemon juice (1 tsp)
Yellow onion (1 medium)
Crystal salt

Shopping List
Fish backbones, fins, heads,
  tails and trimmings—
  usually given free by your
  regular fishmonger, or use

good-quality fish fillets
(about 2 lbs. or 2 quarts);
or if you are really
desperate for time and
must compromise, use
bottled clam juice (1 pint)
Fresh mushrooms (½ lb.)
Parsley (1 bunch)
Dry white vermouth (¾
cup)

Wash fish bits and pieces under running cold water and place in a 6-quart enameled or stainless steel soup pot. (Do not use aluminum or iron, which would cause discoloring of the *fumet.*) Peel and slice the onion and add to pot. Cut off stalks from the bunch of parsley, wash them and add to pot. Do not use the parsley leaves, which would turn the *fumet* green. Chop mushroom stems (save the caps for the Shrimp Butter) and add, with the 1 teaspoon lemon juice, the ¾ cup vermouth, ½ teaspoon salt and enough cold water just to cover everything. Bring up to simmering, removing any scum that rises to the surface, then leave at a gentle simmer, uncovered, for 30 minutes.

Strain off liquid through a fine sieve, taste and add more salt, if necessary. Store in the refrigerator in a screwtop jar until needed for the Lobster à l'Américaine and for the Shrimp Butter. (For longer storage—so that you will have some on hand to use in fish aspics, fish sauces, fish soups, etc.—the *fumet* can be frozen into cubes.)

Still 3 Days Ahead—Classic Preparation of the Lobster in About 1 Hour

For the Lobster à l'Américaine:

Staple Items	Flavorings
Sweet butter (11 Tb)	Bay leaf, garlic (2 cloves),
Fish *fumet* (1 cup)	rosemary, tarragon, thyme,
Glace de viande (2 tsp)	crystal salt, freshly ground
(This is the French name	black pepper
for concentrated meat glaze	
which, if you do not have	*Shopping List*
your own, can be bought	Lobsters, live (2, 1½ lbs.
bottled or canned at fancy	each)
food stores.)	Parsley (enough for ¼ cup,
Carrots (4 medium)	chopped)
Arrowroot or cornstarch	Shallots (2)
(about 1 tsp)	Tomatoes (3 medium)
Olive oil (4 Tb)	Tomato paste (6-ounce can)
	Dry white wine (1 cup)
	Cognac (½ cup)

Begin by humanely killing the 2 lobsters. Put them into a suitably large soup kettle, cover with cold water and add plenty of salt to make them feel at home. Place pot over highest possible heat, so that temperature of water rises quickly and the delicate nerves of the lobsters are painlessly numbed. When temperature reaches 80 degrees, lobsters turn red and are dead.

Take them out of water at once and place them on a large wooden chopping board. Using in turn a small, sharp cleaver and a heavy-duty fish knife, clean and cut up the lobsters. Stretch out one of the lobsters on its back and open up the underside of its head. Remove its stomach, or "lady"—the hard little sac where its chin would be, if it had a chin. Open up the underside of the tail and scrape out black intestinal vein. If lobster is a female "hen" (you can tell by her much wider tailfin), she will have the red "coral" inside her head. These are her eggs, a prized delicacy to be carefully removed and held aside to be used later in the sauce. Both female and male also have in their heads the green tomalley, the liver, also an important delicacy to be removed and held for later use.

Now, chop off the claws and legs and chop them into manageable pieces. Chop off the front part of the head and the tailfin and discard. Chop off remainder of head and split lengthwise. Then, starting along the underside, cut along the center of the body to make two long separate halves. Chop each crosswise into manageable pieces. Repeat with the second lobster.

Set a deep frying pan over medium heat and put in it the 4 tablespoons olive oil, 3 tablespoons of the butter and all the pieces of lobster, lightly salted and peppered. Stir them around and turn them over, to coat well with the butter and oil on all sides, for hardly more than 2 minutes. Meanwhile, on a nearby burner, heat up a lidded casserole or saucepan. Using a slotted spoon or kitchen pincers, transfer the lobster pieces to the second pan. Warm the ½ cup Cognac, pour over the lobster and light it. Shake the pan until the flame dies, then, while continuously stirring and turning the lobster pieces, let liquid simmer about 2 minutes more.

Remove remaining 8 tablespoons butter from refrigerator and set aside to soften. Finely chop the 2 shallots and the 4 carrots. Peel and finely mince the 2 cloves garlic. Peel, seed and dice the 3 tomatoes. Now, add to the lobster in the pan the shallots, carrots, garlic and tomatoes, plus the bay leaf, crumbled, and a pinch or two each of dried rosemary, tarragon and thyme (or a few fresh leaves of each). Return to gentle heat, stir everything together and let simmer, uncovered. Meanwhile, in a mixing bowl, work together the 6-ounce can of tomato paste, the 2 teaspoons *glace de viande*, the 1 cup dry white wine and 1 cup of the fish *fumet*, then gently stir into lobster. Turn up heat slightly, so that everything now bubbles merrily and the sauce begins to reduce and concentrate flavors. Chop enough parsley to fill ¼ cup, add to the pan and continue bubbling until sauce shows definite signs of reducing, usually in about 20 minutes. In the meantime, in small bowl, work together into a smooth paste the red coral, the green tomalley, the 8 tablespoons softened butter and about 1 teaspoon of arrowroot or cornstarch.

When sauce is reduced and beginning to have a fine flavor, fish out lobster pieces and put aside. Now boil sauce hard, to concentrate flavors even more, mashing down vegetables with a spoon to provide a solid body. When everything is smooth and the flavor is coming up to brilliance, turn off heat and quickly work in the coral-tomalley mixture, until sauce is slightly thickened. Turn off heat, put back lobster pieces, stir them around to cover with sauce, then transfer everything to a tightly lidded container and store in the coldest part of the refrigerator until the evening of the dinner. This completes the first day's work. The two days of waiting will mature and actually improve the flavor.

Two Days Ahead—Classic Preparation of Basic Brown Sauce

For the Basic Brown Sauce:

Staple Items
Sweet butter (½ lb.)
Carrots (2 medium)
Yellow onions (2 medium)
All-purpose flour (about ½ cup)
Olive oil (about ½ cup)

Flavorings
Bay leaves, garlic (2 cloves), dried thyme, crystal salt, whole black peppercorns

Shopping List
Beef and veal bones, cut up by your butcher for roasting (2 lbs.)
Green Pascal celery (3 stalks)
Parsley (3 or 4 sprigs)
Tomatoes (3 medium)
Strong beef bouillon (6 cups)
Tomato sauce (1 cup)
Sherry, dry Fino (½ cup)

Prepare the sauce according to the recipe on page 232. After completing it, use it in the preparation of Shrimp à la Bordelaise (see below), which also is to be made two days before the evening of the dinner.

For the Shrimp à la Bordelaise:

Staple Items
Butter (7 Tb)
Brown Sauce (2 cups—
    see above)
Arrowroot or cornstarch
    (a few Tb)
Olive oil (7 Tb)

Shopping List
Crayfish or large shrimp,
    in their shells (16 to 24,
    depending on size)

Heavy cream (a few Tb)
Green Pascal celery (1 small
    stalk, with the leaves)
Parsley (2 sprigs)
Shallots (4)
Peeled Italian plum tomatoes
    (1 lb.)
Tomato paste (2 Tb)
Dry white wine (2 cups)
Cognac (¼ cup plus 1 to 2
    tsp)

Follow the recipe on page 232, omitting the last two steps which tell you to stir in fresh tarragon leaves and serve the hot shrimp over rice. Instead, transfer the shellfish and sauce from the cooking pan to a tightly lidded container and store in coldest part of the refrigerator until the evening of the dinner. This ends the second day's work.

The Day Before—Classic Preparation of the Shrimp Butter in About 1½ Hours

For the Shrimp Butter:

Staple Items
Sweet butter (7 Tb)
Fish *fumet* (½ cup)
Lemon juice (1 tsp)
Carrot (1 medium)
Yellow onion (1 medium)

Flavorings
Bay leaf, crystal salt,
    freshly ground black pepper

Shopping List
Fresh crayfish or shrimp in
    the shell (½ lb.)
Dark-smoked bacon (2
    rashers)
Green Pascal celery (1 stalk)
Button mushrooms (½ lb.)
    or leftover caps
Pernod (1 tsp)
Parsley (enough to fill 1
    Tb, chopped)
Tomatoes (3 small)
Tomato paste (2 tsp)
Dry white vermouth (½ cup)
Cognac (¼ cup)

Wash the ½ pound crayfish tails or medium-sized shrimp, leaving them in their shells, and set them aside. Finely chop and mix together in a bowl: the carrot, the onion, the stalk of celery, the 2 rashers of bacon and 1 crumbled bay leaf. Heat up 1 tablespoon of the butter in a small sauté pan and just soften the bacon-vegetable mixture, adding crystal salt and freshly ground black pepper to taste. Now add the ½ cup dry white vermouth and simmer, uncovered, for about 5 minutes.

Remove the stems from the ½ pound of mushrooms and reserve for some other use. (Or use the caps left over from making the *fumet.*) Finely dice the mushroom caps; peel, seed and dice the 2 tomatoes; and chop enough parsley to fill 1 tablespoon. Heat up 2 more tablespoons of the butter in another sauté pan, and as soon as it has reached gentle frying temperature, put in the mushroom caps and let them soak up the butter for hardly more than 2 minutes. Then add the tomatoes, the shrimp, still in their shells, and the ¼ cup Cognac. Flame it, and when fire dies down, add the 1 teaspoon lemon juice and the chopped parsley, then blend the entire contents of this sauté pan into the bacon-vegetable mixture. Turn up heat slightly, so that liquid bubbles merrily, to reduce sauce and concentrate flavors. Help the evaporation by frequent and gentle stirring. When liquid has almost disappeared, stir in ½ cup of the fish *fumet,* plus 2 teaspoons of tomato paste and, according to your taste, more salt and freshly ground pepper. Once the liquid returns to bubbling, lift out the shrimp and set them on a wooden cutting board. While you work on them, the contents of the sauté pan should continue bubbling.

Shell the shrimp and put shells and tails into a mortar. Pound them very hard with a pestle, until every last drop of juice is extracted. Put the juice, with the broken-up shells, into the sauté pan, disregarding the shrimp for the moment. Turn up heat under the sauté pan and boil hard, stirring continuously, for a couple of minutes, then strain the entire contents through a fine sieve, pressing down firmly with a wooden spoon to squeeze out all the aromatic juices, leaving the solids worn out and almost dry. Even so, you may not get more than ¼ to ⅓ cup of the highly concentrated, brilliantly flavored juice essence.

Now, return to the shrimp. Chop their flesh and put them, by small loads, into the mortar, pounding them with the pestle to a smooth paste, at the same time working in, bit by bit, the remaining 4 tablespoons butter. Finally, blend into this smoothest of pastes the liquid essence from the sauté pan and a dash of Pernod, then spoon it into a screwtop jar and refrigerate overnight to develop and ripen its flavors.

On the Day—About 4 Hours Before Serving—Poaching the Oysters —Active Preparation About 30 Minutes

Shopping List
Fresh oysters (2 dozen)
Dry white wine, preferably
  Alsatian Riesling (2 cups
  or a little more)

Before dealing with the oysters, remove from the refrigerator all the various parts of the great dish and let them come to room temperature: the Lobster à l'Américaine, the Shrimp à la Bordelaise and the Shrimp Butter.

Now, wash the 2 dozen oysters under cold running water and, with a stiff wire brush, scrub off any barnacles, impacted sand or seaweed. Choose a largish soup pot with a tightly fitting lid, and pour into it the 2 cups of dry white wine, or a bit more—just enough to cover the bottom of the pot about ½ to ¾ of an inch deep. Carefully stack the oysters in the pot, each with its curved shell downwards, then place the pot over high heat and rapidly bring wine to a rolling boil. As soon as pot is filled with steam, clamp on lid tightly, leaving heat full on, to build up internal steam pressure. After about 3 minutes, give pot a shake or two, to encourage oysters to open. After 5 minutes, lift lid and, using tongs, lift out all the oysters that have opened and set them aside to cool. Replace lid, shake pot again, and reopen to take out any more opened oysters. Continue in this way until all oysters have opened and are removed from pot. Turn off heat.

As soon as oysters are cool enough to handle, force off the top flat shells and discard. Leave each oyster, now plump from absorbing wine, resting comfortably in its curved inner shell. Let them stand at room temperature with the other dishes for about 3½ hours, to wait for the final assembly.

1 Hour Before Serving—Final Assembly in About 15 Minutes— Unsupervised Reheating About 45 Minutes . . .

For the Final Assembly:

Staple Items	Parsley (several sprigs)
Sweet butter (2 to 3 Tb)	Fresh tarragon, if available
	(several sprigs)
Shopping List	Black truffles (2 or 3)
Sour cream (4 ounces)	Dry white vermouth (about
Button mushrooms (½ lb.)	⅓ cup)

Preheat oven to 350 degrees. Choose a large, handsome ceramic or earthenware *timbale,* or casserole—fairly shallow (perhaps not more than 4 to 6 inches deep), reasonably wide (so that the orderly beauty of the various colorful ingredients will be perfectly displayed) and, most important, with a tight-fitting lid. The *timbale,* of course, must not be so large that it will not fit into the oven.

Now, imagine that the round bottom of the *timbale* is divided into two equal parts. Across one half, place the pieces of lobster, still in their shells, and spread their Sauce à l'Américaine evenly around and between them. Across the other half, place the whole shrimps, also still in their shells, enclosed and surrounded by their Sauce à la Bordelaise. Here, already, is a brilliant contrast of colorings. For the next full layer, put in the oysters, still in their bottom shells, and sprinkle them with a few drops of their poaching wine. Quickly sauté the ½ pound of button mushrooms in a few tablespoons butter and spread them around in the odd spaces of the *timbale.* Next, dot everything here and there with the Shrimp Butter. In a small mixing bowl, lightly beat together ½ cup of sour cream with just enough dry white vermouth to make the cream thick but still runny. Dribble it over the oysters and into odd corners. Finally, decorate everything with, first, a dozen or so thin slices of black truffle, and second, several handsome sprigs of bright green parsley and fresh tarragon. Now clamp on the lid very tightly. It must not under any circumstances be lifted again until the *timbale* is before the guests at table. Place it in the center of the oven and leave everything to get hot, so that all the flavors can blend to a marvelous finish in about 45 minutes.

Serving at Table

Bring in the *timbale,* still unopened, if possible placing it in the center of the table, where the lid can be lifted with maximum ceremony. Supply small nutcrackers for cracking the lobster claws and serve chunks of fresh-baked French or sourdough bread to mop up all the delectable sauces.

SAUTÉED FROGS' LEGS IN CREAM AND WHITE WINE SAUCE
(*Les Cuisses de Grenouilles à la Poulette*)
FOR 4 TO 6 PEOPLE

This is the classic high cuisine method of preparation, but it seemed to me when I was there that nowhere else in the world were the frogs' legs fatter, fresher, or more abundant than in the springtime in the Valley of La Grande Chartreuse. (See menu and wine suggestions on page 74.)

Staple Items	*Shopping List*
Butter (4 Tb)	Frogs' legs (2 lbs.)
Egg yolks (2, possibly 3)	Clear chicken broth (1 cup)
Lemon (1)	Parsley (1 small bunch)
Flour (about 3 Tb)	Shallots (4)
	Dry white wine, preferably
Flavorings	Chablis (1 cup)
Crystal salt, freshly ground	
black pepper, whole bay	
leaves, rosemary, thyme	

About 25 Minutes Before Serving

Into a 2-quart saucepan put the 1 cup each of chicken broth and wine, with a bay leaf, ½ teaspoon rosemary, ½ teaspoon thyme, a few sprigs of parsley, and salt and pepper to taste. Bring quickly up to boiling and put in the frogs' legs, letting them bubble gently for not more than 5 minutes. Meanwhile, mince the 4 shallots and reserve them. Lift out the frogs' legs with a slotted spoon and keep them warm, reserving the cooking bouillon. Melt the 4 tablespoons of butter in a sauté pan, add the minced shallots and quickly sauté the frogs' legs, sprinkling them with the 3 tablespoons of flour, until they are very lightly browned. Strain the reserved bouillon through a fine sieve into a 1-pint measuring jug. As soon as the frogs' legs are perfectly done, lift them out with a slotted spoon and keep them warm. Now complete the Poulette Sauce. Pour 1 cup of the bouillon into the sauté pan and bring quickly up to merry bubbling. Beat the 2 egg yolks lightly with a fork in a small mixing bowl, then beat into them one by one about 4 tablespoons of the hot liquid. Turn down heat to avoid any more boiling and, at once, vigorously work the yolks into the main sauté pan, stirring continuously until sauce begins to thicken. It should finally have the consistency of heavy cream. At first it will be too thick. Thin it by working in, tablespoon by tablespoon, more of the bouillon. Also add the juice of the lemon. If, accidentally, the sauce should become too thin, work in one more egg yolk, in exactly the same way as with the first two. When the sauce is perfect, put back the frogs' legs to absorb and be heated by the sauce—taking great care to avoid any boiling, which would curdle the sauce at once. Serve in a hot dish well sprinkled with more parsley.

MEDITERRANEAN FISH STEW WITH GARLIC MAYONNAISE

(*Bourride à l'Aïoli Provençale*)

FOR 4 PEOPLE

Fine at any time of the year, but especially good as a one-dish summer meal. (See menu and wine suggestions on page 53.)

Staple Items
Butter (4 Tb)
Lemon (½)
Mayonnaise (1 cup)
Yellow onions (2 medium)
Garlic (up to 9 cloves, accord-
ing to taste)
All-purpose flour (1 to 2 Tb)
Olive oil, green virgin (about
½ cup)
Dry white wine (1¾ cups)

Flavorings
Crystal salt, freshly ground
black Tellicherry pepper,
whole bay leaves, whole
cloves, Spanish saffron
filaments, dried or fresh
thyme

Shopping List
A selection of seasonal fish,
say, the following:
Mackerel, whole fish, with
head (about 1 lb.)
Whiting (about 1 lb.)
Eel (about 1 lb.)

(All these fish should be
boned by the fishman,
cut into largish chunks,
and the valuable heads
and bones wrapped
separately.)
Boned fillets, preferably a
mixture of cod, haddock,
flounder, sole, etc. (about
1½ lbs. in all)
Extra fish heads and large
bones, usually a gift from
the fishman (about 2
lbs.)
Orange (1, for its rind)
Small carrots (1 bunch)
Leeks, white parts only (11
medium)
Sweet Bermuda or Spanish
onions (2 large)
Tomatoes (6 medium)
White celery (1 head)
Fennel (1 head)
Fresh parsley (1 bunch)
Potatoes (6 medium)
French loaf (1 long)

About 3 Hours Before Serving (or Even the Day Before)

First, prepare a classic Provençal fish *court-bouillon*—a well-flavored fish stock. Using chopping block and small chopper, cut the 2 pounds of fish heads and bones into chunks, wash, then hold. Slit open the 11 leeks, wash out any remaining sand under fast-running cold water, cut the white parts into chunks, discarding the green, then leave soaking. Assemble and hold in a medium-sized mixing bowl: the 2 large Bermuda or Spanish onions, peeled and sliced, and the bunch of carrots, scraped and chunked. Mince finely 3 cloves of the garlic and hold, covered. Place a large soup pot of 4-quarts capacity over medium frying heat and melt in it the 4 tablespoons of butter with 2 tablespoons of the olive oil, making sure that butter does not brown. Add 4 of the cut-up leeks, plus the sliced onions and the carrot chunks, then sauté, stirring, until vegetables are lightly colored. Sprinkle in 1 to 2 tablespoons of the flour, just enough to absorb juices, and continue to brown, stirring and scraping the bottom continually, for a couple of minutes or more. Now blend in gradually, still stirring vigorously to avoid lumping, 1½ cups of the wine and 2 cups of freshly drawn cold water. Turn up heat, bringing liquid rapidly to a boil, then add fish heads and bones. If necessary, add a little more water to cover bones. Bring rapidly back to a boil, then turn down heat to gentle bubbling and add: the minced garlic, the juice of half a lemon, 2 or 3 sprigs of parsley, 2 whole bay leaves, 6 whole cloves, 1 teaspoon of dried or fresh thyme, plus plenty of salt and pepper. Continue gently bubbling, uncovered, for 1 hour or more.

While the *court-bouillon* is simmering, prepare 1 cup of homemade mayonnaise. (If you are feeling very lazy, you can use commercial mayonnaise, but a good mayonnaise is such an important part of the flavoring of a *bourride* that this is a serious compromise. Have courage! If you have never prepared mayonnaise before, now is the time to learn. It is much simpler than you think.)

Now convert your mayonnaise into a classic Provençal *aïoli* by incorporating into it as little or as much mashed fresh garlic as suits your taste. Use more than you think you will need, remembering that it will be considerably diluted by the fish broth. My own preference is for 6 cloves of garlic, crushed to a mash through a garlic press and completely blended with light strokes into the mayonnaise. Set it in the refrigerator, covered, until needed.

When the *court-bouillon* is ready, taste the liquid for proper seasoning and adjust, if necessary. It should have a good, strong, pleasantly fishy flavor. Now strain through a sieve and discard all the solids. This is the liquid base of the *bourride*. (If you are making it the day before, cool and then refrigerate, covered, overnight.) If it is to be used shortly, set it aside and let cool to room temperature.

About 1½ Hours Before Serving

Choose a lidded saucepan of about 2-quarts capacity and put into it the aromatic herbs and vegetables which will form the thickening of the stew: the 2 yellow onions peeled and coarsely chopped; the 6 tomatoes peeled, seeded and coarsely chunked; the remaining leeks, coarsely chopped; the heart of the celery, with some leaves, washed and coarsely chopped; 2 or 3 sticks of the fennel with some of the green fronds, washed and coarsely chopped; a small handful of fresh parsley; some dried or fresh thyme; 3 bay leaves, crumbled; the 6 potatoes, peeled and sliced; plus the grated outer rind of the orange, and crystal salt and freshly ground black pepper. Pour in about ¼ cup of the olive oil and set the pot over a medium frying heat. As a healthy sizzling begins, turn everything around with a wooden spoon and don't be afraid to crush down the mixture. After 2 or 3 minutes of frying, the vegetables will begin to give out their liquids, with hissing, bubbling and steaming. At this point, clamp on a tight lid, turn down the heat to rapid bubbling and let the vegetables steam until they are edibly soft, usually in 20 to 30 minutes.

Meanwhile, wash the pieces of fish under cold running water, removing any bones and skin, and set aside.

About 45 Minutes Before Serving

As soon as the vegetables are soft, mash them down again with a wooden spoon, then carefully lay all the pieces of fish on top of them. Make sure there is still plenty of bubbling liquid to provide a continuing supply of hot steam, put back the lid tightly and let the fish steam until it is just cooked, usually in about 20 minutes. Reheat the *court-bouillon* until it is just at the boiling point. Mix ¼ teaspoon of the saffron with ¼ cup of the dry white wine, bring just to the boil in a tiny saucepan, then turn off the heat and let the saffron melt into the wine.

About 25 Minutes Before Serving

Set the oven to a keep-warm temperature (150 to 175 degrees) and place in it the large serving bowl in which the golden liquid of the *bourride* will be brought to table and the open bowl or platter in which the fish and shellfish will be served separately. Cut diagonally 8 chunks of bread (each about 1½ inches thick) from the long French loaf, lightly brown them on both sides in a frying pan with a little of the olive oil, and keep them warm also in the oven. Now, working quickly, complete the "assembly" of the *bourride*. The instant the fish is done, carefully lift each piece out of the saucepan with a slotted spoon and place it on the warm serving dish in the oven, arranging all the pieces so as to make a handsome pile. Spoon the mash of vegetables and all their liquid from the pan into the jug of an electric blender and blend at high speed for only a few seconds, until you have a smoothly thick mash, which is at once poured into the large hot serving bowl from the oven. Using a soup ladle, gradually thin this mixture, bit by bit, with enough of the hot *court-bouillon* to make a soup with a texture slightly thicker than heavy cream. Now carefully blend into this liquid, first, the saffron and wine, and second, half the *aïoli*, spoonful by spoonful, stirring firmly to avoid lumping. The *bourride* will now take on its brilliant golden-yellow coloring. Check the seasonings, and carry it instantly, piping hot, to table.

Serving at Table

The *bourride* is served in four parts: the golden-yellow liquid, the pile of mixed fish, the chunks of fried bread and the rest of the *aïoli* in a sauceboat. Into each extremely hot soup bowl or plate, put first a chunk of the bread. On and around it, balance a selection of the pieces of fish. Ladle over it enough of the golden liquid to fill up the bowl or plate and act as the sauce. Each diner, then, according to his taste for garlic, spoons in more or less of the extra *aïoli*. *Bourride* is very much an informal party dish. One uses a soup spoon for the liquid and a fork to break up and spear the pieces of fish and soup-soaked bread.

LA MEURETTE—THE BURGUNDIAN STEW OF FISH IN RED WINE
(*Le Meurette Bourguignonne*)
FOR 4 TO 6 PEOPLE

This is the classic French dish which proves that red wine and fish do sometimes go together perfectly. The secret is that the Burgundians use the rich, oily-fleshed fish from their lakes and rivers to balance their rich red wines. In our saltier part of the world, we can still strike a good balance with a mixture of about 1/3 freshwater fish, about 1/3 oily-fleshed saltwater fish and 1/3 shellfish—always with some eel as an essential ingredient. In our Atlantic, Pacific and Gulf waters the principal oily-fleshed fish are chub, herring, mackerel, pompano, rockfish, salmon, sea smelt, trout and tuna. The wine for both the cooking and the drinking should be a red Burgundy, which does not preclude, of course, a sound and true Beaujolais.

Staple Items
Sweet butter (¼ lb.)

Flavorings
Crystal salt, freshly ground black pepper, whole bay leaf, whole cloves, garlic (5 cloves essential), mace, thyme

Shopping List
A balanced mixture of fresh-water, saltwater, and shell fish (see above), always with some eel, all skinned and boned (total about 3 lbs.)

Fish heads and bones (about 2 lbs.)
Leeks, white part only (3)
Bermuda or Spanish onion (1 large)
Carrots (3 medium)
Green Pascal celery, with leaves (3 stalks)
Parsley (small bunch)
Long loaf of French bread (1)
Red Burgundy wine, say a medium-priced Côte de Beaune-Villages (1 bottle)
Burgundy *marc* brandy (¼ cup)

About 1 Hour Before Serving

We use a stewpot with a tightly fitting lid. Pour into it the bottle of red wine and gently heat it up, adding the fish heads and bones, washed; the large onion, peeled and chunked; the 3 carrots, scraped and sliced; the 3 leeks, slit open, carefully de-sanded under fast-running cold water, and chunked; 1 of the cloves of garlic, peeled and finely minced; 1 whole bay leaf; 4 whole cloves; ¼ teaspoon thyme; the 3 stalks of celery, chunked, the leaves chopped; 4 whole sprigs of the parsley; plus salt and pepper to taste. Stir around and bring up to gentle bubbling, then cover and leave for 30 minutes. Meanwhile wash and trim the pieces of fish, divide into large chunks, and hold. Cut slits in the long loaf and insert butter and mashed garlic, then wrap in foil, but do not put into the oven yet.

About 20 Minutes Before Serving

Turn off heat under the now richly aromatic wine bouillon, strain out all solids and discard them. Rinse out stew pot and return wine bouillon to it, bringing liquid back to gentle bubbling. Stir in the ¼ cup of *marc* brandy, then at once add fish and keep gently bubbling, uncovered, until fish is just opaque and flaky, usually in 15 minutes. Meanwhile, turn on oven to 350 degrees and put in garlic bread. Make sure that fish keeps bubbling merrily, to distribute flavors and reduce liquid slightly. Chop enough parsley to fill ¼ cup.

Serving at Table

A *meurette* is served in the same magnificent manner as a *bouillabaisse.* The bread comes to table on a board, still wrapped in its foil. A chunk is broken off and placed in the bottom of each hot bowl, a variety of fish piled on top of it, and the red bouillon ladled over. Finally, it is all sprinkled with bright green parsley.

MUSSELS POACHED IN RED WINE
(*Les Moules Pochées au Vin Rouge*)

FOR 4 PEOPLE

The use of red wine instead of the traditional white makes this an unusual and robust dish whenever fresh mussels are in season (generally, in the United States, from October through May).

It is always a bit difficult to decide how many mussels to buy, since some fishmongers sell them by the quart and others by the pound. Roughly, 1 quart equals 1 pound, and 1 pound gives just about 2 dozen average size mussels in the shell. If you are serving this dish as an hors d'oeuvre, or first course, you should allow 15 mussels per person; double that as a main course. As a simple rule of thumb, buy 5 quarts, or 5 pounds, for a main course for 4 people. This is the amount used in the recipe below. (See discussion on page 129; menu and wine suggestions on page 128.)

Staple Items
Sweet butter (8 Tb)
Arrowroot or cornstarch (4
   Tb)
Flour (3 or 4 handfuls)

Flavorings
Crystal salt, freshly ground
   black pepper, whole bay
   leaf (1)

Shopping List
Mussels (5 lbs., see above)
Heavy cream (½ cup)
Parsley (1 small bunch)
Scallions (8) or shallots (6)
Light red Beaujolais (2 cups)

The Day Before—The Care and Feeding of the Mussels in About 30 Minutes

Clean and feed mussels according to BASIC RULE FOR CLEANING AND FATTENING MUSSELS from the recipe for Billi-Bi on page 209.

30 Minutes Before Serving—Poaching Mussels in 10 Minutes

Steam mussels according to BASIC RULE FOR STEAMING MUSSELS AND OTHER SHELLFISH, page 209, substituting the 2 cups of red Beaujolais for the white wine used in the BASIC RULE; and add an additional whole bay leaf.

Meanwhile, turn on oven to a keep-warm temperature (about 175 degrees), and heat up, for serving, 4 individual lidded casseroles.

Reserve the aromatic wine in which mussels were poached (now rich with their juices). As soon as mussels are cool enough to be handled, remove and throw away the empty tops of the shells. Now put mussels, like little boats, into hot casseroles, cover, and set in oven to keep warm. Finely mince the 6 shallots (or the 8 white scallion bulbs and ½ cup of the green scallion tops) and hold separately. Chop about 3 tablespoons of parsley and hold. Prepare a thickening *roux* by blending, in a small bowl, the 4 tablespoons powdered arrowroot (or cornstarch) with ¼ cup of the heavy cream, and hold.

15 Minutes Before Serving—Making the Sauce

This is best done in an open 8-inch sauté pan. Gently heat up, in the pan, 8 tablespoons of butter. Add the minced shallots (or scallion bulbs) and let them melt rather than brown. Carefully strain the aromatic poaching wine through a very fine sieve, add to sauté pan, turn heat on full and boil hard for a few minutes to reduce liquid by about half and to concentrate flavor. Then, turn down heat to gentle simmering and add minced scallion tops. Thicken sauce by blending in about 2 tablespoons of the *roux*. Do not add more *roux* than necessary. Now enrich sauce by adding another ¼ cup, more or less, of the heavy cream. If sauce thins, add more *roux*. When sauce has texture of pouring custard, taste and adjust seasoning. Keep heat down so that sauce remains just below bubbling point. Keep stirring continuously to avoid lumping. When sauce is perfect, pour it in equal amounts over mussels in the serving casseroles, sprinkle with chopped parsley and bring at once to table.

Serving Suggestions

This is, happily, a messy dish to eat. Do not be afraid to get the tips of your fingers slightly into the sauce. It is most convenient to pick up each mussel shell, digging out meat with a small fork and, preferably noiselessly, sucking out the sauce. There should be a separate plate on which to place the empty shells. Naturally there should also be a spoon or some chunks of French bread with which to finish the sauce. An ideal accompaniment to the poached mussels is lightly buttered rice which can be spooned into the casserole (or even used as a bed for the mussels) and which nicely absorbs the handsomely pink sauce. To stress the unusual combination of shellfish and red wine (which invariably makes conversation at table) serve with this dish a very fruity, light and young Beaujolais—preferably of last year's harvest. Many producers now label these very young wines as *Primeur*.

LAKE PIKE IN CHAMPAGNE

(*Brochet Braisé au Champagne*)

FOR 4 PEOPLE

Although pike is the perfect fish for this method, other whole freshwater fish can be used at the different seasons of the year when they are available. (Menu and wine suggestions on page 41.) Mademoiselle Ray professionally decorates her fish with flowerets of flaky pastry and hand-carved mushroom caps. Naturally these embellishments are optional. The secret trick is that the flesh of the fish is enriched by being larded with Cognac-soaked salt pork lardoons as if it were a rare piece of game meat.

Staple Items	*Shopping List*
Sweet butter (3 Tb)	Pike or other freshwater whole fish (about 4 lbs.)
Flavorings	Salt pork, cut into long strips as lardoons (about 12 strips)
Crystal salt, freshly ground black pepper	Heavy cream (about 1¼ cups)
Also: small batch of flaky pastry for flower decoration, optional (see recipe on page 197)	Fresh mushrooms (¾ lb.)
	Shallots (4)
	Dry brut Champagne (½ bottle)
	French Cognac (½ cup)

About 1½ Hours Before Serving—Active Preparation in About 20 Minutes—Unsupervised Baking for About 1 Hour

Soak the salt pork lardoons in the ½ cup of Cognac. Clean and dry the fish, then let it stand at room temperature. Choose an oval ovenproof open au gratin dish large enough to easily hold the fish. Place it over gentle heat on top of the stove and melt in it the 3 tablespoons of butter. Peel and finely mince the 4 shallots and lightly gild them in the hot butter. Turn off the heat before they brown. Preheat oven to 400 degrees and set shelf so that fish will be in the center. Lard fish on both sides with the salt pork lardoons, saving Cognac for later use. Lay fish (preferably with heads on, since it greatly helps the cooking by conducting heat inward) on its shallot bed in baking dish.

About 1 Hour Before Serving—Basting Every 15 Minutes During the Baking

Place fish in oven and let it sweat, uncovered, while the lardoons begin melting inside, for 20 minutes. Meanwhile, deal with the ¾ pound of mushrooms. Wipe each clean with a damp cloth. Remove stems, chop coarsely and hold. If you have the patience and skill, carve the mushroom caps in circular, fluted, or spiral designs. Otherwise leave them as they are—they will taste the same. Open the Champagne. At the end of the 20 minutes, working quickly, take fish out of oven, baste it with buttered shallots, lay mushroom caps around it (domes upwards), fill spaces between with chopped stems, sprinkle everything with salt and pepper to taste, pour in entire contents of half-bottle of Champagne and return to oven.

Thorough basting every 15 minutes is the vital key to the success of this dish. Preferably use a bulb baster to avoid displacing the mushrooms. After the third basting (that is, after 45 minutes of cooking with the Champagne), begin testing fish for doneness. As soon as flesh is flaky and opaque right through to center bone, it is perfectly cooked—this usually happens in about 45 minutes, although the time may vary, depending on precise size and weight of fish. Then you may (but need not) remove head and central backbone. You must, however, keep fish warm on hot serving platter while sauce is prepared. This is best done by quickly bringing oven temperature down to 165 degrees and leaving fish inside, with its serving platter lightly covered with foil. You may also have made and separately baked decorative flowerets of flaky pastry.

About 15 Minutes Before Serving—The Sauce

Use whole mushroom caps to decorate fish on its serving platter. Place all remaining contents of baking dish in jug of electric blender and turn on to high speed for a few seconds. Then transfer to a saucepan and over high heat reduce contents until everything is a smooth thick purée. Lower heat to medium and blend in as much of the heavy cream as is needed to produce a smooth and subtle Champagne sauce—usually about 1¼ cups. Check and adjust seasonings if necessary, then pour over fish. Complete decoration with pastry flowerets or in any other way that pleases you.

Preparing Flaky Pastry for Decorative Flowerets—Pâté Pour Fleurons

It is a good deal of trouble, let us admit it, to make a small quantity of flaky pastry just for some decorative flowerets. Obviously the easiest way is to use a small amount removed from some other, larger, flaky pastry job; or to buy some ready-prepared flaky pastry dough from a fancy baker; or to use the frozen flaky pastry cutouts now widely available. But if you want to make a marvelous show of your fish, prepare a batch of flaky pastry according to the recipe given on page 197 for Flaky Pastry Shell and Top, following instructions exactly for the method, through the final 2-hour chilling period. Then, finish as follows.

Final Rolling Out and Cutting of the Design in About 15 Minutes— Additional Chilling 30 Minutes or Longer

Roll out the very well chilled dough about ⅜ inch thick and cut into various shapes with cooky cutters. These can then be fluted with a small sharp knife. Place the cutouts on a cooky sheet and chill for 30 minutes or longer, until you are ready to bake them.

About 20 Minutes Before Serving—Final Glazing and Baking

Preheat oven to 450 degrees and set shelf so that cooky sheet will be in center of oven. Quickly brush flowerets with an egg yolk beaten with 1 teaspoon cold water, then bake until golden brown, crisp and thoroughly puffed up—usually in about 12 to 15 minutes. Use them for all kinds of decoration, remembering that they can also be served as part of the starch accompaniment to the main dish.

SALMON OR SALMON-TROUT IN WHITE ALPINE CRÉPY IN PASTRY CRUSTS
(*La Truite-Saumonée au Crépy sur Croûtes*)

FOR 4 PEOPLE

When Mademoiselle Ray decides to use this method with her fish, she divides it into boneless fillets or steaks and gently poaches them upon a bed of butter and shallots in the crackling white wine of the High Savoy, the Crépy, which is now widely available in the United States. Then she serves the fish with a white wine sauce on individual shells of flaky pastry dotted with black truffles. (See menu and wine suggestions on page 155.)

Staple Items
Butter (¼ lb.)
Egg yolk (1 large)

Flavorings
Crystal salt, freshly ground
    black pepper, tarragon,
    thyme

Shopping List
Salmon, or salmon-trout fillets
    or steaks (4)
Heavy cream (½ cup)
Parsley (small bunch)
Shallots (4)
Black truffle—not essential,
    but excellent if pocketbook
    allows (1)
Dry white Crépy (1 bottle)

Plus ingredients for 1 pint of fish *fumet* as described in the Epicure's Supreme Shellfish Casserole of Curnonsky on page 239.
Plus ingredients for 1 batch of Flaky Pastry Dough as described in Roquefort Cheese Flaky Pastry Pie on page 197.

The Day Before—Total Preparation of Flaky Pastry About 5½ Hours—Unsupervised Resting About 4½ Hours

Prepare the flaky pastry as described in Roquefort Cheese Flaky Pastry Pie on page 197, giving it about 6 turns and then holding it in the refrigerator until needed.

At the same time, boil the bones and heads of the fish with aromatic herbs and vegetables as described in the Epicure's Supreme Shellfish Casserole of Curnonsky on page 239 and hold this (refrigerated if it is to be held longer than 1 hour) until needed.

About 1 Hour Before Serving—Active Preparation of the Fish in About 20 Minutes—Unsupervised Baking for About 20 Minutes

First, preheat the oven to 450 degrees. Roll out the pastry once more and divide it into 4 socles or individual pedestals, each just large enough to hold one of the pieces of fish. Place them on a lightly buttered baking sheet; set them high in the oven to gild and rise, for about 12 to 15 minutes. Then set aside until the fish is baked.

While the socles are baking, choose a shallow open au gratin dish (preferably of tinned copper or enameled iron, since it must be used both on top of the stove as a fryer and in the oven) and butter it liberally. Mince the 4 shallots and spread them over the bottom of the baking dish. Over gentle frying heat on a top burner, lightly sizzle the shallots just until they are transparent—usually in about 3 or 4 minutes. Turn the oven down to 400 degrees. As soon as the shallots have begun to melt, turn off the heat, place the fillets on the shallot bed and hiss enough Crépy into the pan to half-cover the fish —so that the top surfaces will be steamed rather than poached in actual liquid. Cover the pan reasonably tight with foil, then set in the center of the oven and bake until the fish flakes easily and is just done through—usually in 15 to 20 minutes.

Next, heat up the fish *fumet* just to boiling. Thinly slice the truffle (if you have one) and begin preparing the sauce. Lightly beat the egg yolk with a fork and blend it into the ½ cup of cream. Have ready a hot serving platter. The moment the fish and the pastry pedestals are done, set the oven to keep-warm temperature, about 175 degrees, and set the door ajar to hasten the cooling down. Using a slotted spatula, carefully lift each piece of fish out of the baking dish, place it on the serving platter and keep warm, along with the flaky pedestals, in the oven. Place the baking dish with its wine juices over gentle heat on top of the stove. Quickly and thoroughly blend in the cream-egg mixture, making sure that it does not boil. Then work in, spoonful by spoonful, enough of the hot fish *fumet* to make a well-flavored sauce of the consistency of heavy cream. Add salt and pepper as necessary.

A Few Seconds Before Serving

Lift each piece of fish onto the serving platter and slide under it one of the pedestals of flaky pastry. Cover each with the sauce and decorate with the slices of black truffle. Serve instantly.

SALMON OR SALMON-TROUT POACHED IN RED WINE AS THEY DO IT IN GENEVA
(*Saumon ou Truite-Saumonée à la Genevoise*)

FOR 4 PEOPLE

In the language of a French menu, whenever you see a fish prepared à la Genevoise, it always means that it was cooked by the classic method in a light red wine. Remember, however, that the secret trick is to use a rich, oily-fleshed fish, where the slightly tannic quality of the red wine helps to cut the richness, to complement the flavor and to bring out the soft texture of the flesh. On our side the dish is generally best prepared—either with a small whole salmon for a party or with salmon steaks—during the season when truly fresh salmon is available, between April and September. (See note on page 26; menu and wine suggestions on page 25.) The poaching wine can very well be the light, fruity Gamay de Savoie (now being imported into the United States) or an equally light Beaujolais, or an inexpensive regional Bordeaux. The final contribution of all of these wines is the lovely pink-to-red color of the dish when it comes to the table.

Staple Items	*Shopping List*
Sweet butter (¼ lb.)	Salmon or salmon-trout, whole
Carrots (3 medium)	fish (say, 2½ to 3½ lbs.)
Yellow onions (3 medium)	or 4 salmon steaks (say, ½
Flour (2 Tb)	lb. each)
	Mushrooms (½ lb.)
Flavorings	Parsley (small bunch)
Crystal salt, freshly ground	Shallots (6)
black pepper	Anchovy fillets (2-ounce can)
	Light red wine, see above (1
	bottle)

About 1¼ Hours Before Serving—Active Preparation About 15 Minutes—Baking Time About 45 Minutes

Choose an open oval baking dish into which fish will fit comfortably, but do not put fish into it. Liberally butter this dish. Preheat oven to 400 degrees and set shelf so that fish will be in center. Chop the 3 carrots and 3 onions fairly fine and spread them over the bottom of the dish as a bed for the fish. Lightly salt and pepper the fish and carefully lay it on its bed. Place dish, uncovered, in oven and let fish and vegetables sweat for 10 minutes. Meanwhile, finely mince the 6 shallots and chop the bunch of parsley. After 10 minutes, take dish out of oven, sprinkle fish with all of the shallots and about 2 tablespoons of the parsley, then gently (so as not to disturb anything) pour in the bottle of red wine. Now cover dish with aluminum foil and put back into oven, turning temperature down to 350 degrees. After 10 minutes, thoroughly baste fish with the red wine, re-cover and continue simmering. After another 10 minutes, baste again, leave off aluminum foil and begin checking for doneness. Flesh of fish should flake and be just opaque. This happy state will usually be achieved within the next 5 to 10 minutes. Begin warming platter on which fish will be served. Allow 3 tablespoons of remaining butter to soften at room temperature, then thoroughly work into it 2 tablespoons of the flour. This is the classic French *beurre manié* to be used for thickening the red wine sauce. Slice the ½ pound mushrooms, lightly sauté in about 3 tablespoons of the butter, then hold.

About 5 Minutes Before Serving

As soon as fish is done, turn oven down to keep-warm temperature (150 to 175 degrees), carefully lift fish with slotted spatulas, place on serving platter and keep warm. Quickly strain the hot red wine and discard the cooked-out vegetables. Pour 1 cup of the hot red wine into jug of electric blender, add the can of anchovy fillets and blend at high speed for about 30 seconds. Pour this now salty wine into a 1-quart saucepan, add the rest of the hot red wine and bring to a vigorous boil, so as to reduce it and concentrate its flavor. Finally, turn down heat until wine is just simmering, then thicken sauce by working in, bit by bit, the *beurre manié* and vigorously stirring it around until sauce has thickened to the consistency of heavy cream. You will not necessarily have to use all of the *beurre manié*. Add sautéed mushrooms to this sauce. Sprinkle rest of chopped parsley over the fish and carry to table with the sauce served separately in a hot sauceboat. With this dish, of course, drink a light, fruity and refreshing red wine.

SUFFOCATED FILLETS OF SOLE
(*Filets de Sole à l'Étouffée*)

FOR 4 PEOPLE

The French word *étouffée* means, literally, "suffocated"—food gently poached in a pot with such a tight lid that no air whatsoever can get in. The word also appears in the Creole cuisine as *estouffade* and in the Greek as *stiffado* or *stuffado*. This is, of course, a nonseasonal dish; and sole cooked in this hermetically sealed way holds its own flavor juices and absorbs those of the herbs and vegetables. (See note on page 57; menu and wine suggestions on page 56.) Mademoiselle Ray puts her pot among the glowing embers of her log fire in the open hearth, but it works equally well in even the most modern of wall ovens.

Staple Items
Sweet butter (¼ lb.)
Yellow onions (4 medium)

Shopping List
Fillets of sole, 1 or 2 per
    person, according to size
    (about 2 lbs. total)
Fresh parsley (1 bunch)

Flavorings
Bay leaves, whole cloves,
    crystal salt, freshly ground
    black pepper

About 1 Hour Before Serving—Active Preparation About 20 Minutes—Unsupervised Suffocation in About 40 Minutes

Choose the "suffocation pot," preferably of enameled cast-iron, with an extremely tight-fitting lid and a flat bottom, large enough so that the fillets can rest easily without becoming intermingled. Place this pot over very gentle heat and melt 4 tablespoons of the butter, meanwhile slicing the 4 onions and coarsely chopping the parsley. Then add half the onion slices and half the parsley to the melted butter, plus salt and pepper to taste. Without waiting for the onions even to start sizzling, carefully and neatly place the fillets in a layer on top of the onions. Place the remaining onion slices on top of the fillets, then the other half of the parsley. Dot with the remaining butter and add 2 whole bay leaves. Place 2 whole cloves above the center of each fillet, then sprinkle top with a little more salt and pepper. Do not add any outside liquid—the juices of fish and vegetables will provide enough steam. Preheat oven to 325 degrees and place shelf so that "suffocation" will take place exactly in center of oven. Place pot in oven and do not open for first 25 minutes. Then check for perfect doneness, when fish is flaky and opaque —usually in 30 to 40 minutes.

CASSEROLE CHARTREUSE OF FRESH TUNA IN THE STYLE OF PROVENCE

(*La Chartreuse de Thon Frais à la Provençale*)

FOR 4 PEOPLE

The word *chartreuse* as used here only accidentally has anything to do with the valley of the same name, which is the home of the Auberge. A *chartreuse*, in the language of the French high cuisine, is a simple, entirely meatless vegetable dish which might be served to a group of monks in their lonely hideaway as the main dish of their Friday supper. Both the Valley and the dish take their name from their silent house in the woods, their "Chartreuse." This version is from Provence. It would be equally good if made with fresh tuna and salmon: a casserole of layered fish and aromatic vegetables cooked slowly either under the glowing embers of a wood fire or in a tightly lidded dish in a very slow oven—so that all the flavoring juices are released and are amalgamated into an irresistible perfection of aromatic freshness. (See menu and wine suggestions on page 83.)

Staple Items	*Shopping List*
Lemons (4)	Fresh tuna or salmon, in
Yellow onions (6 medium)	1-inch steaks (about 2 lbs.)
Olive oil (about ¼ cup)	Boston lettuce (2 medium
	heads)
Flavorings	Tomatoes (8 medium)
Crystal salt, freshly	Dry white wine (about
ground black pepper	2 cups)

About 3 Hours Before Serving—Active Preparation About 30 Minutes—Unsupervised Cooking About 2½ Hours

First, prepare all the various ingredients and hold each one separately. Peel and thinly slice the 6 onions. Peel, seed and slice the 8 tomatoes. Wash, dry and shred the lettuce leaves. Peel the 4 lemons (saving the peel for some other use) and cut the flesh into paper-thin slices. Choose a tightly lidded casserole or *cocotte*, preferably of enameled iron so that it can be used for frying on top of the stove and for braising in the oven, and one that is also handsome enough to come to table as the serving dish. Set it over medium frying heat, add 2 tablespoons of the olive oil and quickly brown the fish steaks on both sides, then lift them out with a slotted spatula and hold. Preheat the oven to 275 degrees. Now put into the pot half the slices of onion and let them just gild. Then add, in neat layers, half the slices of tomato, half of the shredded lettuce and half the lemon slices. Sprinkle with salt and pepper. Lay the fish steaks on this comfortable bed, then cover them with the same vegetable layers in reverse: lemon, lettuce, tomatoes, raw sliced onions, and at the end, more good sprinkles of salt and pepper. By now the various juices will have gathered at the bottom of the pot. Adjust the heat until you hear a merry bubbling from below and let it continue for about 5 to 10 minutes, to reduce the liquid and concentrate the flavors. Then, add the 2 cups of wine and bring it up quickly to the boil. When wine is boiling, put on the lid and set the pot in the center of the oven to braise, poach and steam the contents very slowly for about 2½ hours. When you bring the pot to the table, do not lift the lid until your guests are assembled—the first puff of the superb bouquet will raise their appetites to a fever pitch. This dish is equally good, hot or cold.

SECTION V

Beef
Aromatic, Small
and Tender

BARBECUED BEEF IN A PROVENÇAL BLANKET

(*Aloyau de Boeuf à la Provençale*)

SERVES 4—I HOT MEAL, I COLD

Good at any time of the year. (See notes page 57; menu and wine suggestions on page 56.)

Staple Items
Butter (2 Tb)
Yellow onions (2 medium)
Olive oil (1 or 2 Tb)
Dry breadcrumbs (about ½ cup)

Flavorings
Whole black Tellicherry pepper, dried or fresh savory and thyme

Shopping List
Beef for barbecuing, short loin or sirloin according to grade, boneless and fatless (about 3 lbs.)
Beef marrow if available (5 ounces)
Bacon, dark-smoked and lean (½ lb. to be ground, either by the butcher or at home, plus 1 lb. in thick slices)
Anchovies, either fresh whole or canned fillets (4 ounces)
Shallots (2 or 3, according to size)
Fresh parsley (small bunch)

About 2½ Hours Before Serving

Cajole your butcher into cutting you a piece of first-class barbecuing beef, of the right shape and size for your turning spit. Let it come to room temperature while you assemble the Provençal "blanket." In a large mixing bowl, assemble and work together: the ½ pound of ground bacon, the anchovies, ground or finely chopped, the 5 ounces of beef marrow, chopped (if available), the onions and shallots, peeled and minced fairly fine, the 2 tablespoons of butter, plus some chopped parsley, savory, thyme and a few grinds of fresh black Tellicherry pepper. (The anchovies take care of the salt.)

This mixture, when worked together, should be about as thick as the average bread stuffing for a turkey—thick enough to stay in place when patted onto the bacon blanket and pressed onto the outside of the beef. If it is too thick, add a tablespoon or two of olive oil. If too thin, add some dry breadcrumbs.

About 2 Hours Before Serving

Working on a flat wooden surface, make the blanket by laying down the slices of bacon vertically, each overlapping the next, until you have formed a square large enough to go around the meat but not around the ends. Next, to strengthen the blanket, lay 3 or 4 slices across horizontally. Now, using a wooden spoon and/or clean fingers, pat and press the anchovy mixture onto the blanket until it is entirely covered with a layer about ¼ inch thick. Place meat horizontally in center of blanket and carefully wrap covering around the entire turning surface—not including the ends. Now bind string around so that every slice of bacon is firmly tied into place. Heat up the rotisserie so that it will be to maximum heat when the beef begins turning. Cover the beef completely with aluminum foil (or parchment paper if preferred). Meat should be totally enclosed, including ends. Stick the spit through the beef, making sure it is properly balanced, and set it turning on the spit. According to whether you want the interior to be rare or well done, leave the beef turning for about 20 to 30 minutes per pound—or from 60 to 90 minutes for our 3-pound chunk. Inside the foil the Provençal blanket will begin melting and impregnating the meat with its salty flavor.

About 30 Minutes Before Serving

When the internal cooking time is up, usually after about an hour, carefully remove the foil (or parchment). Keep the beef turning until the bacon blanket has crisped to a mahogany brown. Remove from rotisserie and let the beef rest for 5 to 10 minutes to develop flavor. Carefully remove the string and bring the beef to table within its dramatically colored and beautifully flavored crust.

FINAL NOTE: This method of preparation is excellent with hickory chips on an outdoor smoker-type grill.

POT ROAST OF BEEF IN THE STYLE OF MADEMOISELLE VIVETTE'S FAMILY
(*Boeuf à la Mode de la Famille Artaud*)
FOR 6 TO 8 PEOPLE

This is a Provençal variation of a pot roast of beef, with a calf's foot to add body and strength to the poaching sauce, while a blend of mountain herbs and a dash of Armagnac brandy supply the aromatic flavorings. Surprisingly for Provence, there is no garlic! (See discussion on page 129; menu and wine suggestions on page 128.)

Staple Items
Butter (about 6 Tb)
Carrots (3 medium)
Yellow onions (2 medium)

Flavorings
Crystal salt, freshly
  ground black pepper,
  whole bay leaves, thyme

Shopping List
Beef for pot roast: chuck,
  or heel of round, or
  shoulder, arm or blade
  (about 3 to 5 lbs.)
Calf's foot or veal knuckle,
  split by butcher (1)
Salt pork, long lardoons to
  lard the beef (about 1
  dozen)
Parsley (small bunch)
Potatoes, small boiling (1
  to 1½ lbs. according
  to size of beef cut)
Beef bouillon (about 4 cups)
Armagnac brandy (½ cup)
Dry white wine (½ cup)

About 6½ Hours Before Serving (or May Be Prepared in Advance and Reheated)—Active Work at the Beginning and the End About 30 Minutes—Unsupervised Marination and Boiling About 6 Hours

Wash as much salt as possible from the lardoons and marinate them for at least an hour in the ½ cup of Armagnac, stirring and turning them to make sure that they absorb as much brandy as possible.

About 5½ Hours Before Serving—Preparing the Beef in About 15 Minutes

Using a French grooved and handled larding sticker, lard the beef, going right through in the direction of the grain. In a frying pan over fairly high frying heat, melt the 6 tablespoons of butter and thoroughly brown the beef on all sides. Now put it into the casserole, *cocotte,* or Dutch oven (with a tightly fitting lid, of course, of a size that will not allow too much waste space once the surrounding vegetables are in). Add the 3 carrots, scraped and cut lengthwise; the 2 onions, peeled and sliced; a *bouquet garni* of about 5 sprigs of parsley; a couple of bay leaves and 2 teaspoons of dried thyme, plus pepper to taste, but no salt yet. Next, push down among these vegetables the pieces of calf's foot. Deglaze the frying pan with a little of the bouillon and add this to the pot with the rest of the 3 cups of the bouillon plus the ½ cup of wine. Heat quickly to boiling; turn down the heat to a merry bubbling to provide plenty of steam inside the pot once the lid is on. Check the saltiness of the Armagnac which was used to marinate the lardoons. It should provide enough salt, as you add it to the pot, for the entire dish, but you can add more if necessary. Now cover the pot and keep it bubbling nicely but gently for about 5 hours (to an internal temperature of about 125 degrees). Meanwhile, prepare the potatoes, either peeling them or scrubbing the skins and leaving them on. Hold the potatoes in cold water until the moment they are due to go into the pot.

About 1 Hour Before Serving

Once more, check the seasonings in the pot and adjust if necessary. If the pot liquid is too low, add 1 cup bouillon. Add the potatoes, re-cover and continue bubbling for the final hour.

About 15 Minutes Before Serving

Set the oven to keep-warm temperature, about 175 degrees, and heat up the serving platter. Put the meat on the platter and surround it with the vegetables and any nice glutinous pieces of veal removed from the bones. Degrease and strain the liquid from the pot into a fairly wide sauté pan (the reduction works faster when there is a larger surface) and boil it hard to concentrate its flavors and thicken it, until it is reduced by at least half and has a good, thickish feel in the mouth. Pour it over the beef and vegetables and serve. This is also marvelous cold.

POT ROAST OF BEEF IN THE STYLE OF MARSEILLES
(Boeuf à la Mode Marseillaise)

SEVERAL MEALS FOR 4, OR ENOUGH FOR A PARTY OF 12 TO 16

This classic dish is hardly worth making in small quantities. For one thing, the flavor and texture of the cooked meat are much better with a largish piece of, say, 5 to 7 pounds. Smaller sizes lose their juices too quickly. The secret trick here is the use of a dry fruit brandy (instead of the more normal Cognac) to give a most delicate and subtle, vaguely fruity touch to both the meat and the sauce. In this recipe I use a very light Alsatian blackberry brandy, but one might equally use the clear dry *eaux-de-vie* (for heaven's sake, not the sweet liqueurs) of Kirsch cherry, *mirabelle* plum, or wild raspberry. A final point—the black and green olives with which the dish is garnished are not the bland, boiled-out, canned kind, but fresh olives preserved in brine or oil, weighed out from huge wooden tubs in Greek or Italian groceries where there are at least a dozen types to choose from—each with its own strong character —to bring variety to any dish.

Staple Items
Butter (4 Tb)
Egg yolks (1 to 2)
Yellow onions (3 medium)
Carrots (5 medium)
Beef bouillon (2 cups)

Flavorings
Bay leaves, 1 to 3 cloves
    garlic (to taste), parsley,
    thyme, crystal salt, freshly
    ground black pepper

Shopping List
Beef pot roast, chuck,
    sirloin, top round or
    rump, according to grade,
    (5 to 7 lbs.)
Salt pork, long solid piece
    for cutting into lardoon
    strips (¾ lb.)
Heavy cream (4 Tb)
Black olives (½ lb.)
Green olives (½ lb.)
Tomato paste (6 ounces)
Dry blackberry brandy
    (1 cup)

About 3 Hours Before Serving—Preparation in About 40 Minutes

Cut about 12 long larding strips from the salt pork and soak them in a bowl in the 1 cup of blackberry brandy. Cut more of the salt pork into large dice to fill 1 cup, then begin frying these dice to bring out their fat and crisp them. Coarsely chop the 3 onions, scrape and dice the 5 carrots, and hold, together. Finely mince as many cloves of garlic as you can stand and hold, covered. Lard the beef with the blackberry-marinated salt pork lardoons, carefully saving the brandy. Using the heel of your hand, pound the beef all over with coarse crystal salt and coarsely cracked black pepper. With a slotted spoon, remove crisp salt pork dice from frying pan and set on absorbent paper. In the hot salt pork fat in the frying pan, quickly brown the beef all around, then hold aside. Then, lightly sauté the chunked onions and diced carrots and spread them, as a bed for the meat, on the bottom of the big, tightly lidded pot in which the beef will be cooked. Place the beef on its bed in the pot. Turn on oven to 325 degrees and set shelf so that big pot will be exactly in center. Now add to pot, around and over the meat, the minced garlic, 3 to 4 whole bay leaves, about a dozen sprigs of parsley and 2 to 3 teaspoons dried thyme. Pour off excess fat from frying pan, deglaze it with the blackberry brandy in which the lardoons were marinated, then add 6 tablespoons of the tomato paste and stir until dissolved. Pour over the beef along with the 2 cups of beef bouillon. Place pot over high heat on top of stove and bring liquids up to boiling, then at once cover and put in oven. I feel strongly that the cooking should not be continued beyond the rare or, at the most, the medium-rare stage; otherwise the joyous juiciness and aromatic accents of the meat are largely lost. Personally, I stop the cooking when an internal thermometer shows 125 degrees, but for medium rare the internal temperature might be allowed to go up to 140 degrees. Cooking time is usually from 2 to 2½ hours.

About 15 Minutes Before Serving—Final Preparations

Bring oven temperature down, as quickly as possible, to 175 degrees. Carefully lift out beef and keep it warm in the oven. Skim off fat from liquid in cooking pot. Put it over high heat on top of stove and boil vigorously about 5 minutes to draw out final juices from vegetables. Then strain hot liquid into an 8- or 9-inch sauté pan (discarding the boiled-out vegetable mash) and continue boiling liquid hard, to reduce it and concentrate flavors. If you wish, it can then be slightly thickened and enriched by carefully blending in, off the fire, 1 or 2 egg yolks beaten up with 3 to 4 tablespoons of heavy cream. At the same time, in the original frying pan, quickly heat up the black and green olives by sautéing them, stirring often, in 3 to 4 tablespoons of hot butter.

Serving at Table

The beef should make a magnificent entrance by being brought to table whole on its large platter, with some of the sauce glistening over it (the rest in a sauceboat); with the black and green olives used as decorative garnish; with the diced salt pork sprinkled on as a crisp contrast; and with the beef circled, perhaps, by the classic Provençal accompaniment of grilled tomatoes.

BEEF STEW À LA SAINTE-TULLE
(Boeuf en Daube à la Sainte-Tulle)

NOT WORTH MAKING FOR FEWER THAN 8, BUT IMPROVES WITH KEEPING

This is an adaptation of a regional dish, not from the southeastern Alps, but from the southwestern truffle country of the Périgord. Near the village of Tulle, beginning in the eighth century, there was a Benedictine abbey whose monks helped to develop the agriculture of the district. Six hundred years later, when Tulle was incorporated as a town, it was known as Sainte-Tulle, in honor of the holy men who had made it famous as a farm and food center. Today, Tulle is known all over France for its blue cheese, its ducks, its pâté de foie gras, its wild mushrooms, its meat and its truffles. These last give their earthy and marvelous flavor to this classic stew. Incidentally, a daube in the French cuisine implies that the meat is cut into pieces, while à la mode is the equivalent of what we call a pot roast. (See discussion on page 152; menu and wine suggestions on page 150.)

Staple Items
Carrots (3 medium)
Yellow onions (3 medium)
Red wine vinegar (¾ cup)

Flavorings
Whole allspice, whole bay
  leaves, whole cloves, 2
  cloves garlic, a slice of
  orange peel, oregano,
  dried sage leaf,
  summer savory, thyme,
  crystal salt and freshly
  ground black pepper

Shopping List
Beef for stew—chuck or
  top round, boneless and
  fatless, cut into large
  chunks (4 lbs.)
Dark-smoked bacon (½ lb.
  of rashers)
Black truffle (1)
Green Pascal celery (1 stalk,
  with leaves)
Red wine (1 quart)

Two Days Before Serving—Preparing the Meat for Marination in About 10 Minutes

Put the chunks of beef into a covered china, earthenware, or glass dish, then add the 3 carrots and 3 onions, all chopped, the quart of red wine, the ¾ cup of vinegar, the sliced black truffle, and the seasonings: 1 teaspoon whole allspice lightly crushed in a mortar, 3 crumbled bay leaves, 1 teaspoon each whole cloves, oregano, dried sage leaf, summer savory and thyme, with salt and pepper to taste. Cover and refrigerate overnight. Stir the meat around with a wooden spoon once before going to bed, again before breakfast in the morning, and then perhaps about every 2 hours until the cooking begins.

The Day Before Serving—Preparing the Stew in About 30 Minutes With 6 Hours of Unsupervised Simmering

Remove the marinating beef from the refrigerator in good time to allow it to come to room temperature before you are ready to cook it. Choose a tightly lidded stewpot, preferably of enameled cast iron, large enough to hold the meat with the vegetables and usable also as a fryer on top of the stove. In it, over medium frying heat, fry out the rashers of bacon until they have given up most of their fat. With a slotted spoon, remove the now crispy pieces of bacon and reserve them. With a slotted spoon, remove pieces of beef from marinade and pat them dry. Quickly brown each piece on all sides in the hot bacon fat in the stewpot. As they are done, take them out and hold them. Again with a slotted spoon, take out all vegetables from marinade, lightly squeeze them in a towel to dry them, and then gently brown them also in the fat. Put back the pieces of beef into the stew pot, pour in the marinade and add 2 finely minced cloves of garlic and the piece of orange peel. Bring rapidly up to boiling, then very gently simmer (the surface of the liquid "just smiling"), tightly covered, for about 6 hours. This can be done over gentle heat on top of the stove, or in an oven at 250 degrees. Taste occasionally and adjust the seasonings. Also, watch the simmering carefully. Any heavy bubbling for this length of time might break up the meat and ruin the dish. When done, let it all cool, then refrigerate, covered, overnight.

On the Day—About 4 Hours Before Serving

Take stew out of refrigerator, skim off every trace of fat and let it come to room temperature. Shortly before serving, crumble in the reserved pieces of bacon, reheat the whole dish, or only part of it, then serve. The balance of flavors improves with repeated reheating. It can also be served cold.

THE GRAND FEASTING POT OF GOVERNOR GENERAL DE LESDIGUIÈRES
(La Grande Marmite de Lesdiguières)

FOR 12 PEOPLE

This is the modernized version of the historic one-dish winter party meal served in the sixteenth century by Governor General de Lesdiguières, who ruled the province of the Dauphiné for King Henry IV. (See discussion as to how it was originally made on page 62; menu and wine suggestions on page 67.) This dish (called a *marmite* after the huge earthenware pot in which it is cooked) is now one of the *grandes spécialités de la maison* at the Auberge and is served on cold wintry nights, when the snow is ten feet deep outside, to large parties of hungry skiers. At the Auberge it is brought to table in an enormous pottery casserole divided into seven partitions which hold the three different meats and the chickens, the huge pile of saffron rice, the traditional pickled cherries and the hot sauce. The different parts, however, can also be separated onto various platters and into serving bowls. I often prepare this *marmite* in New York as a luxurious party supper for a winter Sunday night.

Staple Items	*Shopping List*
Lemon (½)	Lean beef, rump or top round
Yellow onions (6 medium)	(4 to 6 lbs.)
	Chickens (2 whole)
Flavorings	Pigs' feet (12)
Crystal salt, freshly ground	Veal knuckle (1)
black pepper, whole cloves,	Carrots (12 medium)
freshly grated nutmeg	Mushrooms (2 lbs.)
and a *bouquet garni* of	Peeled Italian plum tomatoes
parsley, rosemary	(2 2-lb. cans)
and thyme	Red wine (2 gallons)
	Dry white wine (1 gallon)
	Cognac (1 pint)

The Day Before—Initial Preparation of the Marmite in About 7½ Hours, Including 7 Hours Unsupervised Simmering

Peel the 6 onions and stud each with a whole clove. Split the veal knuckle and the 12 pigs' feet. Scrape the 6 carrots. Then, into the bottom of a very large soup kettle (I use a lidded copper ham boiler of about 6 gallons capacity), put the chunk of beef, the slab of bacon rind, the pigs' feet and the veal knuckle, the carrots, onions and the 2 cans of tomatoes, along with the *bouquet garni* and salt, pepper and nutmeg to taste. Add the 2 gallons of red wine and the 1 gallon of white wine and bring to boiling, skimming off any rising scum, then let it all simmer very gently, covered, for about 7 hours. Then turn off heat and let pot ripen overnight on top of stove.

On the Day—Completing the Marmite in About 2¼ Hours, Including 2 Hours Unsupervised

Return the *marmite* to simmering. While it is heating up, rub the 2 chickens thoroughly with the cut side of the ½ lemon and wipe the mushrooms clean with a damp cloth. Add both to the now gently simmering stew, then carefully stir in the 1 pint Cognac, ½ cup at a time, and leave to cook, the surface of the liquid just smiling until the chicken is done, usually in a couple of hours. To accompany the *marmite,* prepare enough yellow saffron rice (see recipe page 355) and Piquante Sauce (see below) so that every diner can have his fair share. The traditional garnish at the Auberge is Mademoiselle Ray's pickled cherries, but these must be made at least 2 or 3 weeks in advance (see recipe on page 423).

Serving at Table

Serve everything extremely hot in deep soup bowls, with plenty of the richly unctuous broth poured over the meats and each bowl garnished with saffron rice, Piquante Sauce and pickled cherries.

PIQUANTE SAUCE FOR THE MARMITE

Staple Items	*Flavorings*
Sweet butter (10 Tb)	Crystal salt, freshly ground
All-purpose flour (½ cup)	black pepper
Tarragon white wine vinegar	
(1½ cups)	*Shopping List*
Dry white wine (1½ cups)	Heavy cream (2¼ cups)
Broth from the *marmite*	Shallots (16)
(1 quart)	Whole juniper berries
	(1 dozen)

About 1 Hour Before the Marmite Is Served

Skin and finely chop the 16 shallots and crush the 12 juniper berries in a mortar. Put both in a small saucepan with the 1½ cups tarragon vinegar and boil, uncovered, until virtually all the vinegar has evaporated, leaving just a wet mush on the bottom of the pan. In another saucepan, of about 2 quarts capacity, melt 8 tablespoons of the butter, then blend in the ½ cup flour and cook gently, stirring, until the mixture is golden. Now, slowly pour in, stirring all the time, 1 quart of hot broth from the simmering *marmite* and keep on cooking until the mixture is as thick as pouring custard. Blend in the 1½ cups white wine, then the aromatic mush from the small saucepan, and boil, uncovered, for about ½ hour, stirring quite regularly and removing any scum which rises to the surface.

Pass the sauce through a sieve and return to its cleaned saucepan. Gently reheat, adding salt and pepper to taste, then very gradually, tablespoon by tablespoon, blend in the 2¼ cups heavy cream. Finally, melt in the last 2 tablespoons butter. Serve as soon as possible. If this sauce has to be kept hot for longer than 5 minutes, it should be transferred to a double boiler. It must never get too thick.

SECTION VI

*Game
Feather and Fur*

GRILLED SADDLE OF CARTHUSIAN CHAMOIS OF THE ALPS
(Selle de Chamois à la Carusienne)

FOR A PARTY OF 6 TO 8 PEOPLE

The most highly prized local meat of La Vallée de La Grande Chartreuse is the Carthusian chamois, a special breed of the Alpine antelope. It is so difficult to find, leaping from rock to rock among the highest peaks, that the grilling of this marvelously flavorful, juicy and tender meat before the open fire seldom comes more than once a year, even in its home valley. While staying at the Auberge, I have tasted it only on a single occasion. Does this mean that the recipe below is utterly impossible for the United States? Not at all. Carcasses of antelope from various mountainous regions of the world are regularly imported into the United States, and I am sometimes able to get a properly butchered saddle or leg from a private midwestern source. Failing an antelope, this extraordinary dish can be prepared, with some compromise, from a leg or rack of small young venison. (See menu and wine suggestions on page 155.)

Shopping List
Saddle, leg, or loin of
    antelope, or venison (1,
    whole)
Brandy (¼ cup)
Fat salt pork, cut into long
    narrow lardoons (about
    ½ lb.)

For the Marinade in Which Meat Will Soak for 3 Days:

Staple Items	*Shopping List*
Carrots (2 medium)	Parsley (1 bunch)
Yellow onions (2 medium)	Shallots (2)
Olive oil (about ½ cup)	Dry white wine (about 2
Red wine vinegar (about	bottles, according to size
½ cup)	of meat)

Flavorings
Crystal salt, whole bay leaves,
   rosemary, thyme

For the Green Chartreuse Sauce:

Staples	*Shopping List*
Yellow onions (2 medium)	Madagascar whole green
Red wine vinegar (about	peppercorns, now avail-
¼ cup)	able at fancy food stores
	(2 Tb)
Flavorings	Shallots (2)
Crystal salt, whole juniper	Walnut oil (about 2 Tb)
berries	Green Chartreuse liqueur
	(1 ounce)

Three Days Before Serving—Active Preparation of the Marinade and Larding of the Meat in About 45 Minutes

Wash off as much salt as possible from the salt pork, then soak these lardoons in the ¼ cup of brandy for a couple of hours, stirring them around occasionally to encourage them to absorb the spirit. Meanwhile, mix the marinade. Choose a large pot or bowl into which the meat will fit fairly snugly so that you will not have to use too much wine in order to cover it. (Once, when I was marinating an enormous saddle, I used the bathtub!) Into this container put the 2 carrots, the 2 onions, the 2 shallots, all minced, 4 whole bay leaves, 2 teaspoons rosemary, 1 teaspoon thyme, plus about ½ dozen sprigs of parsley. Now moisten these aromatic ingredients with the ½ cup each of olive oil and vinegar, plus the first bottle of wine. Stir in salt (no pepper) until the liquid is pleasantly briny. Now lard the meat, using an efficient French-style needle with a wooden handle, making sure that the lardoons go in with the grain of the meat and right through the center. When they are all in, add their remaining brandy to the marinade. Now gently lower the meat into it, adding as much more wine as is needed to cover. Add more salt, as needed, to compensate for the extra wine. Now leave everything soaking for three days, religiously turning over the meat about three or four times each day.

Allow About 9 to 12 Minutes per Pound for Grilling or Roasting

Take the meat out of the marinade, wipe it dry and either grill it on a turning spit or roast it at a temperature of 400 degrees. Be careful to catch all the drippings in a tray, as they are an essential part of the sauce.

Meanwhile, prepare the sauce. Finely mince the 2 onions and the 2 shallots, then put them into a smallish sauté pan with the 2 tablespoons of walnut oil and lightly gild them over medium-high frying heat. Then, at once, hiss into them ½ cup of the marinade, spooned from the top so as to avoid any bay leaves or sprigs of parsley, etc. (If you are fussy you may prefer to first strain the marinade.) Also add to the sauté pan the ¼ cup of vinegar and then turn off the heat, covering the pan and leaving the sauce to amalgamate its flavors until the meat is ready.

About 10 Minutes Before Serving

Remember that game meats should always be served relatively rare, since overcooking can toughen them to the consistency of leather. I grill my antelope or venison to an internal temperature of 135 degrees. The meat should then be removed from the grilling spit and allowed to stand, to develop flavor, while the sauce is being finished. Put juniper berries into a mortar and coarsely crush. Deglaze the dripping pan with the 1 ounce of Green Chartreuse, plus as many extra tablespoons of the marinade as are needed to complete the job efficiently. While vigorously scraping the bottom of the drip pan, keep it reasonably hot over a top burner of the stove. When the bottom of the drip pan is clean, work its contents into the sauce in the sauté pan. Also add the 2 tablespoons of green peppercorns and the juniper berries, plus salt to taste. Now boil the sauce reasonably hard to reduce and thicken it, adding a few more tablespoons of the marinade if you wish, until you have about 2 cups of sauce with a pleasant salty-sweet flavor which is exactly right for this kind of strong meat. If necessary, strain the sauce before its final reheating and serve it in a very hot sauceboat.

SPIT-ROASTED BLACK ALPINE GROUSE
(*Le Coq de Bruyère Grillé à la Broche*)

FOR 4 PEOPLE

This is another of the great specialties of La Vallée de La Grande Chartreuse which are marvelous but which can be eaten only on very rare occasions—perhaps once or twice a year. The *coq de bruyère* flies so fast and so high among the mountain peaks that it can seldom be brought home to the kitchen. I have successfully prepared this dish in my own kitchen in New York with imported Scottish grouse, usually available from fancy poulterers during the period from Labor Day to Christmas. (See discussion of the *coq de bruyère* on page 91; menu and wine suggestions on page 96.)

Staple Items
Slices of buttered bread, to
catch the drippings (4)

Flavorings
Crystal salt, freshly ground
black pepper

Shopping List
Alpine or Scottish grouse
(2, about 1½ lbs. each)
Fatback, or fat bacon, me-
dium-thin slices (about
¾ lb.)

About 45 Minutes Before Serving—Active Preparation of the Birds
About 15 Minutes—Mainly Unsupervised Grilling About 30 Minutes

Wrap the birds in the slices of fatback or bacon. Set the grilling heat up to high. Salt and pepper each bird inside. Thread them on the spit rods so that they are well balanced. Set 2 slices of the buttered bread under each bird, so that they catch and become soaked with the drippings. Turn them until they are beautifully browned outside, while still remaining slightly rare inside—usually in 20 to 30 minutes. When serving, cut each bird neatly in half and place each half, cut side down, on the soaked bread slice. This flesh, so full of flavor, so generously juicy and so perfectly perfumed, needs no sauce whatsoever. It is ideally accompanied by buttered sautéed mushrooms.

RAGOUT OF HARE WITH GREEN CHARTREUSE
(*Civet de Lièvre à la Chartreuse*)

FOR 4 OR MORE PEOPLE, ACCORDING TO SIZE OF HARE

In France this is a dish of the fall hunting season, but in the
United States, in fancy game shops, hares are also available
throughout the cold winter months. (See notes on Alpine hares
on pages 17 and 90; menu and wine suggestions on page 16.) Our
store-bought hares are usually called "Belgian" or "Canadian,"
which does not mean that they come from those countries (any
more than a Bermuda onion comes from the island)—it's the type
of hare (or onion) that came originally from you-know-where!
Best of all, of course, is when a hunter friend brings back his own
hare.

Staple Items
Bacon, dark-smoked,
    thickly sliced (¾ lb.)
Yellow onions (3 medium)
All-purpose flour (⅓ cup)

Flavorings
Bay leaves, 2 or 3 cloves of
    garlic (to taste), juniper
    berries, rosemary, thyme,
    crystal salt, freshly
    ground black pepper

Shopping List
Whole hare, with its liver,
    see above (usually about
    5 lbs.)
Heavy cream (½ cup)
Shallots (6)
Strong red wine, perhaps
    medium-priced regional
    Châteauneuf-du-Pape
    (1 bottle)
Green Chartreuse liqueur
    (¼ cup)

*Three Days Before—Marinating the Hare—Active Preparation in
About 15 Minutes*

Assuming that the hare has already been cleaned and skinned, cut
it up into pieces as for fricassee. Hold the liver separately. Assemble
aromatics for marinade in a bowl large enough to easily hold hare
pieces: 3 crumbled bay leaves, the finely minced garlic, 1 tablespoon
crushed juniper berries, 1 teaspoon rosemary, 1 teaspoon thyme, the

3 chopped onions and the 6 finely minced shallots. Mix these dry ingredients, then pat them around pieces of hare as you pack them into bowl. Gently pour over the bottle of red wine. Cover and re-frigerate for three days, moving pieces of hare around and turning them over two or three times each day.

On the Day—About 2½ Hours Before Serving

Remove hare pieces from marinade, carefully scrape off adhering herbs and wipe flesh completely dry. Cut up entire ¾ pound of bacon slices into inch-square pieces and fry until crisp. With slotted spoon, remove crisp bits and hold. In remaining hot bacon fat, sauté hare pieces until lightly browned on all sides. Then, piling them up in frying pan, flame them with the ¼ cup of Green Chartreuse. Pack them loosely into a tightly lidded oven casserole and sprinkle them with ⅓ cup flour. Turn on oven to 325 degrees and set shelf so that casserole will be exactly in the center. Put the ½ cup of cream and the liver into the jug of an electric blender and turn on to medium-high speed for only a few seconds, until both are com-bined into a thickish purée. Blend this into the marinade, adding salt and pepper to taste, then gently pour, including all herbs, over hare pieces in casserole. Bring up quickly to boiling over high heat on top of stove, then cover tightly and place in oven to simmer until hare is done—usually in about 2 hours.

Serving at Table

Crumble the crisp bacon and sprinkle over hare on serving plat-ter. Surround with crisp triangles of fried bread and homemade noo-dles (recipe on page 354). The wine to drink can be a domaine-bottled vintage Châteauneuf-du-Pape.

SPITTED OR GRILLED PARTRIDGE
(*Perdreaux à la Broche*)

FOR 4 PEOPLE

The ideal, of course, is to have partridge brought home by the hunter. All across the United States, however, they are now avail-able, at least through the winter months, from fancy game farms and shops. Each cleaned and dressed bird (without the liver which Mademoiselle Ray can use for her partridge dishes) weighs about a pound and provides a single solid serving for a hungry diner. (See discussion of hunting birds in the Alps on page 90; menu and wine suggestions on page 25.) Although Mademoiselle Ray roasts her birds in front of a wood fire, they can equally well be cooked on a rotisserie, under a grill, or in a hot oven. In each case, one should make sure to catch the highly flavorful drippings, which are usually spread on a toasted bread canapé and placed under the bird on the dinner plate. This operation is known in France as the *lèchefrite*—literally, the "lickfry."

Staple Items
Sweet butter (about ½ lb.)
Canapés, square slices of white
    bread, golden-fried in
    butter (4)

Flavorings
Crystal salt, freshly ground
    black pepper

Shopping List
Partridges, cleaned and trussed
    (4, each about 1 lb.)
Salt pork lardoons (24), each
    about 6 inches long
Sour cream (½ pint)
Crisp eating apples (4
    medium)
Sweet black grapes (bunch of
    about 1 lb.)
Filberts or hazelnuts, in the
    shell (16)
Dry Kirsch cherry brandy
    (½ cup)

About 1 Hour Before Serving—Active Preparation About 30 Minutes —Spit-Roasting Time About 20 Minutes

Marinate the 24 salt pork lardoons in the ½ cup of Kirsch cherry brandy. Pit and skin the grapes—best done by cutting them in half— then hold them aside. In a sauté pan, melt 4 tablespoons of the butter. Peel and core the 4 apples, cut each into 8 segments and gently fry in the hot butter until golden. Shell the 16 nuts, grate them and add to the apples in the hot butter, stirring around until nuts also are lightly browned. As butter is absorbed, add more, tablespoon by tablespoon. Then add grape halves. Drain Kirsch from lardoons and add Kirsch to sauté pan and flame. Turn down heat under sauté pan to keep warm and cover.

Lard partridge with salt pork, using 2 lardoons on each side of breast, and 1 lardoon—cut in half and inserted into two incisions—on each leg. (This uses up 6 lardoons for each bird.) Spit and rôtisse partridges (or grill, or bake at high heat), being careful to catch and save the drippings. (If it is possible to put one of the canapés under each turning bird so as to catch the drippings directly onto the bread, so much the better.) Never overcook partridges, or they will dry out. Average time on a turning spit is 20 minutes, but this depends on the age of the bird. Watch them carefully—they must remain juicy.

About 15 Minutes Before Serving

Complete the garnishing sauce by reheating the sauté pan and carefully blending in enough of the sour cream to absorb and thicken the juices. Taste and blend in crystal salt and freshly ground black pepper as needed. When partridges are done, remove trussing strings, balance each bird on top of a canapé with the drippings and pile the garnishing sauce at the side of the plate. The ideal additional accompaniment is matchstick potatoes.

MEAT PIE OF WILD BOAR
(*La Tourte de Marcassin*)

FOR 4 PEOPLE

Of all the recipes printed here, this is perhaps the most difficult to reproduce exactly on this side of the Atlantic. There is something quite marvelous about the meat of a young wild boar that has spent its life feeding on the aromatic plants and roots of the Alpine mountains, then is hung for a few days in Mademoiselle Ray's store room and afterwards marinated. Only then does it give up the best and tenderest of its back strip of lean meat for this extraordinary double-crust flaky-pastry meat pie with the corners filled with an aromatic *velouté* sauce of cream and eggs. It is possible, however, sometimes to get boar meat from specialty butchers or game dealers, and then I have been able to prepare a reasonable reproduction of this very savory *tourte*. It is served with a red wine Bordelaise sauce. (See menu and wine suggestions on page 117.)

Staple Items
Heavy cream (1 Tb)
Egg yolk (1 large)
Butter (about 1 Tb, for butter-
    ing layer pan)

Flavorings
Crystal salt, freshly ground
    black pepper, chervil,
    oregano, savory, thyme

Shopping List
Entirely lean wild boar meat,
    from the tenderest part of
    the black sirloin strip, cut
    into thin slices (1 lb.)
Cognac (½ cup)

Plus one batch of Flaky Pastry for a double-crust pie, as described in Roquefort Cheese Flaky Pastry Pie on page 197:

Sweet butter, chilled (10
    ounces—2½ cups)
Egg yolk (1, for glaze)

All-purpose flour (1½ cups)
High-gluten flour (½ cup)
Salt (1 tsp)

Plus ingredients for the Velouté Sauce, to fill the internal spaces of the pie:

Heavy cream (¼ cup)
Eggs, whole (2 large)

Plus 1 pint of red wine Sauce Bordelaise as described below.

Earlier in the Day or Even the Day Before—Mixing, Rolling and Resting the Flaky Pastry

Prepare a standard double-crust batch of flaky pastry as described on page 197. After it has had its six turns, with proper resting in between, it can be stored, wrapped in wax paper, in the refrigerator until needed.

About 3 Hours Before Serving—Putting the Meat into the Marinade —in About 5 Minutes—Unsupervised Marination for About 2 Hours

Cut the thin slices of boar meat into pieces about 2 inches by 2 inches. Place them in a bowl and pour over them the ½ cup of Cognac. Add salt and pepper to taste, plus 1 teaspoon each of the chervil, oregano, savory and thyme. Stir everything around and leave to marinate for about 2 hours.

About 1 Hour Before Serving—Active Construction of the Pie in About 25 Minutes—Unsupervised Baking for About 35 Minutes

Choose a 9- or 10-inch layer cake pan and butter it well. Divide the flaky pastry into two halves and roll out the first half about ¼ inch thick into a round large enough to line the bottom and sides of the pan. Preheat the oven to 425 degrees. Neatly place the marinated wild boar slices across this pie shell, leaving an outer circle of about 1 inch of naked pastry. Moisten the meat by sprinkling on a tablespoon or two of the Cognac marinade. Roll out the second half of the flaky pastry, also about ¼ inch thick, then cover the pie with it. Lightly beat the egg yolk with the 1 tablespoon of cream and use this mixture firmly to glue together the edges of the pie crust all around. Roll the edges together and pinch them with your fingers. Make a hole exactly at the center of the top and mold the pastry into a small chimney. Using a small, sharp-pointed knife, lightly cut a decorative design in the top, either circles or pinwheels or radiating star lines, then liberally paint the top with the rest of the egg-cream mixture. Place the pie in the center of the oven and let it bake for exactly 15 minutes.

Meanwhile, prepare the Sauce Velouté for the inside of the pie and the Sauce Bordelaise to pour over it at serving time. Break the 2 eggs into a mixing bowl and add the ¼ cup of heavy cream, with salt and pepper to taste. Beat thoroughly until it is fluffy and light. Precisely at the end of the first 15 minutes of baking, using a small funnel, run this sauce into the pie through the central chimney. You may have to use all of the sauce, or the pie may fill up before it is all in. This depends on the expansion of the pastry. Now put the pie back in the oven and leave it until the top is nicely gilded—usually in not more than another 20 minutes.

Meanwhile, prepare the Sauce Bordelaise as detailed below. Finally, serve the *tourte* very hot with the red wine sauce brought to table separately in a hot sauceboat. An ideal vegetable accompaniment to this dish is the Eggplant Baked in Cream on page 368.

SAUCE BORDELAISE
FOR 4 PEOPLE

This is one of the most universal and useful meat sauces made with French red wine. It is excellent with all kinds of grilled steaks and oven roasts.

Shopping List   Shallots (2)
Beef marrow, if available (¼   Good red wine (½ cup)
   lb.)
Parsley (enough for 1 tsp,
   chopped)

Plus 1 cup of Brown Sauce prepared as described in the recipe for Crayfish or Shrimp à la Bordelaise on page 232.

Finely mince the 2 shallots and put them into a small saucepan with the ½ cup of red wine. Boil hard until the wine reduces to about one quarter of its volume and is just beginning to glaze and thicken. Work in the 1 cup of Brown Sauce and simmer gently for about 10 minutes. Meanwhile, drop the beef marrow into hot but not boiling water; as soon as the marrow is firm enough to handle, lift it out with a slotted spoon and dice it on a cutting board. Stir these dice into the sauce. At the last moment before bringing it to table, stir in the 1 teaspoon of chopped parsley and check for seasoning, adjusting if necessary.

SECTION VII

Goat

YOUNG SPRING KID STEWED WITH WILD MUSHROOMS

(Daube de Jeune Chevreau de Printemps aux Morilles)

FOR 4 PEOPLE

This is a happy alternative method to the grilling of a young kid (see Lamb, page 298) in which the maximum flavor is brought out by slow aromatic poaching. It is called a *daube* because the meat is not pot-roasted whole but cut into sizeable chunks. In the Valley of La Grande Chartreuse, of course, they garnish the meat with the local wild black mushrooms called *morilles*, or morels. I find I do fairly well with our large domesticated mushrooms. (See menu and wine suggestions on page 77.)

Staple Items	Shopping List
Butter (7 Tb)	Boned lean meat of young kid
Yellow onions (2 medium)	(about 3 lbs.)
Flour (about 2 Tb)	Sour cream (½ to ¾ cup)
	Large mushrooms (1 lb.)
Flavorings	Shallots (4)
Crystal salt, freshly ground	Parsley (1 small bunch)
black pepper	Dry white wine (1 cup)

About 1 Hour Before Serving—Active Preparation About 30 Minutes —Unsupervised Simmering About 30 Minutes

Preheat the oven to 350 degrees. Cut the meat into the neatest possible pieces, each weighing about ¼ pound. Lightly flour each piece. Finely mince the 2 onions and the 4 shallots, reserving them separately. Choose a lidded casserole or *cocotte* which can be used on top of the stove over fairly high frying heat. Melt in it the 7 table-spoons of butter, then quickly sauté the pieces of meat, at the same time sprinkling them with the minced onions, until the meat is lightly browned. Then turn down the heat to medium frying, add the minced shallots and let them just gild, turning the meat over and over to absorb flavor. Pour in the cup of wine and bring it up to boil-ing. As soon as the wine boils, cover the casserole and put it in the center of the oven to stew until the meat is very soft—usually in about 30 minutes.

When the meat is just done, put the casserole back on top of the stove over medium heat, adding the cleaned mushrooms, which should be allowed to stew merrily for not more than 10 minutes. Leave off the lid during this process, so that the sauce will boil down and reduce, thus concentrating the flavors.

Just Before Serving

Finally, thicken the sauce by working in the ½ cup of sour cream (or a bit more, if necessary, to achieve proper thickness), then taste and season with salt and pepper as necessary. Serve directly from the casserole or from a hot dish, with everything well sprinkled with bright green chopped parsley.

SECTION VIII

Lamb

YOUNG SPRING LAMB OR KID, SPITTED AND GRILLED

(*Agneau ou Chevreau de Printemps, Grillé à la Broche*)

ANY NUMBER, ACCORDING TO SIZE OF CUT

This basic technique will work either with a whole baby lamb (which Mademoiselle Ray often prepares in the spring and as I sometimes do at Easter time in New York), or for a leg with the main bone in, or for a boned and rolled shoulder. The leg is the most practical for year-round menu planning, so I give this version below, but it will immediately be obvious how the method can be adapted to other cuts or to the whole baby animal. The method applies to a spring baby kid either whole or in cuts. At the Auberge, naturally, they use a fruitwood fire in the great open hearth, but I use either a charcoal grill on the terrace or, indoors, the electric rotisserie in my all-glass oven. If you decide the first time to try a leg of lamb, get one that is short and fat, with the flesh a light rosy tan rather than a brownish dark red. Leave in the shank bone at the narrow end as a handle for later carving, but the bone at the wide end should be removed from the knee joint. Then push through the spit rod close to the shank bone, making sure that the weight of the leg is nicely balanced as the spit turns. (See discussion on page 75; menu and wine suggestions on page 74.)

Staple Items
Olive oil (about ½ cup)

cloves), oregano, rosemary, savory, thyme

Flavorings
Crystal salt, freshly ground black pepper, garlic (4

Shopping List
Leg of spring lamb, or other cut, see above (4 to 7 lbs.)

The Day Before—Preparing the Meat in About 10 Minutes for Overnight Marination

Peel the 4 garlic cloves and slice each lengthwise into 3 or 4 slivers. Push 2 or 3 deeply into the space alongside the shank bone.

298

Place others in the space left by the removal of the knee bone. For the remaining slivers, make ½-inch-deep cuts here and there in the thickest parts of the flesh and push slivers in. Mix together 1 teaspoon each of the oregano, rosemary, savory and thyme, then press small amounts into the cavities with the garlic slivers and into any other available interior spaces. Now, thoroughly rub the meat all over, almost as if massaging it, with the olive oil, letting some dribble into the spaces with the garlic and herbs, where it will encourage the infusion of the flavoring oils. Finally, tightly wrap the meat in aluminum foil and refrigerate overnight.

On the Day—At Least 5 Hours Before the Grilling Is To Begin

Unwrap the meat and again massage it with more of the olive oil. Leave it, uncovered, to come to room temperature.

Between 2 and 3 Hours Before Serving—According to Weight of Meat

For the finest flavor, juice and texture, young lamb should always be grilled to a medium-rare pink; this means, with the grill heat at about 400 degrees, a timing of about 15 minutes to the pound—with a final central internal temperature of 130 degrees. Push the spit rod through alongside the shank bone and bring it out at the other end at a point which ensures an even turning balance. Only after the meat has formed a good crust—when the spit has been turning for about 20 minutes—should the salt and pepper be patted on. After the grilling is complete, the roast should rest for 20 to 30 minutes in a warm place to develop flavor and texture.

Carving and Serving at Table

Using a cloth or glove, I hold the shank bone in my left hand and, following Mademoiselle Ray's French method, cut fairly thick slices, on the slant, from the fleshy side—1 slice per person. Then, again following the thrifty French method, I cut 1 small slice per person from the narrow shank end. (Mademoiselle Ray calls each of these *La Souris*—"The Mouse.") Be sure to catch all the magnificent juices and spoon a tablespoon or two over each serving. Always keep the meat in a warm place to be ready for second servings.

SURPRISE PACKETS OF LAMB AND TRIPE AS THEY DO IT IN MARSEILLES
(*Pieds Paquets à la Marseillaise*)
FOR 4 TO 6 PEOPLE

This is probably the least well known of all French regional specialties—a hearty, "rib-sticking," peasanty, extremely inexpensive Sunday-night-supper-style one-dish meal—best for cold winter nights. (Menu and wine suggestions on page 64.) Mademoiselle Ray served it to parties of young skiers from a huge black iron "witches' cauldron" hanging from a hook above the log fire in the open hearth. The dish works equally well in an enameled-iron casserole in the oven or in a big stewpot on top of the stove. It is one of those dishes that gets better and better the longer it is simmered and then goes on improving the longer it is kept.

Staple Items
Carrots (3 medium)
Yellow onions (2 medium)

Flavorings
6 garlic cloves (they disappear
    in the long cooking)

Shopping List
Prime young tripe, in sheets,
    for cutting at home into
    squares (4 to 5 lbs.)
Lambs' feet (8)
Knuckle of veal (1)
Salt pork (½ lb.)
Bacon, dark-smoked, thickly
    sliced (½ lb.)
White leeks (2)
Fresh parsley (1 bunch)
Beef bouillon (1 quart)
Dry white wine (1 quart)

Best Made in Advance and Reheated—Active Preparation About 30 Minutes—Unsupervised Simmering at Least 4 Hours

Finely mince the 6 cloves of garlic, chop the entire bunch of parsley and hold both. Slice the 3 carrots, coarsely chop the 2 onions and the 2 white leeks and set them all aside. Cut tripe into neat 4-

inch squares and soak in cold water while you prepare stuffing. Pass the ½ pound salt pork through coarse cutter of meat grinder, then assemble it in a mixing bowl with the minced garlic and the chopped parsley, plus plenty of salt and pepper. Mix thoroughly. Now dry the tripe squares and fold each into a small envelope—with 4 flaps, like the envelope for a small Christmas card—and fill each with about 1 tablespoon of the aromatic stuffing. Tie each filled envelope with string and hold for the moment.

This is the kind of dish that you "construct" in its tightly lidded big pot. Line bottom with the ½ pound of bacon slices. On top of this make a layer of the sliced carrots, the chopped onions, the chopped leeks, plus more salt and pepper. Wash the 8 lambs' feet and criss-cross them over the vegetables. On top of the lambs' feet, balance the tripe surprise packets. Put pot on fairly high frying heat on top of stove and, when the bacon on the bottom is thoroughly sizzling, pour in the quart of beef bouillon and the quart of wine. Bring quickly up to boiling, then turn down heat to gentlest simmering (as French cooks say, "just smiling" on the surface), put on tight lid and keep simmering, either on top of stove or in the oven, for at least 4 hours. The soup will be gradually thickened by the gelatin from the feet, and all the flavors will develop and blend in a quite marvelous way.

Serving at Table

This dish requires, of course, an extremely informal service. Ladle the soup into large bowls, adding some of the surprise packets (with string removed) and a complete lamb's foot, bone and all. For slightly more formality, first remove the gelatinous meat from each lambs' foot. Serve with it a light refreshing wine of Provence, or the gay red Gamay de Savoie, or a good Beaujolais.

SECTION IX

Mutton

MADEMOISELLE RAY'S LEG OF MUTTON OF THE SEVEN HOURS

(*Gigot de Mouton de Sept Heures*)

FOR 4 TO 6 PEOPLE

This can, of course, be prepared with a leg of lamb, but there is rather more of an aromatic flavor in the older flesh of the mutton, which can nowadays be ordered from specialty butchers. For this dish, it is boned and poached in dry white wine, with the flavorings of smoky bacon, aromatic vegetables and a knuckle of veal to enrich the sauce, which is finally flamed with Armagnac. The ideal accompaniment is a dish of the White Beans of Soissons (page 364) and a fine bottle of red Bordeaux. (See discussion on page 94; menu and wine suggestions on page 93.)

Staple Items
Sweet butter (3 Tb)
Bacon, thick-sliced, dark-smoked (1 lb.)
Carrots (6 medium)
Green peppers (2 medium)
Sugar (1 Tb)

Flavorings
Crystal salt, freshly ground black pepper, garlic (2 cloves)

Shopping List
Leg of mutton or lamb, boned (about 5 to 7 lbs.)
Knuckle of veal, cut in half (1)
Beef bouillon (2 cups)
Eggplant (2 medium)
Onions, small white boiling (2 lbs.)
Tomatoes, medium, skinned, or Italian plum, peeled (2 lbs.)
Dry white wine (2 cups)
Armagnac brandy (¼ cup)

About 8 Hours Before Serving—Active Preparation in About 1 Hour —You Guessed How Much Unsupervised Poaching

Open up the boned leg and, into all the odd corners and spaces left by the removal of the bones, neatly tuck slices of bacon, using about ¾ pound. Make sure that, as the bacon melts, its smoky flavor will be absorbed into every part of the meat. Then tie it all up with

304

string into a neat package. Choose if possible a tightly lidded large oval *cocotte*, preferably of enameled iron, which can be used as a fryer on top of the stove and can then go into the oven. Set it first over medium-high frying heat and melt in it the remaining ¼ pound of bacon cut into inch squares. As soon as the bottom is covered with fat, put the meat in to brown on all sides, then take it out and brown the two halves of the knuckle of veal. Then put back the meat and begin packing the vegetables around it: the 2 pounds of tomatoes, the 6 carrots, scraped, the 2 green peppers, quartered, the 2 eggplants, thickly sliced, plus the 2 cloves of garlic, finely minced. Turn down heat and let all this simmer and sweat, covered, so that the juices will flow and intermingle, on top of the stove for about half an hour. Meanwhile, skin the 2 pounds of white onions. In a sauté pan over medium-high frying heat, melt the 3 tablespoons of butter, then sprinkle in the 1 tablespoon of sugar and quickly brown the onions. Preheat the oven to 250 degrees.

7 Hours Before Serving

Combine the 2 cups each of wine and beef bouillon and bring them just to the boil. Using a slotted spoon, neatly pack the onions around the meat in the main *cocotte*, then pour over the boiling wine-bouillon, season with salt and pepper to taste, put on the lid and place the *cocotte* in the center of the oven. Let it cook, as slowly as possible, for 7 hours.

Serving at Table

Have ready a large, very hot platter. Remove the string from the meat and place it in the center of the platter. Neatly surround it with all the vegetables. Preferably using a bulb baster, remove as much as possible of the fat from the *cocotte*, then ladle the wonderfully aromatic meat and vegetable juices over everything on the platter. To try to thicken this natural sauce would be a crime. At the last moment, at table, warm up the Armagnac to just above blood heat, pour it over the meat and flame it. Then carve into fairly thick slices.

SECTION X

Pork
Les Cochonnailles

WHOLE COUNTRY OR SMITHFIELD HAM BAKED WITH MADEIRA

(*Jambon Crû de Montagne au Madère*)

FOR 8 TO 12 PEOPLE, ACCORDING TO SIZE OF HAM

Mademoiselle Ray, of course, uses the sun-dried hams of the Alpine mountains, which are similar in some ways to our great American Smithfield. A raw Smithfield ham would fit beautifully into this recipe. Or you could use a genuine "country ham," available from fancy food stores or direct by mail from farm producers in many states. Do not, however, use one of those mass-produced standard supermarket hams, which are bland, too soft in texture, and are deliberately injected with water, allegedly to keep them "moist." In this recipe the ham is finally covered, not with the usual coating of molasses and mustard, but with the French Sauce Anglaise. This is a savory paste which decorates as well as flavors the ham and is not to be confused with a Crème Anglaise, which is a dessert egg custard!

Staple Items
Butter (8 Tb)

Flavorings
Freshly ground black pepper, whole allspice, whole bay leaves, whole cloves

Basic Ingredients for Sauce Velouté:

Butter (4 Tb)
All-purpose flour (4 Tb)
Strong chicken bouillon (2 cups)
Crystal salt

Shopping List
Smithfield or country ham, uncooked (usually 10 to 16 lbs.)
Anchovy paste (a few tsp)
Clear honey (1¼ cups)
Mushrooms (2 lbs.)
French Dijon mustard (5 Tb)
Tomato paste (5 Tb)
Madeira, dry Sercial (1¼ cups, or more to taste)
Sherry, dry Fino (1 bottle)

Plus Basic Ingredients to Convert Sauce Velouté to Sauce Anglaise:

Eggs, hard boiled (4)   Lemon juice (a few tsp)

The Day Before—Preparing the Ham in About 30 Minutes and Simmering It, Unsupervised, for Several Hours

Prepare ham according to maker's instructions, then lay it, skin-side down, on the bottom of a large deep pan. Thoroughly moisten ham by dribbling all over it about ⅓ of the bottle of Sherry; allow it to soak for 5 minutes. Then dribble on, next, ⅓ of the Sherry and let it soak 5 minutes more. Then add the remaining Sherry and again leave it for 5 minutes. Now moisten ham with ½ cup of the honey and let it soak 15 minutes, meanwhile adding the flavorings: 2 teaspoons whole allspice, 5 whole bay leaves, 2 teaspoons whole cloves. After the 15 minutes, turn stove heat on high (it will probably be necessary to use 2 burners to distribute heat to such a large pan) and run in freshly drawn cold water—at side of ham so as not to disturb honey—until the level of liquid is about ¾ of the way up the ham. Heat to gentle simmering, then at once run in more cold water, again at the side, until the liquid gently laps over ham and rises to about ½ inch above it. Continue with heat on full until it returns to gentle simmering. It is absolutely vital that the liquid should not bubble at any time but should gently simmer, "just smiling." With such a large quantity of water, the heat will have to be turned down slightly several times. Cover and keep simmering gently for a total time calculated at 20 minutes per pound. Then turn off heat and leave ham soaking in the cooking liquid overnight to absorb flavors.

About 2 Hours Before Serving—Active Preparation in About 1 Hour Plus 1 Hour of Relatively Unsupervised Baking

Take the ham out of its cooking liquid, skin it, score the fat into the usual diamond shapes, stick a whole clove into the center of each diamond and place ham on a roasting pan in the oven at about 200 degrees to begin to warm up.

Meanwhile, prepare a Sauce Velouté and convert it into a Sauce Anglaise. Begin by making a classic velouté.

BASIC RULE FOR SAUCE VELOUTÉ: In a 2-quart saucepan melt the 4 tablespoons of butter and work in the 4 tablespoons of flour. While they are gently cooking together, heat up in another pan the 2 cups of strong chicken bouillon. When the butter-flour *roux* is perfectly smooth, begin working in the chicken bouillon dash by dash, stirring all the time. Blend in salt to taste. Let this *velouté* simmer very gently to develop flavor and thicken. As *velouté* simmers, skim off any liquid butter which may rise to the top. Continue simmering until *velouté* is quite thick—usually in about 30 minutes. Then pass it through cheesecloth or a fine strainer. This is your Sauce Velouté.

Now convert the *velouté* into the Sauce Anglaise.

BASIC RULES FOR CONVERTING SAUCE VELOUTÉ TO SAUCE AN-GLAISE: While the *velouté* is simmering, hard-boil the eggs and cut them into small dice. When the *velouté* is ready, work the diced eggs into the sauce, with enough of the anchovy paste and the lemon juice alternately, teaspoon by teaspoon, to give it a good salty-sour flavor, brought up with a pinch or two of pepper and a few grinds from the nutmeg grater. This Sauce Anglaise should be thick enough so that it may be dribbled without running over the ham. If it is not thick enough, continue bubbling it over medium heat, stirring continuously, until the right consistency is achieved. Finally, work in ¼ cup of the honey and 3 tablespoons of the mustard.

Take the ham out of the oven and put up the oven temperature to 350 degrees. Thickly dribble the top of the ham with the Sauce Anglaise, using a small, flexible spatula to spread it evenly, but taking care not to disturb any of the cloves. Put ham in its roasting pan back in the center of the oven and let.it glaze and heat for about 1 hour. Combine 1 cup of the Madeira with the remaining ½ cup of the honey and 2 more tablespoons of the mustard, then baste the ham every 15 minutes with this mixture.

About 15 Minutes Before Serving—The Mushrooms and the Madeira-Tomato Sauce

Wipe clean the 2 pounds of mushrooms and separate stalks from caps. In your largest sauté pan, melt the remaining 8 tablespoons butter and quickly sauté the mushroom caps, then remove them with a slotted spoon and set them aside to keep warm. While mushrooms are sautéing, quickly chop the mushroom stalks. As soon as caps are re-moved from sauté pan, put in the chopped stalks, stir them around, then begin working in the 5 tablespoons of tomato paste. As sauce bubbles and begins to thicken, stir in about ¼ cup of the Madeira and about the same amount of pan juices from the ham. Keep stirring the bubbling sauce until it thickens again. You may add more Madeira and pan juices, tablespoon by tablespoon, until the flavor of the sauce is exactly to your taste. It should not be salted; there will be enough salt from the ham.

Serving at Table

Carve the ham into fairly thick slices, so that each guest gets a share of the now-crusty Sauce Anglaise. Cover the slices with the tomato sauce and garnish with the mushroom caps. An ideal accompaniment is puréed spinach, which could be spooned in little piles into the upturned mushroom caps.

PORK FILET BRAISED IN CREAM WITH PORT
(*Le Filet de Porc Braisé à la Crème*)

FOR 4 PEOPLE

This is one of the near-perfect ways of cooking pork until it melts in the mouth, with the concentrated richness of the cream and the aromatic subtlety of the wine. Remember to allow about 1 pint of the cream-Port mixture per pound of meat.

Staple Items
Butter (about 4 Tb)
Light cream (3½ cups)
Yellow onions (2 medium)

Flavorings
Crystal salt, freshly ground
  black pepper, basil, whole
  coriander seed, fennel seed,
  garlic, marjoram

Shopping List
Pork fillet steak, without bone
  or rind, about 1½ inches
  thick, preferably cut from
  the leg (2 lbs.)
Boiled ham (¼ lb.)
Port, ruby (½ cup)

About 2½ Hours Before Serving—Active Preparation About 30 Minutes—Unsupervised Simmering About 2 Hours

This should be prepared in a heavy casserole (preferably enameled cast iron) on top of the stove. Do not use a thin aluminum, copper, or stainless steel pan because toward the end, as the cream begins to thicken, there is always the danger of burning or scorching. Finely mince 1 clove of garlic, the 2 onions and the ¼ pound of ham, re-serving them separately. Place the casserole over medium-high frying heat and melt in it the 4 tablespoons of butter. Lightly sauté the ham and onions. Place the pork steak on a wooden board and sprinkle the top side with the minced garlic, a couple of pinches of basil, about 6 whole coriander seeds, with a pinch each of fennel and marjoram. When ham and onions are golden, turn off heat, remove them with a slotted spoon and spread evenly over the pork. Now roll it up like a jelly roll and tie with string. Using the heel of the hand, pound into its outer surface crystal salt and coarsely ground pepper. In a separate saucepan, bring the 3½ cups of cream almost to the boil. Again turn on heat under casserole to medium-high frying and quickly brown pork roll on all sides. Then pour in hot cream and add the ½ cup of Port, stirring to mix. Adjust heat to bring liquid up to gentlest simmering. Finely mince another clove of garlic and drop into the cream. Continue gently simmering, uncovered, turning meat over after the first hour, until liquid has boiled down to a thick cream —usually in about 2 hours. A golden skin will form, of course, on top of the cream. This is an essential part of the cooking process and it should not be broken during the first hour.

About 1 Hour Before Serving

Now, break up the skin and scrape all the congealed cream from the sides of the casserole, stirring all the bits down into the liquid, which should now be just beginning to thicken. Again, turn over the meat and thoroughly baste it with thick cream. Continue very gently simmering.

About 30 Minutes Before Serving

The pork should now be covered by a golden crust and the liquid should be becoming very thick at the bottom of the casserole. From this point on, watch everything carefully; if the liquid should dry out, there would be a serious danger of the flavor being ruined by burning. Stir the cream often, around and over the meat, scraping the bottom to make sure that nothing is sticking. The meat may be turned, to keep it warm on all sides.

Serving at Table

When the cream is thick enough, the dish is ready to serve. (If a smoother sauce is desired, purée in an electric blender.) Place the pork roll on a warm platter and cover it with the cream that has been spooned and scraped from the bottom of the casserole. The meat will be crusty on the outside, melting and moist inside; and the cream will have a marvelous concentration of all the flavoring juices. It is all equally good served cold the next day.

THE SAUSAGES OF THE VALLEY AND THE AUBERGE

Once you have tasted the homemade sausages of the Valley of La Grande Chartreuse, you will never want to eat any others. Whether they are made by Mademoiselle Ray at the Auberge; by the wives of the farmers of the Valley; or by Georges Cloitres, the *charcutier* or pork butcher of the village of Saint-Pierre-de-Chartreuse, they are always strong in character, color and flavor. Freshly made, entirely filled with pure meats and aromatic spices and vegetables, with no "fillers" of cereals or preservatives, they are quite unlike the pale pink plastic-covered additive-filled bland mass-products of our American meat markets and groceries. In the Alpine valleys around the Auberge there are at least two dozen types of sausage, from the chocolate-brown *boudin noir* to the creamy-white *boudin blanc,* with as much variety in shapes and sizes as in the aromatic ingredients, which may be wild nuts, onions or shallots, hot or sweet peppers, pistachios, young sage or other aromatic leaves, truffles, and sometimes even Champagne or locally distilled brandy. On the day when pigs are being slaughtered at one of the farms in the Valley, Mademoiselle will be on hand to collect the cuts of meat she wants for her sausage making; and the internal tubes of the animals (which will be the casings of the sausages) will be taken down to the river to be cleaned, scraped, thoroughly washed and salted. The exact recipe will vary according to the resources of the season: if the apple trees are loaded with ripe *reinettes,* or there are ripe chestnuts for the picking in the woods, or a good row of young spinach in the kitchen garden. . . .

Many types of Alpine sausage (for example, the *boudin noir* and the *boudin à la crème*) include the fresh blood of the newly slaughtered animal, but since the retail sale of animal blood is prohibited by United States law, these types of "blood sausage" or "black pudding" cannot be homemade here. However, Mademoiselle Ray's *boudin blanc,* or "white pudding," can easily be prepared from chicken, pork, or rabbit, or a combination of all three. The putting together of the filling involves no more complication than the use of a good meat grinder. No need to discuss here the techniques of filling the casings by means of a funnel or a tube or a "sausage stuffer" attachment to the home meat grinder or food mixer. Books have been written on the subject. But even if you do not have the proper machinery and cannot find a local fancy butcher who stocks salt-preserved hog or sheep casings, you can buy sheets of "caul skin" and use them to wrap hamburger-shaped patties (called *crépinettes*) ready to bake, deep-fry, pan-fry, or grill. Or some of the firmer textured mixtures (see recipe below) can simply be rolled into meatballs and then cooked in the standard way. Personally, I get more fun out of making sausages than I ever had shaping play putty.

To start on the right track with Mademoiselle Ray's recipes, you should begin by preparing a supply of her basic flavoring mix. Quite apart from its use in sausage, it is a valuable multipurpose staple for the spice cabinet or store cupboard.

MADEMOISELLE RAY'S SAUSAGE FLAVORING OF FIVE SPICES
(*Cinq Épices de Malemoiselle Ray*)

A SUPPLY TO KEEP ON HAND

This is the basic spice mixture for several of Mademoiselle Ray's homemade sausages (including the recipes below), but it also has other valuable uses. The classic accompaniment to *boudin blanc* is a creamy mash of potatoes and a nicely aromatic coarse-textured applesauce. Try blending a few pinches of this *cinq épices* into the potatoes. Sprinkle a little of it into the stuffing for a chicken or turkey. Rub the outside of a pork loin with it an hour or so before the roasting begins. Add some to the molasses-mustard glaze of a baked ham. You will discover dozens of uses.

The preparation of *cinq épices* is simply a matter of putting the five spices, in precisely the right proportions, into a mortar and grinding, pounding and stirring them around until you have a finely powdered, perfectly mixed blend. I give the amounts in "parts" which you can translate into half-teaspoons, teaspoons, tablespoons, or ounces, according to how much you want to make and store away in a tightly lidded jar. The mixture: 9 parts of freshly ground black pepper, 1 part ground cinnamon, 1 part ground clove, 2 parts ground ginger and 3 parts freshly ground nutmeg.

WHITE SAUSAGE WITH CHICKEN AND PORK
(*Boudin Blanc au Poulet et au Porc*)

FOR 4 PEOPLE

Staple Items
Heavy cream (about ½ cup)
Eggs (3)
Yellow onions (enough to fill 3 cups, chopped—usually about ¾ lb.)
Breadcrumbs (about 1 cup)

Flavorings
Crystal salt, freshly ground black pepper, *cinq épices*

Shopping List
Chicken, boneless white meat, either leftover roasted or uncooked breasts (½ lb.)
Pork, whitest lean meat, boned from loin (½ lb.)
Beef kidney fat, whitest available (10 ounces)
Lean salt pork, presoaked to remove salt (10 ounces)

Complete Preparation in About 30 Minutes

Measure ¼ cup of the cream and heat it up, but keep it well below boiling. Measure ¾ cup of the breadcrumbs and thoroughly mix into a smooth paste with the hot cream, then reserve. Using the finest cutting disk of the meat grinder, put through the ½ pound chicken, the ½ pound pork, the 10 ounces beef fat and the 10 ounces salt pork and assemble in a large mixing bowl. Sprinkle over 2 tablespoons of salt, 1 teaspoon pepper and 1 teaspoon *cinq épices*. Add the 3 cups of chopped onions and work everything together, most efficiently with clean hands. Pass everything once more through the meat grinder. Finally, work in the 3 whole eggs and the bread-cream paste. It should all be thick enough to hold any required shape. If too thick, work in a few more dashes of cream. If too thin, work in more breadcrumbs. Also, check seasonings and adjust if necessary. The *boudin* mix should be good and peppery—it will lose some of its spiciness during the later cooking. Stuff the mix into sausage casings, or wrap in caul skin as *crépinettes,* or roll into meatballs. To serve, they may be gently baked, deep-fried, pan-fried, or grilled until done through. Uncooked, they will keep perfectly in the coldest part of the refrigerator for 4 or 5 days—or frozen for at least a month.

WHITE SAUSAGE WITH RABBIT
(*Boudin Blanc au Lapin*)

FOR 4 PEOPLE

Staple Items
Butter (2 Tb)
Light cream (about ¾ cup)
Eggs (2)
Breadcrumbs (about 2 cups)
Yellow onions (2 medium)

Flavorings
Crystal salt, freshly ground
 black pepper, *cinq épices,*
 tarragon

Shopping List
Rabbit, boned light meat, with
 liver (½ lb.)
Pork, boneless white lean,
 from loin (¼ lb.)
Lean salt pork, presoaked to
 remove salt (¼ lb.)
Shallots (4)
Fresh chives (enough to fill
 1 Tb, chopped)
Parsley (enough to fill 2 Tb,
 chopped)

Complete Preparation in About 30 Minutes

Measure ½ cup of the light cream and heat it up, but keep well
below boiling. Measure 1½ cups of the breadcrumbs and, when cream
is hot, work together, stirring vigorously, until you have a smooth,
thick *panade*. Keep stirring over heat until it dries out and comes
away from the sides of the pan. Then, turn off heat and leave to cool.
Finely grind together the ½ pound rabbit, the ¼ pound pork and the
¼ pound salt pork and assemble in a large mixing bowl. Sprinkle
over 1 tablespoon salt, ½ teaspoon each pepper and *cinq épices,* plus
the 1 tablespoon chives, the 2 tablespoons parsley, and the 2 teaspoons
dried tarragon or ½ cup chopped fresh tarragon leaves. Work into this
—most efficiently with clean hands—the bread *panade* and let it all
rest. Finely mince the 2 onions and 4 shallots, then quickly sauté them
in the 2 tablespoons of butter. Add the rabbit liver to the onions, and as
soon as it is stiff enough to handle, chop it finely. Add it, the contents
of the sauté pan and the 2 whole eggs to the main mixing bowl and
work everything completely together. Adjust thickness with extra
breadcrumbs or cream, as described in the previous recipe. Check and
adjust the seasonings if necessary. Fill sausages, shape and wrap
crépinettes, or roll into meatballs exactly as described in the previous
recipe. Cook in the same way, or refrigerate or freeze in the same way.

THE SAVORY MEATBALLS OF THE VALLEY
(*Les Caillettes de La Vallée*)

FOR 4 PEOPLE

In summer, when these meatballs are on the menu of the Auberge,
Mademoiselle Vivette climbs to the fields on the upper slopes
around the edges of the forest and picks the young leaves of the
wild strawberry spinach, which are then finely chopped and used
to spice the ground pork. In New York, having no forests or strawberry spinach, I pick out the small young leaves of our domestic
spinach and. find that they serve me very well. They seem to
balance and lighten the aromatic strength of the *cinq épices* homemade seasoning.

Staple Items
Olive oil (about 2 Tb—for
oiling the baking dish)

Flavorings
Crystal salt, freshly ground
black pepper, *cinq épices*

Shopping List
Pork loin meat, boneless and
entirely lean (½ lb.)
Pork liver (¼ lb.)
White pork fat (¼ lb.)
Young spinach leaves (about
¼ lb.)
Pigs' caul skin (several sheets)

About 1¼ Hours Before Serving—Active Preparation About 30 Minutes—Unsupervised Baking About 45 Minutes

Fill a 2-quart saucepan with freshly drawn cold water, salt it and bring to boiling. Put the ¼ pound of spinach leaves into the boiling water, dunk them thoroughly and let them blanch for exactly 5 minutes. Drain at once, "refresh" them by covering with cold water, thoroughly dry them, then chop fairly finely on a wooden board and hold. Using the finest cutting disk of the meat grinder, pass through the ½ pound of lean pork, the ¼ pound of pork liver, the ¼ pound of pork fat and mix them all lightly but thoroughly (preferably with clean fingers), adding the spinach, 1 tablespoon of salt, ½ teaspoon of pepper and ½ teaspoon of *cinq épices* or more to taste. Preheat the oven to 325 degrees. Now divide the meat mixture into 4 parts, rolling each quarter into a round the size of a tennis ball and carefully wrapping each in several thicknesses of the pigs' caul. Thoroughly oil an open baking dish, stand the *caillettes* in it, making sure that they do not touch each other, then bake in the center of the oven until they are just done through, usually in about 40 minutes. They are equally good hot or cold. They will keep in perfect condition in the refrigerator for 3 or 4 days, or in the freezer for several weeks.

SECTION XI

Veal

POACHED VEAL WITH GARDEN VEGETABLES IN THE STYLE OF AIX-LES-BAINS

(Le Carré de Veau à l'Aixoise)

FOR 4 PEOPLE

If you are one of those gourmets who think that veal is often a relatively dull and tasteless meat—who insist on their scallopine being slathered half an inch thick with cheese and tomato sauce—this is the recipe to give you an entirely new idea of the meat of a young calf. A solid cut of loin or leg is slowly simmered in an aromatic wine broth, absorbing the flavoring juices of chestnuts and vegetables, while they in return take on a meaty richness. This digestible and light dish is a regional specialty of the High Savoy and its Alpine resort city, Aix-les-Bains (see menu and wine suggestions on page 114).

Staple Items
Butter (about 4 Tb)
Egg yolks (1 or 2)
Carrots, small (12)
Onions, small white (12 to 16)
Celery, white (2 heads)
Olive oil (about 6 Tb)

Flavorings
Crystal salt, freshly ground black pepper

Shopping List
Veal, boneless loin, rolled and tied (about 3 lbs.)
Good, strong chicken bouillon (2 cups)
Heavy cream (about 2 Tb)
Celery root (1 medium)
Fresh chestnuts in their shells (24)
Dry white wine (1 bottle)

About 3 Hours Before Serving—Active Preparation of Meat and Vegetables About 1 Hour—Unsupervised Simmering About 2 Hours

Choose a casserole or French *cocotte* with a tightly fitting lid (perhaps of enameled iron) large enough to take the 3-pound boned and rolled loin of veal plus all the vegetables without being overfilled. In this *cocotte*, first melt 2 tablespoons of the butter and 2 tablespoons of the olive oil, heat up to a good frying temperature, then thoroughly brown the veal on all sides. Sprinkle it with crystal salt and black pepper to taste. Gently pour in the 2 cups chicken bouillon plus as much wine as is needed to come about ⅔ of the way up the meat. Bring up to gentle simmering, cover tightly with lid and let the meat gently poach on top of stove, turning once, for about 1 hour. Preheat oven to 350 degrees.

Meanwhile, prepare the vegetables and assemble them in a large bowl. Remove and save for some other purpose the tough outer stalks and half the leaves of the 2 medium heads of white celery; separate the tender inner stalks, and coarsely chop the remaining leaves. Peel the 12 to 16 small white onions, then quickly sauté them whole in a couple of tablespoons of an equal-part mixture of butter and oil until lightly brown. Top, tail and scrape the dozen small carrots, leaving them whole, then also lightly sauté them. Peel a medium-sized celery root, skin it and cut it into bite-size chunks. Shell and skin the 24 chestnuts.

BASIC RULE FOR SHELLING AND SKINNING CHESTNUTS: Make 3 deep cross-gashes on the flat side of each chestnut with short-bladed oyster knife and put them in a pan over medium high heat on top of the stove. Sprinkle them with the remaining 2 or so tablespoons of oil and stir them around until they are all well coated. When they start merrily sizzling, set pan in center of the oven and bake them until they begin to crackle and pop. Then shell and skin them. As soon as chestnuts are out of oven, lower its temperature to keep-warm, 175 degrees.

About 1½ Hours Before Serving

Carefully pack all these vegetables in the bouillon around the meat. If necessary, add more wine just to cover the vegetables. Check again for seasoning and adjust if necessary. Continue simmering, tightly covered, for at least 1 more hour.

About 30 Minutes Before Serving

Check the meat for doneness, either roughly by testing its tenderness with a fork, or more accurately by plunging in a meat thermometer, which should read 155 degrees. Also test the vegetables for doneness. If necessary, continue simmering a little bit longer. Again, correct seasoning. Choose a flat, oval serving platter and set it to warm.

About 15 Minutes Before Serving

Place veal in center of the platter, carefully lift out vegetables with slotted spoon and arrange them handsomely around the meat. Keep the meat and vegetable platter warm in the keep-warm oven while you make the sauce. Remove about 3 cups of the bouillon from the cooking pan, strain it through a fine sieve, then put it into a 1-quart saucepan and boil down rapidly to reduce the liquid and concentrate the flavor. Thicken this sauce with an egg yolk or two as needed, beaten with the tablespoon or 2 of heavy cream. Serve this sauce separately in a hot sauceboat.

BONED AND ROLLED GALANTINE OF VEAL IN ITS OWN ASPIC

(Le Veau des Montagnes en Gelée)

FOR 4 TO 6 PEOPLE

This is a true French *galantine*, with the veal rolled around an aromatic filling and poached in a winy bouillon, with a veal knuckle to provide a natural jelly and everything then cooled in a long, handsome mold. The meat for this magnificent production cannot be picked out from a supermarket freezer cabinet. It requires the cooperation of a friendly custom butcher. He should cut for you, preferably from the breast, a slab of entirely lean meat about 12 inches long, and then he should flatten it with his big wooden hammer until it is about 9 inches wide and 2 inches thick. He should also let you have about 2 pounds of chopped veal bones and about 1 pound of reasonably lean veal trimmings. (See discussion on page 152; menu and wine suggestions on page 150.)

Staple Items
Carrots (3 medium)
Yellow onions (2 medium)

Flavorings
Crystal salt, freshly ground
black pepper, whole all-
spice, whole bay leaves,
garlic (2 cloves), whole
black peppercorns, mace,
marjoram, thyme

Shopping List
Veal breast, entirely boneless
and lean (3 to 5 lbs.), but
bring home bones (2 lbs.)
and trimmings (1 lb.)
Veal knuckle, split by butcher
(1)

Ham, preferably dark-smoked
country style (½ lb., in one
piece)
Bacon, dark-smoked (½ lb., in
one piece)
Leeks, white part only (2
medium)
Parsley (small bunch)
Shallots (2)
Black truffles—optional, if
pocketbook allows (1 or 2,
according to size)
Beef, chicken, or veal bouillon
(about 6 cups)
Cognac (½ cup)
Madeira, dry Sercial (1 cup)
Dry white wine (best to have
1 bottle available to fill up
pot)

*Prepare, of Course, 1 or 2 Days in Advance—Active Preparation in
About 1 Hour—Unsupervised Marination and Simmering About 8
Hours*

Prepare the meats for the marination. Lay the slab of veal in a
baking or roasting pan large enough so that it will not have to be
folded over on itself. Cut the ½ pound of ham into half-inch cubes
and fit them neatly around the veal. Sprinkle very lightly with salt
and also add here and there about half a dozen whole allspice, 2
crumbled bay leaves, about 4 whole black peppercorns, plus, if you
have them, the diced truffles. Thoroughly moisten all this by pouring
over the ½ cup of Cognac and ½ cup of the Madeira. Cover tightly
with foil and leave to marinate at room temperature for about 5 hours.

Meanwhile, prepare the stuffing. Using the fine cutter on the meat
grinder, pass through the ½ pound of bacon and the 1 pound of veal
trimmings. Thoroughly mix together with ¼ cup of chopped parsley,
the 2 shallots, minced, plus salt and pepper to taste. Hold this mixture,
refrigerated, until the moment for stuffing the veal.

Stuffing and Rolling the Veal in About 30 Minutes

You will need a piece of cheesecloth large enough to give you a double-thick square of about 18 inches each way. Lay it out on the working table and place the slab of veal exactly at its center. Wipe the veal with a paper towel to make sure that none of the marinating spices are sticking to it. Strain the marinating liquid into the ground meat mixture. Also add to it the cubes of ham and dice of truffles. Mix thoroughly. Then, preferably with clean fingers, place this stuffing, as a sort of backbone about 2 or 3 inches wide, down the length of the veal slab at its center but stopping about 1½ inches from each end. Everything should be very neat. Now carefully roll the veal lengthwise around this central backbone of stuffing. You should finish up with a fat, long, almost jelly-roll sausage. While still holding it firmly together, wrap it tightly in the cheesecloth and tie it with string. Also, fold over and firmly tie the loose ends of the cheesecloth, so that the *galantine* cannot possibly lose its innards or its shape in any direction. Now put it aside while you prepare its boiling pot.

Preparing the Pot in About 20 Minutes—Simmering for About 2½ Hours

The size of the covered pot is important. The *galantine* should of course lie flat, and there must be enough room around it for the various flavoring ingredients, but not much more than that. Otherwise, if you have a huge pot which has to be filled up with vast quantities of liquid, you will not get a good aspic jelly. The ideal is to have a minimum of liquid, just covering the meat. Set the *galantine* in the bottom of the pot and pack around it the 2 pounds veal bones; the pieces of veal knuckle; the 2 leeks, washed and chunked; the 3 carrots and 2 onions, all chunked; the 2 cloves of garlic, minced; 2 teaspoons each of marjoram and thyme; a few sprigs of parsley; 2 whole bay leaves; about a dozen whole black peppercorns; ½ teaspoon of mace, plus salt to taste. Now pour in the bouillon until the *galantine* is just covered with liquid. If the bouillon is not enough, add as much as necessary of the wine. Bring quickly to the boil, then turn down to gentle simmering, "just smiling," keeping it going, covered, for 2½ hours.

Cooling and Molding, With at Least 24 Hours of Refrigeration

Turn off the heat and let the pot cool enough so that there is no risk of burning your fingers. Gently lift out the *galantine* and set it on a platter to drain, still in its cheesecloth. Place a board on top of it with a heavy weight, so that the *galantine* will be firmly pressed as it cools. Strain the liquid from the pot and, if you want to be fussy for a special party, clarify it by the basic rule described in Cushion-Terrine of Pheasant on page 174. Then add the final ½ cup of Madeira. This aromatic broth should cool into a firm jelly. If it is not quite firm enough, boil it down to reduce it. Finally, when the *galantine* is quite cool, carefully unwrap it from its cheesecloth and place it in a handsome mold in such a position that the seam of the meat, after unmolding, will be at the bottom. Reheat the jellied broth until it is just liquid again and then fill up the mold with it. Wrap in foil and refrigerate at least 24 hours. Then unmold onto the serving platter and decorate the *galantine* simply or lavishly as the party demands.

VEAL KIDNEYS SPIT-ROASTED WITH DEVILED SAUCE

(Les Rognons de Veau Grillés à la Broche, Sauce Diable)

FOR 4 PEOPLE

One of the most attractive ways of preparing veal kidneys—giving them a slightly crispy crust on the outside, while keeping them juicy and soft inside. You can make the deviled sauce exactly to your taste—either mouth-burning hot, or just gently aromatic (menu and wine suggestions on page 86).

> *Shopping List*
> Veal kidneys, each enclosed
>   in its white fat (8 to 12,
>   whole, according to size and
>   the appetite of the guests)

For the Sauce Diable:

Butter (2 Tb)

Tomato paste (2 Tb)

Red wine vinegar (2 Tb)

Worcestershire sauce (about
  1 tsp)

Flavorings

Crystal salt, whole black
  peppercorns, red Cayenne
  pepper

Horseradish, grated (about
  2 tsp)

Parsley, chopped (¼ cup)

Shallots (3)

Dry red wine (¼ cup)

Plus one-half batch of the Sauce Velouté as described in the recipe for Whole Country or Smithfield Ham on page 308.

About 40 Minutes Before Serving—Active Preparation of Kidneys and Sauce About 30 Minutes—Unsupervised Grilling About 10 Minutes

Begin by preparing the kidneys. Carefully slice off the fat around each one, leaving it fully covered by about a ⅜-inch thickness of fat. Cut each kidney open almost halfway through and neatly remove the internal tubes and any other tough bits. Tie each kidney back together with a single thin piece of string, then slide them onto the grill rod of the rotisserie and hold them until the sauce is almost ready. They will take about 10 minutes to cook. Prepare the Sauce Diable. First, prepare a half-batch of the Sauce Velouté on page 308, then reserve it. Mince the 3 shallots, sauté them quickly in the 2 tablespoons of butter, then put them into a small saucepan with 2 tablespoons each of the vinegar and wine, plus 8 whole black peppercorns, then boil hard, uncovered, stirring occasionally, until the mixture reduces to a gooey paste. Then, at once, work in the remaining 2 tablespoons of wine, the 2 tablespoons of tomato paste, the cup or so of the Sauce Velouté, the ¼ cup chopped parsley, the 1 teaspoon Worcestershire, plus salt and as much Cayenne as you think fit. Continue a gentle bubbling, uncovered, stirring almost continuously until the sauce is exactly as strong and thick as you like it.

About 20 Minutes Before Serving

Turn on the grill and let it heat up.

About 15 Minutes Before Serving

Start gently grilling the kidneys until they are just done inside, but be careful not to overcook them, or they will become leathery tough. With average-sized kidneys, this usually takes about 10 minutes.

About 5 Minutes Before Serving

Strain the sauce to get rid of the peppercorns. Work into it one or two teaspoons of the grated horseradish, and as much more of the red Cayenne pepper as your desire for fire-in-the-mouth demands. Quickly reheat and serve the sauce separately in a very hot sauceboat.

SECTION XII

Poultry
Les Volailles

FRICANDEAU OF CHICKEN IN RED WINE VINEGAR
(*Fricandeau de Poulet au Vinaigre de Vin Rouge*)

FOR 4 PEOPLE

This is an ancient recipe from the Loire Valley which in recent years has spread all the way across France. During the hot, steamy summers along the River Loire, every local winemaker had the unpleasant experience of finding that some of his wine had turned to vinegar. (Incidentally, this is why the city of Orléans on the upper Loire became the "vinegar capital" of France.) However, the thrifty wives of the winemakers insisted on using up some of the good red wine vinegar by putting it into the pan while sauté-ing a chicken. The result is unusual and delicately refreshing. The chicken flesh becomes, so to speak, a lightly flavored salad—in fact, the authentic accompaniment is a tossed salad with walnut oil and a contrasting white vinegar. For this dish you must of course use only the best quality of wine vinegars.

Staple Items
Unsalted butter (about 6 Tb)
Garlic, unpeeled (4 cloves)
Tomato paste (2 Tb)
Red wine vinegar (about 1½ cups)

Flavorings
Crystal salt, freshly ground black pepper, tarragon (dried, if fresh not available), thyme

Shopping List
Roasting chicken, cut up for fricassée (about 3½ lbs.)
Clear chicken broth (2 cups)
Good strong veal broth, or demi-glace (½ cup)
Heavy cream (¾ cup)
Fresh chervil leaves, if available, optional (small bunch)
Chives (small bunch)
Parsley (small bunch)
Fresh tarragon leaves, if available (small bunch)

About 1½ Hours Before Serving—Active Preparation About 40 Minutes—Unsupervised Simmering About 45 Minutes

This dish is entirely prepared in a sauté pan with a well-fitting lid and large enough to hold all the chicken pieces, with some extra room to be able to move the pieces around easily. If you first dry the chicken pieces, they will brown better. Rub the chicken pieces with salt and pepper. Set the sauté pan over medium-high frying heat and quickly melt in it 4 tablespoons of the butter. Then put in the chicken pieces and quickly sauté them to a good, deep brown. As soon as the chicken begins to brown, put in the 4 unpeeled cloves of garlic. This is the "secret trick," since, if the garlic is peeled, it will burn and give a bitter flavor to the sauce. Also, do not be afraid of the large amount of garlic. By frying it with the chicken, much of its oil is evaporated and the end result is about equal to 1 clove. Stir the garlic cloves around and see to it that their skins become lightly browned and crisp. Also add to the pan 3 or 4 sprigs of parsley, about 2 tablespoons of chopped chives, a small handful of fresh tarragon leaves (or 1 teaspoon dried), plus 1 teaspoon dried thyme. Stir everything around for hardly more than a couple of minutes, turning over the chicken pieces to absorb the flavors on all sides. Add more butter if necessary. When the browning is complete, turn down the heat to simmering, put on the lid and let the juices bubble gently for 25 minutes.

About 30 Minutes Before Serving

Set the oven to keep-warm temperature, about 175 degrees, and heat up a covered bowl for the chicken pieces. Take the pieces out of the sauté pan and keep them warm in the bowl, covered, in the oven. Turn up the heat under the sauté pan and hiss into it ¾ cup of the red vinegar, vigorously scraping and deglazing the bottom of the pan. Add the 2 cups of chicken broth, the ½ cup of veal broth or demi-glace, and the 2 tablespoons of tomato paste. Let it all boil hard, stirring often, to reduce and concentrate flavors. Taste the sauce as it reduces. When the nip of the vinegar has changed from mouth-puckering to agreeably zinging in the back of the mouth and throat, the sauce is ready. Strain it and put it back in the sauté pan. If it now has enough garlic flavor for your taste, discard the garlic cloves from the strainer, but for my preference I would pick them out and squeeze them so that their insides (now a soft mash) go back into the sauce. The garlic skins, of course, are discarded. Work into the sauce the ¾ cup of cream, and from this point onward keep the sauce always just below boiling, or it may curdle. Check and adjust the seasonings, adding more vinegar and/or more tomato paste until you have exactly the flavor that fits your taste. Put the chicken pieces back into this sauce, letting them warm up in it and absorb its flavors, covered, for about 10 minutes. Make sure that sauce does not boil. Serve on a very hot platter, with the sauce poured over and chopped fresh leaves of chervil, parsley and tarragon sprinkled on top.

CHICKEN ROUSILLE OF THE VALLEY
(*Le Poulet Rousille de La Vallée*)

FOR 4 PEOPLE

This is not even a regional specialty of the Alps—it is virtually a local and parochial dish of the Valley of La Grande Chartreuse. The name comes from the local dialect word *roussi*, meaning "slightly burnt." This is what is done to the chicken before it is then "soothed" by being poached with an aromatic combination of the freshest of fresh vegetables. This recipe is easy and quick to prepare and the result is a typical country dish with all the attractive freshness of food in a country kitchen.

Staple Items
Butter (4 Tb)
Arrowroot or cornstarch
    (1 to 2 Tb)
Olive oil (6 Tb)

Flavorings
Crystal salt, freshly
    ground black pepper

Shopping List
Chicken, quartered (3 to
    3½ lbs.)
Lean, dark-smoked bacon
    (½ lb. of rashers)
Heavy cream (a few Tb)
Mushrooms (½ lb.)
Small white onions (12)
Tomatoes (6)
Fresh chervil (for garnishing)
Parsley (for garnishing)
Armagnac (½ cup)
Chambéry vermouth (½
    cup)

*About 1 Hour Before Serving—Active Preparation About 30
Minutes—Unsupervised Poaching Another 30 Minutes*

In a heavy iron skillet over very high heat, bring up to almost-smoking frying temperature the 6 tablespoons of olive oil, then plunge in the chicken quarters and fry until they are a good, dark brown. Meanwhile, have ready a tightly lidded casserole or *cocotte*, large enough to hold the chicken quarters and the surrounding vegetables, preferably of enameled cast iron so that it can be used on top of the stove as well as in the oven. Set it, empty, over medium heat, and the moment the chicken quarters are brown, switch them to the casserole, pour over the ½ cup of slightly warmed Armagnac and flame. As soon as the fire dies down, turn heat down to reasonably gentle simmering, clamp on the lid and let chicken poach in its own juices while you prepare the vegetables.

Skin and chunk the 6 tomatoes and add to the chicken. Into a sauté pan over medium frying heat, put the 4 tablespoons of butter and the ½ pound wiped-clean mushrooms to quickly sauté for hardly more than 3 minutes, then remove with a slotted spoon and also add to chicken. In the same sauté pan, brown the 12 peeled small white onions and also add to chicken. Cut the ½ pound of bacon rashers into ½-inch squares, sauté for a couple of minutes, then remove with slotted spoon and add to chicken. Now, finally, add the ½ cup of dry Chambéry vermouth—the local vermouth of the Alps. Adjust the heat under the covered casserole so that there is a merry bubbling until chicken and vegetables are perfectly soft and done— usually in 20 to 30 minutes. Check seasoning, adding salt and pepper as needed.

Just Before Serving

Pour all the accumulated juices from the casserole into a separate saucepan, bring up to gentle simmering and thicken by vigorously working in a tablespoon or two, as needed, of the arrowroot or cornstarch diluted with a little heavy cream. When it is thick enough just to coat the spoon, pour it back over the chicken and vegetables in the casserole. Serve from the casserole if it is attractive enough, or from a very hot covered dish. Decorate with chopped green parsley and (if available) chopped fresh chervil.

SHAKEPOT OF CHICKEN IN CREAMED WINE OF THE PRINCE OF ORANGE
(*Hochepot de Poule du Prince d'Orange*)

FOR 4 PEOPLE

The extraordinary background of this historic dish, which is perfectly in season every month of the year, is on page 34. See also menu and wine suggestions on page 33. It is best when made with a boiling hen—an old bird with flesh full of flavor juices (as with aged beef)—but since they are less often available these days, the alternative is a fairly large roasting chicken.

Staple Items
Sweet butter (¼ lb.)
Egg yolks (4)
Yellow onions (2 medium)

Flavorings
Crystal salt (2 tsp),
    freshly ground black pepper

Shopping List
Boiling hen or roasting
    chicken, see above (4 to
    6 lbs.)
Calf's foot, cut in half
    lengthwise (1)
Sour cream (¼ cup)
Green Pascal celery (1 head)
White leeks (6)
Fresh parsley (1 bunch)
Dry white wine (1 bottle)

About 2¾ Hours Before Serving—Active Preparation About 30 Minutes—Unsupervised Cooking for 2 Hours

Wash calf's foot, put into lidded saucepan with just enough cold water to cover and gently boil to soften for 15 to 20 minutes while other ingredients are being prepared. Choose a large soup kettle or stewpot with a tightly fitting lid, then gently melt in it the ¼ pound butter and add the best stalks of the celery, finely chopped; the carefully washed white parts of the 6 leeks, chunked; the 2 onions, chopped; the bunch of parsley, chopped; plus salt and plenty of pepper to taste. Stir everything around and let it all lightly gild about 10 minutes. Cut up the chicken as for fricassée; when vegetables are done in stewpan, drop chicken pieces (laying the back, thighs and legs on bottom, ending with the more tender breasts on top) on this aromatic layer and then shake pot once or twice to encourage chicken to bed down. Pour in ¾ to one bottle (depending on your pan) of white wine. Add the calf's foot and 1 cup of the liquid in which it was poached. If there is not enough liquid to cover everything, add a small extra quantity of cold water.

About 2¼ Hours Before Serving

Bring rapidly to the boil over high heat on top of the stove, then cover and continue simmering until chicken is absolutely tender— usually (with an old and tough bird) in about 2 hours. If preferred, entire pot may be cooked in oven at 325 degrees.

About 15 Minutes Before Serving—Preparing the Sauce

When chicken is done, take out pieces and keep warm on hot serving platter. Also take out calf's foot, remove and cut up pieces of gelatinous meat and place around chicken. Discard bones. Strain liquid from stewpot into bowl and hold. Place remaining cooked vegetables in jug of electric blender, then turn on to high speed for a few seconds until vegetables are finely puréed and hold. In a medium-sized mixing bowl, beat together the 4 egg yolks with the ¼ cup of sour cream, then blend into it, spoonful by spoonful, whipping all the time with a small wire whisk, the vegetable purée from the blender jug. When it is all in and the mixture is perfectly smooth, transfer to a saucepan and place over gentle heat. Next, while continuing to use the wire whisk, add, ladle by ladle, as much of the liquid (which has been degreased) as is needed to make about 3 cups of sauce the thickness of heavy cream. Taste for seasoning and add more salt and pepper as needed. When sauce is smooth and thick, pour over chicken and bring to table at once.

DUCKLING GARNISHED WITH FRESH PEACHES AND FLAMED WITH ARMAGNAC

(*Caneton Glacé aux Pêches à l'Armagnac*)

FOR 4 PEOPLE

This is one of Mademoiselle Ray's dramatic party dishes, but of course her French ducks do not have nearly so much fat underneath their skins as do our Long Island Pekin birds. So I have had to adapt her recipe with a preliminary step for defatting the duck before the main cooking begins. (Incidentally, this dish can also be made with wild ducks, but then the roasting technique must be adjusted, because they are not fat.) You should prepare the veal stock the day before so that it can be skimmed and defatted. The classic Bigarade Orange Sauce can be prepared earlier on the day of your party and reheated just before serving. (*Bigarade,* by the way, is the French name for a particular variety of small, slightly bitter orange.) Finally, on the day, there remains only about 1½ hours needed for the preparation and braising of the duck, which is magnificently flamed at table (see discussion on page 42—menu and wine suggestions on page 41).

The Day Before—Preparing the Veal Stock in About 10 Minutes With About 3 Hours of Unsupervised Simmering

Staple Items	*Shopping List*
Carrots (2 medium)	Veal bones (1 lb.)
Yellow onions (2 medium)	Giblets of the duck

Flavorings
Garlic (2 cloves), sweet
marjoram and thyme

Put about 1 pound of veal bones into a pot with the giblets of the duck. Add 2 medium carrots and 2 medium onions, both chunked, 1 or 2 minced cloves of garlic, to your taste, plus ½ teaspoon each of dried sweet marjoram and thyme. Just cover with freshly drawn cold water, bring quickly up to boiling, skimming as the scum rises, then gently simmer, covered, for about 3 hours. When it is cool enough to handle, strain the liquid from the solids (crushing the vegetables to extract the last drops of their juices) and refrigerate the stock, covered, overnight. Next morning, every last bit of fat should be skimmed off. This stock is deliberately unsalted so that it will not affect the flavor of any dish to which it is added.

The Next Morning—Preparing the Bigarade Sauce in About 30 Minutes

Staple Items	*Flavorings*
Veal stock (see recipe above, 6 Tb skimmed and at room temperature)	Crystal salt, freshly ground black pepper
Butter (2 Tb)	*Shopping List*
Flour (1 Tb)	Oranges (2)
Brown sugar (4 Tb)	Sweet Madeira, Port, or
Pan juices from duck (a few Tb)	cream Sherry (to taste)

Using a sharp potato peeler, carefully cut the thin yellow outer rind from the 2 oranges (Mademoiselle Ray calls this *le zest*) and cut the strips, on a chopping board, into fine threads. Drop them into a small pan of boiling water for not more than 3 minutes to blanch them and remove some of their bitterness. Strain them out at once and reserve them. Cut 1 of the skinned oranges in half, extract its juice and reserve it. In a 1-quart saucepan, prepare a brown *roux* by melting the 2 tablespoons of butter over medium heat, working in the 1 tablespoon of flour and cooking them together, stirring continuously with a wooden spoon, until the mixture is satin smooth and has the color of light coffee. Now begin blending in, spoonful by spoonful, 6 tablespoons of the veal stock. Simmer gently, still stirring, for about 5 more minutes. Add salt and pepper to taste, the 4 tablespoons of brown sugar, the strained orange juice and the orange zest. Now, have fun balancing the flavors and seasonings exactly to your taste. Dribble in a dash or two of sweet Madeira, Port, or cream Sherry, but do not let the sauce become too sweet. For more orangy tartness, add, a few drops at a time, some of the strained juice from the second skinned orange. Finally, after the duck has been braised, work into this sauce a few tablespoons of the pan juices from the bird. Meanwhile, refrigerate this Bigarade, tightly covered, until the final preparations of the duck begin.

About 1½ Hours Before Serving—Active Preparation of the Duck
About 30 Minutes—Unsupervised Oven Cooking About 1 Hour

Staple Items	Shopping List
Butter (8 Tb)	Duck (3½ to 5 lbs.)
Lemon (½)	Peaches (4 whole fresh or 8
Carrots (3 medium)	canned halves)
Yellow onions (3 medium)	Parsley (6 sprigs)
Shallots (6)	Tarragon—fresh (4 to 5
Maple syrup (up to 2 Tb)	sprigs) or dried (2 tsp)
Olive oil (2 Tb)	Apricot jam (up to 2 Tb)
Tarragon white wine vinegar	Armagnac (5 ounces)
	Curaçao (5 ounces)
	Dry white wine (1 cup)

Remove Bigarade Sauce from refrigerator to come to room temperature. Then clean and defat the duck. Preheat oven to 400 degrees.
With fingers and a small, sharp knife, get out as much as possible of
the solid yellow fat from under the skin—especially from the breast.
Rub duck inside and out with the cut side of half a lemon. Using
sharp trussing pins, fix legs and wings firmly in place. Prick the skin,
not deeply but frequently and regularly, all over the bird to allow
remaining fat to run out. Place duck on raised rack over roasting pan
in hot oven and let fat run out for exactly 15 minutes.

Meanwhile, choose a covered oval roasting pan large enough
to hold the duck, and make up on the bottom of the pan the bed
on which the duck will lie. Place roasting pan over medium frying
heat on top of stove, melt in 4 tablespoons of the butter and lightly
sauté, until just beginning to gild, the 3 medium onions and 3 medium carrots, all chopped, with the 6 minced shallots. Turn off
heat and put in the 6 sprigs of parsley and the 4 or 5 sprigs of
fresh tarragon, or if not available, sprinkle in 2 teaspoons of dried
tarragon. After the 15 minutes, remove the defatted duck from
oven and place it, breast down, on its aromatic bed in roasting pan.
Using a pastry brush, paint the exposed parts of the duck with the
2 tablespoons olive oil. Now clear the oven by removing (with extreme care) the hot pan of duck fat. Duck will already be partly
browned, and to complete the process place roasting pan in oven, uncovered, until duck is fully browned—usually in 10 to 15 minutes more.

Meanwhile, if you are using 4 fresh peaches, cut each in half and
remove stone. If using canned halves, drain 8 solid halves. In a sauté

pan over medium frying heat, melt 4 tablespoons of the butter and lightly sauté peach halves until edges are just tipped with brown. Then add 2 ounces each of Armagnac and Curaçao and flame. When fire dies down, remove peach halves with slotted spoon and let drain, cut side down, on warm platter. Turn off flame under sauté pan. Put the 1 cup of dry white wine into a saucepan and heat up, but do not let it boil.

Now deal with the duck. The moment it is properly browned, turn oven down to 250 degrees and remove roasting pan from oven. Turn duck breast side up. Pour over it the heated wine, put on lid and return pan to oven to let duck braise until flesh is perfectly tender—usually in about another 40 to 45 minutes.

Meanwhile, complete and combine the various sauces. Turn on heat again under sauté pan and bring back peach butter to gentle simmering, then thicken it slightly by working in, 1 tablespoon at a time, alternate additions of the apricot jam and the maple syrup. Do not add more than 2 tablespoons of each. Next, begin working in the Bigarade Sauce. Finally add, tablespoon by tablespoon, the tarragon wine vinegar until you have achieved a well-balanced sweet and sour taste. Keep it bubbling to reduce it and concentrate the flavors, until it reaches the consistency of a thoroughly syrupy glazing sauce. Then keep it just warm, covered, until the duck is done.

When duck is perfect, place it on its hot serving dish, decorate it with the 8 peach halves and keep it warm. Turn off oven and turn on grill. Strain juices from roasting pan into a glass measuring jug and, using a bulb baster, draw off some of the duck juices from below the top layer of fat. Add about ½ cup of these juices to the sauce in the sauté pan, bringing everything back to merry bubbling. When sauce is perfect as to flavor and thickness, dribble it over the duck and place under the grill, with the breast about 2 inches below the heat, until everything is bubbling and brightly glazed.

Serving at Table

Pour over the duck and around the serving dish the 3 remaining ounces each of Armagnac and Curaçao. Set on fire, basting the duck with the flaming juices.

BRAISED DUCK OF THE WATERFRONT OF MARSEILLES
(*Canard Braisé du Port de Marseilles*)

FOR 4 PEOPLE

Duck is a favorite dish of the Marseillais who work in the great port and eat in the small bistros along the waterfront. Mademoiselle Ray brought this recipe from her native city and I have adapted it as I did the Duckling Garnished with Peaches to allow for the extra fat on our Long Island ducklings, now available around the year.

Staple Items	*Shopping List*
Sweet butter (4 Tb)	Duck (about 3½ to 5 lbs.)
Carrots (3 medium)	White leeks (3 medium)
All-purpose flour (2 to 3	Fresh parsley (1 bunch)
Tb)	White turnips (3 medium)
	Peeled Italian plum tomatoes,
Flavorings	(1-lb. can)
Crystal salt, freshly ground	Dry white wine (1 cup)
black pepper, garlic (2 or 3	
cloves according to taste)	

About 1½ Hours Before Serving—Active Preparation About 30 Minutes—Unsupervised Defatting and Cooking About 1 Hour

Cut up the duck as for fricassée and take the three essential steps to get rid of the oversupply of fat layered under the skin. First, using a small sharp-pointed knife, cut away as much visible fat as possible. Second, lay pieces of duck, fattiest side downwards, in a heavy frying pan and fry over medium-high heat to melt out more fat. As skin begins to brown, turn pieces over. They will be well browned and much of the fat will have run out in 8 to 10 minutes of frying.

Meanwhile, choose a tightly lidded oven casserole large enough to hold duck pieces with extra room for vegetables; put this casserole, empty and unlidded, into center of oven and turn on to 500 degrees. As each duck piece is properly fried, rub with salt and pepper and hold until all are done. Then put them all into the very hot casserole in the oven and bake them, uncovered, at this very high heat until more fat is melted out—usually in 15 minutes.

Meanwhile, prepare aromatic vegetables. Melt the 4 tablespoons of butter in a sauté pan and lightly gild, all together, the carefully washed and sliced whites of the 3 leeks, the scraped and sliced 3 carrots and the 3 peeled, thinly sliced turnips. When defatting of duck in oven is completed, take out extremely hot casserole, remove all duck pieces and get rid of all fat from bottom of casserole. Put back duck pieces, lightly sprinkle them with the 2 or 3 tablespoons of flour, and pack in, between and around duck pieces, the vegetables from sauté pan, including any remaining butter. Add the finely minced 2 or 3 cloves of garlic, the 1 pound of tomatoes and the cup of white wine. Cooking of duck may now be completed over simmering heat on top of stove, or in oven with heat reduced to 325 degrees.

About 45 Minutes Before Serving

Set casserole over high heat on top of stove and bring liquid to a rolling boil. Then, tightly cover and, either on top or in oven, gently poach everything in steam until duck is perfectly soft and done—usually, depending on age of duck, in about 30 to 40 minutes.

Serving at Table

In the bistros on the Marseilles waterfront, they serve this dish on soup plates with the natural juices poured over each portion. If you prefer, however, you may strain off these juices into a saucepan and thicken them into a sauce in the usual way. An ideal accompaniment is a dish of just-cooked young green peas lightly tossed in butter. For a handsome appearance, liberally sprinkle the dark brown duck pieces with the bright green chopped parsley.

DODINE OF BONED AND STUFFED DUCK WITH COGNAC AND MADEIRA
(*Dodine de Canard au Cognac et Madère*)

FOR 4 TO 6 PEOPLE

The word *dodine* comes from the French language of the four-teenth century and is applied to any bird served cold, boned and stuffed with an aromatic mixture and laced with spirits. In this version it is filled with pork, veal, chicken and duck livers, eggs, mushrooms, shallots and truffles. Mademoiselle Ray took out every bone, then magically reshaped the duck around its stuffing, sewing it at the seams, then gently roasting it, and finally glazing it with Port. At table, it looked so much like a real duck that the guests were amazed to find that they could slice it straight through, as if it were a terrine. (See menu and wine suggestions on page 150.)

Staple Items
Eggs (2 large)
Carrots (3 medium)
Yellow onions (3 medium)

Flavorings
Crystal salt, freshly ground black pepper, whole bay leaves, whole nutmeg

Shopping List
Duck, with its liver (3½ to 5 lbs.)
Veal, lean meat, sliced as for scallopine (1 lb.)

Pork, lean meat, also sliced (¾ lb.)
White pork fat, or fat bacon (10 ounces)
Chicken livers (½ lb.)
Mushrooms (¼ lb.)
Parsley (small bunch)
Shallots (2)
Black truffles, optional, if pocketbook allows (1 or 2, according to size)
Cognac (½ cup)
Madeira, dry Sercial (½ cup)
Port (½ cup)

*Total Preparation Time About 4 Hours—Active Work About 1 Hour
—Unsupervised Marination and Baking About 3 Hours*

Neatly and completely bone the duck, removing as much fat as possible using the technique described in Great Terrine of Grandmother Artaud on page 166. When it is all opened up and flattened out, lay it skin-side down across the bottom of a large mixing bowl. Cut the 1 pound of veal into narrow strips 3 to 4 inches long and the thickness of your finger. Lay them on top of the duck in the mixing bowl. Put in the liver of the duck, the ½ pound of chicken livers and the truffles, thinly sliced, then wet everything thoroughly with the half-cup each of Cognac and Madeira. Cover the mixing bowl with foil and leave everything to marinate for about 1 hour.

Meanwhile, using your meat grinder with its finest cutter in place, prepare the stuffing. Put through the grinder and assemble in a large mixing bowl the ¾ pound of lean pork and the 10 ounces of white pork fat or bacon. Add to this, in turn, the ¼ pound of mushrooms, chopped, the 2 shallots, minced, the 2 eggs, plus salt, pepper and freshly grated nutmeg to taste. Mix everything lightly but thoroughly and hold, covered, until the marination is completed.

*About 2½ Hours Before Serving—Stuffing the Duck in About 30
Minutes*

Pour the remaining liquid marinade into the stuffing and mix it in. Lay the duck, again skin-side down, onto a wooden board and work it back into its original shape around the stuffing. Divide the stuffing mixture in half, and spread this first half inside the duck. Then neatly put in a middle layer of veal strips running the length of the duck, pieces of chicken and duck livers and slices of truffle, all finally covered and enclosed by the second half of the stuffing. When the duck is back in shape, sew it at the seams with a needle and strong thread, completing the job, also, as required, with small trussing skewers and outside string. Now preheat the oven to 300 degrees and prepare on aromatic bed for the duck in a suitably sized open roasting pan. Spread across its bottom the 3 carrots and 3 onions, chopped, plus 2 or 3 whole bay leaves and about half a dozen sprigs of parsley. Set the duck, breast-side up, on this comfortable couch.

About 2 Hours Before Serving—Baking and Glazing the Duck

Set the duck in the center of the oven and let it roast slowly to a beautiful brown. Baste it every 20 minutes, by removing from the roasting pan with a bulb baster as much as possible of the fat and juices, then mixing these in a small bowl with the Port wine and dribbling this mixture over the duck. The Port adds the deep and rich coloring. When the duck is done it will look so beautiful that you will be tempted to eat it at once—and it can be served hot—but to my mind the flavors develop, mingle and sharpen their subtle composition as it cools. You cannot imagine a more dramatic and elegant centerpiece for a cold buffet.

ESCALLOPS OF TURKEY BREASTS IN THE STYLE OF SAVOY
(Les Escalopes de Dinde à la Savoyarde)

FOR 4 PEOPLE

This is obviously a variation of the Italian scallopine—a recipe that probably came across the Italian border at Nice and then, over the centuries, spread, in one form or another, across southeastern France. These thin slices of turkey breasts are filled with the local Reblochon cheese and slices of the sun-dried mountain ham. It all finishes up as a golden-fried sandwich, crackly crisp on the outside but filled with a luxuriously hot melted cheese mixture on the inside. (See menu and wine suggestions on page 150.)

Staple Items	*Shopping List*
Butter (about 6 Tb)	Turkey breasts, large (2, from
Eggs (2 large)	the two sides of 1 turkey)
Breadcrumbs (1 cup)	Ham, thickish slices (4)
	French Reblochon cheese
Flavorings	(1 whole)
Crystal salt, freshly ground	Parsley, chopped (¼ cup)
black pepper	

About 40 Minutes Before Serving

Cut the turkey breasts lengthwise into 8 slices of about the same size and thickness. Next, cutting horizontally across the top of the round Reblochon cheese, cut 4 slices of a size to fit the turkey slices, each about ⅜ inch thick. Now construct your sandwiches. Around each slice of cheese fold a slice of ham and tuck in the sides to make an envelope. Carefully place this on a slice of turkey. Salt and pepper very slightly. Place a second slice of turkey on top and tie the whole contraption lengthwise and crosswise, like a package, with thin string. Break the 2 eggs into a wide soup plate and beat them lightly with a fork. Spread the cup of breadcrumbs on another soup plate. When your 4 sandwiches are ready, heat up 4 tablespoons of the butter over medium-high frying heat in a large sauté or crêpe pan. Dip each sandwich first in egg, then in breadcrumbs, and quickly fry on both sides until they are crispy and golden brown. Add more butter to the pan as needed. Remove the strings and serve at once, very hot, sprinkled with the chopped parsley.

SECTION XIII

The Glory of the Potato—
The Great Gratins
of Le Dauphiné
and La Haute Savoie;
Also Pasta and Rice

CASSEROLE OF POTATOES IN CREAM
(*Gratin Dauphinois*)

FOR 4 PEOPLE

This is the great specialty of the Dauphiné region—probably the most famous French way of cooking potatoes at any time of the year. Some of my friends think that this is a helluva wasteful way of using up a pint of heavy cream. I disagree. I think the cream does more for these potatoes—in terms of luxury and richness—than it ever did whipped on a birthday cake.

Staple Items	*Shopping List*
Sweet butter (4 Tb)	Potatoes, good, waxy (2 lbs.)
Milk (1 cup)	Heavy cream (½ pint)

Flavorings
Garlic (2 cloves), freshly
  ground nutmeg, crystal salt,
  freshly ground black pepper

About 2½ Hours Before Serving—Active Preparation About 25 Minutes—Unsupervised Baking About 2 Hours

Skin potatoes and slice them in even rounds about ¼ inch thick. Wash thoroughly at once to get rid of starch and pat dry in towel. Put slices loosely into heavy iron skillet, with two or three liberal turns of the nutmeg grinder, plus salt and pepper, to taste. Pour in the 1 cup of milk and bring up to boiling. Peel and finely mince 1 clove of garlic and sprinkle into milk. When it boils, turn down heat and keep simmering moderately, uncovered, turning potatoes quite often to coat all sides, until all the milk is absorbed—usually in about 15 minutes.

Meanwhile, prepare ovenproof lidded earthenware casserole in which potatoes will be baked. Thoroughly rub inside with the other cut clove of garlic, then spread liberally all around with butter. Turn on oven to 300 degrees and set shelf so that casserole will be in center. When potato slices are ready, put them into casserole in interleaved layers, thoroughly soak them with the ½ pint of cream and dot the top with remaining butter. Cover casserole and set in oven in a larger dish filled with water about 1 inch deep. When potatoes are thoroughly soft—usually in 1½ to 2 hours—check for seasoning and if necessary add more salt and pepper, then quickly brown top surface by placing casserole for a couple of minutes under a hot grill. All the cream will generally have been absorbed into potatoes, making them unbelievably soft and velvety.

GRATIN OF POTATOES SAVOYARD
(*Le Gratin Savoyard*)

FOR 4 PEOPLE

Here is another of the marvelous Alpine ways of casserole-baking sliced potatoes. (Notes on page 58; suggested menu on page 56.)

Staple Items	*Shopping List*
Butter (3 Tb, plus enough to liberally grease baking dish)	Potatoes, good, waxy (2 lbs.)
	Gruyère cheese (1 cup, grated)
Eggs (2)	Double-strength chicken
Flour (2 Tb)	bouillon (2 cups)

Flavorings
Garlic (2 cloves),
  freshly grated nutmeg,
  crystal salt, freshly ground
  black pepper

The method for this dish is the same as for the Gratin Dauphinois, above, but with the following differences:

1. The sliced potatoes are *not* first cooked in milk, but are cooked entirely in the oven.

2. Slice the 2 pounds of peeled raw potatoes thinner if possible than for the Gratin Dauphinois, and instead of placing them directly

into the baking casserole, put them first into a large mixing bowl and, working very gently so as to break as few potato slices as possible (some breakage doesn't matter), thoroughly blend into them, so that each slice is well coated, 2 eggs, first lightly beaten, 1 cup grated Alpine Gruyère cheese, 2 tablespoons flour, ¾ teaspoon grated nutmeg, with salt and pepper to taste. Then, as described for the Gratin Dauphinois, above, layer these coated potatoes in a previously buttered and garlicked oven casserole.

3. Instead of covering them with heavy cream, pour in 2 cups double-strength chicken bouillon, then cover with a second ½ cup of Gruyère cheese, dot with about 3 tablespoons of butter and bake as for the Dauphinois. Because the precooking of the potatoes is eliminated, the Savoyard version may require a slightly longer baking time than the Dauphinois—perhaps 2 to 2½ hours in a 300-degree oven.

One might say, finally, that the Savoyard is a low-calorie version of the Dauphinois!

FEMININE GRATINÉE OF POTATOES À LA SAVOYARDE

(*La Gratinée à la Savoyarde*)

FOR 4 PEOPLE

Since my return from my explorations of the kitchens of the Alps, I have discovered that the large majority of people, even of expert gourmets, are not aware that there exists also a feminine version of the Gratin Savoyard—feminine, perhaps, because it is more sensuous, softer to the touch of the lips. There is only one main difference from the masculine Gratin Savoyard, above:

Add to the shopping list ½ pound of mushrooms (at the Auberge in the Alps they would probably be wild *bolets*) and, before preparing the potatoes, slice these mushrooms and quickly sauté them in 3 or 4 tablespoons of butter and hold. Then, when you start layering the coated potato slices in the oven casserole, interleave each layer of potatoes with a layer of the mushroom slices. Then continue exactly as for the masculine Gratin Savoyard.

POTATO PANCAKES OF THE MOUNTAINS

(*Le Farçon de Pommes de Terre*)

FOR 4 PEOPLE

Good at any time of the year. (See menu with wines on pages 74 and 142.) Can be the potato accompaniment to a main dish, or the main part of a light Sunday night supper.

Staple Items	*Shopping List*
Butter (4 Tb)	Potatoes (4 whole medium—
Eggs (3)	to make about 1 quart of
Peanut oil (2 Tb)	pulp)
	Heavy cream (up to 2 Tb)
Flavorings	Parsley (enough to fill 2 Tb,
Garlic, rosemary leaves,	chopped)
crystal salt, freshly ground	Scallions (4)
black Tellicherry pepper	

About 1½ to 2½ Hours Before Serving (Depending Entirely on the Unsupervised Baking Time of the Potatoes)

Bake the 4 potatoes in their skins in your favorite way. (At the Auberge and in my New York kitchen, the potatoes are baked in a handmade ceramic *diable* made of unglazed pottery, which takes about 2 hours, but draws the moisture out of the potatoes, so that they are wonderfully fluffy, with the flavor concentrated. Other methods of baking, with a metal spike for the potatoes to conduct the heat to the center, may take only 1½ hours or even less. Meanwhile, break the 3 eggs into a bowl, but do not beat them. Coarsely cut the 4 green stalks of scallions, mince 2 cloves of garlic, chop enough parsley to fill 2 tablespoons and, in a mortar, pound enough rosemary leaves to fill ½ teaspoon. Clarify 3 tablespoons of the butter and hold.

About 15 Minutes Before Serving—The Only Work Involved

As soon as the potatoes are done, cut them open, dig out the pulp and drop it into a 1-quart mixing bowl. While it is still hot, mash it (but not too smoothly) and mix in the 3 eggs, the scallions, garlic, parsley and rosemary, about 1 tablespoon of the butter, with crystal salt and freshly ground black Tellicherry pepper to taste. Now adjust the thickness of the mash by adding up to 2 tablespoons of the heavy cream. The final texture should be nice and mushy, while remaining thick enough to be shaped into pancakes. Heat the 3 tablespoons clarified butter and the 2 tablespoons oil in a 10-inch sauté pan. (If your pan is a different size, just be sure that there is enough combined oil and butter to cover the bottom of the pan by about ⅛ inch.) Shape pancakes about ¼ inch thick and about 2 inches across. Lay them carefully, with a spatula, in the hot butter and oil. Fry on both sides until there is a brown and crisp crust, with the insides still juicy and soft. Serve very hot. This dish is obviously a first cousin of the famous *rösti* potato pancakes of Switzerland. As usual, the recipe was changed as it crossed the border. Which version is better? Don't ask me to decide. France and Switzerland are both irresistible countries. Try both recipes and then decide for yourself!

MADEMOISELLE RAY'S SAFE AND SURE METHOD FOR SOUFFLÉED POTATOES
(Les Pommes de Terre Soufflées de Mademoiselle Ray)

FOR 6 PEOPLE

This most dramatic way of serving potatoes—each puffed up as if it were a hollow cylinder—requires some practice, with two deep-fat fryers, each at a different temperature, but is easy to repeat once you have mastered the technique.

Staple Items	*Shopping List*
Oil for frying (3 quarts)	Baking potatoes, Idaho or
Salt	Maine (8)

About 1 Hour Before Serving

This method requires a small amount of practice and skill, so that it may take longer the first time. But once you have the hang of it, on your own cooker and with your own equipment, it can easily be repeated again and again. If you have two electric fryers, each thermostatically controlled, so much the better. Otherwise you *must* use two deep-fat thermometers, so that one fryer can be kept continuously at 275 degrees and the other at 400 degrees.

(If you are a beginner and want absolutely precise instructions, here is how you start. Use two 4½-quart Dutch ovens and into each pour 6 cups of the frying oil so that each pot will be about half full and the oil about 3 inches deep. Heat the first pot until the temperature is 275 degrees. Using a second thermometer, heat the second pot until it reaches a temperature of 400 degrees. Then, adjust the heat so that these temperatures remain constant. Now you are ready to begin the souffléing!)

In my part of the world, during most of the year, Idaho or Maine baking potatoes work for me extremely well. I peel them thinly, then cut them lengthwise into absolutely even (and this is most important) slices barely ⅛ inch thick. Cut these, again lengthwise, into strips about ¾ inch wide. They should all be as nearly as possible exactly the same size. I wash them immediately under running cold water and pat them dry in a folded cloth towel.

Drop these strips, 5 or 6 at a time, into the 275-degree oil. Turn them over with a slotted spatula every 15 seconds or so, so that they heat evenly all around, until they are just barely browned and beginning very slightly to puff—usually in 5 or 6 minutes. Lift them out immediately and let them drain and cool for 5 minutes on paper towels. Now they can be held until you are ready for the precise timing of the final operation. (When you get to know this job extremely well, you can even do the frying the day before and hold the strips overnight in the refrigerator. They must be allowed to come back to room temperature at least an hour before the final frying.)

About 20 Minutes Before Serving

Drop the potato strips, in batches as before, into the 400-degree oil (if you prefer, you can now use a frying basket). Again, keep them moving and turning over with a slotted spatula. They will quickly brown, and then like magic they will blow up into small air-filled crispy crackly sausages. Sprinkle them at once with salt and rush them to table wrapped in a snow-white napkin in a pretty basket. Danger! They are habit-forming.

MADEMOISELLE RAY'S HOMEMADE EGG NOODLES
(*Les Nouilles de la Maison*)

FOR 4 PEOPLE

These were prepared especially to go with the Civet de Lièvre (menu and wine suggestions on page 16), but they are worth the small extra effort with any dish on any day of the year. Here they are made the day before and "hung out to dry"—for what an Italian cook would call *pasta secco*. But they can also be made an hour or two before eating, and served in the style of *pasta fresca*. In this recipe, the noodles are rolled out and cut by hand. If you have one of the small home pasta machines, so much the quicker.

Staple Items	*Shopping List*
Butter (for tossing with pasta when serving, about 4 Tb)	All-purpose flour (1 lb., to fill, after sifting, 4 cups)
Eggs (4)	
Walnut oil (a few tsp)	
Crystal salt	

The Day Before—About 30 Minutes of Active Preparation—With Some Resting in Between

Mademoiselle Ray sifted and measured 4 cups of the all-purpose flour and made a small pyramid in the center of her marble-topped work table. She broke the 4 whole eggs into a bowl, added 1 teaspoon of salt and beat lightly with a wire whisk. She made a small crater in the top of her pile of flour and poured in the eggs. At once she began working together the flour and the liquid with the tips of her fingers. As the stiff dough formed and she needed more liquid to keep it workable, she added first one, then a second teaspoon of walnut oil. After that, as more liquid was still required, she added first one, then a second teaspoon of warm water. Finally, after hardly more than 5 minutes, she had a rubbery-smooth ball of dough.

She carefully cleaned off her marble top, sprinkled it lightly with more flour and began kneading. She pushed and pulled. She pressed with the heel of her hand. She slapped vigorously. She continued until the dough was perfectly smooth. This second phase took another 5 minutes. Once more she had a ball. She placed a bowl over it in the center of the worktable and let it rest for 30 minutes.

Again she cleaned and floured the marble. She divided her ball into 4 parts. Using a tapered French pastry rolling pin, she rolled out the dough into the thinnest possible sheet. Then, with the point of a sharp knife, she cut it into strips about ½ inch wide. She hung these, slightly separated so they would not stick together, over a long wooden bar and let them dry out overnight.

On the Day—About 15 Minutes Before Serving

As many noodles as were needed immediately (about 1 pound by weight) were set aside. The rest were taken off the wooden bar, rolled up and packed in plastic bags for storage in the refrigerator. Ours were cooked in the usual way, dropped into a couple of gallons of salted water at a rolling boil and pulled out, for instant draining, as soon as they had reached the *al dente* stage. Then they were tossed in melted butter and brought to table in a very hot covered serving dish.

BOILED SAFFRON RICE FOR THE MARMITE

(*Riz au Safran*)

Mademoiselle Ray has her own rule of thumb for calculating the amount of rice required for any particular party of diners. She allows ¼ cup of raw rice for each lady and ½ cup for each gentleman. She denies that this represents any discrimination between the sexes. Her secret trick in boiling rice is to use slightly less water than the normal rule of two to one. Instead of the usual 2 cups of water to 1 cup of rice, she adds only 1¾ cups of water and claims that this makes for a fluffier final result. The recipe below is for two ladies and two gentlemen. If, however, the recipe is to be used with the Marmite de Lesdiguières, which is for 12 people, then this recipe should be multiplied by three.

Staple Items
Sweet butter (1½ Tb)

Flavorings
Saffron, preferably Spanish
   type in strands (1½ tsp),
   crystal salt (2 tsp)

Shopping List
Rice (1½ cups, raw, about
   ¾ lb.)
Dry vermouth (1½ Tb)

About 35 Minutes Before Serving

Mademoiselle Ray also has a rule of thumb for the correct amount of saffron to make bright yellow rice: 1 teaspoon of the finest Spanish stranded saffron to each cup of raw rice. To get the best from this saffron, in terms of its coloring and flavoring power, it should first be steeped in a warm, not hot, alcoholic bath. If it were to get too hot, or to boil, the essential oils would be evaporated off and lost. Put the 1½ teaspoons of saffron into a tiny butter-melting saucepan and moisten it with the 1½ tablespoons of dry vermouth. Over the gentlest possible heat, bring it up to just above blood temperature so that it feels slightly hot, but not stinging, to the tip of the finger. Keep it at this temperature, stirring occasionally, while you prepare the rice. Put the 1½ cups of raw rice into a heavy saucepan, preferably enameled iron, with a tightly fitting lid. Pour in, according to Mademoiselle Ray's rules (see above), exactly 2⅝ cups of cold water and add the 2 teaspoons salt. Stir and set over high heat. While it is heating, float on top the 1½ tablespoons butter to prevent water's frothing up and boiling over. As it comes up to boiling, stir in the saffron and vermouth, rinsing out the tiny saucepan with a couple of spoonfuls of the rice water. Stir the rice once more, then clamp on the lid, turn down heat to simmering and do not even peek for 15 minutes.

About 5 Minutes Before Serving

Using a wooden fork, lift rice around edges and check if there is any water left at bottom. If so, replace lid and continue simmering for 2 or 3 minutes longer. Rice will be perfectly done at the precise moment when water is all absorbed. Then finally dry out rice by leaving saucepan open over gentle heat for last 2 or 3 minutes before serving.

TIAN OF ZUCCHINI WITH RICE
(*Tian de Courgettes au Riz*)

FOR 4 PEOPLE

A most excellent Provençal combination of starch and vegetable, fine to make whenever zucchini is available. (The background of the *tian* is explained on page 42; menu with wines on page 41.)

Staple Items	Shopping List
Sweet butter (4 Tb plus 1 Tb to butter baking dish)	Zucchini (3 lbs.)
Eggs (4)	Light cream (1 cup)
Rice (½ lb.)	Fresh parsley (enough to fill 4 Tb, finely chopped)
Olive oil (2 Tb)	

Flavorings
Garlic (2 cloves), thyme,
   crystal salt; freshly ground
   black pepper

About 1½ Hours Before Serving—Active Preparation in About 30 Minutes—Unsupervised Cooking of Rice and Baking for About 1 Hour

Clean zucchini, cut off ends and, without peeling them, coarsely grate into a strainer set over a bowl. Sprinkle with salt and let drain for 15 minutes. Meanwhile, cook rice in any way you prefer, drain it, fluff it and hold. While rice is cooking, mince the 2 cloves of garlic and finely chop enough parsley to fill 4 tablespoons, and hold both. Preheat oven to 425 degrees, setting shelf so that *tian* will be in the center. Squeeze and discard excess juice from the zucchini and dry zucchini on paper towels. In a large frying pan, over medium-high heat, melt 4 tablespoons of the butter with the 2 tablespoons olive oil. Sauté the zucchini for about 10 minutes. Remove from heat and add the minced garlic, 2 teaspoons thyme, and the 4 tablespoons chopped parsley, plus salt and pepper to taste. As soon as rice is ready, fold it into the grated zucchini and mix thoroughly.

In a 2-quart mixing bowl, lightly beat the 4 eggs just until yolks and whites are blended, then beat in the 1 cup of light cream. Choose an open shallow 3-quart ovenproof baking dish (the Provençal *tian* is always square), rub it with the remaining 1 tablespoon butter, put in the rice mixture, then pour over the eggs and cream. Gently mix so that cream is evenly distributed. Set in the oven and bake until everything is firmly set into a Spanish-flan-style savory custard—usually in about 45 minutes. Test with a silver knife, which should come out dry when center is done. The *tian* is a most excellent accompaniment to roast duck or any other strongly flavored main dish. It also makes a good Sunday night main-course supper all on its own.

SECTION XIV

*Salads and Vegetables
From Coco of Savoy
to Zucchini*

ARTICHOKES À LA BARIGOULE
(Les Artichaux à la Barigoule)

FOR 4 PEOPLE

This is an extremely flexible way of preparing small young artichokes by poaching them with aromatic vegetables in a mixture
of olive oil and white wine. They can be served hot as the accompaniment to a main meat; or cold as a refreshing salad just before the cheeses; or as the hors d'oeuvre at the start of the meal.
This is a regional dish of Provence, and the name *Barigoule* comes
from the Provençal dialect word *Berigouliero*, the land where the
artichokes and mushrooms grow. (See menu with wines on page
96.)

Staple Items
Carrots (2 medium)
Yellow onion (1 medium)
Olive oil (about 3 Tb)

Shopping List
Artichokes, small, young
    (about 2 lbs.)
Dry white wine (about 1 cup)

Flavorings
Crystal salt, freshly ground
    black pepper, garlic (2
    cloves)

*Preparation Usually Well Ahead in About 2½ Hours—Active Work
About 20 Minutes—Unsupervised Simmering More Than 2 Hours*

Wash the artichokes, cut off their thorny tips and dig out their
chokes in the standard way. Scrape the 2 carrots, peel the onion and
mince both together. Choose a lidded sauté pan large enough to take
all the artichokes with a little extra room to move them around.
Place it over medium frying heat, put in the 3 tablespoons of olive
oil and quickly gild the minced carrots and oinion. Add the artichokes,
reduce heat to gentle bubbling, grind in salt and pepper to taste, then
cover and let artichokes simmer and sweat for just about 10 minutes.
    At the end of this preliminary time, add the 1 cup of wine and
the 2 cloves of garlic, finely minced. Adjust the heat to gentle simmer-

ing, then re-cover and keep everything going for about 2 hours. Occasionally, with a wooden spoon gently stir the artichokes around and turn them over. When they are beautifully soft and very aromatic, they may be served either hot or cold, with the pan juices poured over them.

ASPARAGUS WITH RED WINE
(*Les Asperges au Vin Rouge*)

FOR 4 PEOPLE

An unusual way with what is to me one of the greatest of all vegetables. (See menu with wines on page 74.)

Staple Items	Shopping List
Homemade mayonnaise (1 cup)	Asparagus (about 2 bunches) Good dry red wine (½ to ¾ cup)

About 20 Minutes Before Serving—Assuming Mayonnaise Was Made Ahead

Boil and steam the asparagus spears by the classic method, in a stand-up lidded boiler, with the lower two-thirds of the spears standing in boiling water and the tips in hot steam, just under the lid. Depending on the age and thickness of the spears, both the stalks and the tips will be done to perfection in somewhere between 12 and 18 minutes. Meanwhile, begin gradually working the wine into the 1 cup of mayonnaise, tablespoon by tablespoon, beating lightly in between, until you have achieved a charming pinkish-red color and a nice winy taste. Serve both the asparagus and the mayonnaise warm, but not hot.

GREEN BEANS SAUTÉED IN CREAM
(*Les Haricots Verts Sauté à la Crème*)

FOR 4 PEOPLE

This is one of the most luxurious ways of preparing green beans for an important dinner menu. They are sautéed in a mixture of butter and cream, then richly coated with egg yolks beaten with chopped chives. (See discussion on page 157; menu with wines on page 155.)

Staple Items	*Shopping List*
Butter (4 Tb)	Green beans, French cut (1 lb.)
Egg yolks (2 large)	
Flour (about 1 tsp)	Heavy cream (¼ cup)
	Chives, finely snipped (about 1 Tb)
	Parsley, chopped (about 2 Tb)

About 15 Minutes Before Serving

Only just, just cook the 1 pound of French-cut green beans by dropping them into boiling water and leaving them for hardly more than 1 minute. They must remain crisp and chewy. Drain them at once and hold them. In a casserole (preferably of tin, copper, or enameled iron which can be used as a fryer on top of the stove and is still handsome enough to be brought to table) over medium frying heat, melt the 4 tablespoons of butter and then work in the 1 teaspoon of flour plus the ¼ cup of cream. Add the beans and sauté them for hardly more than a minute or two, making sure that they are all well coated with the sauce. Now work in the 2 egg yolks, first lightly beaten with a fork, plus the tablespoon of chopped chives. Keep on sautéing for perhaps one minute longer, just to thicken the eggs. Sprinkle with the 2 tablespoons of parsley and bring the casserole at once to table.

SALAD OF GREEN BEANS WITH RAW MUSHROOMS
(*La Salade des Haricots Verts aux Champignons*)

FOR 4 PEOPLE

At the Auberge, Mademoiselle Vivette often serves this as an appetizing and refreshing first course—in typical French country style. The dressing is so light that the salad can be accompanied by one of the robust white Alpine wines, say, the charming Apremont (discussion on page 94—menu with wines on page 93.)

Staple Items	*Shopping List*
Sweet butter (4 Tb)	Green beans (1½ lbs.)
Lemon (1)	White button mushrooms,
Tarragon white wine vinegar	sliced (½ cup)
(2 Tb)	Fresh herbs, a few sprigs, if
Walnut oil (1 Tb)	available:
	Basil
Flavorings	Parsley
Crystal salt, dried herbs if fresh	Rosemary
not available	Summer savory

Several Hours Before Serving—Active Preparation About 15 Minutes —Unsupervised Boiling About 15 Minutes

In a 2-quart saucepan bring 1 pint of cold water up to boiling with 2 or 3 sprigs of fresh summer savory or 1 teaspoon of dried. Then let it simmer, covered, for as long as it takes to wash and cut the beans. If they are small, merely top and tail them. If large, they may be snapped, chunked, or frenched through a cutter. Drop them into the simmering water, adding a little more hot water, if necessary, just to cover them. Add 2 or 3 sprigs of fresh rosemary, or 1 teaspoon dried, then keep the water bubbling merrily, uncovered, so that the beans steam as the water gradually boils down, until they are just done but still nicely crisp—usually in 12 to 15 minutes. Meanwhile, soften 4 tablespoons of butter by pressing it around in a mortar and work into it about a quarter cup of fresh basil leaves, chopped, or 2 teaspoons dried, plus 1 tablespoon of the vinegar. Toss the ¾ cup of thinly sliced white mushrooms lightly with the 1 tablespoon of walnut oil plus the remaining tablespoon of vinegar. Chop about ¼ cup of parsley. Hold all these until the beans are served.

As soon as beans are perfectly done, pour off any remaining water (saving it for stock) and put saucepan back over low heat for 2 or 3 minutes for beans to dry out. Pick out and discard any remaining sprigs of rosemary or savory. Finally, pile beans into a hot salad serving bowl and toss into them the basil butter, the mushrooms and the parsley. Serve at once.

THE WHITE BEANS OF SOISSONS WITH WATERCRESS CREAM
(*Les Haricots Blancs de Soissons au Cresson*)

FOR 4 PEOPLE

The giant white beans (each almost ¾ inch long) that I have held in my hand in the Farmer's Market of Grenoble are, sadly, not a part of our fall harvest in the United States. But I have prepared this dish quite satisfactorily with our large white marrowfat or lima beans, and this recipe is adapted to their use. It is an ideal and handsome accompaniment to roasted lamb or mutton, with its creamy smoothness and contrasting colors of bright green and white. (See discussion on page 94; menu with wines on page 93.)

Staple Items
Butter (about 4 Tb)
Carrots (2 medium)
Yellow onions (2 medium)

Flavorings
Crystal salt, freshly ground
  black pepper, garlic (1
  clove), dill, oregano, savory

Shopping List
Large marrowfat or lima
  beans (1 lb.)
Watercress (1 large bunch
  or 2 small)
Heavy cream (1 cup)

*The Day Before—Set the Beans to Unsupervised Soaking for About
12 Hours*

Bring 3 pints of freshly drawn cold water up to a rolling boil in
a 2½- or 3-quart lidded saucepan. While it is boiling hard, dribble the
pound of beans through your fingers into the hot water, but slowly
enough so that they do not take the water off the boil. Let the hard
boiling continue for 2 minutes, then turn off the heat, put on the lid
and leave the beans to soak for 12 hours or more. (If you are using
limas, they sometimes froth up and boil over—so watch them and be
ready to turn down the heat.)

*About 1½ Hours Before Serving—Active Preparation About 15
Minutes—Entirely Unsupervised Simmering*

Some of the skins of the beans will have floated to the top
of the soaking water. Skim these off and throw them away. The
beans will have expanded and more cold water will have to be added
to keep them covered. They should be about 1 inch, not more, below
the surface of the water. Bring them back up to gentlest simmering,
"just smiling," adding to them the 2 carrots and the 2 onions, both
chopped, the clove of garlic, finely minced, plus 1 teaspoon each of
dill, oregano and savory. Again, if you are using limas, it is best to
melt a tablespoon of the butter on the surface of the water to stifle
any possible frothing and boiling over. Keep the gentlest simmering
going steadily, with the pan covered, until the beans are beautifully
soft and flavorful—usually in 1¼ to 1½ hours.

Meanwhile, wash the watercress, cut away the harder stalks and
coarsely snip the remaining leaves and baby stalks with sharp kitchen
scissors, then hold them. Put the 1 cup of cream into a 1-quart saucepan, add the remaining 3 tablespoons of butter, but do not heat them
up yet.

About 15 Minutes Before Serving

Gently heat up the butter and cream, but be careful not to let the
mixture boil. When it feels hot to the touch, put in the watercress,
stirring it around and adding salt and pepper to taste.

About 5 Minutes Before Serving

Drain the beans and put them into a hot serving bowl. Pour the
watercress cream evenly over the top for maximum decoration.

CARDOONS WITH BEEF MARROW
(*Cardons à la Moelle*)

FOR 4 PEOPLE

The Italian-originated *cardone*, which looks and tastes rather like a silvery green globe artichoke on a long stem, is one of the favorite winter vegetables of gourmets in France and Italy. It also grows in California and is distributed nationally during the winter months. One eats the leafy, fleshy and tender, delicately flavored midribs of the plant, and this is one of the best methods of preparing them. (Menu with wines on page 56.)

Staple Items

For the Béchamel Sauce:

    Sweet butter (4 Tb)
    Milk (1¼ cups)
    All-purpose flour (4 Tb)

For the Blanching Bouillon:

    Lemon (1)
    All-purpose flour (¼ cup)
    Olive oil (3 Tb)

Flavorings

Crystal salt, freshly ground
    black pepper

Shopping List

Cardoons (1 or 2, according
    to size)
Beef marrow (½ lb.)
Parmesan cheese (¼ lb.—
    about ½ cup, grated)

About 3 Hours Before Serving—Active Preparation About 30 Minutes —Unsupervised Simmering and Baking About 2½ Hours

Have ready a French-style *blanc de cuisson*—blanching bouillon— a white blanching and poaching liquid in which to soften the cardoon slices. For this, put about 1 pint of cold water into a 2-quart saucepan and stir in ¼ cup of the flour, the juice of the lemon and the 3 table-spoons of olive oil, and bring up to gentle simmering. Skin the fleshy midribs of the cardoons, slice them fairly thin, drop slices into sim-mering liquid and cook gently until they are quite soft—usually in about 2 hours.

Preparing Béchamel Sauce in About 15 Minutes

In a 1-quart saucepan, over medium heat, melt the 4 tablespoons of butter and blend in the 4 tablespoons flour. Stir until fully blended and very smooth. Then leave on low heat to cook the flour while you heat up the 1¼ cups of milk in another saucepan. Now, again stirring continuously, begin gradually blending the milk into the butter-flour *roux*, continuing to stir until it all thickens and is very smooth. Cook very gently, stirring, until it achieves the consistency of thick cream.

Poach the beef marrow in simmering water for about 5 minutes, then slice and hold.

About 15 Minutes Before Serving

Into an ovenproof open au gratin dish, lightly buttered (with sweet butter), put first a single layer of cardoon slices, then a thin layer of white sauce, a few slices of the beef marrow with salt and pepper, then repeat layers in the same order until all cardoons, sauce and marrow are used up. Then cover the top with the ½ cup grated Parmesan cheese. Preheat oven to 400 degrees and set shelf so that cardoons will be in center. Put dish into oven and bake until everything is bubbling hot and cheese is melted and lightly browned—usually in 10 to 15 minutes.

WILTED DANDELION SALAD WITH SALT PORK
(*La Salade de Pissenlit aux Lardons*)

FOR 4 PEOPLE

At the Auberge this is a spring salad made with young dandelion leaves picked by Mademoiselle Vivette in the fields in the Valley. I pick up mine from a basket on the stand of my favorite greengrocer. Incidentally, this is the traditional accompaniment, on Alpine farmhouse menus, to the Omelette à la Savoyarde (page 189) so often served for Sunday lunch. (See menu with wines on page 77.)

Staple Items
Eggs, hard-boiled (4)
Tarragon wine vinegar (about
2 tablespoons)
Garlic-rubbed croûtons fried
in olive oil (½ cup)
French-fried potatoes—
optional (enough for 4
people)

Shopping List
Young dandelion leaves
(enough to fill a quart
measure, about ½ to ¾
lb.)
Lean salt pork, diced (enough
to fill about ½ cup)

Flavorings
Freshly ground black pepper,
garlic for croûtons

About 10 Minutes Before Serving

Fry the salt pork dice until they have given up most of their fat and are crackly crisp. See that there is plenty of garlic on the croûtons. Wash and dry the dandelion leaves, then put them into the salad bowl and sprinkle with pepper (the salt comes from the pork) and a tablespoon or so of the vinegar. Add the croûtons and pour over the salt pork dice with the hot fat that they have given up. Quickly toss the salad, decorate with slices of the hard-boiled eggs and serve at once, accompanied ideally (but not necessarily) by the hot French-fried potatoes.

EGGPLANT BAKED IN CREAM

(*Les Aubergines à la Crème*)

FOR 4 PEOPLE

This is a rich preparation of the vegetable, and very good as an accompaniment to game meats. (See menu with wines on page 117.)

Staple Items	*Shopping List*
Butter (6 ounces)	Eggplants (about 3, according to size)
Flavorings	Sour cream (½ cup)
Crystal salt, freshly ground black pepper	

About 40 Minutes Before Serving—Preparing and Frying the Egg-plants in About 20 Minutes—Unsupervised Baking for up to 20 Minutes

Cut off the stalk ends of the eggplants, peel them and cut them lengthwise into slices just under ½ inch thick. Lightly brown each slice in hot butter in a sauté pan over medium frying heat. They will absorb a lot of butter, so you must keep adding it, tablespoon by tablespoon, to the pan. Neatly lay the gilded slices in a flat, open baking dish or ceramic casserole ready to go into the oven. Preheat the oven to 400 degrees. Salt and pepper the ½ cup of sour cream to your taste and spoon it evenly over the eggplant. Place the baking dish in the center of the oven and bake until the eggplant slices are thoroughly soft and have enriched themselves with a good part of the cream—usually in 15 to 20 minutes. Just before serving, set the baking dish under a hot grill until the top surface is flecked with brown—usually in 2 to 3 minutes.

SALAD OF BELGIAN ENDIVE WITH CRISPED-BACON DRESSING
(*Salade de Cornette au Lard*)

FOR 4 PEOPLE

Excellent whenever the endive is in season—usually from October through April (menu with wines on page 16). The Salade de Cornette of the Alps is not exactly the same variety as the Belgian endive imported into the United States, but the general ambiance of this salad as we can make it here is almost exactly the same, as they are very close—both members of the *chicorée*, chicory, family.

Staple Items
Bacon, dark-smoked, thickly
  sliced (8 rashers)
Tarragon wine vinegar (8
  tsp)
Garlic croûtons, fried in
  advance (1 cup)

Shopping List
Belgian endive (6 average
  size)
Green scallions (4)

Flavorings
Crystal salt, freshly ground
  black pepper

About 10 Minutes Before Serving

Wipe the 6 endives clean with a damp cloth, cut them into ½-inch chunks and separate the leaves directly into the salad bowl. Finely chop the green tops and white bulbs of the 4 scallions and toss them in the bowl with the endives. Cut the 8 rashers of bacon into small pieces and fry until crisp. Let cool slightly, then add the 8 teaspoons of vinegar and pour everything—fat, vinegar and crisp bits —over the endive. Toss lightly with the 1 cup of croûtons, plus salt and pepper to taste, then serve at once.

MUSHROOMS (CULTIVATED OR WILD) SAUTÉED IN CREAM

(*Chanterelles, ou Trompettes des Morts, Sautées à la Crème*)

FOR 4 PEOPLE

An excellent opening course or a side-dish accompaniment to a main course whenever fine mushrooms are available.

Staple Items	*Shopping List*
Sweet butter (8 Tb)	Small button mushrooms
Toast slices (4)	(1 lb.)
	Heavy cream (1 cup)
Flavorings	Parsley (about 4 Tb,
Crystal salt, freshly ground	chopped)
pepper	

About 15 Minutes Before Serving

Carefully wipe each mushroom clean with a damp cloth. Never wash mushrooms by soaking in water—it dilutes the flavor oils inside the gills. Put mushrooms into dry frying pan over medium-low frying heat and stir them around, so they get rid of their water. If bottom of pan actually runs with water, pour it off. Put in the 8 tablespoons of butter and keep stirring to coat all mushrooms. Continue gently sautéing mushrooms, so that they absorb butter, for about 7 minutes. Then add the 1 cup of cream, the chopped parsley, plus salt and pepper to taste. Keep stirring around for about a minute more, then serve at once, with the pan sauce, on toast slices, on very hot plates.

WILD MOUNTAIN MUSHROOMS IN THE PEASANT STYLE

(*Les Hygrophores de Neige à la Paysanne*)

FOR 4 PEOPLE

Naturally, Mademoiselle Ray's little "snow mushrooms" are not available in the United States (or for that matter anywhere else in France), but I have found that our button mushrooms work extremely well prepared in this excellent way. The secret trick of the recipe is still valid. You expel their own water from the mushroom so that a tiny vacuum is created inside, and they suck in the aromatic butter and the attractively tart peasant-style egg and lemon sauce. (See discussion on page 71—menu with wines on page 74.)

Staple Items
Butter (7 Tb)
Egg yolks (2, possibly 3)
Lemon (1)

Shopping List
Tiny button mushrooms
   (1 lb.)
Good chicken broth (1 cup)

Flavorings
Crystal salt, freshly ground
   black pepper

About 15 Minutes Before Serving

Wipe the mushrooms clean. Do not wash away their internal juices by wetting them with water. Melt the 7 tablespoons of butter in a sauté pan and quickly sauté the mushrooms over fairly high heat until the bubbling stops, showing that all the water has first been expelled and then boiled away. Sprinkle on salt and pepper. Add the juice of the lemon and the 1 cup of chicken broth. Bring up to gentle bubbling and continue for about 3 minutes. Break 2 of the yolks into a small mixing bowl, beat lightly with a fork, then beat into them, one by one, 4 tablespoons of the hot broth from the sauté pan. Then, at once, vigorously work the yolks into the main sauté pan, stirring strongly until the sauce begins to thicken slightly. It should, finally, have the consistency of heavy cream. If it does not get thick enough, work in, in the same way, a third yolk. When mushrooms and sauce are exactly right, serve at once on very hot plates.

MUSHROOMS À LA SAVOYARDE

(Les Chanterelles à la Savoyarde)

FOR 4 PEOPLE

At the Auberge, Mademoiselle Ray changes slightly the cooking of her wild mushrooms, since the size and texture vary among those she picks in the spring, summer and fall. She uses this cheesy-creamy method with the bright yellow *chanterelles* of July and August. I find that the recipe works almost equally well with our domestic mushrooms. (See menu with wines on page 86.)

Staple Items
Butter (about 6 Tb)
Yellow onions (2 medium)

Shopping List
Mushrooms (1½ lbs.)
French Alpine Gruyère cheese,
   grated (about ¼ lb.)
Sour cream (about ½ cup)
Parsley (1 small bunch)
Salt pork (¼ lb.)

About 1¼ Hours Before Serving—Active Preparation About 15 Minutes—Unsupervised Simmering About 1 Hour

Wipe the 1½ pounds of mushrooms clean, separate the caps and stalks, cut off and discard any dried ends and hold everything for the sautéing. Wash as much salt as possible from the ¼ pound of salt pork, dice it and hold. In a sauté pan over fairly low frying heat, melt 4 tablespoons of the butter, add the diced salt pork, the mushroom caps and stems and let them sizzle for a few minutes to give up their moisture and absorb the flavors of the butter and pork. Mince the 2 onions and sprinkle into the sauté pan. Then, cover the pan and let everything inside it simmer gently for about an hour.

About 5 Minutes Before Serving

Stir the contents of the sauté pan gently but thoroughly. Work in, first, the ½ cup sour cream, then the ¼ pound of grated cheese. Turn up the heat slightly and keep stirring until the sour cream is thoroughly heated and the cheese melted. Serve at once on very hot plates —either as a supper dish or as an accompanying vegetable for a main meat dish—with plenty of bright green parsley sprinkled on top.

THE AUTHENTIC RATATOUILLE OF NICE
(*La Salade de Ratatouille à la Niçoise*)

FOR 4 PEOPLE

The *ratatouille* has become such a normal and universal dish on American tables across the country that many people who eat it regularly are unaware of the fact that it originated as the great specialty of the city of Nice, where of course there is an unlimited supply of garlic, olive oil and tomatoes—the basic ingredients of what has come to be called *La Cuisine Niçoise*. The other point that is often forgotten is that in Nice the *ratatouille* is served in two distinctly different ways. It is brought to table hot as a vegetable accompaniment to a main meat course, or it comes cold as a salad, a separate course between the main entrée and the inevitable cheeses. Mademoiselle Ray's version is the authentic original Niçois recipe—simple, earthy, with no added folderols or luxurious overtones. (See discussion on page 152; menu with wines on page 150.)

Staple Items
Butter (4 Tb)
Yellow onions (3 medium)
Olive oil (½ cup)

Flavorings
Crystal salt, freshly ground
    black pepper, garlic (1
    clove)

Shopping List
Tomatoes, perfectly ripe (6
    medium)
Eggplant (2 medium)
Green pepper (1 medium)
Zucchini (6 medium)
French Alpine Gruyère cheese,
    grated (⅓ cup)

About 2½ Hours Before Serving—Active Preparation ½ Hour— Unsupervised Simmering 2 Hours

Chop the 3 onions and lightly gild them in the ½ cup of olive oil over medium frying heat. Be careful not to let them brown. Skin the 6 tomatoes, cut them into ⅛ sections and then add them to the onions. Turn down the heat and let them simmer gently, uncovered. Skin and slice fairly thinly the 2 eggplants and the 6 zucchini, then lightly sauté them in the 4 tablespoons of butter in a sauté pan over medium frying heat. When they are just gilded, add them to the tomatoes in the main casserole and gently blend them in. Also work in the green pepper, chopped, and the clove of garlic, finely minced, with salt and pepper to taste, then let everything continue gently simmering, covered, for at least 2 hours. Gently stir and turn the contents over every 20 minutes. Toward the end of the cooking, if there is too much liquid, boil it off by turning up the heat and bubbling it a little harder, uncovered, until the excess liquid has steamed away.

About 10 Minutes Before Serving

Turn the *ratatouille* out into a shallow serving bowl, sprinkle it with the ¼ cup of grated cheese and place it under a farily hot grill for a couple of minutes to brown the top lightly. Serve at once hot, or let it cool to room temperature.

SECTION XV

Desserts
The Wild Mountain Fruits

CLASSIC UPSIDEDOWN APPLE TART

(Tarte aux Pommes des Belles Demoiselles Tatin)

FOR 4 TO 6 PEOPLE

This is the most famous apple tart of France, and once you have mastered its special technique, you will probably never want to make any other. (For the story of the sisters Tatin and the accident that led to their invention, see page 35—menu with wines on page 33.) The tart will, of course, have a different character with different kinds of apples. Try it especially with Greening, Rome Beauty, Northern Spy, Winesap or York Imperial. . . .

Staple Items	*Shopping List*
Sweet butter (4 Tb)	Pie apples, see above (3 lbs.)
White granulated sugar (½ lb.)	
Also: French pie pastry (1 batch, see recipe below)	

About 1½ Hours Before Serving—Active Preparation About 30 Minutes—Unsupervised Baking and Resting About 1 Hour

Much earlier (see recipe below) you will have mixed, kneaded and rested a batch of standard French Pâte à Tarte, short-crust tart pastry. Now, peel and core the apples, then cut them into ¼-inch-thick slices. The shape of the baking pan is very important. It must have straight sides like a layer-cake pan, not sloping sides like a normal pie plate. It must be about 9 inches across and 2½ to 3 inches deep. This type is imported from France in either tinned copper, aluminum, or stainless steel. There are also American-made counterparts in Pyrex.

Begin by making a caramel. Cook ½ cup of sugar with 3 tablespoons of water in a heavy skillet over fairly high heat until the sugar turns to a golden caramel. Pour the caramel into the bottom of the baking pan you have selected and tilt the pan so that the caramel coats the bottom evenly. On this, carefully and precisely lay the slices of apple. Sprinkle over them all the sugar that remains. Then, dot them with the butter. Preheat oven to 375 degrees and set shelf so that tart will be only about one third up from the bottom. Roll out pastry about ¼ inch thick and cut a circle of it about 11 inches across. Carefully lay this on top of the apples, then fold edge downwards, as if you were tucking in a blanket around the sleeping apples. Press against sides of pan so that apples will be as hermetically sealed as reasonably possible.

About 1½ Hours Before Serving

Set tart in oven. The baking time is usually from 45 to 50 minutes. It is important to learn to recognize the exact moment of doneness. First, the pastry crust should be golden brown. If crust shows signs of browning too quickly, cover pan lightly with aluminum foil. In metal pan, check whether sugar has caramelized by tilting pan slightly. The liquid which will appear at edge of crust should be thick brown syrup—not light and thin. With a glass pan you can check the brownness through the bottom. At this point, take the tart from the oven. Let it cool about 30 minutes. Then turn it out onto a serving platter, so that crust forms the base, shiny caramelized apples are on top and browned liquid sugar forms a glaze.

BASIC FRENCH SHORT-CRUST PASTRY FOR APPLE TART
(*Pâte à Tarte*)

FOR ONE 9-INCH TART

Staple Items	All-purpose flour (1¾ cups,
Sweet butter (5 Tb)	after sifting)
Egg (1)	Salt (1 tsp)
White granulated sugar	
(¼ cup)	

At Least 4 Hours Before Starting the Tart—Active Preparation About 15 Minutes—Unsupervised Chilling and Resting of Dough in Remaining Time

The technique of mixing this dough with the tips of the fingers and of kneading it with the heel of the hand is exactly the same as described for Pâte à Foncer, page 175. When it hangs together enough to make a ball, wrap in wax paper and rest in refrigerator for about 4 hours. Then roll out about ¼ inch thick, as required by main recipe above.

MOUSSE OF FRESH APRICOTS
(*La Mousse aux Abricots*)

FOR 4 PEOPLE

This is *the* dessert for the time when fresh apricots are at their freshest and ripest. They are made exciting, light and luxurious here by the balanced addition of whipped cream, orange Curaçao liqueur, the zest of lemon and the fluffy whites of eggs. (See discussion on page 130; menu with wines on page 128.)

Staple Items	*Shopping List*
Egg, white only (1)	Fresh apricots, ripe and soft
Lemon juice and grated	(about a dozen for the
outer rind (½ lemon)	mousse, plus a dozen for
Superfine sugar (1½ cups)	garnishing)
	Heavy cream (1¼ cups)
	Orange Curaçao liqueur
	(2 ounces)

About 1½ Hours Before Serving— Can Be Made Well Ahead and Held—Active Preparation About 30 Minutes—Unsupervised Minimum Freezing Time About 1 Hour

Prepare the first dozen apricots by washing, halving and stoning them, then boil them in a very small amount of water until they are thoroughly soft and mashable—usually in about 10 minutes. Then purée them through a food mill or sieve and let them cool. Only then add the juice and grated rind of the half lemon, plus 1 cup (or less, if you have less of a sweet tooth) of the sugar, working everything together steadily for about 5 minutes, until it is absolutely smooth. Stiffly whip the 1¼ cups of cream and gently fold ⅔ of it into the mousse. Stiffly whip the white of the egg and fold this into the remaining ⅓ of the whipped cream. Now, gently spoon the mousse into your chosen serving dish, spread it evenly and cover it with a layer of the cream and egg-white mixture. Wrap the dish tightly in aluminum foil and put it in the freezer for about 45 minutes, then transfer it to the coldest part of the refrigerator and hold until serving time. Never freeze it solid.

Meanwhile, wash, halve and stone the remaining dozen apricots and marinate them in a mixture of the remaining ½ cup of sugar and the 2 ounces of orange Curaçao. Leave it for about an hour.

Just Before Serving

Handsomely decorate the top of the mousse with the most color-ful sides of the apricot halves and lightly sprinkle on the remaining marinade. Serve very cold.

BANANAS FLAMED WITH RUM
(*Bananes Flambées au Rhum*)

FOR 4 PEOPLE

I have often noticed that there seems to be a fine affinity between the fruits and the distilled spirits or wines of a single area or region. For example, peaches grow beautifully in Portugal and can be wonderfully married to Port. Again, bananas are the prime fruit of the Caribbean, and they go superbly with the spirit of the local sugar cane. Here we use the extraordinary dark French-style *rhum* of Martinique, which Mademoiselle Ray always keeps on hand in her kitchen at the Auberge. (See menu with wines on page 96.)

Staple Items	*Shopping List*
Sweet butter (4 Tb)	Large ripe bananas (6)
Lemon (1)	One of the great rums
Dark brown sugar (about	(½ cup)
⅓ cup)	

About 25 Minutes Before Serving

Preheat oven to 450 degrees. Peel and cross-cut bananas into ½-inch chunks. Choose a shallow, open ovenproof dish, handsome

enough to come to the table. Put into it the 4 tablespoons of butter
and set in the oven for 2 or 3 minutes for the butter just to melt.
Put in the banana chunks, gently working them around, until each
is thoroughly coated with butter. Put back in oven and bake until
banana is quite soft, usually in 15 minutes. Then sprinkle bananas
with the brown sugar and a few squeezes of lemon juice to taste, and
put back into until sugar is melted, usually 3 to 4 minutes
longer. Pour in the ½ cup of rum (no need to heat it in such a
hot dish), set it alight and rush it flaming to the table.

CHERRY BATTER PIE, LIMOUSIN STYLE
(*Clafouti Limousin*)

FOR 4 PEOPLE

A *clafouti* is a baked batter pie, a classic recipe of the Limousin
region of southern France, where cherries are abundant. Mademoiselle Ray, of course, uses the famous Alpine cherries of Allevard.

Staple Items	Confectioners' sugar (a few
Sweet butter (1 tsp, to grease	Tb)
dish)	Crystal salt (½ tsp)
Eggs (3 large)	Vanilla extract (1 Tb)
Milk (1¼ cups)	
All-purpose flour (1 cup)	*Shopping List*
Granulated white sugar	Sweet, ripe cherries (1½ lbs.)
(about ½ cup)	Crystallized ginger (2 oz.)

Well Ahead of Time

Pit enough cherries to fill about 3 cups, fairly tightly packed;
the exact amount is not critical. Chop the ginger and set aside.

About 1¼ Hours Before Serving

Preheat oven to 350 degrees. The batter can be beaten by hand
or made in an electric blender. In the second case, put into the
blender container the 3 eggs, the 1¼ cups milk, the 1 cup flour,
⅓ cup of the granulated sugar, ½ teaspoon salt and the tablespoon

of vanilla extract. Stir ingredients together before switching on the machine, cover and run at high speed for about 30 seconds.

Choose an open baking dish in which the batter will stand deep enough to cover the cherries. Nine by 9 by 2 inches is the ideal size. Butter the dish and pour in enough batter to cover the bottom with a layer ¼ inch deep. Place the dish on a top burner over medium frying heat until the batter is lightly set, usually in about 2 minutes. Turn off heat at once and drop cherries on this batter foundation, making a solid single layer. Sprinkle with the chopped ginger and the remaining granulated sugar to taste. Pour over the rest of the batter, submerging the cherries. Put the dish in the center of the oven and bake until the top is brown and puffy. A silver knife plunged into the center at this point should come out dry. The total baking time is usually 1 hour. Immediately sprinkle the top with the confectioners' sugar and serve piping hot.

TÔT-FAIT BAKED CUSTARD WITH THE GLAZED CHERRIES OF ALLEVARD
(*Le Tôt-Fait aux Cerises d'Allevard*)

FOR 4 PEOPLE

The word *tôt-fait* means, literally, "all done" in a relatively few minutes of preparation. It is a specialty of the region—technically I suppose, a dessert, but solid enough to be a main course for someone with a slightly sweet tooth and a taste for the marvelous mountain cherries of Allevard. Obviously this dish is a variation of the Spanish *flan,* so probably in the distant past it traveled across the Pyrenees and was adapted to the ingredients of the Alpine mountains. (See menu with wines on page 142.)

Staple Items	*Shopping List*
Butter (2 Tb)	Brandied cherries, drained
Eggs (4 large)	(½ cup)
Flour (4 Tb)	Light cream (1 quart)
Superfine sugar (½ cup)	Cherry brandy (1 ounce)

*About 45 Minutes Before Serving—Active Preparation in About 15
Minutes—Unsupervised Baking for About 30 Minutes*

Break the 4 eggs into a mixing bowl and beat them lightly with
a fork. Work into them the ½ cup of sugar and the 4 tablespoons
of flour. Then mix in the quart of light cream, the ½ cup of drained
cherries and the ounce of cherry brandy. Preheat the oven to 425
degrees. Pour the mixture into a 2-quart buttered soufflé dish and
bake at the center of the oven until a silver knife comes out clean to
indicate that the custard is completely set—usually in about 30
minutes. Serve it very hot.

FRIED CHESTNUT CROQUETTES
(*Croquettes de Marrons*)

FOR 4 PEOPLE

A dramatically good dessert whenever fresh chestnuts are available, usually in the winter months, but can also, with some compromise, be made with dried chestnuts or with canned French
chestnut purée. (See discussion on page 43; menu with wines on
page 41.)

Staple Items	*Shopping List*
Egg (1)	Fresh chestnuts, in their
Milk (7 ounces)	shells (about 30—or
Confectioners' sugar	alternative, see above)
(about ¼ cup)	French *marrons glacés*,
Crystal salt	sugar-glazed chestnuts,
Fine breadcrumbs (½ cup)	canned (6 whole)
Olive oil (4 Tb)	Whole vanilla bean (1)
Peanut oil for deep-frying	

*About 1 Hour Before Serving—Active Preparation About 30 Minutes
—Unsupervised Cooking About 30 Minutes*

Preheat the oven to 350 degrees. Using a short-bladed oyster
knife, make 3 deep cross-gashes on the flat side of each chestnut
and put them in a fairly large roasting pan over medium-high fry-

ing heat on top of stove. Sprinkle them with 3 tablespoons of the olive oil and stir them around until they are all well coated. When they start merrily sizzling, set pan in oven and bake them until the inside flesh is just soft—usually in about 20 to 30 minutes.

Meanwhile, measure exactly the 7 ounces milk (1 cup, less 2 tablespoons) and bring it almost, but not quite, to boiling. Slit the vanilla bean in half lengthwise and drop both halves into the milk, with a couple of pinches of salt. Keep everything hot, but still just below boiling, stirring occasionally, so that milk will absorb vanilla flavor.

When chestnuts are ready in oven, shells will have puffed out and will be quickly removable, while furry inner skin will be crisp and can be easily flaked off, even from crevices. As each chestnut is bared, drop it into the vanilla milk, turning heat up slightly, so that liquid is now very gently simmering. As soon as chestnuts are soft enough to purée—usually in about 15 to 20 minutes—remove both halves of vanilla bean, then thoroughly mash chestnuts into the milk. (Or the job may be done mechanically by passing through a food mill.)

Continue cooking purée in saucepan, stirring almost all the time, until it is stiff and thick. Be careful that it does not burn. Then spread it out on a large platter in a layer about 1 inch thick, so that it will cool and set.

Meanwhile, pick out from the *marrons glacés* 6 well-shaped specimens and carefully cut each in half. Around each of these halves, as soon as the chestnut mash is cooked, build a ball of the purée about the size of a medium plum.

Lightly beat the egg in a bowl and add to it 1 teaspoon of the remaining olive oil. Spread the ½ cup of breadcrumbs on a dinner plate. Dip each chestnut ball in the egg, then roll in the crumbs and place in refrigerator to await the moment for frying. Preheat deep-frying oil to 375 degrees.

About 10 Minutes Before Serving

Place chestnut balls in frying basket and lower into hot oil. Make sure that balls do not touch each other. When they are golden brown and have crisp crusts—usually in about 3 or 4 minutes—drain them on absorbent paper, sprinkle them liberally with confectioners' sugar and bring them, still hot, to table.

THE ENTREMET OF WHIPPED CREAM CHEESE
(*L'Entremet au Petit Suisse*)

FOR 4 PEOPLE

The Petit Suisse is probably the most universal of all bland, creamy, soft cheeses in the homes of France. It is called "Little Swiss" because it was invented by a Swiss cheesemaker working on a farm near Paris. It comes in small cylinders rolled in wax paper and open at each end and is eaten everywhere, either with salt as a savory, or with sugar as part of the dessert. Since there is never enough of the farm-made stuff to go around, there is also a manufactured version, which comes (like our own Philadelphia type) in foil-wrapped rectangular packages and is called Gervais. Both of these French cream cheeses are imported into the United States but apparently are not very widely distributed. So if you cannot get the French products, our American cream cheese will do very well, and in this recipe it is whipped up with egg whites into a frozen dessert of irresistible fluffiness and lightness. (See discussion on page 120; menu with wines on page 117.)

Staple Items	*Shopping List*
Eggs (4 large)	Cream cheese, see above
Sugar, superfine (¾ cup)	(12 ounces)
	Sour cream (1 cup)
	Cherry Kirsch (3 ounces)

About 2 Hours Before Serving—Active Preparation About 30 Minutes—Unsupervised Freezing About 1½ Hours—Or May Be Prepared Longer in Advance and Kept Frozen

Bring the cream cheese to room temperature. Separate the 4 eggs and put the yolks into a fairly large mixing bowl. Add ½ to ¾ cup sugar (according to your taste) and beat vigorously until the mixture is creamy and smooth. Then add, piece by piece, the cream cheese (which should now be thoroughly soft) and, using an electric beater, break it up and cream it into the egg mixture. When all the cheese is incorporated, work in the 1 cup of sour cream and the 3 ounces of fine quality Kirsch. Now, thoroughly beat the mixture until it is very glossy and smooth. Next, in a separate mixing bowl, whip the 4 egg whites until they are stiff enough to stand up in peaks, then fold them lightly into the cheese mixture. Now carefully spoon everything into the serving bowl, wrap it tightly in foil, then set in the freezer so that it finally takes on the consistency of soft ice cream. (If you are making it far in advance, you may prefer to freeze it in a covered icebox container.) Always serve it very cold.

LES CRÊPES SURPRISES

FOR 4 PEOPLE

Mademoiselle Ray's surprise is the fluffy filling, strongly flavored with dry cherry brandy and textured with lightly burned almonds. (See menu and wines on page 64.)

Staple Items	*Shopping List*
One batch of Crêpe Batter (as described in Pannequets au Fromage on page 191)	Almonds, blanched and slivered (¼ lb.) Kirsch dry cherry brandy, not a sweet liqueur (4 ounces or 2 jiggers)

For the Crème Pâtissière, pastry cream filling:

Butter (7 Tb)	All-purpose flour (⅓ cup)
Egg yolks (3, from large eggs)	Confectioners' sugar (¾ cup)
Milk (1 cup)	

About 50 Minutes Before Serving—Preparing the Crêpe Batter in About 5 Minutes

Prepare the batter exactly as described for Les Pannequets au Fromage on page 191, but this time, since these are dessert crêpes, also beat into the batter 3 teaspoons of the sugar. Let batter rest.

About 45 Minutes Before Serving—Preparing the Pastry Cream in About 20 Minutes

Put the 3 egg yolks into a mixing bowl and gradually beat into them ½ cup of the confectioners' sugar until the mixture is pale yellow and ribbons—usually in 2 to 3 minutes. Next, beat in the ⅓ cup flour. Bring the 1 cup milk almost to boiling, then add it, dash by dash, beating continuously, to the egg mixture. When everything is smooth and just beginning to thicken, transfer it to a saucepan, over moderate heat, still beating and scraping the bottom of the pan. As the sauce comes to the boil, it will get lumpy, but will smooth out as you continue beating. Keep beating for 2 or 3 minutes more, as it gently bubbles, to cook the flour. Keep scraping the bottom to avoid danger of scorching. Now turn off heat and, at once, beat in the 7 tablespoons of butter. Also beat in, ounce by ounce, the Kirsch, until you have achieved a cherry brandy flavor exactly to your taste. Mademoiselle Ray always uses the full 4 ounces, or even more. Now set aside the cream sauce in the saucepan, first lightly pressing down onto its top surface a fitted round of wax paper. This prevents the formation of a skin. Leave it to keep just warm.

About 20 Minutes Before Serving—Griddling and Filling the Crêpes in About 15 Minutes

Heat up and lightly butter your pancake griddle. Control doses of batter so that each crêpe is very thin and about 2½ inches across. Spread each crêpe fairly thickly with the Kirsch pastry cream, then roll up and place neatly in a grill pan. Set the grill to heat up. When all the crêpes are in the pan, side by side in a single layer, cover them with the remainder (or part of it) of the pastry cream, sprinkle thickly with the ½ cup of slivered almonds and put under the grill until almonds are nicely browned. Serve very hot on hot plates.

FRESH GOOSEBERRY TART
(*La Tarte aux Groseilles*)
FOR 4 TO 6 PEOPLE

The secret trick here is that the gooseberries are hardly cooked at all but are burst open and instantly sweetened by being dropped into a burning hot, thick sugar syrup before being spread into a prebaked fluffy and rich tart shell. The fruit mixture gels almost immediately as it begins to cool, forming a luscious, refreshing yet rich, sour-sweet filling. (See menu with wines on page 83.)

Staple Items
One batch of basic yeast-raised tart pastry, Pâte à Tarte Levée, as described for Tart of Fresh Raspberries Sealed In Cream on page 402.
Sweet butter (9 Tb)
Eggs (2)
Extra egg yolk (1)

Milk (⅓ cup, plus 1 Tb for glaze)
White granulated sugar (4 Tb)
All-purpose flour (2 cups, after sifting)
Salt (½ tsp)

Shopping List
Yeast (1 envelope)

Plus Ingredients for the Filling:

Superfine sugar (1¾ lbs.)
Fresh gooseberries (2 lbs.)

Total Preparation Time About 1 Hour—Active Preparation of Shell and Filling About 30 Minutes—Unsupervised Baking of the Shell About 30 Minutes

Prepare the yeast-raised pastry, line the tart pan and bake the shell exactly as described in the raspberry tart recipe on page 402. Meanwhile, pick over the gooseberries, removing the stalks and pits. Put them into a heavy saucepan over medium-high heat with the 1¾ pounds of sugar, and stir continuously as it heats up, slightly crushing the gooseberries so that their juices will liquefy and dissolve the sugar. The instant it is all syrup, remove the solid gooseberries with a slotted spoon and put them into a holding bowl. Turn up the heat under the saucepan and boil the sugar hard, stirring every 2 or 3 minutes, until the syrup shows clear signs of thickening. As soon as the tart shell is baked, spread it evenly with the gooseberries, then cover them with the sugar syrup. As soon as the tart begins to cool, the syrup will become a firm jelly, sealing in and solidifying the gooseberries, while excess juice will be absorbed by the rich and spongy pastry. Thus, the whole tart becomes a luxuriously solid unity.

THE FLAMING ICE CREAM MOUNTAIN OF CHAMECHAUDE
(*Le Chamechaude Flambé*)

FOR A PARTY OF 8 TO 10

This is a piece of dessert nonsense on a monumental scale— but fun! The Chamechaude is the mighty mountain, almost 8,000 feet high, which dominates the Valley of La Grande Chartreuse. If you sit near the main window of the dining room of the Auberge, Chamechaude seems to tower over you—its lower slopes green with meadows, speckled with mountain flowers; its middle slopes dark with pine forests; its heights brown and grey with outcroppings of granite; its peak glistening and white with ice and snow. So perhaps it was hardly a surprise, one day several years ago when Mademoiselle Vivette was trying to think of a dramatic and large dessert for a local wedding party, that she should look out of the window and decide to make a model of Chamechaude in various colors and flavors of ice cream. Then she decorated it lavishly, using green sticks of angelica to simu- late the trees, glacéed fruits for the flowers, nougat for the rocks, icing sugar and whipped cream for the snow . . . and, just to make a monster joke of it, as it was brought into the dining room she poured over it lashings of local brandy and set the whole darn thing on fire! It was such a success that she has been making it for parties ever since. (A full description of the action is on page 181.)

For the *Génoise:*

Staple Items
Eggs (6 large)
Sweet butter, clarified (½ cup)

All-purpose flour, sifted (1 cup)
Granulated sugar (1 cup)
Vanilla extract (1 tsp)

About 2½ Hours Before Serving—Active Preparation About 50 Minutes, Including Icing After Baking

Preheat oven to 350 degrees. Butter and lightly flour a jelly-roll pan (11 by 16 inches) or a pan close to that size. The cake, when baked, should be quite wide and relatively flat, to make a firm foundation for the mountain of ice cream.

To clarify the ½ cup butter, place it in a small, deep saucepan to melt over low heat, then continue cooking it until the foam disappears from the surface and a brownish sediment collects on the bottom of the pan, usually in no more than 10 minutes. When butter looks perfectly clear, remove from heat, skim off any crust from the top and strain the butter through a muslin-lined sieve, or simply pour the clear butter off the top, leaving the sediment behind in the bottom of the pan. Set the clarified butter aside to cool.

In a large bowl, stir the 6 eggs with the 1 cup sugar just until combined. Place the bowl over a saucepan containing about 2 inches of hot water and set the pan over low heat until the eggs are lukewarm, usually in 5 to 10 minutes. Stir several times during this period to keep the eggs from cooking and sticking to the bowl. Then, remove from heat and begin beating the eggs vigorously (an electric mixer would be useful here). Continue beating the mixture until it is light, fluffy and almost tripled in bulk, with the appearance of whipped cream. This usually takes 10 to 15 minutes with an electric mixer and about 25 minutes by hand. Don't be lazy and settle for less beating than necessary—the lightness of the *génoise* depends on the proper completion of this step.

Now, sift the 1 cup flour and sprinkle it, tablespoon by tablespoon, over the beaten eggs, folding it in gently and adding the ½ cup clarified butter, cooled but still liquid, and the 1 teaspoon vanilla extract. Do not overmix. Pour the batter into the pan and bake until the cake is lightly browned and pulling away from the sides of the pan, usually in 25 to 30 minutes. Remove immediately from pan and set aside on a rack to cool completely. Transfer the cake to a large, attractive platter or tray before putting on the icing.

For the Icing:

Staple Items	*Shopping List*
Egg white (1)	Sweet cherry liqueur (2 Tb)
Lemon juice (1 tsp)	
Confectioners' sugar, sifted	
(1½ cups, or a bit more)	
Salt	

In a medium bowl, combine the 1½ cups confectioners' sugar, sifted, with a pinch of salt, the 1 egg white and the 1 teaspoon lemon juice. Then beat well until the mixture is light and fluffy and standing in peaks. Beat in the 2 tablespoons cherry liqueur and then, if necessary, add a bit more sugar to correct the consistency—the icing should not be too stiff. The longer it is beaten, the better it is. Spread immediately in a thin layer on the well-cooled *génoise,* then put the cake aside for a few minutes to allow the icing to set before constructing the Chamechaude on it.

About ½ Hour Before Serving—Preparation for and Construction of the Chamechaude

For the Whipped Cream:

Staple Items	*Shopping List*
Confectioners' sugar (3 Tb)	Heavy cream (1 cup)
Vanilla extract (½ tsp)	Kirsch (2 Tb)

For the Final Assembly:

Shopping List	
Pistachio ice cream (½ gallon)	Almond paste (½ lb.)
	Glacéed angelica (6 ounces)
Coffee ice cream (½ gallon)	Cognac (1 cup)

Whip the 1 cup of cream until very stiff, then fold in the 3 tablespoons confectioners' sugar with the ½ teaspoon vanilla extract and the 2 tablespoons Kirsch. Put in the refrigerator to chill until needed.

Now, take a moment to read the recipe and to think through the pending act of creation, so that you won't be held up later trying to make decisions while the ice cream "snow" melts away beneath your hands. If at all possible, find a cool place in which to work and enlist the aid of a helper to "plant" the angelica trees on the lower slopes while you are completing the topmost peaks.

Set out the *génoise,* now cooled and glazed and resting on its serving tray. You will begin building the mountain, on the cake foundation, with a layer of pistachio ice cream, to represent the grass-covered lower slopes. In a bowl, work the ½ gallon of ice cream with a wooden spoon to soften it slightly, then spread it somewhat irregularly on the *génoise,* leaving a border of cake about 1½ inches wide showing all the way around. Do not smooth the top—the line where this green layer ends and the next layer of brown coffee ice cream "rock masses" begins should be not straight but, as in nature, relatively uneven. Soften in a bowl the ½ gallon of the coffee ice cream and begin adding it on top of the pistachio, gradually narrowing the mass the higher it goes. As soon as you have completed this layer, you—or your helper—can begin distributing the green sticks of angelica, pressing them slightly into the ice cream over the lower slopes, like tiny trees growing up from the green-covered earth and occasionally defying nature to appear, higher up, growing amidst the rocks.

Mold the very highest peak, the proud summit, of almond paste, pressing it down gently into the brown ice cream layer at the point where the ice cream mass is highest and most narrow. Now, take the whipped cream out of the refrigerator and pile it on thickly, swirling it into peaks here and there. Leave the lower tree-covered slopes green, and allow part of the almond paste summit, where the wind would blow the snow away, to remain uncovered, "pointing like a sharp tooth up at the sky."

Bear the Chamechaude to table and, while your guests are admiring it, quickly heat up the cup of Cognac. Then, with a flourish, pour the warmed Cognac over the mountain and set a match to the whole affair.

LEMON CREAM TART OF THE ATRE FLEURI
(Tarte au Citron à l'Atre Fleuri)

FOR 6 PEOPLE

This is one of Mademoiselle Ray's *grandes spécialités*—a near-perfect balance between the acid tartness of the lemon and the richly sweet smoothness of the egg cream. (See discussion on page 69; menu with wines on page 67.)

> *Staple Items*
> One batch of Pâte à Tarte,
>   French pie-shell pastry
>   (page 379)

For the Lemon-Cream Filling:

Sweet butter (6 Tb plus	Milk (2 Tb)
a bit to rub on tart pan)	Lemons (2)
Whole eggs (2 large)	Arrowroot or cornstarch (2 tsp)
Egg yolks (3, from large eggs)	Confectioners' sugar (½ cup)

About 1 Hour Before Serving—Prebaking the Pie Shell and Preparing the Filling in About 25 Minutes

Make the pie pastry (as described on page 379), roll it out about ⅛ inch thick and line a 9- or 10-inch lightly buttered French tart pan, preferably with removable bottom. Preheat oven to 375 degrees. Prick bottom of pie shell and weight it down with dried beans, marbles, or a second pan one size smaller. (Mademoiselle Ray puts in small round clean pebbles which she picked up on the beach near Marseilles and has used again and again for years.) Set shell in center of oven and bake for 6 minutes, then remove pebbles (or whatever) to give the shell a chance to bake to a good golden color—usually in 5 to 7 minutes longer.

Meanwhile, prepare the lemon-cream filling. Using a sharp potato peeler (or a French zest scraper), thinly slice off the yellow outer rind of the 2 lemons, chop finely and reserve. Squeeze the juice from the 2 lemons and reserve. Blend 2 teaspoons of the arrowroot or cornstarch with the 2 tablespoons milk and reserve. Just melt the 6 tablespoons of butter and reserve. Put the 2 whole eggs and the 3 extra yolks into a mixing bowl and, using a wire whisk, beat with the ½ cup confectioners' sugar until thoroughly blended and smooth. Next, beat in the lemon juice, the lemon rind, the blended arrowroot or cornstarch and the melted butter. As soon as the pie shell is ready, fill with this mixture, reduce oven to 350 degrees and bake tart until it is quite set and the top is faintly brown—usually in 25 to 35 minutes. Tastes equally good hot or cold.

BLACK NOUGAT WITH PINE HONEY
(*Le Nougat Noir au Miel de Pain*)

FOR 4 PEOPLE

The recipe for this extraordinary and irresistible traditional Christmas candy was brought by Mademoiselle Vivette from her native Provence, but was then changed by Mademoiselle Ray to include the strange mountain honey produced by the bees of the Valley in the springtime, when the tiny flowers appear on the pine trees. The pine blossom honey adds its delicate and subtle taste to the browned almonds and the dark nougat. This is one of the thirteen "Christmas Desserts" of Provence, where "The Twelve Days" are increased to thirteen by being extended through the day of Epiphany, with one particular dessert in honor of each day. Here is the original recipe, which I prepare with Linden honey in place of the Alpine pine. (See Mademoiselle Vivette's description of the Provençal Christmas on page 91.)

The pine honey, which is a delicious specialty of the Chartreuse Valley, may be replaced by any good flower honey such as raspberry or buckwheat. The preparation is extremely simple —only the temperature has to be watched, and for this a candy thermometer is a most useful watchdog.

Staple Items
Butter (about 2 Tb)

Shopping List
Flower honey (1 pint)
Whole almonds (3 cups or
about 16 ounces)
Fresh thyme (a small
handful)

Preparation in About 45 Minutes

Into a 1½-quart saucepan, preferably of heavy iron (or any other type which will stand the high heat of candy-making), slowly heat the 1 pint of honey. As the temperature begins to rise, drop in a small handful of the thyme and the 3 cups whole almonds with their skins on (very carefully dried, if you have washed them) and continue cooking slowly, bringing up the temperature, stirring the contents almost continuously until the honey begins to turn dark brown and the almonds begin to crackle. This will usually take about 30 minutes and you must be prepared to keep stirring for that length of time.

Choose a square cake tin, large enough to hold 2 quarts—9 by 9 by 1½ inches in size, for example. Line it carefully with well-buttered, heavy wax paper or aluminum foil. When the almonds and honey are ready, pour them into this mold. Press another piece of buttered paper or foil on top of the hot mixture. On top of that, place a light wooden board of a size just to fit inside the mold and put a reasonably heavy weight on top of the board, so that the candy mixture will be pressed down and solidified. Let it cool gradually to room temperature. Do not refrigerate. When it is cool, take it out of the mold, peel off its covering, lay it on a wooden board and, with a heavy, sharp knife, cut it up into bite-size squares. Store these in a tightly lidded jar. At room temperature they will be chewy. From the refrigerator they will be crackly. This candy will have a different flavor for every kind of honey used. You can literally make hundreds of different experiments, because there are hundreds of honeys.

MOCHA PARFAIT WITH MARTINIQUE RUM
(*Le Parfait Mocha au Rhum de Martinique*)

FOR 6 PEOPLE

This is the classic French version of a frozen dessert with a base of egg yolks beaten with coffee, cream and vanilla sugar, flavored with the superb dark French rum and served in narrow, tall glasses. (See menu with wines on page 150.)

Staple Items	Vanilla sugar (1 cup)
Egg yolks (8 large)	Vanilla extract (1 tsp)
Milk (2 cups)	
Coffee, coarsely ground (1	*Shopping List*
cup)	Heavy cream (2 cups)
Coffee extract (1 Tb)	Martinique rum, dark (4 Tb)

Can Be Made at Any Time in Advance—Active Preparation in About ½ Hour—Unsupervised Freezing and Ripening for About 2½ Hours

It is best to make this in a rotary ice-cream freezer—either the old-fashioned kind with ice and salt in a wooden bucket, or the modern small electric machines which fit inside the refrigerator freezer. You can, at a pinch, freeze it in ice trays—scraping and stirring it around frequently as it hardens—but there is always the danger of a rough, crystalline texture. Begin by beating the 1 cup of vanilla sugar into the 8 egg yolks until you have a smooth cream. Put the 2 cups of milk into a 1-quart saucepan, add the 1 cup of freshly ground coffee, bring up just to boiling and let simmer, uncovered, stirring frequently, for about 5 minutes. Then, when you have a nicely colored and strongly flavored coffee milk, strain out the coffee grounds through a sieve lined with double cheesecloth. When the milk has cooled to about blood heat, gently beat it into the egg-sugar mixture. Put back into the saucepan and reheat gradually, stirring continuously, until it is close to boiling and fairly thick—but under no circumstances let it actually boil. Turn off the heat, let everything cool, and when it has again reached blood heat, stir in the 1 tablespoon of coffee extract and the 1 teaspoon of vanilla. In a beating bowl, preferably by hand with a wire whisk, beat the 2 cups of heavy cream until quite stiff and, when the egg custard is down to room temperature, lightly fold in the whipped cream. Now freeze the mixture by whatever method you have available and, after it is completely solid and needs no more turning, let it rest and ripen in the freezer for at least another two hours. Serve it in parfait glasses with 1 tablespoon of the dark rum poured over the top just as it goes to table.

PEARS POACHED IN SWEETLY AROMATIC RED WINE

(Les Poires au Vin Rouge)

FOR 4 PEOPLE WITH SOME LEFT OVER

This is one of the finest and simplest ways of cooking pears—either the summer Bartletts, or the winter Anjou, Bosc, or Comice—as an elegant, handsome and irresistibly aromatic dessert. The actual poaching takes only about 10 minutes, but it must be done several hours ahead, so that the pears can slowly cool in the wine, absorbing its color and balance of flavors. (See discussion on page 95—menu with wines on page 93.)

Staple Items
Lemon (1)
Superfine sugar (¾ cup)

Flavorings
Stick cinnamon, whole cloves,
  1 whole vanilla bean

Shopping List
Whole pears, perfectly ripe
  (12)
Good red wine (about 4 cups)

At least 3 to 4 Hours Before Serving—Active Preparation in About 10 Minutes—Unsupervised Simmering About 10 Minutes

This should be prepared in an enameled saucepan, as the acid of the fruit and wine might react with metal and spoil the color. Peel the pears, cut them in half, remove the hard core, pits and stalk, rub them at once with the lemon juice to avoid discoloration, rinse them lightly in cold water and neatly stack them in the saucepan. Sprinkle the pears with the ¾ cup of sugar (or less, if the pears are quite sweet, according to your personal taste) and add to the saucepan: one 2-inch stick of cinnamon, 4 whole cloves and the vanilla bean cut in half lengthwise. Then pour in enough of the wine to cover everything, bring up to gentle simmering and continue, covered, for hardly more than 10 minutes. Turn off the heat at once and let the pears cool in the wine. The whole concoction may, if you wish, be refrigerated overnight.

Final Preparation Just Before Serving

Carefully remove the pear halves from the wine and place them neatly, preferably standing up and in line, in the serving dish. Fish out from the red wine the cinnamon stick and the vanilla bean halves, both of which can be dried off and put away to be used another time. The wine will now have slightly thickened and some of it should be strained as the sauce over the pears.

SOUFFLÉ OF FRESH RASPBERRIES
(Le Soufflé aux Framboises)

FOR 4 PEOPLE

The secret trick of this exceptional recipe is that the flavor and texture of the fresh raspberries is held by sealing them with sugar syrup and giving them only a minimum of cooking. Because of the solidifying influence of the sugar, this soufflé holds up beautifully and may be served hot or cold. (See discussion on page 88; menu with wines on page 86.)

Staple Items
Butter (about 1 Tb)
Egg whites (6)
Superfine sugar (1 cup)
Cream of tartar (½ tsp)

Flavorings (optional)
Lemon zest, minced (1 Tb),
   or walnuts, grated (¼ cup)

Shopping List
Raspberries (1 lb.)

About 40 Minutes Before Serving—Active Preparation in About 25 Minutes—Unsupervised Baking For 15 Minutes

Measure 7 ounces (14 tablespoons) of the sugar into a heavy saucepan, add 1 tablespoon of water and bring it up to a solid boil, stirring it continuously with a wooden spoon to prevent the sugar from burning, until it is all melted and continues boiling down to a syrup. Put in a candy thermometer and keep it boiling until the "large hardball" stage, when the thermometer should read between 250 and 255 degrees. At once turn off the heat and stir into this hot syrup the 1 pound of fresh raspberries. Let them just soak in it while you beat the eggs. Preheat the oven to 400 degrees and set the oven shelves so that the lower will be about 2 to 3 inches above the floor of the oven, with a space of about 8 inches between the lower and upper shelves. On the upper shelf, place a 10-inch cake pan upside down so that it will reflect heat downwards onto the top of the soufflé. Choose a 1½-quart soufflé dish about 7½ inches in diameter, lightly butter its bottom and sides, then sprinkle with the remaining superfine sugar and knock out excess. Quickly beat the 6 egg whites, preferably in a copper bowl by hand with a ballon whisk, at the same time beating in the ½ teaspoon cream of tartar, until the whites stand up in firm peaks. Using a rubber spatula, quickly fold in the still-hot raspberries and syrup and the optional 1 tablespoon minced lemon zest or ¼ cup grated walnuts, using folding rather than stirring strokes. Avoid overdoing it—do not try to mix everything perfectly. At once, empty the mixture into the soufflé dish and place on the lower shelf of the oven. Make sure that the reflecting pan is immediately above the soufflé, with about 4 inches of space for the soufflé to rise. Close the oven door gently and do not open it again for at least 15 minutes. After that time, test it by pressing the top lightly with the finger. If it is firm and springy to the touch, it is done. If not, give it another 5 minutes. Do not slam the oven door. Serve this magnificent soufflé at once, very hot. Or, it may be allowed to cool very slowly at room temperature. As the sugar syrup hardens, it will support the soufflé, which, once it is set, can then be refrigerated until needed.

TART OF FRESH RASPBERRIES SEALED IN CREAM
(*Tarte à la Crème aux Framboises*)

FOR 4 TO 6 PEOPLE

This French version of a fresh-fruit pie is only possible, in its most resplendent form, during the short spring season of fresh raspberries. (Discussion of Mademoiselle Ray's techniques on page 55—menu with wines on page 53.) There are two secret tricks to the dazzling success of this dessert: first, the full flavor and freshness of the raspberries is preserved by simply not cooking them at all but layering them raw in the prebaked tart shell and sealing them under a covering of custard cream; second, by surrounding the fruit and cream with a uniquely original absorbent yeast-raised tart crust which, without ever becoming over-soggy, soaks up the inevitable raspberry juice and prevents the fruit from becoming mushy even after several days of storage. The basic technique for making this most unusual tart crust (also useful for other juicy fruits) is in the next recipe below.

Staple Items	*Shopping List*
Eggs (2)	Fresh raspberries (2 cups,
Extra egg yolks (3)	about 1 lb.)
Milk (2 cups)	
White granulated sugar (7 Tb)	
All-purpose flour (about 1 Tb)	

Also: 1 prebaked tart shell (see recipe below)

About 2½ Hours Before Serving—Active Preparation About 30 Minutes

Remove one batch of Mademoiselle Ray's special yeast-raised tart pastry from refrigerator where it has been resting overnight. Roll out chilled dough, let rise, and bake according to basic recipe below.

Remember that French tarts are never baked in our type of sloping-sided pie plate but always in straight-sided pans of the kind that we use for baking cake layers. For easiest handling, use either a spring-form pan or an open *flan* ring on a cooky sheet.

While the tart shell is baking, prepare the custard cream. In a 1½-quart saucepan, heat up the 2 cups of milk, but under no circumstances allow it to boil. In a mixing bowl, using a wire whisk, beat together the 2 whole eggs and the 3 extra yolks and then beat into them the 7 tablespoons of sugar and the 1 tablespoon of flour. Continue beating until everything is fluffy and light.

When milk is hot enough so that it slightly stings the finger, gradually pour it into the eggs, beating furiously all the time, until it has all been added. Transfer mixture back to saucepan and place over medium heat, continuing to beat and religiously scraping bottom and sides of saucepan, until mixture thickens to consistency of heavy custard. Cover and keep warm.

As soon as firmly baked tart shell has come out of oven and has been slightly cooled, fill it with a layer of all the raspberries, then cover them with the hot custard cream. Put tart back in oven for not a second more than 4 minutes, to set the custard cream. Serve at once.

BASIC YEAST-RAISED PASTRY FOR FRESH-FRUIT TARTS
(*Pâte à Tarte Levée de Mademoiselle Ray*)

FOR ONE 9- TO 10-INCH TART

See explanation at beginning of recipe above.

Staple Items	All-purpose flour (2 cups,
Sweet butter (9 Tb)	after sifting)
Eggs (2), plus 1 yolk	Salt (½ tsp)
Milk (⅓ cup, plus 1 Tb for	
glaze)	*Shopping List*
White granulated sugar	Yeast (1 envelope)
(4 Tb)	

The Day Before the Pastry Shell Is Needed for the Above Recipe—Active Preparation 20 to 30 Minutes

Gently heat the ⅓ cup milk until it feels just warm to the touch of the fingertip, then stir dried yeast into it and leave to develop and dissolve, stirring occasionally. Assemble in a large mixing bowl the 2 cups of sifted flour, the 4 tablespoons sugar, the 9 tablespoons butter cut into small bits, plus ½ teaspoon salt. The technique for working these things together with the tips of the fingers is described in detail at the very end of the recipe for Cushion-Terrine of Pheasant, page 175—the section of the method subtitled Mixing and Kneading Dough in About 15 Minutes. When you have achieved the consistency of whole-kernel corn, add liquids: the 2 eggs lightly beaten with 2 teaspoons of water, plus the warm milk-yeast mixture. The dough at this point will be extremely sticky and must be kneaded by lifting and slapping back into the bowl until it pulls away clean—usually in about 7 to 8 minutes. Form into a ball, put into a clean mixing bowl, cover with a cloth and set in a place where the temperature is between 70 and 75 degrees. (At a warmer temperature, the butter would melt and ooze out of the dough.) Leave to rise for 3 hours, during which time it will double or triple in bulk, then stir down with a wooden spoon, roll into a ball, cover, and leave to refrigerate at least 4 hours, or preferably overnight.

About 2½ Hours Before Serving—Unsupervised Final Rising of Dough in About 2 Hours—Baking of Shell in About 20 Minutes

When chilled, roll out dough to fit buttered spring-form pan or *flan* ring, then leave to rise another 2 hours, again at a temperature of 70 to 75 degrees. Shortly before the end of the 2-hour rising time, preheat oven to 400 degrees and set oven shelf in middle slot. Combine the egg yolk and the remaining 1 tablespoon milk and hold. When dough has finished rising, line the empty pastry shell with aluminum foil punched with small holes and fill it with a layer of dried peas or beans, to keep pastry from puffing as it bakes.

Set shell in center of oven and bake for the first 10 minutes. Meanwhile, prepare the filling according to the preceding recipe. After 10 minutes, lower temperature to 350 degrees, brush rim of shell with egg and milk glaze and continue baking until firm and very lightly golden, usually in another 5 to 10 minutes. Then remove beans and foil, cool shell slightly and fill as described in the recipe above.

TART OF QUEEN CLAUDE GREENGAGE PLUMS
(*La Tarte aux Reine Claudes*)

FOR 4 TO 6 PEOPLE

The Queen Claude plums in the Valley are magnificently scented and sweet. When you cook them, their bouquet fills the entire house. This fine dessert, however, can be made with many of our varieties, provided they are absolutely ripe and soft. After being skinned, stoned and chunked, they are briefly sealed in a very hot sugar syrup, exactly as in the recipe for Soufflé of Fresh Raspberries, page 399. Plums should then be removed to a holding bowl. For the shell to hold the plums, prepare Mademoiselle Ray's yeast-raised brioche-style pie shell as described in the above recipe for Tart of Fresh Raspberries Sealed in Cream. All other details of preparation—for thickening syrup and assembling tart —are the same as in the recipe for Fresh Gooseberry Tart, page 389. (See discussion on page 116; menu with wines on page 114.)

SNOWY SOUFFLÉ WITH GREEN CHARTREUSE
(*Neige à la Chartreuse*)

FOR 4 PEOPLE

I consider this one of the finest liqueur-filled soufflés I have ever tasted. (See menus with wines on pages 25 and 155.) The secret trick is that the soufflé must be baked very quickly at an unusually high oven heat, so that the liqueur does not evaporate. For this reason it should not be baked in a normal soufflé dish, which is too deep, but in an oval or round open baking dish, preferably with straight sides and not more than 2½ inches deep. This magnificent soufflé then comes to table looking like a miniature mountain range of golden brown peaks, while the inside is like fluffy snow marbled with pale green.

Staple Items	*Shopping List*
Sweet butter (2 to 3 Tb)	Green Chartreuse sweet
Eggs (4)	liqueur (½ cup)
Egg whites (4 extra)	
Lemon (1)	
Confectioners' sugar (6 Tb)	
Salt (about ½ tsp)	

About 30 Minutes Before Serving—Active Preparation About 15 Minutes—Unsupervised Baking About 15 Minutes

Separate the 4 whole eggs; put the yolks into a mixing bowl and the 8 whites into a round beating bowl, preferably copper, which has first been lightly rubbed with lemon juice. Using a small wire whisk, beat the 6 tablespoons of sugar into the 4 yolks, until they are lemon-colored and lift up in ribbons. Then beat into the yolks the ½ cup of Green Chartreuse. Sprinkle about ½ teaspoon of salt over whites and beat, preferably by hand, until they glisten and stand in firm peaks. Do not overbeat. Turn on oven to 400 degrees, setting lower shelf about 2 inches from bottom of oven and upper shelf near the top. Butter the open baking dish (see above). Spoon about ⅓ of the whites into the yolks and quickly fold with rubber spatula. Then pour yolk mixture into remaining whites in beating bowl and continue quickly folding. Do not worry if there are some remaining white streaks. Then, pour at once into baking dish and set on lower shelf in oven. Adjust upper shelf so that it is about 3 inches above the surface of the soufflé. Place a shiny cooky sheet, inverted, on upper shelf so as to reflect heat down onto top of soufflé. Without opening oven door, bake for 10 minutes, then check. Soufflé is done when top is golden brown and springy to the touch—usually in 10 to 15 minutes. Serve instantly on very hot plates.

HOMEMADE WALNUT ICE CREAM
(*Glace à la Noix de Grenoble*)

FOR 4 PEOPLE

When I first went to the Alpine region of the Dauphiné—which is the "walnut capital" of France—I had difficulty with the word *noix.* It means, in general, a "nut"—any nut, of any kind—but in the Dauphiné it also means, quite specifically, the walnut for which that region is famous. A warning: This ice cream can only be made with fresh walnuts, still in their shells, within a few months of the harvest. The secret trick is that the halves of nut-meat must be fresh enough and oily enough so that they can be skinned. This slightly tricky operation is simply not possible with old nuts or pre-shelled nutmeats. So—in France, this is a seasonal fall dish. (Menu and wines on page 16.)

Staple Items
Heavy cream (2⅔ cups)
Milk (1⅓ cups)
Egg yolks (9)
Confectioners' sugar (3 cups
    —about ¾ lb.)
Cornstarch (1 tsp)

Shopping List
Fresh walnuts in shells (1 lb.,
    to provide ½ lb. of nut-
    meats)

Active Preparation in About ¾ Hour—Freezing in 1 Hour—Several Hours of Ripening

Rope in as much help as possible for the shelling of the walnuts and the skinning of the halves. Pound them to a purée with a pestle and mortar. (Some cooks do this job in an electric blender, but this involves some loss of the vital oil.) Mix the 2⅔ cups heavy cream and the 1⅓ cups milk, bring up almost but not quite to boiling, then add the walnut mash. Turn off the heat and leave the walnut oil to permeate the liquid.

Beat the 9 egg yolks with the 3 cups of sugar until mixture is smooth, and so thick that it forms ribbons on the beater. Then, working gradually and stirring all the time, incorporate into the eggs the warm nut-milk and the 1 teaspoon cornstarch. Now heat the mixture very gradually over a low flame, stirring continuously and carefully scraping the bottom and sides of the pan, until you have a thick pour-ing-custard that runs lazily from the spoon. Remove from heat and continue stirring for a few minutes to cool. Then pour into icebox bowl and cool in refrigerator.

Freeze by any of the standard methods—in rotary machine, in ice-box freezer or in an electric or hand-turned tub freezer—with ice and salt. Then let the ice cream ripen in the freezer for several hours before serving.

FIRST VARIATION: One extra cup heavy cream, whipped, may be folded into the cooled mixture just before freezing.

SECOND VARIATION: One or 2 cups of extra walnut meats, coarsely chopped, may be worked into the ice cream as it thickens in the freezer.

THIRD VARIATION:

HOMEMADE FILBERT ICE CREAM
(*Glace aux Noisettes*)

FOR 4 PEOPLE

This is basically the same as for the Walnut Ice Cream, with only the difference in the nuts and in the manner of handling them.

Replace the walnuts in the above recipe with 1 pound of filberts in their shells, which will produce about ½ pound of nutmeats. These also must be skinned before pounding, and this is done most easily by first lightly sautéing the nutmeats in butter over a medium-high frying heat until the skins become crisp and flaky—usually in about 5 minutes. Then remove every last little bit of skin before pounding the nutmeats to a purée, continuing as described in the recipe above for the Walnut Ice Cream.

SECTION XVI

*Breads and Cakes
and Petits Fours
with Walnut Bread
and Gâteau de Savoie*

BABY BRIOCHES—SUNDAY BREAKFAST

(Petites Brioches)

<small>A FEAST FOR 4, WITH MAYBE SOME REMAINING FOR NEXT DAY</small>

Staple Items
Sweet butter (13 Tb)
Vegetable oil (about 1 tsp)
Eggs (5)
Milk (1 Tb)
Flour, all-purpose (about 2
  cups, plus more for flouring
  board)

Confectioners' sugar (1½
  Tb)
Salt (1 tsp)

Shopping List
Dry active yeast (1 packet)

The Day Before—Active Preparation About 40 Minuets—
Unsupervised Proofing of Dough About 5 Hours

Lightly butter a 3-quart mixing bowl. Cut up 12 tablespoons of the butter into small pieces and allow to come to room temperature. The butter should be soft but not melted. Also, allow about 1 table-spoon to soften, to be used for brushing dough. Dissolve the yeast in ¼ cup fairly warm water—not hot to the tip of the finger—about 100 degrees. Then let yeast mixture rest for 5 minutes.

Into a 2-quart mixing bowl, break 3 whole eggs and 1 more egg yolk; add the 1½ tablespoons sugar and 1 teaspoon salt. Mix together, add the yeast mixture and blend. Preferably using an electric beater, blend at low speed and slowly add 1 cup of the flour. Increase the beating speed to medium, or continue by hand, and gradually add another cup of flour and the 12 tablespoons softened butter, 1 table-spoon at a time. Beat until well blended.

Reduce speed and, using a dough hook on the mixer if available, continue beating until dough retracts and pulls away cleanly from the bowl—usually in about 10 to 15 minutes.

(The beating of brioche dough is very important, because it is too soft and rich to knead by hand. If you have to beat by hand, do so by lifting pieces of the dough out of the bowl and slapping them back until they begin to hold their shape and pull cleanly away from the bowl. This is a messy job because the dough is extremely sticky, and, if at all possible, an electric beater should be used.)

Turn dough out onto a floured board, shape into a ball, and place in the buttered mixing bowl. Brush top with the softened butter,

<small>410</small>

cover and set in a warm place, 70 to 75 degrees, where dough will rise and triple in bulk—usually in 4 to 5 hours. This rising must not be hurried by allowing the temperature to exceed 75 degrees or the dough will take on a yeasty flavor.

Four to 5 Hours Later—Punching and Proofing About 12 Hours

When dough has risen, punch down, turn out onto a floured board and shape again into a ball. Return to bowl, cover and refrigerate at least 12 hours. The dough will rise again and may double in bulk.

The Next Day—Shaping and Proofing the Brioche in About 2½ Hours—Baking About 25 Minutes

Lightly butter the insides of 12 small fluted brioche molds. From this point on work quickly on a cool, lightly floured surface (if possible on a pastry marble). If the temperature is too warm and the butter softens, the dough will become a sticky mess and will have to be refrigerated again before continuing.

Take the dough from the refrigerator and punch it down. Form the dough lightly into a 12-inch-long roll. Working from one end, cut off 12 pieces, each weighing about 2 ounces, plus 12 pieces, each weighing about ½ ounce. Working quickly, form the 12 large pieces into tight balls and press one into each of the 12 molds. Press down firmly enough so that they are squeezed and fill each mold about ⅔ full. With a fairly blunt pointed instrument (perhaps a fairly fat larding needle), push a conical-shaped hole down into the center of each molded brioche. One by one, mold the smaller pieces of dough into teardrop shapes and lightly press each into the conical hole in each molded brioche. This, after baking, forms the *tête*, the "head" that is the traditional shape of a true French brioche. Each little head must be precisely at the center, or it will bake and rise crooked.

Using aluminum foil, make 12 small collars, each as high as one of the little heads. Lightly oil the insides of the collars and gently wrap them around the little heads. Pinch the collars slightly so that they will firmly hold the shapes of the heads. Now set the brioches to rise in a warm place (about 70 to 75 degrees) until the dough has completely filled each mold—usually in about 2 hours.

About 15 Minutes Before Baking

Preheat the oven to 450 degrees. With a fork, lightly beat an egg yolk with 1 tablespoon of milk. Carefully remove the aluminum collars and brush the entire top surface of each brioche (including the head) with the egg glaze. Try to avoid having the glaze run down between the dough and the mold, or into the crack between the head and the base, or it will cause distortion of the shape. Set the 12 brioches on a shelf at the center of the oven and bake for 10 minutes. Then lower the heat to 350 degrees for the remaining 15 minutes. About 10 minutes before they are due to be done, check them and, if they seem to be browning too quickly, loosely cover them with aluminum foil. They are perfectly done when they are a good shade of gold.

WALNUT WHOLEWHEAT BREAD
(*Le Pain de Noix*)

2 MEDIUM LOAVES

Since the lower slopes of the Alps and the Dauphiné Plain to the west of the city of Grenoble are the main centers in France for the growing of walnut trees, it is hardly surprising that Mademoiselle Ray bakes a superb wholewheat whole-nut walnut bread. She gives it the strong character of the nuts by first blending into the dough a substantial amount of finely ground nutmeats and then folding in the uncut nut halves. The dough itself is made with a relatively coarse wholewheat flour, so that it has an attractive chewy country texture. It is a relatively easy recipe and there are no problems whatsoever about reproducing it on this side of the Atlantic.

Staple Items
Sweet butter (2½ Tb)
Egg yolk (1)
Milk, scalded (1¾ cups, plus
    1 tsp for glaze)
White unbleached high-
    gluten flour (3 cups)

Flavorings
Crystal salt, powdered ginger

Shopping List
Fresh, whole walnuts (2 cups)
Grated walnuts (⅔ cup)
Wholewheat high-gluten
    flour (3 cups)
Wild huckleberry honey, or
    other dark honey (¼ cup)
Wheat germ (¼ cup)
Dried yeast (1 package)

Total Preparation Time About 5 Hours—Active Work About 45 Minutes—Remaining Time for Unsupervised Rising and Baking

Combine the package of dried yeast with ¼ cup warm water and set aside. Bring the 1¾ cups milk almost to boiling, then remove from heat, stir in the ¼ cup honey, 2 tablespoons of the butter, 2 teaspoons salt and ¼ teaspoon ginger and leave to cool. Then, in a large mixing bowl, combine the now-bubbly liquid yeast with the milk and honey mixture, then add 1 cup of the white flour, the 3 cups wholewheat flour, the ¼ cup wheat germ, and the ⅔ cup grated walnuts. Stir thoroughly before adding another cup of the white flour. The dough at this point will be somewhat sticky and too stiff to stir. Add more flour if necessary.

Spread ½ cup of the remaining white flour on a flat surface and turn the dough out onto it. Knead vigorously until the dough is elastic and no longer sticky, usually in 10 to 15 minutes. Clean and lightly butter the bowl and return the dough to it. Set aside, covered, in a warm place (about 80 degrees) until doubled in bulk, in 1½ to 2 hours.

Then, punch the dough down and divide it into 2 halves. Roll each into a ball, cover and let rest on the lightly floured work surface for about 20 minutes, before flattening each ball to a large pancake. Scatter the 2 cups whole walnuts over the rounds of dough, pressing the nuts in slightly, then roll each pancake into a loaf shape. Pinch at the seam to seal and place the loaves in 2 pans, 5½ by 9½ inches. Leave them to rise in a warm place until again nearly doubled in bulk, usually in about 1 hour.

Preheat oven to 375 degrees. When the loaves have risen, set in the oven to bake. After 35 minutes, brush the tops with a glaze of 1 egg yolk beaten with 1 teaspoon milk, then continue baking until browned and a knife inserted in the center comes out clean, usually in about 10 minutes more.

CREAM PUFFS WITH GREEN CHARTREUSE
(*Les Petits Choux à la Chartreuse*)

ABOUT 24 PUFFS

These little pastry balls, each about the size of a walnut, are what Mademoiselle Vivette serves to her guests as a midnight snack with cups of mint tea. The first time I bit into one, the mint-green whipped cream squished all down the front of my shirt. Moral: Always stuff a puff whole into your mouth. This is one of the most classic of French recipes, involving the preliminary preparation of a batch of basic *pâte à choux,* "cream-puff pastry," filled after baking with Crème Chantilly—whipped cream flavored, in this case, with the famous liqueur of the Valley. (See Mademoiselle Ray's discussion on page 60.)

For the Cream-Puff Pastry:

Staple Items
Sweet butter (6 Tb, plus a bit to rub on baking sheet)
Eggs (4, possibly 5)
Egg yolk (1 for glazing, if desired)
All-purpose flour, sifted (1 cup plus 2 Tb, and a bit more to dust baking sheet)
Granulated sugar (2 tsp)
Salt (¼ tsp)

Preparing the Pastry and Filling in About 20 Minutes—Unsupervised Baking for About 30 Minutes

Put into a 1-quart saucepan 1 cup of cold water and bring quickly to the boil. As it heats up, drop into it the 6 tablespoons of butter, one by one, plus the 2 teaspoons sugar and the ¼ teaspoon salt. Stir around to make sure that they melt. Meanwhile, break each of the 4 eggs into a separate cup and set aside. As soon as the water in the saucepan is boiling and the solids are melted, turn off heat and instantly throw in, all at once, the 1 cup plus 2 tablespoons of flour. Work together vigorously with a wooden spatula or spoon until you have a compact, solid, thick paste. Turn on heat again, medium-high, while continuing to stir strongly, continuously scraping the bottom and sides of the pan, so that the paste cooks without burning. Keep on going until the paste no longer sticks to the pan or the spatula but conglomerates into a single ball—usually in about 3 minutes. Instantly turn off the heat again. Now, while it is still very hot, work in the eggs, 1 at a time. Each egg should be completely blended in before the next is added. The final pastry should be flexible and soft, firm enough to hold its shape, not at all runny. If it is almost right after the addition of the third egg, add another egg only 1 teaspoon at a time and stop as soon as the pastry is of the right consistency. On the other hand, if it is not soft enough after the 4 eggs, add a teaspoon or 2 of a fifth. After making this pastry a couple of times, you will recognize the signs and signals for the perfect consistency, when the pastry is satiny and shiny and draws easily into strands. Do not overbeat. Stop at once if the pastry seems to be shrinking.

Baking and Filling the Puffs

Preheat the oven to 375 degrees. Lightly butter and flour a cooky sheet. Drop the puffs, by rounded tablespoons of the pastry, onto the sheet about 2 inches apart. (Incidentally, if you like your cream puffs shiny, each may be painted, before baking, with a pastry brush dipped in a mixture of an egg yolk beaten with 1 teaspoon of cold water.) You can make them any size, from marbles to plums, but I think each should be a single pop-in mouthful. Bake them in the center of the oven until they are golden (with all their sweat beads dried off) and firm when lightly squeezed—usually in about 30 to 40 minutes. Do not underbake. (See further instructions following preparation of the filling.)

For the Filling:

Staple Items	*Shopping List*
Confectioners' sugar (¼ cup)	Heavy cream (1 cup)
Vanilla extract (1 tsp)	Green Chartreuse liqueur (about 2 Tb)

BASIC RULE FOR CRÈME CHANTILLY: Chill a bowl and wire whisk in the refrigerator. Then, beat the 1 cup of heavy cream in the bowl with the whisk until cream is stiff. Gently fold in the ¼ cup of confectioners' sugar, the 1 teaspoon vanilla extract and between 1 and 2 tablespoons of the Green Chartreuse, enough to give a mint-green color. If the cream loses a little of its stiffness, beat again. Hold in refrigerator until puffs are ready.

As soon as they are, turn off oven and prick each puff with a pointed knife, so that internal steam can escape. Leave them in the turned-off oven for 20 minutes longer, to cool slowly while drying out centers. Then, bore a hole in the bottom of each puff and pipe in the

Chartreuse cream with a pastry tube. Or, if you do not have a tube, cut puffs in half with a very sharp knife to avoid crushing them, then fill with cream and put halves back together. Keep refrigerated until the moment for serving.

THE PUFF OF A NUN FROM CHAMONIX
(Le Pet de Nonne de Chamonix)
ABOUT 2 DOZEN

This irreverent name for a light-as-air, very restrained little deep-fried fritter has been shocking diners for almost 300 years. Some pastry chefs have tried to change it to "The Sigh of a Nun," but the old classic name has stuck and is printed officially in all the major high cuisine reference cookbooks. It is a simple small pastry ball, as fluffy as a little puff of wind. Indeed, even a sigh might blow it off your plate! (See discussion on page 127 and menu with wines on page 125.)

Staple Items
Sweet butter (6 Tb)
Eggs (4, possibly 5)
Lemon rind (enough to fill
   1 tsp, finely minced)
All-purpose flour, sifted (1
   cup plus 2 Tb)
Superfine sugar (1 Tb)

Confectioners' sugar (to coat
   fritters after frying)
Salt (¼ tsp)
Vanilla extract (1 tsp)
Oil for deep-frying

Shopping List
Orange flower water (1 tsp)
Dark rum (1 tsp)

At Any Time Beforehand—Active Preparation About 40 Minutes—Last-Minute Frying in About 10 Minutes

Prepare your cream-puff pastry (Pâte à Choux) following the exact method described in detail in Cream Puffs with Green Chartreuse, page 414, with this additional step: immediately after working the 1 cup plus 2 tablespoons of flour into the melted water-butter-sugar-salt mixture, beat in the 1 teaspoon each of orange flower water, rum, lemon rind and vanilla extract. Again following the detailed method, finish preparing the pastry. Let the pastry rest in the warm kitchen, covered with a cloth, for 2 hours or longer, until the *pets* are needed.

About 30 Minutes Before Serving—Deep-Frying the Pets

Heat up the deep-frying oil to 370 degrees. Take about 1 tablespoon of the cream-puff pastry for each *pet* and shape into a ball. Drop each gently into the hot oil. As it browns on one side, roll it over. As soon as each one is blown up and crackly, lift it out with a slotted spoon and let it drain for a few seconds while keeping it hot. Finally, a few seconds before serving, liberally sprinkle it all around with the confectioners' sugar. Serve extremely hot.

THE GÂTEAU OF SAVOY (The Classic Sponge Cake of the Region)

(*Le Gâteau de la Savoie*)

FOR 4 PEOPLE

This is, of course, only the basic cake. It can be decorated, iced, filled with fruit, or "fancied up" in any conceivable way. It is, however, so light and lovely in itself that I prefer it with coffee or liqueur and no other embellishments. (Discussion on page 76; menu with wines on page 74.)

Staple Items
Eggs (6)
Lemon juice (for rubbing copper bowl)
Cake flour (1¾ cups)
Confectioners' sugar (1¾ cups, plus ¼ cup to dust cake pan)
Cream of tartar (¼ tsp)
Salt (½ tsp)
Vanilla extract (1½ tsp)

About 2 Hours Before Serving

Preheat oven to 300 degrees. Slightly warm a 10-inch demountable pan, so as to make it easier to butter every surface and corner of the inside. Put in ¼ cup confectioners' sugar and shake pan until interior is completely coated, then shake out excess. Separate the 6 eggs, putting the yolks into a mixing bowl and the whites into a copper beating bowl which is absolutely clean, entirely without a speck of grease, and has been lightly rubbed with lemon juice. Sift the 1¾ cups cake flour and hold. Hand-beat the yolks until they ribbon, gradually incorporating into them the 1¾ cups confectioners' sugar, a little more or less, according to your sweet tooth. Bring ¼ cup water to boiling and beat it in, 2 teaspoons at a time. Then beat in the sifted flour, ¼ cup at a time, and the 1½ teaspoons vanilla extract. Now, hand-beat the egg whites, at the same time incorporating the ½ teaspoon of salt and the ¼ teaspoon of cream of tartar, until whites stand in stiff peaks but are not dry. Stir ¼ cup of the whites into the yolk mixture to lighten it, then, working quickly, fold in the remaining whites with a flexible rubber spatula. Pour, scrape and spoon the mixture into the tube pan, filling it not more than two-thirds full. Smooth out surface with spatula. Bake in the precise center of the oven until cake is springy to the touch, usually in about 1 hour. Upturn at once onto a cake grid and let cool to room temperature. Then, demount tube pan and remove cake.

BABY MERINGUES WITH ALMONDS AND CREAM
(*Les Meringues aux Amandes à la Crème*)

ABOUT 4 DOZEN

Each of these little meringues makes about one creamy, nutty, sweet mouthful to be served either as dessert or among the *petit fours* with the coffee. These meringues are a specialty of the ancient Dauphiné province, where nuts grow in abundance.

For the Meringues:

Staple Items
Butter (about 1 Tb to grease the baking sheet)
Egg whites (12)
Confectioners' sugar (to sprinkle on baking sheet)
Superfine sugar (2¼ cups)
Cream of tartar (1 tsp)
Salt

Shopping List
Almonds, blanched and slivered (9 ounces)

For the Filling:

1 batch Crème Chantilly (see page 415)	Coffee (1 to 2 Tb double-strength, chilled)

The Day Before—Preparation in About 30 Minutes—Unsupervised Baking in About 1 Hour—They Must Dry Out Overnight

First toast the slivered almonds. Preheat oven to 350 degrees. Spread the almonds in a single layer on the bottom of an ungreased 9- or 10-inch layer cake pan, place in center of oven and stir frequently until almonds are an even, light brown—usually in 7 to 10 minutes. Do not let them blacken, or they will give the meringues a burnt flavor. Preferably using a copper beating bowl and a large balloon whisk, beat the 12 egg whites until they stand up in firm peaks and do not slide around in the bowl. Shortly before this point is reached, beat in two pinches of salt and the 1 teaspoon of cream of tartar. Then, sprinkle the 2¼ cups superfine sugar, ¼ cup at a time, over the beaten egg whites, quickly folding it in, using a flexible rubber spatula in circular strokes from bottom to top. Before all the sugar is in, also incorporate the toasted almonds and the 3 teaspoons of vanilla extract. Set the oven down to 225 degrees. Cover a large cooky sheet with wax paper, lightly greasing it with butter and sparsely sprinkling it with confectioners' sugar. Drop the meringue mix onto the sheet by small tablespoons so that each will be hardly larger than a walnut, and keep them in regular rows about 2 inches apart. Place in center of oven and leave oven door very slightly open to avoid any concentration of steam. When they are crispy and dry, gently unstick them from the paper, poke in their bottoms with your finger to help them dry out inside and keep them overnight in a dry, warm place.

On the Day—An Hour or So Before Serving

Prepare a batch of whipped Crème Chantilly according to the BASIC RULE FOR CRÈME CHANTILLY in the recipe for Cream Puffs with Green Chartreuse, page 415, only this time flavor it with the 1 to 2 tablespoons of very strong coffee instead of the Chartreuse, and spoon the cream between a matched pair of meringues.

SECTION XVII

*Pickles and Preserves
From Savory Cherries
To Bleeding Mushrooms*

MADEMOISELLE RAY'S INFUSION OF MINT TEA
(Infusion de Menthe)

PER PERSON

There are now available, both in France and in the United States, dozens of labels of dried mint tea which can be brewed with hot water just like normal tea leaves. However, with rather typical subtlety, Mademoiselle Ray has a secret trick with the cups of mint tea, which she brings into *le salon* for sipping just before going to bed (see page 28). She combines the flavors of two different kinds of mint by using one variety for making the tea in a china teapot and then pouring this over a single leaf of a second kind of mint in each cup.

Staple Items	*Shopping List*
Sugar (1 or 2 lumps)	Peppermint leaves, either fresh, in season (about 1 Tb) or dried (about ½ tsp)
	Spearmint leaves, whole, either fresh or dried (1 leaf)

About 7 Minutes Before Serving

Never use a metal pot—it reacts against some of the acid oils in the mint and spoils the flavor. Put the required amount of the peppermint in a china teapot and pour in absolutely boiling water. Stir and let it steep for about 5 minutes. Place a single spearmint leaf in each cup and pour the hot tea over it, adding sugar to taste. Obviously, if the tea is too strong or too weak the first time, adjust the amounts used in later brewings. Also, it is well worth experimenting with other types of mint leaf when you can get them; for example, apple mint, lemon mint, orange mint, and pineapple mint.

SWEET-SOUR CHERRY PICKLE
(*Cerises Griottes aux Vinaigre*)

MAKES ABOUT 7 PINT JARS

When the sour cherries arrive for their summer season, Mademoiselle Ray bottles enough of this irresistible pickle to last all winter. (See menu use on page 67.) These cherries are an outstanding pickle accompaniment to almost all cold and many hot meals.

Staple Items
White wine vinegar (3 cups)
Brown sugar (1 lb.)

Shopping List
Sour cherries, fresh, pitted (4 lbs., or 2 quarts)

Flavorings
Stick cinnamon, whole cloves

At Least 3 Weeks Before You Need Them—Active Preparation for About 30 Minutes Spread Over 6 Days

Sterilize seven 1-pint Mason jars. Carefully pit cherries so as to damage them as little as possible. Then divide them equally between the seven Mason jars. In a 2-quart saucepan, bring rapidly to the boil the 3 cups of vinegar and stir in, until it dissolves, the 1 pound of sugar. Put ½ cinnamon stick, plus 6 whole cloves, with the cherries in each Mason jar. When sugar is completely dissolved in the vinegar, fill up each Mason jar with the hot liquid. Let it cool slightly, then screw on the lids and keep jars at room temperature for 2 days.

Strain liquid from all jars back into the saucepan, leaving cherries, cinnamon and cloves in jars. Bring liquid again to boiling, then pour back into jars, let cool slightly, screw lids back on and, again, leave at room temperature for 2 more days.

On the fifth day, exactly repeat the operation. Then, screw on lids extra tight and leave jars at room temperature for 15 days. Cherries are then ready to eat but will continue to improve with longer keeping. From this point onward, I prefer to store jars in refrigerator.

CORNICHONS À LA FRANÇAISE
(*Pickled Cucumbers*)

A SUPPLY TO STORE

Surely every gourmet interested in the French cuisine has, at one time or another, bought a jar (usually imported from the Loire city of Orléans) of these excellent tiny pickled cucumbers called *cornichons*. Mademoiselle Ray taught me how to make my own— a method as simple as boiling an egg. The only problem is to get hold of the miniature cucumbers, usually available as "pickling babies" in the spring or early summer. The "black spine" type are best, and they should average about 1½ inches long and should be freshly picked and slightly underripe. Try to get them with a tiny bit of the stem still attached. You should ideally have a stone crock in which to store them, but a heatproof jar will also do. Make sure that the vinegar you buy is of first quality and has an acidity of at least 6 percent. Otherwise, if the vinegar is too weak, the *cornichons* may lose their crispness and may even spoil. Here is Mademoiselle Ray's method.

Thoroughly brush and clean the baby cucumbers, then soak them overnight in heavily salted water. Next day, drain and dry them, then pack them neatly and tightly into the stone crock that will be their storage home. Fill up the crock with white wine vinegar, using enough so that the cucumbers are covered, with about an inch to spare. Now, pour off the vinegar into a large enameled heating pan (never use any kind of metal pan, which would react chemically with the vinegar) and bring it to a rolling boil, adding an extra ½ cup of fresh vinegar. At once, pour it, still at the boil, over the cucumbers in the crock and let them soak, covered, for a full 24 hours.

Again, pour off the vinegar into the heating pan, bring it back to a rolling boil, adding an extra ½ cup of fresh vinegar, then

. pour it back over the cucumbers and leave them to soak, covered, for another 24 hours.

Repeat exactly the same operation for the third time. This time, however, the preparation job is done, the cucumbers have become *cornichons* and are stored, covered, of course, soaking in their vinegar. After leaving them alone for 6 weeks, you take them out as you need them. Always make sure that the remaining *cornichons* are covered by the liquid. Add more vinegar at any time, as necessary. If you are going to keep them for a long time, it is a good idea to put into the crock with the cucumbers a few fresh grape leaves, which will help keep them crisp.

WILD MUSHROOMS VINAIGRETTE
(*Lactaires Délicieux Sanguins Vinaigrette*)

A REFRIGERATOR SUPPLY FOR SEVERAL MEALS

One of the several hundred types of wild mushrooms which grow in the Valley of La Grande Chartreuse is colored bright orange and known in English as the Lactaire Blood Root because when it is cut it oozes reddish juice. It is in fact delicious, but of course entirely unavailable in the United States. Mademoiselle Ray's method of preparing them as a slightly tart hors d'oeuvre, however, works almost equally well with our American button mushrooms. This method of boiling and marinating all kinds of vegetables in an oil and vinegar mixture is classically known in the high cuisine as *préparation à la Grecque.* (See discussion on page 84—menu and wines on page 83.)

Staple Items
Lemon (1)
Olive oil (¾ to 1 cup)
Tarragon white wine vinegar
   (¼ to ½ cup)

Shopping List
Small button mushrooms (1
   lb.)
Fresh parsley (3 or 4 sprigs)
Fresh watercress (1 bunch)

Flavorings
Bay leaves, whole fennel seeds,
   thyme, crystal salt, freshly
   ground black pepper

Prepare the aromatic marinade in the same way as in the recipe for Cold Artichoke Hearts *à la Grecque* (page 178). Before adding the pound of mushrooms to the simmering marinade, wipe (never wash) them, cutting off stems level with the caps, getting rid of any dried ends on stems and reserving remaining good parts to be cooked with the caps. Caps, if small enough, should be left whole. The mushrooms should be simmered, covered, just until cooked through, usually in 10 to 15 minutes. To check progress the first time, fish out one cap and cut it in half. The flesh should be dark and soft through the center. When done, store and serve in the same way as the artichoke hearts.

PRESERVING THE SUMMER FRUITS OF THE VALLEY
(*Les Conserves de Fruits de la Vallée*)

A SUPPLY TO STORE

During July and August (remember that the harvest seasons are always late in the high Alpine mountains) Mademoiselle Ray spends a part of each day in her kitchen "conserving" and bottling the magnificent fresh fruits of the region. She has her own ideas as to the techniques—somewhat different from our American ways—and her results are so good that even her midwinter menus, when the Auberge is snowed in almost to the second floor, can include fruit soufflés and tarts which seem to hold in suspension the crispness and freshness of high summer. Mademoiselle Ray says that the fruits to be "conserved" must be only just ripe—even a shade underripe—and they must be boiled as quickly as possible after the picking. She is so fussy about the degree of sweetness and thickness of her sugar syrup that she uses a Baumé saccharometer and stops the boiling when the meter shows 28 degrees of sweetness. Her general rule for quickly reaching this optimum level of sweet syrup is to use between 2¾ and 3¼ cups of water to each 2 pounds of sugar—adjusting slightly, one way or the other, according to the sweetness or tartness (and the juiciness) of the fruit. I have translated her methods into the possibilities of my New York kitchen with such success that I am now entirely sold on *les conserves,* even with the commercial fruits available in our local markets. When one "bottles one's own" (to borrow a famous Prohibition phrase), one can fill one's shelves for the winter dog days with fruits of a far better quality and at a much lower price than anything in the commercial cans or frozen packages. Here are my adaptations of Mademoiselle Ray's basic rules.

Apricots and Peaches

Use firm, well-shaped, slightly underripe, nicely sweet fruit. If they are peaches, peel them; if they are apricots, leave the skin on. Cut them in halves and take out the stones. Crack open 2 stones for each jar to be filled, remove the kernels and hold them. Choose an enameled boiling pan. Do not, under any circumstances, use a pan of aluminum, copper, iron, or steel, as the metal is likely to react with the acid of the fruit, causing discoloration and taking the edge off the flavor. Use about 3 cups of sugar to each quart jug (fairly tightly packed) of fruit. Layer the fruit, packing it in neatly, in the boiling pan, with the measured amount of sugar spread over each layer. When the pan is loaded, let it stand, covered, at room temperature for about 2 hours. Then add water and bring up to gentle simmering and continue until the fruit is just transparent—in about 10 minutes. Have ready the requisite number of sterilized screw-top glass jars and, using a slotted spoon, fill each about ¾ full of the fruit, packing it down neatly and tightly.

When there is nothing but syrup left in the boiling pan, bring it back up to a good boil and put in a candy thermometer. When all remaining water has boiled away and the syrup has just about reached the "large thread" stage, with the candy thermometer showing 218 to 220 degrees, turn off the heat. For each measured quart of fruit with which you started, now stir into the boiling syrup 2 tablespoons of lemon juice. Fill up each jar with the hot syrup to within about ½ inch of the top. Add 2 of the reserved kernels to each jar. Seal the jars according to the instructions for the particular type you are using.

Sweet Bing Cherries

Basically, the same rules as above. Wash, stem and stone the cherries. Measure them in a quart jug and layer them in the enameled boiling pot with 2 to 3 cups of sugar per quart of cherries—according to the sweetness of the fruit. When the pot is loaded, let it stand, covered, at room temperature, for about 8 hours. Then, add water and bring it up to gentle simmering, stirring it regularly, continuing the simmering, covered, until the cherries are soft—usually in 6 to 10 minutes.

Using a slotted spoon, fill each sterile jar about ¾ full of cherries, packing them down neatly and tightly. Bring the syrup back to a good boil and keep it going, until all water has boiled away and the candy thermometer shows 218 to 220 degrees. Fill each jar with syrup to within about ½ inch from the top. With a hammer, crack one cherry stone for each jar and drop it in just before sealing according to instructions with the jar.

Reine Claude, or Greengage Plums

Again, the same basic rules. Wash the plums, halve them and discard the stones. Measure the fruit, pack it tightly into a quart jug and layer it in the enameled boiling pot with an equal amount of sugar, quart for quart. Let it stand, covered, at room temperature for about 12 hours. Add some water and simmer until the plums are just soft—usually in 15 to 20 minutes. Fill the sterile jars ¾ full of fruit, packing neatly and tightly. Boil down syrup until the candy thermometer shows 218 to 220 degrees. Fill each jar to within ½ inch of the top. Seal.

INDEX